PRAISE FOR
THE WAY OF THE INTELLIGENT REBEL

'Olivier does a brilliant job in this book to show you that not to feel well integrated in the old system is a strength, if you know how to play your cards right. And he gives you the proper mindset, and the right tools and strategies so you can thrive while creating your own adventure through life, and become a happy intelligent rebel. I highly recommend this book. Go read it!'

ROBERT GREENE, AUTHOR OF THE *NEW YORK TIMES* BEST-SELLER *THE 48 LAWS OF POWER* AND *THE 33 STRATEGIES OF WAR*

'Some people seem to fit naturally into the "get a degree and get a 9–5 job" world. This book is for the rest of us. For more than a decade, I've watched Olivier Roland ask the questions and take the actions that have shaped his iconoclastic (and extraordinarily successful) life. Now with this book he shows us how he's done it, and how we can do the same.'

JEFF WALKER, #1 *NEW YORK TIMES* BEST-SELLING AUTHOR OF *LAUNCH*

'This book is about how to set yourself free from average and live an extraordinary life... whatever that may mean to you. It's about how to see different, think different and live different. If you've ever felt like you were made for more but just didn't know how to achieve it, read this book and follow Olivier's advice. He has crafted a life on his terms – and this is his playbook showing you how to do it too!'

STU MCLAREN, CO-FOUNDER, SEARCHIE.IO

'In his brilliant book, Olivier Roland takes your hand and shows you how to navigate our complex and modern society. Work smarter, not harder, is the key philosophy. By becoming an Intelligent Rebel you will learn time-tested principles on how to better influence and convince people, how to use and leverage modern technology to your advance, and how to turn your passion into profit. All while minimizing the risks and living your life to the fullest. Enjoy these golden drops of "street-smart" nectar and go change the world.'

STIG SEVERINSEN, PH.D., FOUNDER, BREATHEOLOGY, 4 X FREEDIVING WORLD CHAMPION AND EXPLORER

'Growing up, I always heard this voice talking to me... coaching me... motivating me to ask different questions, take different chances, go in an opposite direction. It was lonely, and people didn't understand me. I didn't know what to call it – until I read Olivier's book. I am an Intelligent Rebel! I only wish I had this amazing context when I was younger, and hope that every young entrepreneur finds their way to this book!'

JASON FRIEDMAN, FOUNDER AND CEO OF CXFORMULA, AND 2 X INC. 5000 FASTEST GROWING COMPANY

'No matter where you are in your life, if you feel like you are in a work-driven rat-race and yet not building much for yourself, read this book. Olivier is proof that you can be so much more than you ever thought possible, whether you graduated from college and followed all the conventional rules or not. His story will inspire you, and the strategies he shares in this book will help you succeed beyond your dreams.'

RUTH BUCZYNSKI, PH.D., LICENSED PSYCHOLOGIST, PRESIDENT AND CEO, THE NATIONAL INSTITUTE FOR THE CLINICAL APPLICATION OF BEHAVIORAL MEDICINE

'Incredible! I have read many books, but this one is a piece of art. You will read without stopping! It looks big, but when you start reading it becomes small and you want to return again and again. It really shows the way for entrepreneurs who want a business that designs the life they desire. Olivier is the living proof of that life. If you want freedom and a life that is fun and amazing, this book is your bible! Read it NOW!'

RICARDO TEIXEIRA, #1 REFERENCE IN DIGITAL MARKETING IN PORTUGAL AND 2 X WORLD CHAMPION OF KARATE

'I grew up poor, barely graduated high school and was denied admission to every university I applied for. And I became a millionaire before I turned 30... There is no book (or author) that encapsulates my own journey better than this one. A must-read for those who know they haven't yet lived up to their potential.'

DYLAN FROST, CREATOR OF THE WHOLESALE FORMULA

'Watch out! Read this book and you might find yourself on the path to lucrative, lifestyle-focused self-employment! *The Way of the Intelligent Rebel* is packed chapter by chapter with insight, shortcuts, actions you can take immediately, and even the math of how your new business will thrive from the start. A riveting instruction manual to boost your intelligence, improve your life, and launch your dream business.'

MARGARET LYNCH RANIERE, SPEAKER, ENTREPRENEUR AND BEST-SELLING AUTHOR OF *TAPPING INTO WEALTH* AND *UNBLOCKED*

'A rebel can be defined as a person who resists convention. When you think about it, there is no way to forge your own path and reach your dreams without resisting convention. Therefore, being a rebel is essential for success in today's world. In this book, Olivier Roland reveals the map for the extraordinary adventure that is entrepreneurism. Though I wish I had this book when I started, I'm glad to have it now as intelligent rebels never stop sharpening their tools.'

JOHN GALLAGHER, FOUNDER, LEARNINGHERBS

'I never wanted to give the best hours, days, and years of my life to some random business. I wanted to use that time to build my own thing and have my own adventures. Olivier's the guy to show you how to do that.'

WILL HAMILTON, FOUNDER, FUZZY YELLOW BALLS

'I have had the honor of knowing Oliver for over a decade and he has always lived true to his word. He is proof that the rebel life is possible. In this manual of opportunity he offers us one of the most authentic and honest views that you will not experience elsewhere. This is not your standard off-the-shelf business success book. This is an encyclopedia of success. A detailed instruction set for living a life of learning and freedom. Oliver shows how to create a life of freedom and then actually "live" that life.'

RICK MCFARLAND, SERIAL ENTREPRENEUR AND CREATOR OF VOICE4NET

'*The Way of the Intelligent Rebel* is one of the most powerful business books ever written. It's loaded with breakthrough strategies to win in business so you can have an amazing life. Start reading it immediately.'

CHRISTIAN MICKELSEN, AWARD-WINNING ENTREPRENEUR, BEST-SELLING AUTHOR, HUMANITARIAN, AND CREATOR OF LIVELIMITLESS.COM

'From all those years meeting all sorts of entrepreneurs who leverage the Internet to achieve financial and location freedom (the freedom to live and work from whatever part of the world) I have yet to meet someone who achieved this on a higher level than Olivier. I am glad his knowledge is now available in such a detailed and easy-to-digest way as in this book.'

ERICO ROCHA, ONE OF THE BIGGEST REFERENCES IN DIGITAL MARKETING IN BRAZIL

'This book is a gift to the outsiders, a love letter to the rebels who will change the world. Other authors try to tell you how to succeed. But Olivier shows you – because he's been proving it in his own life, day after day, for decades. Don't waste another minute on an outdated system's definition of success. Read this book now and start creating your own future.'

SHELLEY BRANDER, *WALL STREET JOURNAL* BEST-SELLING AUTHOR OF *MOVE THE NEEDLE*

'Like Olivier, I'm an entrepreneur with a business that grows at a fast pace year after year. Most of what I learned in school is of no use to me today. I have known Olivier for quite a few years, and I know that he does what he says and says what he does. His book is awesome if you want to live life on your own terms. Go read it! Thanks Olivier for the inspiration and for allowing me and others like me to be and belong.'

VICTOR DAMASIO, CREATOR OF GRUPO MAESTRIA AND VIDA DE MENTOR

'To anyone who has ever felt "there must be more," this book is a must-read! Olivier Roland is "awake" to what it's like to live a life of passion, freedom, and purpose. Through his real-life experience as a successful entrepreneur, global citizen, and forward thinker, he gives us a how-to manual for "waking up" and embracing our own Intelligent Rebel within. This book is a relief. I wish I had read it years ago. You will want to give it to everyone you care about.'

MICHELLE FALZON, FOUNDER, WE ARE CONTENT AND CREATE WITHOUT BURNOUT

'If you have an inkling that there could be more to life than "get the best education you can, land a job, do the commute-work-sleep-repeat for 40 years and then maybe have a little fun before you die" – this book is for you. *The Way of the Intelligent Rebel* is the ultimate guide on how to create and live your own wild, wealthy, and wonderful life adventure. A life where you flourish, add a lot of value to the world, make a lot of money, have a blast, and experience true freedom.'

ANN WILSON AUTHOR OF *THE WEALTH CHEF*

'Since I was a child I always felt different. I always believed there had to be more to life. There had to be another way. Was life really just about working hard at school, going to college, getting a job, working harder, climbing the ladder, and looking forward to having freedom in the future when I would eventually retire. I wanted to make a difference. I wanted to be different and do differently. I wish I had met Olivier and read *The Way of the Intelligent Rebel* 25 years ago. It would have saved me so much time and money. It would have given me comfort that although I was different, maybe my thinking was right.'

DES O'NEILL, FOUNDER, OMNIPRO, PROFITPRO, AND CPDSTORE.COM

'For anyone who has ever struggled with not fitting into the workaday world (but wanting to have an impact), with knowing you are meant for more (but not knowing where to find it), with wanting time and money freedom (but not knowing where to start). This book is a guide to living a life without boundaries or borders. Olivier shows you how to take everything that has made you stand apart from the crowd and turn it into what makes you stand out from the crowd. Olivier is a living example, and in this simple (and accessible) guide he gives you the inside track so you can do the same – faster, simpler, easier.'

BARI BAUMGARDNER, CREATOR OF SAGE EVENT MANAGEMENT

'This book has the potential to change more lives than any other I have read. The World has changed. It needs new leaders. It needs entrepreneurs. It needs people who don't just follow the old way of doing things. I have been an entrepreneur, "free" from the corporate world, for 15 years, but I still had so many eye-opening, "aha" moments reading this book. It was like going back to "lifestyle school" and I loved it. This book is about taking action and making it happen, to live a life on your own terms, free and inspired, and I cannot think of a better teacher than Olivier.'

ROSS BRIDGEFORD, FOUNDER, LIVEENERGIZED.COM AND AUTHOR OF *THE ALKALINE RESET CLEANSE*

'*The Way of the Intelligent Rebel* addresses how to solve your work-life imbalance with methods personalized to work for you. Olivier pulls from both familiar and new narratives with strategies that will help the reader carve out their own adventure in creativity and independence.'

ROGER FARLEY, FOUNDER, ALWAYSINVERT.COM

THE WAY OF THE INTELLIGENT REBEL

Succeed Outside the System, Teach Yourself Anything, and Achieve Ultimate Freedom

OLIVIER ROLAND

HAY HOUSE

Carlsbad, California • New York City
London • Sydney • New Delhi

Published in the United Kingdom by:
Hay House UK Ltd, The Sixth Floor, Watson House,
54 Baker Street, London W1U 7BU
Tel: +44 (0)20 3927 7290; Fax: +44 (0)20 3927 7291; www.hayhouse.co.uk

Published in the United States of America by:
Hay House Inc., PO Box 5100, Carlsbad, CA 92018-5100
Tel: (1) 760 431 7695 or (800) 654 5126
Fax: (1) 760 431 6948 or (800) 650 5115; www.hayhouse.com

Published in Australia by:
Hay House Australia Pty. Ltd, 18/36 Ralph St, Alexandria NSW 2015
Tel: (61) 2 9669 4299; Fax: (61) 2 9669 4144; www.hayhouse.com.au

Published in India by:
Hay House Publishers India, Muskaan Complex,
Plot No.3, B-2, Vasant Kunj, New Delhi 110 070
Tel: (91) 11 4176 1620; Fax: (91) 11 4176 1630; www.hayhouse.co.in

Text © Olivier Roland, 2021

Originally published in French as *Tout Le Monde N'a Pas Eu La Chance De Rater Ses Etudes* © 2016, 2019, Alisio, une marque des éditions Leduc.s

English language translation by Simon Knight, 2020

The moral rights of the author have been asserted.

A catalogue record for this book is available from the British Library.

Tradepaper ISBN: 978-1-78817-517-3
E-book ISBN: 978-1-78817-550-0
Audiobook ISBN: 978-1-78817-608-8

Interior illustrations: 380: ALDECA studio / Shutterstock.com; 391: Laurent Breillat; all other images and illustrations Olivier Roland and Éditions Leduc

Printed and bound in Great Britain by
TJ Books Limited, Padstow, Cornwall

To all the world's intelligent rebels, whose inner fire
inspires them to do something different.

CONTENTS

CREATING YOUR OWN BUSINESS AND BREAKING FREE 131

ON GIANTS' SHOULDERS

This book would never have seen the light of day without the work of entrepreneurs, scientists, authors, intelligent rebels, and explorers of talent, so numerous I can't name them all here.

Here is a list of the most significant in alphabetical order: Jay Abraham, David Allen, Oussama Ammar, Leo Babauta, Roy F. Baumeister, Warren Buffett, Robert Cialdini, Stephen Covey, Vincent Delourmel, Hermann Ebbinghaus, Tim Ferriss, Philippe Gabilliet, William Gibson, Seth Godin, Benjamin Graham, Nicolas Guéguen, Chip and Dan Heath, Claude Hopkins, Salman Khan, Josh Kaufman, Ray Kurzweil, Michael Masterson, Kelly McGonigal, Samuel Michelot, Xavier Niel, David Ogilvy, Frank Oz, Vilfredo Pareto, Steve Pavlina, Neil Rackham, Gregory Retz, Eric Ries, Ken Robinson, Olivier Seban, Sénèque, Simon Sinek, Peter Thiel, Henry David Thoreau, Jeff Walker, Richard Wiseman, Mariana Zanetti.

And thank you to all those who, directly or indirectly, have helped me write this book. In particular: Karinny Ank, Romain Bastide, Laurent Breillat, Vincent Delourmel, Isabelle Dépatie, Pierre De Vreyer, Dr Chantal Dutron, Michael Ferrari, Pauliina Jämsä, Édith Lassiat, Martin Latulippe, Samuel Michelot, Attila Pongor, Aurélie Sergy, Benoît Wojtenka and, of course, my publishers – Éditions Leduc and Hay House – and their teams.

And everyone else! Thank you!

ADDITIONAL RESOURCES

The time when books were only available in hard copy format is over. In addition to this book, you will also find free videos offering further training, and many other additional resources, beginning with the missing chapter, by going to:

https://en.olivier-roland.com/formation

Or by scanning this code:

FOREWORD

The purpose of education is to enable young people to discover their talents and passions and transform them into skills that benefit society while ensuring they flourish.

Sadly, though, the reality often falls far short of the ideal. The education system is struggling to adapt to the modern world and becoming increasingly expensive. As Olivier explains later in this work, many people work jobs that leave them uninspired.

Having left school at 17 to set up my first business and begun self-learning computing on a PC given to me by my father, I have long been aware of the gap between what the education system promises and what it actually delivers.

And as I believe it is essential not only to have a critical spirit but also to apply it, I have very much wanted to propose a new model of education, at my own level, offering viable solutions. So, a few years ago, some friends and I founded a school, Campus 42, that breaks with many conventions and helps thousands of young people to learn a useful occupation.

Believe it or not, at our school:

- No academic qualification is required for admission. You may have left school at 16, like Olivier, or have a doctorate in nuclear physics; it doesn't matter. All you have to do is demonstrate your skills by taking some tests, and be comfortable with our school's methods, with the emphasis on free inquiry and personal responsibility.

- There is no rigid timetable. The school is open 24 hours a day, 365 days a year because it is made to fit the student, not the other way around. The idea that everyone has to study the same thing at the same age and at the same time is obsolete.

- There is no preset curriculum, but rather a common core and many options. You can complete your modules as and when you like, within a gamified educational system. Some students take two years to complete their studies, others five. You work at your own pace.

- There are no teachers: the students mark one another's work.

- We teach our students to learn for themselves to encourage autonomy, creativity, a can-do attitude, and a healthy rebelliousness and critical spirit, with the emphasis on practical application.

- We encourage cooperation among our students. Working together is often regarded as cheating in a conventional school, but in real life, very little is achieved in isolation.

- We don't award formal qualifications; we provide practical training and seek to create a state of mind. Our students have no trouble finding work when they leave, and 400 of them have decided to start their own businesses since Campus 42 was founded.

This system works so well that, after starting in Paris, we opened another school in California, in conscious opposition to the absolutely outrageous cost of education in the USA.

Of course, I am not claiming that this model is the ultimate solution to the US system: not everyone is receptive to a method based on the independence of mind. And Campus 42 focuses on computer programming and so omits many other fields.

Even so, I think a system of this kind is right for a certain percentage of the population – Olivier calls them 'intelligent rebels' or mold-breakers – who are suffocated by the traditional education system, sometimes to the point of never flourishing as they might have done. And for those who aren't tempted by computer programming or by Campus 42, this book is an excellent guide to devising your own course of studies, your own 'school of life,' one much better suited to your needs.

And entrepreneurship is, in my opinion, a route that more intelligent rebels should be exploring. It is an excellent way of short-circuiting fossilized systems and archaic monopolies, achieving social mobility, engaging in exciting projects, making a valuable contribution to society, and fulfilling your potential.

I am also convinced that an entrepreneur is more likely to change the world than a politician at all levels of society, whether your aim is to set up a simple business to support your family or establish an empire that will transform your country and the world.

Of course, not everything will be hunky-dory: you will have to face difficult challenges, but I am confident that you will also enjoy plenty of success. It is through challenges and achievements that you will grow and, by adopting some of the strategies set out in Part 2 of this book, you will be able to minimize the risks and the consequences of temporary failure.

The philosophy of the book you are now holding has many points in common with mine: 'Not everyone is fortunate enough to drop out of school' will encourage you to think outside the box, understand the limitations of conventional schooling and be liberated, learn how to study, engage in life-long learning, throw yourself into a project dear to your heart, and live a worthwhile and rewarding life while adding value to society.

In short, it will encourage you to train your own mind and act intelligently.

Enjoy!

Xavier Niel
Internet billionaire and founder of Campus 42

WHY I WROTE THIS BOOK

The main reason I wrote this book is simple: I think that life has better things to offer than 'getting a degree and then experiencing 40 years of daily grind until you can finally enjoy life when your best years are behind you.'

The best way to live a worthwhile life is to have the freedom and sufficient financial resources to do so, and running your own business is still the best way of achieving these things. Entrepreneurship is the royal road for intelligent rebels who dislike the system and seek fulfillment by a different route.

All too few young (and older) people fail to consider this route because no one has suggested it. Many talented people could accrue enormous wealth for their countries and themselves if only they were aware that setting up a business is possible, that it can be great fun. It is also possible to do so on a part-time basis in tandem with their studies or present job, thus minimizing the risks involved. Even those who are tempted to take this route are often unaware that it is possible to establish 'quality-of-life' businesses that serve them (rather than being slaves to their business).

I have written this book for you, dear reader, to make your brain bubble with new possibilities as you explore ideas that will change your life and broaden your horizons. My ultimate purpose is to enable you to put into practice as much of what you glean from it as you possibly can so that you can live a more fulfilled life than you have ever dreamed.

ABOUT THE ENGLISH EDITION

In the French-speaking world, this book met with unexpected success: 100,000 copies sold in less than five years[1] (in France, a first-time author is considered fortunate if they can sell a thousand copies).

I was therefore very pleased when Hay House offered to publish this work in English. I have had to adapt it to some extent, slimming it down a bit and changing some aspects to make it more compatible for readers in the UK and USA. Otherwise, this is the same book that has already helped thousands of French-speaking readers, and I hope you will draw inspiration from it, too.

---

1   In all formats: hard copy, digital, and audio.

BREAKING FREE

How to Live Life to the Full and Succeed Outside the System... While Enhancing Your Life and the Lives of Others

As you will find out in this book, by using modern technologies, intelligent rebels who dream of something other than the daily grind can:

- Educate themselves

- Set up a business with a minimum of risk

- Ensure that the business serves them rather than making them its slave

- Live out their passions while enhancing their own lives and the lives of others

- Embark on an exciting adventure

- Live a really worthwhile life!

And, for all this, academic qualification is an optional extra.

Wow. It seems too good to be true.

Of course, this path isn't without risk, and at various stages of your adventure, you are sure to fear the worst, but I will show you how to mitigate the risks and face down your fears. In any case, an adventure that doesn't make your hair stand on end occasionally wouldn't be an adventure, would it?

If I were able to set up my first business at the age of 19, when I was far less experienced, handsome, self-confident, and well-dressed than you, there is no reason why you can't do the same.

And if I managed to set up a second business – alongside the first, requiring 60 to 70 hours' work a week – which now means I can travel around the world for six months of the year while helping thousands of people each month, it's a sure thing you can launch your business project while doing your present job, don't you think?

You just need to have a dream, transform it into a project based on a good idea, then take the first step and get on with it. It is in working through these stages that many aspiring entrepreneurs meet with disaster. But if you are an intelligent rebel, I will already have grabbed your attention, and I'm prepared to bet you want to know more. So let's begin with my story...

GETTING AIRBORNE

My Story and Why You Should Read This Book

'OK, now park the plane on the taxiway and let me get out.'

Hearing these words, I was aware of my hands grasping the controls more tightly. I braked to complete the landing as quickly as possible and steered the plane onto the taxiway. Vincent, my instructor, was effectively saying he thought I was ready for my first solo flight. My first flight with no one else on board.

As Vincent opened the door and shouted his final instructions, part of me couldn't help wondering whether he was right, whether I was really ready or whether I would crash miserably into a tree or a farmer's field.

With my instructor safely on the ground, I moved slowly back up the taxiway, trying not to let my mind wander, repeating aloud the various procedures I had to follow on take-off, then on landing. Forgetting any one of them could be fatal.

I turned and lined the plane up on the runway, took a deep breath, announced that I was about to take off over the radio, then opened the throttle. I was airborne.

I've had several similar experiences in the course of my life.

Leaving school at 18 and setting up a business wasn't very sensible. It was the same sequence of events: A strong determination to make a dream come true, several months of careful preparation, then a leap in the dark. The upside? Greater freedom, a wonderful sense of excitement, an extraordinary adventure. The downside? Greater responsibility, including the burden, despite all my preparations, of possible failure.

Like setting up my first business, my first solo flight was a success. The only difference was that absolutely nothing went wrong. I took off smoothly, made a circuit of the airfield, marveling at finding myself all alone in the air, and landed again without a bump, to be congratulated by my instructor. What a relief! That day saw the conclusion not only of months of pilot training but also of a reorientation of my life that had begun some years earlier.

By contrast, running my first business hardly left me the time and energy to take the flying course. Instead, I was the typical overstressed businessman with a disastrous work-life balance, if you see what I mean.

FROM SPOTTY ADOLESCENT TO FREE, HAPPY BUSINESS LEADER

1995: At age 14, I invested almost all my meager savings in buying my first PC. It was one of the best investments I have ever made. I taught myself how to use it. The Internet was in its infancy, and I hadn't heard of it, so I borrowed books to supplement what I was learning by experimentation. This was the first time I used books to learn anything useful.

1999: 'A little computer genius,' as people said at the time. In fact, I was a rather shy 'geek,' hardly daring to speak to girls. A friend and I noted the worrying lack of companies offering to carry out home computer repairs and decided to provide this service to private individuals. We were only 18 and had no idea how to set up and manage a business. We made a lot of mistakes but earned more money than we had ever thought possible.

This was the trigger that convinced me to leave school and set up my own business. I was two years away from graduating. My friend decided to be sensible and complete his course of studies.

2000: After working on my project for a year and getting help from a business mentoring network in Lille, I finally scraped together the money I needed and officially launched Hypro on July 3rd, 2000. I had just turned 19, and I was over the moon at successfully completing this stage of my adventure.

Six months later, I was on the verge of bankruptcy.

Having failed to devise a proper marketing strategy, I was rushing around like a headless chicken. With the terrible naivety of a 'geek' discovering the harsh realities of life, I had invested heavily in ineffective advertising and had to admit to failure: I had no idea how to find new customers affordably. I was embarking on a long learning curve.

Fall 2001: After a period of struggling to make ends meet, one of my customers gave me a piece of advice that was to change my life and finally make my business profitable: 'Olivier, some people are happy when they have a big win, but a real businessman knows that serious money is earned from repeat sales.'

Of course! Instead of offering one-off repairs, I decided I would also provide maintenance contracts. And it worked: I was at last able to pay myself the minimum wage. And none too soon.

2005: Having rushed around like crazy developing my business, I began to realize that slaving away for 60 or 70 hours a week was not an incredibly fulfilling lifestyle. At around this time, someone asked me about my hourly earnings. I worked it out and, to my dismay, found I was earning less than minimum wage! Hardly what I had aspired to, given the risks involved.

So I looked for a solution and realized that the business I had set up to enjoy personal freedom was, in fact, a gilded cage. It was my only source of income, I couldn't sell it on and, like all French entrepreneurs, I was not entitled to unemployment benefit if the business came crashing down. What should I do? For two years, I cast about for an answer.

Mid-2008: I came across a practical book on entrepreneurship with an arresting title: *The 4-Hour Work Week*. It was a salutary slap in the face that completely changed my view of being an entrepreneur, even though I had now been running my business for eight years.

I abandoned my pride in being a self-made man who had no need to learn because he is so intelligent, and did what any normal adult would do in his position and embarked on a quest for exceptional reading material.

I began with *The E-Myth* by Michael Gerber, a book recommended by Tim Ferriss, author of *The 4-Hour Work Week*. This book described in precise detail the problem besetting my business and causing me to work such long hours. Another slap in the face!

Two salutary shocks in under a month; I was definitely on to something. I drew up a list of the best books on running a business and engaged with material that would change my life: my own tailor-made MBA. This reading list also gave me the idea of launching a blog, the move that was to ensure my online success: the French version of *Books That Can Change Your Life*.

Late 2009: The income from my blog suddenly jumped from €300 to €3,000 per month, once I asked my readership what sort of help they needed. Their answer: Training to help them set up a business. So I strove to create this product, something that would perfectly meet the needs of future entrepreneurs – needs with which I was so familiar. As well as running my own business, for eight years, I had been on the jury of a business project funding panel and had presided over at least 100 cases. The training I was offering, therefore, exactly matched the expectations of my readers and began to sell like hotcakes.

March 2010: After I had pulled out all the stops in promoting this training and published the first positive feedback, my turnover increased to €14,000 a month. At last, the fruits of a successful business! So I began making plans to sell on my first business enterprise, Hypro.

September 2010: Having got rid of my most awkward customers and sold a third of my client portfolio, I entrusted the rest of the business to my employees and left Europe for the first time to spend a month on the other side of the world. Wallis and Futuna and Fiji, here I come! I enjoyed the trip so much that I made up my mind to travel – a lot. On my return, I sold the remainder of the business.

Nine years later: I have gone on a month's road trip through California that took me to San Francisco and San Diego via Las Vegas and Death Valley. I have contemplated the Hindu funeral pyres of Varanasi and seen Sikhs bathing in the sacred lake of the Golden Temple at Amritsar. I have driven the Ford Mustang of a millionaire friend from Montreal to Quebec and visited Niagara Falls with the world dog-dressage champion. I have learned paragliding on the island of Réunion, a paradise for this sport. I have been initiated into yoga in the Indian city of Rishikesh, the world yoga capital. I have met more US best-selling authors than I can count on my fingers of both hands (and even more brilliant entrepreneurs). I have been no less charmed by the warm beers of London than by the volcanic marvels of Santorini. I have earned my diver's license in Morocco, watched a Thai boxing match in Bangkok, and, several weeks later, witnessed the Rio carnival parade in the Sambodrome. I have tasted the difference between the sangrias of southern Spain and the Canaries, and discovered an earthly paradise while living on islands with white sandy beaches in the Philippines for two months. I have participated in the crazy *Burning Man* festival in the Nevada Desert, met French-speaking natives of Louisiana, and listened to New Orleans jazz bands. I learned Portuguese, so I could give lectures in Brazil and Portugal, was introduced to meditation and the art of the Japanese saber by a Samurai master in Kyoto, discovered the joys of cruising in the Caribbean with some fantastic entrepreneur friends, and learned to kitesurf in one of the best spots in the world, Jericoacoara in Brazil. And I built up a worldwide network of friends from these travels, not to mention other amusing and magnificent adventures.

I just love my new life.

Early 2021: My four main blogs[2] and YouTube channel[3] help more than 500,000 people each month to discover life-changing books, make them happier and more serene in their daily round, help them earn more money and be more productive, and have more time for their family and friends. In addition, I have helped thousands of

---

2   https://des-livres-pour-changer-de-vie.com; https://blogueur-pro.net/, http://www.habitudes-zen. net/; https://devenez-meilleur.co/

3   https://www.youtube.com/c/OlivierRoland in French

clients to make further progress in some of these fields – an impact I could never have imagined when I set up my first business.

Despite all this, I am not a billionaire and have no desire to be.

I am an entrepreneur whose business serves me, whereas many entrepreneurs are in service of their businesses. I enjoy to the full the four key aspects of freedom that many businesspeople dream of: The freedom to do what I want, where I want, with whom I want, and when I want.

Michael Masterson, in his superb book *Ready, Fire, Aim*, explains just how much such freedom is preferable to being rich and having a hellish time schedule. Tim Ferriss confirms this in *The 4-Hour Work Week*, building his whole book – and his life – around this principle.

How right they are! Since I adopted this model, in combination with life-long self-study and several effective business strategies, my life has been turned inside out.

Basically, I am still the young rebel who wants to enjoy total freedom, fired up with enthusiasm to live his own life rather than a life dictated by someone else. It's just that I have learned to channel this energy and my time in a much more productive way, entirely directed toward the goal I have set myself.

This book is for iconoclasts, rebels who, like me, dream of having something other than the tedious routine of a wage-slave and a retirement that won't happen until the better part of their lives is over. It is for those who doubt the capacity of the system to offer the 'successful' ones anything more than a comfortable little daily existence, for those who cannot fit into this model or make a success of it, for those who really want to live life to the full, without waiting for 'pie in the sky.'

I will teach you how to break free of the system with a minimum of risk, make a success of things while having fun, live life to the full and be able to say at the end: 'I have really lived.' Follow this guide.

GETTING THE ADVANTAGE

Three Vital Principles for All Intelligent Rebels

'As to methods, there may be a million and then some, but principles are few. The man who grasps principles can successfully select his own methods. The man who tries methods, ignoring principles, is sure to have trouble.'

HARRINGTON EMERSON

These three principles will enable you, as the estimable Harrington explains, to select your own methods and use them effectively. 1) By being able to distinguish which ways are more effective, 2) by testing them to find out whether they are useful for you, and 3) by focusing 80 percent on the benefits they bring and 20 percent on the work they require, you will then become very good at applying methods that are in themselves excellent. This double leverage will give you an enormous advantage over others who have not understood the principles and/or have not applied them. Let's see what this entails.

PRINCIPLE 1: HEALTHY SKEPTICISM

The Mexico Olympics, 1968: A gangly young man is shifting his weight nervously from one foot to the other, in total concentration, clenching and unclenching his fists. The crowd holds its breath. He hesitates, then begins his run-up and clears the bar with ease. The stadium erupts in a thunder of applause. For this young man had adopted a technique that no one had ever tried before. And he had just set a new Olympic record for the high jump. His style was so novel that, at first, the jury was inclined to disqualify him. The tension was sky-high: was his exploit going to be ruled illegal?

Finally, after the adjudicators had re-read the regulations and found that there could be no objections, his jump was validated. And Dick Fosbury became part of history. He won the gold medal, having brought about a radical change in the practice of high-jumping. And so the technique pioneered by an outsider became the norm. In 1980, 13 of the 16 finalists used the 'Fosbury-flop,' and nowadays, it is the only technique used in high-jump competitions.

Imagine you were a high-jumper in the 1960s, and you heard stories of people who had adopted a technique that seemed to give them a clear advantage, enabling them to jump an inch higher. It is contrary to everything you have been taught: rather than straddling the bar face down, the jumper leads with his back. Unprecedented. No one has done this during the seven decades of the discipline's official history. Faced with something so radically new in 1968, you could react in one of three ways:

- Straightforward denial: Pull the other one: after all, if it were so effective, someone would have tried it long ago, wouldn't they?

- Polite curiosity: *Really? This could be something interesting*, you think. You discuss it with your coach during the coffee break. He welcomes the idea with a groan, and life returns to normal.

- Keen interest: You know that new developments in sport sometimes arise from counterintuitive discoveries. So you arrange to meet people who have adopted the new method, see how they perform, measure their progress. If you are convinced that the new technique could be advantageous, you undertake some training and see where it leads.

Your own reaction will depend in part on the available evidence: is the proof plentiful, reliable, and easily visible?

In the high jump, a more effective method will gain traction very quickly, given the motivation of the athletes involved and the ease with which the effects of a new approach can be measured.[4]

But how can you determine the actual effectiveness of methods when there is less evidence? For instance, a book on a subject that has very little in the way of results? Maybe if a popular book advocates an effective method, you may think it will be easy enough to find the results on the Internet. But that, unfortunately, is not necessarily true. For example, one of the world's best-sellers on communication and personal development is *How to Make Friends and Influence People*[5] by Dale Carnegie, written in the 1930s and read by tens of millions of people. And many of them have simply:

1. Rejected it with some degree of disdain

---

4   Even so when I say 'quickly,' everything is relative. After all, in 1980, 12 years later, three of the 16 finalists were still using the old method.
5   More than 15 million copies have been sold, according to *The Financial Post*.

2. Bought it and read only a section or two, or nothing at all

3. Found it interesting, then tidied it away and forgot about it

Given the book's global success, it is likely that most purchasers fall into the third category. But that means that most readers merely read the book, found it interesting, tried out one or two of the author's ideas, then put it on their bookshelves where it gathered dust.

This behavior is due to several factors, not least the common human tendency to put off things until tomorrow. And we may have doubts. We hear about an interesting method, wonder what to make of it, and end up entertaining serious misgivings concerning the theory as a whole:

- What if the author were lying, even to some extent? He or she might be doing it for selfish purposes (fame, money).

- And what if the author were simply wrong? If, like Don Quixote, he or she were mistaking windmills for giants?

These doubts are a powerful and insidious form of demotivation: who would want to invest their efforts in a method whose efficacy is in doubt? This kind of pessimism is healthy and entirely normal, much more so than rejecting an idea out of hand as impossible. 'If it were all so simple, it would be obvious!' But how can we harness this doubt intelligently, to motivate rather than paralyze, and work out whether the method is effective or not?

Let's take a concrete example to point the way to an answer, the example of Warren Buffett.

Buffett, a US entrepreneur and investor, is one of the world's wealthiest men.[6] He has proved to be a successful stock-market investor and has given billions of dollars to charitable causes. In the long run, he plans to give away 99 percent of his fortune. But how did he get started? One of the foundations of his success was not only his discovery of *How to Make Friends and Influence People*, but also how he tested the book's principles to decide whether Carnegie's method was viable.

Buffett first read the book when he was eight, having come across it in his grandfather's library.[7] He found it inspirational but, like most of us, applied a few

---

6   Warren Buffett was the world's wealthiest man in 2008 and, after giving $27 billion to charities, he
     was still the third wealthiest in 2018.
7   See Warren Buffett's biography, *The Snowball Effect*, by Alice Schroeder.

of the concepts, then forgot them, came back to them later, then forgot them again. Some years later, he decided to test the method scientifically to determine whether it really worked (and if it was worth applying the principles).

How did he go about it? It was very simple: half the time, he applied the book's principles; the other half, he behaved 'naturally.' 'Naturally' in his case meant 'timidly and with reserve' – as an adolescent, Buffett was something of a 'geek,' before the term had been invented.

The results were striking: when he applied the book's principles, people reacted far more positively than when he didn't. Buffett was delighted: though so shy, he had acquired a method that would help him form better relationships with others, and he had proved the efficacy of the Carnegie method. Of course, this doesn't mean that he was immediately able to apply it as written. But he kept coming back to it, trying, failing, succeeding, and taking up each of the principles more effectively until they were an integral part of him, in the process sharpening his mind and his social skills.

There you have a fine example of what I call 'healthy skepticism.' Warren Buffett realized that having doubts about the system undermined his motivation, so he performed a practical test to determine whether the system would be effective for him. This may seem black and white, but for me, there are two categories of skeptics: healthy skeptics and unhealthy skeptics.

The unhealthy skeptics are those who, when they come across a new theory that challenges their preconceptions, immediately reject it with the words: 'That's just not possible. It goes against everything I have learned to date, and if it really yielded the positive results described, everyone would know about it.' The healthy skeptics are those who, when they encounter a new theory that challenges their received ideas, says: 'That's interesting, and the results are encouraging. But is it true? Let me think... What simple experiment could I perform to test one of two of the method's principles?'

It's not a question of carrying out a randomized, double-blind scientific survey with hundreds or thousands of participants, because: 1) this is beyond the capacities of 99.9 percent of the Earth's inhabitants; and 2) even if a survey of this kind showed that it benefited a minority, you might be one of them and, by using it, you might be able to help thousands or millions of people.

Of all the people who have read *How to Make Friends and Influence People*, how many have applied it practically and repeatedly, and have benefited from it?

It is difficult to know, possibly only a (tiny) minority – but if they have used it effectively to create value for themselves and others, like Warren Buffett, the fact that the majority have got nothing out of it hardly matters. You need to test things for yourself to see if they will be of practical benefit.

Of course, it is impossible to test everything because time is limited, and not all methods lend themselves to such testing. But as far as humanly possible, you should do so. So, please, be skeptical when reading this book. But be a healthy skeptic, testing it to see if it works for you.

While reading, I would suggest taking notes to focus your mind on points for action. As soon as you come across something you could put into practice immediately, for testing purposes, note it down and do it at the earliest opportunity. You will find that this book is stuffed with these types of suggestions.

Do your testing and, if the results are positive, make these new tools and methods an integral part of your life. As for Warren Buffett with *How to Make Friends and Influence People*, this will require considerable motivation and perseverance. It won't be easy. But it's well worth it.

And if you are not sufficiently motivated to use a learning hack and test out at least a few simple activities to set up your own business, I would advise against persisting with this book. Unless you are happy to increase your general knowledge without any practical pay-back, carrying on without the necessary motivation would be a waste of time.

PRINCIPLE 2: SOME METHODS ARE MORE EFFECTIVE THAN OTHERS

Spare a few moments to look around you. Spend some time contemplating each of the objects in your field of vision. Go on. Really take your nose out of this book.

OK. All the human-made objects you have been looking at were manufactured using a method that, at any given time since humans developed their first tools, was more effective than any previous method. Your car, your phone, your computer, the book you are holding, the chair you are sitting on, all these objects were manufactured using a method that, over the centuries, proved to be more effective than others. Even the most ethereal works of art, for which material effectiveness is irrelevant, were created with tools designed to be more effective than the first natural pigments, bare fingers for applying the paint, or the first rudimentary tom-toms for making music.

Do you think there are fields in which some methods are not as effective as others?

Try as you might, you can't think of any.

Of course, not all the methods used are necessarily the best. For example, it might be possible to invent a better method of musical notation. But, as all musicians worldwide use the current system, adopting a more effective strategy would be a slow business, given that the present one performs its task quite well enough. That doesn't prevent you from inventing another, suggesting improvements, or learning a more effective one suggested by a brilliant but mad inventor. Well, OK, in the case of musical notation, no doubt the challenge is somewhat ambitious!

To sum up, in all fields there are methods which work better than others, including those closest to your heart, such as:

- Being happy

- Educating yourself, learning

- Being and remaining motivated

- Developing a business

- And even earning money...

- Or making love!

And even if some methods are better only for a minority of people, how do you know that you are not one of them? You need to test the situation, adopting the healthy skeptic approach.

Let's take a practical example in a field where many people think, without ever having considered the matter seriously, that if there was a more effective method, they would know about it. I'm talking, of course, about earning money.

So what process do most people follow for making money? Being in salaried employment. But is there a better way of earning money than being an employee? Definitely. Hundreds of better ways, thousands. Indeed, if you are an employee and you find earning money disheartening, you are on the right track, because being an employee is the least effective way of earning money, for two main reasons:

1. You are exchanging your time for money, with no leverage. In other words, you are trading the most precious thing you have in the world, your

time – each moment which you don't use to promote your happiness is irredeemably lost – for something that is soulless and cannot give you joy as such. Employees, then, are those who really put money on a pedestal since they are prepared to accept so disadvantageous an arrangement to earn it.

2. For an enterprise to be profitable, it must always pay its employees less than they actually bring in. This is pure mathematics, and it means that, if you are an employee, you will never be paid according to your full potential.

There are so many more effective ways of earning money, yet so many people don't believe it because they are unhealthy skeptics and unwilling to try anything different.

Let's take a concrete example of the intelligent application of an effective way of earning money, illustrated once again by the master in this field, Warren Buffett.

In 1950, Buffett read Benjamin Graham's *The Intelligent Investor*. In this book, Benjamin Graham advocates a particular form of investing on the stock exchange, later known as 'value investing.' This is a complex subject, but to simplify, it means buying shares that are being sold at below their intrinsic price, i.e., at below their true value.

This method was presented as superior to all existing forms of investing in stocks and shares, and Buffett was fascinated by it. Having already some experience of stock-market investing at 20 years of age, Buffett immediately decided to test the method by buying 200 shares in an enterprise whose share price seemed to him lower than its intrinsic value. He then enrolled at university solely to attend Graham's courses and applied his method. He was soon convinced of its effectiveness, and his obstinate and brilliant application of it laid the basis of his fortune. Indeed, Graham's approach was so critical to his success that Warren Buffett is fond of saying he is '85 percent Graham and 15 percent Fisher.'[8]

But Buffett's success didn't silence his critics. In 1984, Buffett responded[9] to those who said he was a kind of statistical anomaly and had just been lucky because it is impossible to beat the market in the long run. In his article, Buffett posited a game of heads-or-tails in which 225 million orangutans[10] were required to throw one coin

---

8   Philip Arthur Fisher, another brilliant investor, inventor of a method described in his book *Common Stocks and Uncommon Profits*.
9   In an article entitled 'The Superinvestors of Graham-and-Doddsville,' published in Hermes, the magazine of the Columbia Business School, 1984.
10   Buffett took this figure because at the time the population of the USA was 225 million.

in the air every day. After 20 days, there would be as few as 215 monkeys who had won (i.e., got 'heads') on 20 consecutive days, the others having been eliminated. In this case, said Warren Buffett, these 215 monkeys had won by pure chance. But what if it was found that, of these 215 monkeys, 40 came from the very same zoo? In this case, Buffett argued, it would be statistically impossible for the 40 to have won by pure chance: there would have to be a common factor among the monkeys of this zoo that ensured they got 'heads' so many times in a row.

And this was precisely what had happened with the Graham method. In the rest of the article, Buffett energetically demonstrated that this method was a more effective way of making money on the stock exchange than randomly investing. He took the example of nine investors who had invested in very different sectors and had nothing in common apart from the fact that they used Graham's method and had beaten the market by a clear margin over several decades. He ended the article with these memorable words:

> *In conclusion, some of the more commercially minded among you may wonder why I am writing this article. Adding many converts to the value approach will necessarily [reduce the gains I get from my investments].*
>
> *I can only tell you that the secret has been out for 50 years [...], yet I have seen no trend towards value investing in the 35 years that I have practiced it. There seems to be some perverse human characteristic that likes to make easy things difficult. [...] It's likely to continue that way. Ships will sail around the world, but the Flat Earth Society will flourish.*[11]

Thirty-five years after he wrote this article, Warren Buffett is still prospering – clear proof that his method works. He became the world's wealthiest man in 2008. From 1965 (when he acquired the Berkshire company) until 2018, his investments made average returns of 20.5 percent per annum, while the market made average gains of only 9.7 percent.[12]

This is an enormous difference: $1,000 invested in Warren Buffett's company in 1965 would have grown to $19 *million* in 2018, compared with $135,192 if they had

---

11   Indeed, 30 years after this article was written, the Flat Earth Society still exists, with a website promoting its bizarre theory: https://theflatearthsociety.org/home/
12   '2018 Letter to Shareholders,' Warren Buffett.

been invested in the market as a whole, or $7,994 if placed in a 4 percent savings account. Such is the power of compound interest. This clearly proves how right Warren Buffett was in 1984. If he had already been lucky to the point of being a statistical anomaly in 1984, how could his run of luck have continued for a further 30 years?[13]

You might reply by saying that Buffett is a brilliant fellow, capable of inventing sliced bread if someone had not already done so.

But let me first remind you that this book is addressed to intelligent rebels. That doesn't mean I am writing only for geniuses like Buffett, but for anyone prepared to defy the status quo by using their intelligence to personally test the best methods in a given field and then apply those that work for them.

This means that instead of looking at the average results people achieve in a particular field and thinking that you will probably achieve similar results, you need to put the question in these terms: 'What methods regularly enable intelligent rebels who practice them to beat these results?'

Then do some research. As a beginner, you will sometimes come across charlatans, and you may not realize this until it is too late. This is one of the risks of the game. But by using your common sense and a dose of healthy skepticism, together with active research into what works best, you will more easily detect the methods that will give you a decisive advantage in life.

Do you want another example of a miracle technique to:

- As much as double your influence, i.e., double your chances of getting someone to comply with a request, whether you are buying a product or asking for someone's telephone number?

- Make people appreciate you more, remember you, and see you as more attractive?

And this:

- In just a couple of seconds?

---

13   N.B. In 2007, at the company AGM, Warren Buffett recommended to 'Sunday investors' (which to his mind includes many people, even professionals in the sector) that they invest in indexed (or passive) funds, simply because these funds are cheap and low-risk, and only a small number of fund managers are able to beat the market on a regular basis (a mere 4 percent). Moreover, the advent of 'high-frequency trading' by computer in the 1990s had also changed the rules of the game, enabling professionals to perform millions of transactions per second! It is difficult to beat experts with such resources at their disposal.

- Without you having to expend energy, time, or money?

- And after a very, very short period of learning?

Does that seem too good to be true? Another of those miracle schemes designed to deceive gullible people.

At this stage, you are undoubtedly suspicious and thinking that, if I am writing this, it must be because there really is such a method, and I can prove it. And if that is what you are thinking, you are quite right.

The miracle method in question is as follows: all you need do is touch the shoulder or forearm of the person you are speaking to (at most for a second or two) to get the results described above.

Just to be clear: it is a light, respectful, friendly one-time touch, and socially as accepted as hugs are in the USA. And, yes, even if you are asking for money or proposing a date. According to the scientific studies on this subject:

- Touching someone in the street when you ask them for a dime or two increases your chances of being rewarded from 29 to 51 percent.[14]

- Touching a woman in the street when asking her to answer a questionnaire about a product increase the chances of getting what you want from 43.1 to 67.1 percent.[15]

- Touching a bus driver when requesting a ticket and you are 7 percent short of the full fare increases your chances of his agreeing to your request from 35 to 60 percent.[16]

- Touching a young woman you have met in the street when asking for her telephone number increases the chances of a positive response from 10 to 19.2 percent.[17]

- A waitress touching a customer when asking what they want to drink increases the percentage of customers leaving a tip from 10.8 to 24.6 percent.[18]

---

14 'Compliance to Requests Made by Gazing and Touching Experimenters in Field Settings,' Kleinke C. L., *Journal of Experimental Social Psychology*, 1977.
15 'Touch, Awareness of Touch, and Compliance with a Request,' Guéguen N., *Perceptual and Motor Skills*, 2002.
16 'Another Evaluation of Touch and Helping Behavior,' Guéguen N. et al., *Psychological Reports*, 2003.
17 'Courtship Compliance: The Effect of Touch on Women's Behavior,' Guéguen N., *Social Influence*, 2007.
18 'The Effect of Touch on Tipping: An Evaluation in a French Bar,' Guéguen N. et al., *International Journal of Hospitality Management*, 2005.

There are many other studies of this subject, almost all of which conclude that just touching the other person for a second or two considerably increases the chances of getting a positive response to a request.[19]

Now, do you think it is extraordinarily difficult to touch someone for a second or two on the forearm or shoulder, and that you would need several years' training and the IQ of Einstein?

Of course not. It is a straightforward technique that anyone can perform, requiring very little practice before it embeds in your daily behavior (I do it without even thinking). If a respectful touch of this kind is well accepted socially and makes people like you more and feel more comfortable around you, can you think of any good reason not to adopt this behavior, which very soon becomes completely natural?

Like Graham's stock-market investing method, the secret has been in the public domain for many years: the first study of the subject dates from 1977. Yet, many people have still not heard of it. And many people will read this and say 'Wow! That's a great idea,' then forget about it and move on to something else without taking the time to embed this technique in their day-to-day behavior.

Don't be like them. Be an intelligent rebel. Just remember this: miracle methods do exist. They are often clearly identified and well known. It is merely, as author William Gibson puts it, that 'the future is already here – it's just not evenly distributed.'

Of course, learning some new methods may demand a significant input of your time and energy. And not all are good for you. As well as Warren Buffett, there is Bernie Madoff. But the fact that Madoff exists doesn't mean that Buffett doesn't. When you start out in a new field, how can you distinguish the Madoffs from the Buffetts?

It's not always easy. But keep in mind that the Madoffs are the exceptions that confirm the rule, and crooks who survive for so long without getting caught are extremely rare. Even Charles Ponzi, the fraudster who gave his name to the infamous pyramid investment schemes, could only keep it up for a year before being apprehended in 1919. Once again, common sense and healthy skepticism will help you to separate the wheat from the chaff.

---

19   For further information: 'Contact tactile et acceptation d'une requête: une méta-analyse,' Guéguen N. et al., *Cahiers internationaux de Psychologie sociale*, 2008.

PRINCIPLE 3: THE PARETO PRINCIPLE

In the early 20th century, an Italian economist and sociologist discovered a principle that was to make him famous. A principle that is simple but incredibly powerful.

Wanting to understand how the rich and powerful came by their wealth and power, he analyzed the income figures for several countries in different centuries and made a striking discovery. At all times in history, a minority of the population has enjoyed the lion's share of the wealth. Although the proportions varied slightly, Vilfredo Pareto noted that, on average, 20 percent of the population enjoyed 80 percent of a country's wealth. And 20 percent of the world's countries enjoyed 80 percent of global wealth. However, Vilfredo Pareto didn't suspect that this economic law might have a far more universal application.

In the 1940s, the great engineer and consultant Joseph M. Juran, whose theories and teaching were a significant factor in Japan's post-war economic miracle, came across the Pareto principle and realized it could also be applied to many quantity-related problems. In particular, that 80 percent of issues were produced by 20 percent of causes. From this time on, a series of discoveries relating to what was already known as the 'Pareto principle' or the '80/20 rule' began to emerge.[20]

The Pareto principle could, in fact, be applied in many fields, some of them of great interest to entrepreneurs. For example:

- Eighty percent of your profits derive from 20 percent of your customers.

- Eighty percent of the complaints and problems you experience derive from 20 percent of your customers.

- Eighty percent of your profits derive from 20 percent of the time you spend running your business.

- Eighty percent of your sales derive from 20 percent of your products.

- Eighty percent of your sales derive from 20 percent of your sales agents.

The rule or principle can be summed up as follows: 80 percent of effects are produced by 20 percent of causes.

Of course, the figure isn't exactly 80/20. But once you start analyzing the world around you with this principle in mind, you will be surprised to find how often the

---

20   Like the 'scarcity law of the vital few' or 'principle of factor sparsity.' Slightly more complicated than the '80/20 rule.'

most effects are produced by a limited number of causes. Most of your happiness derives from the few people you associate with. Vice-versa, most of your troubles are caused by a relatively small number of people. Most of the stress you suffer is produced during a limited amount of your time. And so on.

When I first discovered this principle, I immediately analyzed the simplest and yet the most important figure I could think of: the proportions of income from my business deriving from different customers. I was literally shocked by what I discovered: 17 percent of my customers accounted for 81 percent of my business turnover. Obviously, I knew that some customers were more profitable than others, but I had no idea of the extent of the phenomenon. And I was surprised to find how close this income distribution was to the 80/20 rule.

In making a more subjective (but equally interesting) analysis, I also found that most of my problems and stress were due to a tiny minority of customers. And that, strangely, very few of them were among the 17 percent of customers who were generating 81 percent of my income...

What followed wasn't rocket science: I got rid of the difficult customers and began working out what my best customers had in common so I could find others like them. I shall explain how to go about that in this book.

Meanwhile, take on board that you can get 80 percent of the results you are aiming for by focusing on 20 percent of your most important activities. Regularly in this book, I shall be highlighting what I consider those most important activities to be, to help you achieve the results you are after as quickly and with as little effort as possible.

THE ADVANTAGES OF THESE THREE PRINCIPLES FOR INTELLIGENT REBELS

Can you see the extent to which these three principles work together and how intelligent rebels can take advantage of them to stand out from the crowd?

If you have accepted the idea that in every field some methods are more effective than others, you will have understood that it could be advantageous to discover them. Once you have identified them, it is up to you to test them out with a healthy dose of skepticism (rather than concluding from the word go that such methods must be useless, or everyone would have adopted them...). Finally, when you have identified the strategies that work for you, you should apply them and enjoy the benefits.

Since these methods are far more effective than those used by most people, they will give you a much greater return on investment than others derive for the same expenditure of time, energy, and money. The 80/20 rule will also help you decide which methods to invest in and which to avoid. Moreover, as you discover and adopt new methods, you will learn to master them and gradually find out which of the 20 percent yields 80 percent of the results you are aiming for.

As I said at the start of this section, you will then become very competent in methods which are in themselves excellent. If that doesn't give you an edge in life, what else will?

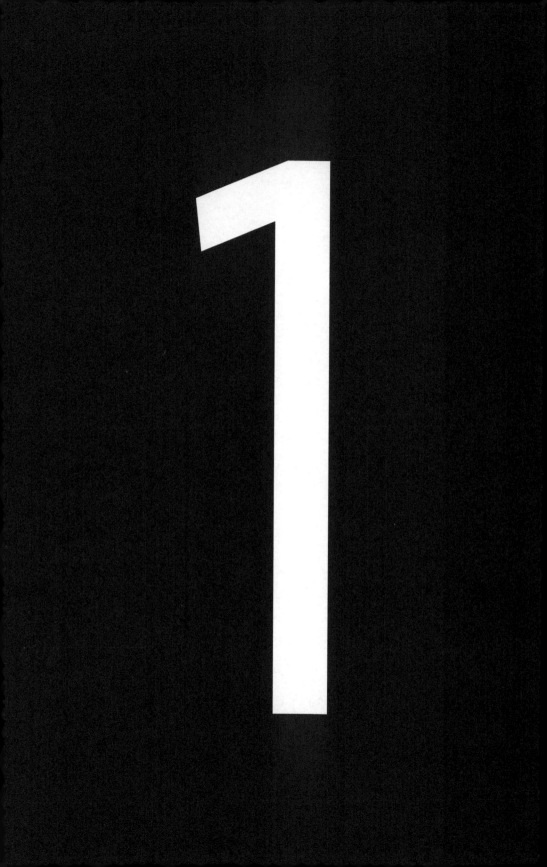

LEARNING WITH ENJOYMENT

(OR HOW TO EDUCATE YOURSELF EFFECTIVELY IN THE 21ST CENTURY)

CHAPTER 1
EDUCATING THE REBEL
Why Traditional Schooling Isn't Ideal for the Intelligent Rebel

'33 percent of all our regrets are the result of decisions we took concerning our education.'

KATHRYN SCHULZ

I would like to start by sharing the story of Caroline, told in her own words, and thousands of others who were a coach but transformed into a pumpkin.

'At last, after five years' study – including two years of cramming for the competitive entrance examination, I got my degree – a hard-earned master's in business studies, which, I thought, would open doors for me. I was over the moon. This was the fulfillment of a dream.

A year later, I had come down to earth with a bump: the only doors that had opened were those of a large retail chain, which took me on as a part-time check-out operator, on minimum wage. They wanted to test my capacity for work and, after four months, I was promoted to departmental sales assistant, a job which brought in €1,500 gross in a good month.

I was promised further opportunities and wanted to become a sales manager for my department because I was interested in management. My boss promised me an appraisal to decide whether I was ready for this, but he was transferred elsewhere a few weeks before it was due.

Inevitably, the store manager hadn't been informed of my application and said he hadn't made me any promises, which I found somewhat discouraging. And as I have a new manager each year, it's always back to square one. The result? After six years, I am still no further forward.'

Caroline gave me a rueful smile, eying me over her teacup and concluding: 'And as for all the knowledge I crammed into my head over those five years of study, I've barely used any of it.'

Naturally, I felt sorry for her. Here was yet another of the many stories I had heard of brilliant studies, undertaken with the utmost application, that turned out to be pumpkins rather than a gilded coach to success.

It's the same thing time and again: academic qualifications are supposed to open doors and ensure a certain level of income, as well as giving you a sound basis of knowledge to draw on in your future occupation. In reality, the doors tend to remain stubbornly closed, salaries are low, and all that knowledge is forgotten in just a few months as it wastes away in the corner of your brain. What is more, the loans to finance your studies and the time spent getting a degree rather than working can be very costly compared with taking a shorter course and starting work sooner. Even though it is true that you can hope to earn a slightly better salary after a more extended program of study.

Nevertheless, by enrolling in this business school, ranked twelfth in her country – a good compromise between reputation and value-for-money – Caroline thought she was giving herself a head-start in her professional career.

Maybe Caroline's is an isolated case. *Maybe* Caroline could have shown more initiative or been savvier; she could perhaps have made multiple applications, or pulled more strings, or created a buzz on social media with a photograph of herself and a seal in a bikini on an ice floe. Maybe. However, in reality, hers is by no means an isolated case. Here follows a few facts:

According to a 2018 report by analysts Burning Glass Technologies,[21] 43 percent of US college graduates are overqualified for their first job. Two-thirds of these students are still doing a job for which they are overqualified five years later, while three-quarters are still doing a job that is beneath their abilities after 10 years.[22] The situation is even worse in the UK, where 49 percent of graduates started in a position for which they were overqualified in 2017.[23] So, Caroline is just one example among millions of a new generation promised the moon provided they didn't break the sacrosanct rule: 'Get your high school diploma and go as far as you can in your studies.'

---

21 Burning Glass Technologies, 2018: 'Pomp and Circumstances: New Study Finds Most College Graduates Who Start Out Underemployed, Stay There'
22 Burning Glass Technologies, 2018: 'The Permanent Detour: Underemployment's Long-Term Effects on the Careers of College Grads'
23 According to the Office of National Statistics: https://www.ons.gov.uk/employmentandlabourmarket/peopleinwork/employmentandemployeetypes/articles/graduatesintheuklabourmarket/2017

Does that mean that undertaking an extended program of studies is pointless? Not necessarily. All the statistics show that, as a general rule, the higher the qualification a person achieves, the higher the likelihood of their being in employment, and the higher the salary they can expect. Of course, in some professions, such as the law or medicine, it is impossible to practice unless you have followed the prescribed career path and passed certain competitive examinations. So, I'm not trying to say that studying is a waste of time, that it doesn't give you an edge, or it isn't the right solution for some people. But:

- A long course of studies doesn't guarantee success; it only improves your chances of finding suitable employment.

- The job you get may not match up to your expectations; it will not necessarily enable you to use the knowledge you have gained, nor bring in a salary commensurate with your qualifications.

- Analysis shows that, as a general rule, the higher your educational qualification, the higher the income you can expect to earn. But such analysis overlooks an essential point. It doesn't take into account the cost of studying, or debts acquired to support you through college, in calculating the actual benefit of high school studies plus five years of higher education, as compared with just graduating high school. The final result is very instructive, as you shall see.

Moreover, aren't these statistics subject to another bias? What if most people who undertake a long course of study were more intelligent or more hard-working than the average? Maybe they would be just as successful without an academic qualification, earning a good income, without having to get into debt, simply *because* they were more intelligent and/or hard-working. It is almost impossible to carry out a study that would confirm or contradict this hypothesis. But the question is worth asking.

Is this 'classic' way of 'succeeding' in life really the one that suits you best? An academic qualification followed by 40 years of commuting/the daily grind until you retire? Is that what an intelligent rebel like you really wants?

THE CONCRETE SLIPPERS TRAP

'Those who would give up essential Liberty to purchase a little temporary Safety, deserve neither Liberty nor Safety.'

BENJAMIN FRANKLIN

'The reason why so many people end up looking for a job is that the economy needs people who end up looking for a job.'

Seth Godin

Let's imagine a typical and relatively positive scenario: long years of study have enabled you to secure a managerial position in a dynamic multinational company, at the cost of getting heavily into debt to pay your school fees, accommodation, IT equipment, and daily expenditure over five years. Your parents have helped you to some extent, but you have had to bear most of these costs yourself, with the help of a minor bursary, a summer job, and a big loan from the bank.

You gradually discover the joys of working for a large corporate entity: the in-house rivalries, the political tensions, the vagaries of fashion, a new boss who arrives out of nowhere and makes your life hell, your slow progress through the ranks of the hierarchy, the rumors, and gossip, not to mention the bad jokes you have to listen to during coffee breaks.

Your salary increases little by little, but you always feel you don't earn enough, especially since you married and took out a mortgage to buy a house. Not to mention the fact that your spouse is perhaps freer with money than you are (and you may have become a big spender yourself), and children arrive and soon account for a large slice of your budget. Then there is your pet dog, your well-deserved vacations, leisure activities of one kind and another, and so on.

Finally, aged 40, you hold a good position in the company and earn a decent salary. Even though your expenditure has inexplicably kept pace with all your raises, you are slightly overweight, suffer from back pain, and wrinkles are beginning to appear. All of which is not surprising considering the stress and overwork that went into making it to your present position.

Even so, you feel you have been stagnating for some time, your superiors seem less enthusiastic when you raise the issue of career progression. You sometimes catch yourself dreaming of something different, maybe a less formal working environment where you could blossom more and enjoy a better work/life balance. And – fantasy of fantasies – maybe no boss always on your back.

The years go by and, by dint of your effort, you secure a higher position. But it entails a big sacrifice: a move to a region you don't like, fortunately paid for in part by your company, longer working hours, and the realization that you find this kind of work less and less congenial. You dream of a less stressful, boss-free life. But your job is well paid, and your current lifestyle makes it difficult to countenance any diminution in income, especially given the exorbitant cost of your children's studies.

And you fought tooth and nail to get this job. Surely you are not going to give it up just like that when many people dream of being in your position – even though you hate where you are living. And then, you are settled with this company, its political conflicts, and petty disputes, and after all, you, too, have made some bad jokes during coffee breaks. At least they reduce the tension somewhat.

So you put your dreams aside and, for better or for worse, you put up with the stress, the tensions, and the downsides of your job. A few years later, you try for another promotion, but your superiors are really unenthusiastic, and you realize you have gone as high as you can in the hierarchy. So you ask to be transferred to a region that would suit you better. A few months later, your boss offers you a 'sideways' move to a quieter position in an area you like and, the cherry on the cake, without taking a pay-cut, though without a raise either. The job is uninteresting, but definitely less stressful and will allow you to relax a bit before you retire, an event which you await with growing impatience. Maybe, at last, after decades spent working for someone else, you will be able to realize your dreams and start enjoying life.

An attractive scenario, I'm sure you will agree? Not exactly what you expected when you graduated, but no doubt you know someone whose experience has been very similar.

If you have been employed for some time, maybe you are already a prisoner of these 'concrete slippers.' Perhaps you are experiencing this comfortable servitude, but when you read these lines, an inner voice cried out that something wasn't right, that this lifestyle is not really what you originally dreamed of. And maybe you immediately suppressed it.

How sad! If this is the case, the good news is that I have devoted several sections of this book to the art of escaping from a boring job while minimizing the risks – and maximizing the chances of success. I shall explain how you can launch despite your fears, and how to give that little voice all the space it needs to express itself.

THE RAT RACE

> *'There are thousands and thousands of people out there leading lives of quiet, screaming desperation, where they work long, hard hours at jobs they hate to enable them to buy things they don't need to impress people they don't like.'*
>
> NIGEL MARSH

The term 'rat race' was coined in the 1950s to describe the unbridled competition people engage in to get the best degree, then the 'top job' – often a stressful, soul-destroying job that brings few rewards, apart from superficial material satisfactions. The rat race metaphor alludes to laboratory rats made to race through a labyrinth to get a piece of cheese, observed with cynical amusement by scientific researchers.

We are always being told that it is vital to choose a career in a field for which we have genuine enthusiasm but just look around you. Do a mental survey of all the people you know. Are most of them in an occupation they are passionate about? Or are they instead in a job which, at best, 'has some interesting aspects,' and offers a 'nice little annual bonus'? The fact is that very few people really love their job.

One of the most authoritative studies on this subject[24] reveals that a mere 15 percent of employees worldwide are emotionally invested and happy in their company, while 18 percent are actively disengaged. In other words, they see their job as no more than an unpleasant way of earning their daily bread. The USA has one of the best scores, with 33 percent of employees who say they love their job and 16 percent who hate it; in Canada, the respective figures are 20 percent and 14 percent; in the UK, 11 percent and 21 percent. Wherever you look, the percentage of those who say they love their job is a (small) minority. And this is the greatest failing of modern society.

Of course, it wasn't long ago that most of the population was obliged to work in the fields or in animal husbandry. Few people had the opportunity to practice an occupation they felt passionately about. On the other hand, most of history's farmers were not subject to enforced working hours. They had to work hard to prepare their land and sow crops and then harvest them, but for the rest of the year, their work was less burdensome. Can you imagine never seeing a watch? Never knowing the exact time.

But that's how people lived until the late Middle Ages, when clocks began to appear in towns, followed by portable timepieces in the 17th century. Not until the 19th-century industrialists wanted to get the maximum productivity from their workers were clocks made mandatory in workplaces, with a minimum number of hours to be worked every day. Before the Industrial Revolution, people worked an average of just 25 hours a week over the whole year.[25] It is, therefore, only very recently that weekly working hours have been imposed and regulated.

---

24 Gallup, 'Report: State of the Global Workplace,' 2017. It is based on a far higher number of informants than other surveys on this subject: no fewer than 155,000 employees in 155 countries: http://olivier-roland.com/state-global-workplace/
25 Étienne Martin Saint-Léon, 'Histoire des corporations de métiers depuis leurs origines jusqu'à leur suppression en 1791,' 1897.

But intelligent rebels like you realize that life has more to offer than a rat race to get the best degree, then 40 years of the daily grind, with the occasional vacation thrown in to sweeten things, until you can finally enjoy retirement when your best years are behind you. And it really is possible to live life to the full and enjoy all the wonderful experiences it offers.

WHY INTELLIGENT REBELS WANT TO LIVE OUT THEIR HEART'S DESIRES

'I may die rich, or I may die broke. But I won't die with my music still in me.'

STEVE PAVLINA

Life is short, as we all know. Much too short to be lived within systems – schools, big corporations – that suppress your talents and aspirations. Too short to be wasted trying to fit into a system that stifles your creativity and silence the inner voice that aspires you to live and shout its message from the rooftops. Because within themselves, intelligent rebels have a voice that is overflowing with insistent, powerful energy, telling them there are alternatives to the daily grind, that they must break with the status quo.

You want something other than a tedious occupation that enables you to survive and buy the latest fashionable gadgets. You know material goods only give temporary satisfaction and fail to feed your inner voice, which won't be satisfied with anything except the fulfillment of your potential. With this awareness, intelligent rebels are always seeking quicker, more effective, and often unorthodox ways of achieving their objectives.

But they don't necessarily know where to look. They may feel all alone in the world, especially if they are young or haven't yet heard this voice telling them to explore, leave the beaten track, and encounter kindred spirits. But they all have something in common, even if they are not really aware of it. What matters for them is to express what they have inside them, to live out their heart's desires and, above all, not to 'die with their music still in them.' They have a mission to accomplish, one which hardly anyone points out to them, and that fills them with excitement, felt by themselves alone. They want to live life to the full, as powerful beings who make their own unique contribution, not as robots ordered what to do.

Intelligent rebels are aware that what they want to do has to be done by someone. They know if they fail to respond to the call, they will perish, put on their concrete slippers, and that others will never benefit from what they could have accomplished – a dead loss for the human race, and for themselves.

This awareness propels intelligent rebels to make their contribution differently. As a result, they may earn more than the average, which will help them to reach more people, make a more significant contribution, disseminate their message more widely. But intelligent rebels also understand that the most important thing is to live life to the full because life is short. Money is just a way of saving time, as time cannot be stored for later use. Time wasted on pointless activities is lost forever.

This book will guide you in your quest to find the desires that make your heart sing and learn to express them by venturing off the beaten track and making the most of your potential.

HOW THOMAS QUIT THE RAT RACE TO LIVE OUT HIS HEART'S DESIRE IN AN EARTHLY PARADISE

Paris, 2000: Thomas was a graphic designer for a French newspaper. It was his first role, and he was very proud of his position. Unfortunately, the business got into difficulties, and his job was one of the first to go as part of a cost-cutting exercise. His wife, Céline, who also worked in media, was made redundant at roughly the same time. Unfortunately, they hadn't contributed long enough to qualify for unemployment benefits. So they had to accept stop-gap jobs, just to keep the wolf from the door.

They were well on the way to becoming victims of the rat race when one day, Céline asked a question that was to change the course of their lives: 'Do you still have contacts in China? That's a country I'd love to visit.'

Thomas had spent a year in China as part of his university course and had made an effort to learn Mandarin. He told Céline he'd been waiting for her to ask this question for the last five years. Having nothing to lose, keen to live his dream and deepen his knowledge of China, he downed tools and left with his very supportive wife, without any clear plan except to explore the country for a while, drawing on their €2,000 of savings.

In China, among French expatriates he found less competition, more solidarity: it was easier to avoid the rat-race scenario. In fact, both of them were able to find interesting, well-paid work. They were barely settled when they had to make a difficult decision: at roughly the same time, both received offers of decent jobs in Paris.

They each took time to think it through. They were happy, making frequent trips within China and to other Asian countries, which they loved. Thomas was able to develop several of his hobbies: he had become a diving instructor. And life was an endless adventure. What they feared most was having to exchange all this for the daily grind back in Paris, the commuting, the slavery of working to pay back a mortgage loan contracted to buy a tiny apartment.

As Thomas put it, with the determination of a person committed to his values: 'I didn't want to get tied up in any way. I prefer total freedom, even if it means things may come crashing down in flames at any time. I don't have a mortgage; I don't owe anyone anything. I'm my own boss; what I have is what I have built up myself. This is what I've dreamed of doing. I don't owe money. I've never claimed a social security benefit.'

They both turned the proposed jobs down. Such is the power of those who have opted out of the rat race.

And that is not the end of the story. After six years in China, they experienced itchy feet once again. So they began exploring different parts of Asia during their vacations, looking for their very own Garden of Eden. Two years later, they found what they were looking for: El Nido, a corner of paradise consisting of tropical islands, white sandy beaches, and crystal-clear waters, with an average annual temperature of 82°F (28°C) and a water temperature of 78°F (26°C). They knew immediately that this was their Shangri-La. Thomas and Céline opened a restaurant there with a partner with catering experience. Having worked there for some time, they completely automated the operation, so that it brought in money without their having to do all the work (we shall see how to do that later in the book).

They had a child who is now three years old and already trilingual in French, English, and Tagalog. Thomas opened a diving center, further advancing his dream of the good life. His customers pay him to do what he loves best, going out diving every day. With his partners, Thomas established another restaurant in Manila in the Philippines, which also makes money without them having to set foot in the place. He no longer needs to work, and nor does Céline. They devote time to their child and enjoy a lifestyle they could not even have dreamed of back in Paris.

The strangest thing about this story?

They earn roughly €600 a month. A sum which seems ridiculously inadequate, but enables them to live very comfortably in the Philippines, without having to slave away in a soulless job, suffering the daily stress of traveling to work in a crowded metro carriage, and competing for a place in a two-bit press organization.

Thomas has remained in touch with a few acquaintances in Paris; most think he is mad. They tell him, for example, that he won't earn a pension, so what will he do in his old age? They don't understand that Thomas is enjoying his retirement already, living his heart's desire while still in his prime, while they won't be able to enjoy retirement until they are over the hill. They don't understand that Thomas is developing an amazing talent, setting up businesses that function even in his absence, enabling him to generate an income and invest in other enterprises that will keep him in old age. Some of his friends envy him, would like to do something similar, but can't summon up the courage. So they stay in Paris.

Thomas ends his story with these words: 'And yet anyone can do what I have done. I completely lacked the skills to set up a business on the other side of the world and live the life I am living. I just did it. And I learned as I went along, never taking outrageous risks.'[26]

TRADITIONAL SCHOOLING, OR WHY YOU FORGET MOST OF WHAT YOU EVER LEARNED

'I have never let my schooling
interfere with my education.'

Mark Twain

Let me clarify my position: I'm a great fan of education. Education is a light to guide us in the darkness, enabling us to make wiser decisions into a broader frame of reference. But there is education and education. Spending years learning things you mostly won't use and that will leak out of your brain without any benefit is not very efficient. Especially if you consider the 'opportunity cost': the things you could have learned and used effectively if you had benefited from a more efficient educational experience.

What do you remember now from your lessons on ancient Egyptian history at high school? From your geography lessons on the economy of Burkina Faso? From your biology lessons on the sex life of mice? If you had to sit an exam paper on these topics now, what grade would you get?

---

26   Thomas has since opened a bar, Angle Bar, at El Nido. Drop in and greet him on my behalf if you happen to be in the vicinity.

The thought is depressing. But it's even more so if you ask yourself the two following questions: What percentage of everything I learned at school have I remembered? And what percentage of what I learned do I now use in my daily life and occupation?

I have searched high and low for any scientific studies investigating these two questions. I have even enlisted the help of several research assistants. And the answer is that no serious research has been done on so important a subject.[27] No one knows what percentage of the knowledge we acquired at school is retained and actually used in daily life. And yet we generally spend between 10 and 20 years sitting on our backsides in a school classroom. Is that really a constructive use of our time?

On the other hand, many studies have been undertaken on remembering and forgetting, going back many years.

In 1885, a German psychologist, Hermann Ebbinghaus, developed his famous 'forgetting curve,' testing his own capacity to memorize meaningless words.[28] The principle he discovered is simple: we quickly forget most of the knowledge we don't use. It is hardly an earth-shattering discovery, of course, but he was the first person to have accurately measured our forgetfulness and provide scientific evidence.

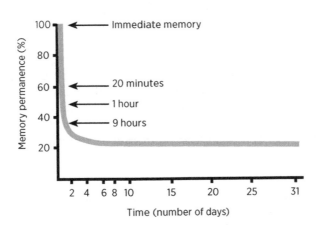

Figure 1: The forgetting curve[29] – with time, we forget an increasing percentage of what we once learned. After nine hours, we have forgotten more than 60 percent.

---

27 As far as I know. I have done some research on this with the help of four assistants, but if you know more about it, please get in touch.
28 See his essay on *Memory*, 1885. I shall be returning to his idea in greater detail later.
29 Reproduction of the curve as presented in the article: 'Play It Again: The Master Psychopharmacology Program as an Example of Interval Learning in Bite-Sized Portions,' Stahl S. M. et al., *CNS Spectrums*, 2010.

Piotr Wozniak, the Polish inventor of SuperMemo, the first mass-market software application to aid learning, conducted an experiment in the early 1980s to measure his memorization of English vocabulary and facts or concepts on biology. After attempting to learn 3,000 English words and 1,400 things about biology, he reached the following conclusion. If he really wanted to study these subjects, he definitely wasn't going about it in the right way.[30]

The problem wasn't that he couldn't learn; it was not forgetting what he had learned. Wozniak discovered that 40 percent of the English vocabulary he had acquired dissipated over time. And the figure was even higher for biology: 60 percent. Finally, he calculated that to master 15,000 words of English, he would need to work at it for two hours each day. And it would take him twice as long to learn 30,000 words. Hardly a practical endeavor.

There was nothing particularly surprising about his discovery, as many people before him had realized it was easier and quicker to learn a language by immersion – living in the country where the language was spoken – than by spending hours in a classroom. But he clearly established that, without revision, any knowledge is eventually forgotten after a longer or shorter period. He concluded that the reason why people become experts in a particular field is simply that they intensively practice what they have learned, which keeps their memory fresh. In Chapter 2, I will share some techniques that will help you overcome the forgetting curve and discuss some other ways of learning more quickly and efficiently.

There are, of course, things we have learned at school that we use throughout our lives: reading, writing, the basic arithmetic of daily life, interacting, discussing, and so on. These skills are essential, and school makes an enormous social contribution by teaching us them. But on the whole, school has one great failing: it lacks practicality. And because it teaches us things without practical application, we forget them, having wasted thousands of hours learning them in the first place.

THE PRACTICAL/PRACTICE PROBLEM WITH TRADITIONAL SCHOOLING

'Some people get an education without going to college. The rest get it after they get out.'

MARK TWAIN

---

30   'Want to Remember Everything You'll Ever Learn? Surrender to This Algorithm,' Wolf G., *Wired Magazine*, 2008: http://olivier-roland.com/remember-everything/

What is practicality in education? Simply to teach us things that we will find really useful, that we won't forget *precisely* because we will use them, and that in the final analysis, will help us to lead a better life.

For this to be the case, what we learn must correspond to the skills we will need on the ground and the society in which we live. So what is the point of learning trigonometry or the imperfect subjunctive if, once our school days are over, we don't use them again? On the other hand, how do you explain the fact that the education system is woefully inefficient in teaching languages (*see p.17*) when nowadays this is a vital skill?

The problem is that society is changing at increasing speed and schools, which have been falling behind for decades, are failing to close the widening gap between the academic curriculum and the realities of modern social life. School is effectively educating young people for a world that no longer exists.

In the past, the objective of mainstream education was to produce workers and employees who were content with their lot, able to read and write, and proud of their country and its history. Circumstances were very different: it wasn't unusual to spend your whole career working for the same company, and surfing the net wasn't a required skill, to give one example.

Suddenly, skills that are now of vital importance and enable us to impact the world around us are inadequately taught, or not taught at all. In my view, there are three areas of competence that are being neglected, with the consequence that schools are turning out a generation of 'new illiterates.'

ARE YOU ONE OF THE 'NEW ILLITERATES'?

If you were among the 11 percent of Americans who couldn't read or write in 1900, you would have been faced with many problems in your personal and working life – limitations we can barely imagine nowadays. For example, can you imagine not being able to read a newspaper or public notices, not even being able to sign your name? What would your life be like if you had never read a single book?

Being illiterate, then and now, makes you dependent on 'those in the know.' Those who will read on your behalf, write on your behalf, sign on your behalf. Nowadays, not being able to read and write has been largely overcome (even though that doesn't necessarily make people very literate!). But a new generation of illiterates is beginning to emerge. They can read, write and do arithmetic, but are 'illiterate' in four areas of increasing importance. In these four areas, they are very much dependent on 'those in the know.'

1. Information technology/computing

Just as everyone needs to read, write, and do basic sums to cope with daily life, everyone now needs a basic knowledge of computing. If, by some miracle, you have so far avoided the need to master this skill, the galloping digitization of our society will sooner or later oblige you to give in and get some training. Unless, of course, you want to be classed as one of those illiterates who needs someone to read, write, and sign for them. And be increasingly cut off from your children and grandchildren, their opinions, and subjects of conversation.

The concept of the 'digital divide' is no mere abstraction: there is a real difference in terms of success in career and in life generally between those who can use a computer and those who cannot. Indeed, a new term has been invented to describe people afflicted with this problem: 'information illiteracy.'

2. Life-long learning

There is a problem even more widespread than computer illiteracy: far too many people think that, once they have got their degree or other qualification, they no longer need to go on learning, apart from the vocational training courses laid on by their company. This is a monumental mistake.

Between someone who reads even one practical book a month and another who just watches television and doesn't read at all, there is an enormous difference: after 10 years, the first person will have read 120 books, the other none. Even if the first person had learned and applied only a small proportion of what he or she had read, in your opinion, which of these two individuals will:

- Have broader intellectual horizons?

- Be most likely to have progressed in their career and personal life?

- Be better protected against political and other forms of manipulation?

- Be better placed to lead a better, more fulfilling life?

- Be better placed to help others and serve as an example?

And reading isn't the only way to go on learning: there are thousands of others.[31] Stop for a moment and have a think.

---

31   We shall be exploring some of these later in this book, particularly in Chapter 6.

How many of the people you know are making an effort to go on learning? How many read, enroll for courses, and apply their knowledge to better themselves, rather than behaving like couch potatoes in front of the television every evening? How many think of using some of the time they spend traveling on business to educate themselves by listening to course materials or audiobooks?

This is increasingly important nowadays as the technological revolution gathers pace, and the world is changing at breakneck speed. If you don't engage in lifelong learning, you will end up like an illiterate among your smarter contemporaries. Your more learned friends will seem to belong to another world, speaking of fields of which you have absolutely no understanding or do not even suspect the existence.

Begin with small steps. Read a book a month, in audio format, which need not take much time. Decide to reduce your television viewing by half-an-hour a day and study something interesting instead.

3. Learning at least one foreign language

'If there is one accomplishment anyone can achieve
by their own efforts, it is a good spoken command of
a foreign language. There is no excuse for not having
this ability. [...] Even idiots can manage it.'

DANIEL JOUVE

This is going to make some people grind their teeth, but it's true. Being satisfied with speaking one language means having a narrower view of the world, limiting your knowledge and open-mindedness, being unconsciously guilty of provincialism (unthinkingly believing that the values you grew up with are universal and superior and that foreigners view things in the same way as you do).

Learning a foreign language is like growing a new eye on your forehead, allowing you to see the world differently. It is the gateway to discovering another culture and all its peculiarities without the filter of translation and editorial choice (you might be surprised how many foreign publications are never be translated into English). Some things have a different taste, a different hue, a different texture.

You will be able to think in the new language and think differently from the way you do in your own. Not only because each language has a different relationship with reality but also because, by immersing yourself in a different culture, you will have the fascinating experience of viewing your own culture with detachment. You will discover and understand, sometimes with quite a shock, that what seems normal (or abnormal) in your culture may not be so in another. This has the amazing effect of opening up your mind and giving you greater independence, greater freedom to think, imagine, and innovate – enormous advantages for an entrepreneur.

Moreover, research increasingly shows that living abroad makes us more flexible, creative, and capable of complex thinking. In a word, more intelligent, which boosts our chances of success in life.[32]

•••

Does school do a good job of teaching us these three skills? Obviously not, and the fact that the teaching of languages is a serious problem in the English-speaking world won't come as a surprise. In the USA, for instance, only 17.89 percent of the population can hold a conversation in a foreign language, while the figure in the UK is 39 percent.[33] The inertia of the school system is such that it would be idle to expect it to reform itself and overcome its limitations. Therefore we need to do so ourselves.

4. Personal finance

> *'Students can graduate from the top universities with starry academic titles, but with little more financial education than an eighth grader. Once they enter the workforce, they might as well be walking outside naked during a winter's blizzard.'*

> Andrew Hallam

There is one further subject which traditional schooling completely overlooks: personal finance. We live in a society where money is everything – a means of exchange, saving, and investment. It can cause us untold problems if it is not well managed, and at no time during our school days are most of us taught a practical course on this subject. Such oversight is barely credible. The financial skills students need to acquire are, in my opinion, the following:

- Being able to distinguish between an asset and a liability, an income item and an asset, and a debt and a liability

- Learning to immediately set aside 10 percent of salary and view only the remaining 90 percent as expendable (and understand why)

---

32 'Expanding Opportunities by Opening Your Mind,' Maddux W.W. et al., *Social Psychological and Personality Science*, 2014, and 'When in Rome ... Learn Why the Romans Do What They Do: How Multicultural Learning Experiences Facilitate Creativity,' Maddux W.W. et al., *Social Psychological and Personality Science*, 2010.
33 European Commission Eurobarometer, 2012.

- Learning to gradually build up an emergency fund in case a problem arises, amounting to between three- and six-months' salary, not to be touched for any other reason

- Learning the basics of investment:

  - Compound interest and how it works (money invested at an interest rate of 10 percent per annum, if the interest is re-invested, will double in a little over eight years, will quadruple after a further eight years, and will then take only seven years to increase by a factor of eight)

  - Investing in real estate (and the traps to avoid)

  - Investing in the stock market (and the traps to avoid)

  - Inflation, and why all investment is a race to beat it

- Learning the dangers of getting into debt

These skills could be learned in just a few hours at high school and prevent countless people from experiencing money troubles at a later stage. Maybe a more practical approach to education would even have prevented many people from getting into the hellish spiral of debt.

One of the great scams of our age: how financial advisers take advantage of our lack of financial education

> 'The goal of the non-professional should not be to pick winners – neither he nor his 'helpers' can do that – but should rather be to own a cross-section of businesses that in aggregate are bound to do well. A low-cost S&P 500 index fund will achieve this goal.'
>
> WARREN BUFFETT,
> IN HIS 2013 ANNUAL LETTER TO SHAREHOLDERS

To learn the basics of what they didn't teach you at school on the art of investing your money in the stock market that could save you from many hassles in later life, download further information in PDF format from https://olivier-roland.com/en/big-scam/.

CHAPTER 2
AN OUTDATED SYSTEM
The 'Modern' Education System, Designed for the 19th Century

> *'Why at school are you not allowed to copy from your neighbor, while in the rest of the world that is known as cooperation?'*
>
> OUSSAMA AMMAR, FOUNDER OF THE FAMILY

At the end of the 19th century, most developed countries made schooling free and compulsory for everyone. At the time, access to knowledge was restricted. The available media (mainly books and teachers) were few in number and unevenly distributed, much more easily found in large towns than in the countryside, and acquiring knowledge was a long, expensive, and specialized process. Of course, provided someone could read, they could purchase a book on a given subject. Still, bookshops and libraries were not well stocked with specialized works, and the problem of uneven distribution applied to them as well: it was much easier to find reference works in the bookshops and libraries of major towns than elsewhere.

In the 19th century, the employment an average school-leaver could aspire to was either:

- Agricultural work

- Factory work

And making education compulsory up to a certain age was in direct opposition to powerful economic interests. Industrialists were alarmed at the prospect that the loss of convenient cut-price labor would be disastrous for the national economy.

So they were sold the idea that educated children would be more docile and productive. And here lies the main problem affecting the education system: it was designed to train agricultural and industrial workers, people content with their lot and sufficiently educated to meet the economic demands of the period, and obedient soldiers to serve in the country's wars.

From the word go, this was a production-line system, with children sitting in rows, subject to a supreme authority handing down instructions that they absolutely must obey. Since then, school curricula may have changed, but the basic principles have remained the same.

This is no doubt why personal finance, creativity, and entrepreneurship are not taught in school: schools have no place for creatives, entrepreneurs, and people who know how to manage a budget and invest. Even today, schools are geared to turning out passive employees enthused by the idea of having a brilliant career by instilling knowledge still regarded as sacred and precious.

Nowadays, though, farm and factory workers account for only a small proportion of the workforce in the developed world.[34] Anyone can access first-class courses from home via the Internet and test out business ideas with minimal investment of time and money. However, schools – supposedly training young people for life in 21st-century society – are still churning out workers with methods and a vision dating from the 19th century.

What matters today, and will matter more and more as time goes by, isn't a willingness to follow instructions, nor the ability to amass tons of knowledge, most of which will be forgotten and which, in any case, can be accessed in a couple of seconds via a telephone cable.

No. Creativity, flexibility, the ability to adapt, independence, innovation, practical skills to develop a project rather than just dream, willingness to challenge the status quo – these are the qualities that are vital in the 21st century.

At this point, I should clarify that some private schools – I'm thinking of Montessori schools, but there are plenty of other exciting examples – are working in this direction. In many cases, they offer a bilingual education, which also encourages children's autonomy and creativity from a very young age. Sadly, such schools are beyond the financial reach of most families and are not to be found in every town. But what about public schools, those which most children attend? Do you now believe they develop in their pupils the skills required to succeed in modern society?

---

34   The primary and secondary sectors accounted for only 20 percent of employment in the USA in 2017 – CIA Factbook.

RECRUITMENT INTERVIEWS GEARED TO FINDING THE 'RARE PEARLS'

The major Internet and IT companies are quite right in asking questions that might seem outlandish at recruitment interviews but designed to identify the most creative and resourceful candidates seeking jobs in their employ. Here are a few examples of the kind of questions they ask at Google, Apple, Microsoft, and the like.[35]

- You shrink to the size of a 5-cent piece and are thrown into a blender. Your mass is reduced so that there is no change in your density. The blades will start turning in 60 seconds. What do you do?

- When a wind is blowing, does a return flight take longer, a shorter time, or the same as usual?

- Think up an evacuation plan for San Francisco.

- Please check that Bob has your telephone number. You cannot ask him directly. So, instead, you need to write him a message on a card you will hand to Eve, your go-between. Eve will give the card to Bob, who will convey his message to Eve, who will pass it on to you. You don't want Eve to know your telephone number... What question do you put to Bob?

THE LIMITATIONS OF GENERAL KNOWLEDGE AND ROTE LEARNING

'Has knowledge become obsolete?'

SUGATA MITRA, INITIATOR OF
THE 'HOLE-IN-THE-WALL' PROJECT IN INDIA

'Teachers are no longer the fountain of knowledge; the Internet is.'

DON TAPSCOTT, CANADIAN AUTHOR AND BUSINESSMAN

---

35 Taken from *Are You Intelligent Enough to Work for Google?* by William Poundstone, J.C. Lattès, 2013.

We have seen how the education system lacks practicality and stuffs us with knowledge we will never use and are likely to forget. Does that mean we should learn only about practical/utilitarian matters and completely neglect general knowledge?

Not really. I'm not trying to suggest you need to become an ultra-specialized but soulless robot to succeed! And learning for enjoyment can be a fantastic leisure activity that will make you a better human being. Provided that this desire to learn is inspired by your own inner passion. Instead, I'm just questioning the notion of general knowledge. Not everything is worth learning. As Seneca remarked, almost 2,000 years ago:

> *No one doubts that those who apply themselves to pointless literary studies are wasting their time: there are already enough such people among us Romans.*
>
> *It was the Greek sickness to try to find out the number of Ulysses' oarsmen; whether the Iliad was written before the Odyssey, or whether both epics are by the same author; and other questions of this stamp, which, if you keep them to yourself, can give you no real satisfaction, and which you could not communicate to others without seeming not more erudite but merely more boring.[36]*

Deepening your knowledge of critical subjects is an intelligent use of your time. Doing so to learn details of no interest is like racking your brains to find out how many angels can dance on the head of a pin, as people might have done in pre-scientific times.

Here, though, are some questions from a general knowledge test a prestigious prep (private) school published on its website to prepare future students:

- How many scooters are there in circulation in Taipei?

- What did the acronym OAS stand for in the early 1960s?

- Which statesman first spoke of an 'iron curtain' the Soviets had put in place between the areas they had liberated and those liberated by the USA?

Good Lord! Can you see the contrast between these pedantic questions and the creative ones asked by the Internet companies at their job interviews? What's the use of being able to answer questions of this sort from memory when a simple search on your mobile phone can come up with the answer in under a minute? And

---

36   *On the Shortness of Life*, Seneca.

when you can subcontract the work of finding information for next to nothing, as I shall be showing you in the second part of this book?

Learning facts develops the brain and its capacity for absorbing and retaining information. It is a useful activity, but much less so nowadays than creativity, determination, and the ability to learn, among other valuable skills.

It's not just me that's saying this: according to the OECD,[37] education today should be much more focused on the ability to reason, and in particular, on learning to:

- Be more creative.

- Develop a critical spirit.

- Solve problems effectively.

- Be better at decision-making.

These are the skills we need nowadays, more than the ability to memorize things. These are the skills tested by Google, Apple, Facebook, Microsoft, and all the major companies of the digital economy trying to attract the most talented individuals. According to many specialists, however, schools are not doing a very good job of developing these skills.[38] And to the list, I would add:

- Concentrate fully on a task.

- Stay motivated and/or disciplined in the medium and long term when working on an ambitious project.

Moreover, these final two points relate to the main problem thrown up by our new digital tools. We have got into the bad habit of multitasking – switching attention rapidly from one thing to another – and undermining our ability to concentrate fully on one thing at a time.[39] This, in turn, drastically reduces our productivity.

Let's return for a moment to the 'opportunity costs' of rote learning. Opportunity costs are the cost of the opportunities lost when you perform a particular task rather than engaging in another activity.

---

37 'The Case for 21st-Century Learning': http://en.olivier-roland.com/plaidoyer-pour-un-enseignement-moderne/
38 For example, Sandra Enlart and Olivier Charbonnier (authors of *Faut-il encore apprendre?* Dunod, 2010), Professor Richard E. Mayer (educational psychologist) or Pierre Giotto (French historian), who was already criticizing rote learning in the 1970s.
39 Gary Small, *iBrain: Surviving the Technological Alteration of the Modern Mind*, 2009.

There are many passions you might develop if you were not exclusively focused on the 80/20 of general knowledge: learning a musical instrument, which has proven benefits for intelligence and creativity;[40] practicing a sport, which again has countless benefits; learning an art or craft; launching a challenging project that really matters to you; not to mention starting a business, setting up a YouTube channel or writing a book.

SCHOOL DESTROYS CREATIVITY

> *'All children are born artists. The problem is to*
> *continue being an artist as you grow up.'*
>
> PICASSO

Creativity is essential if you want to be successful, and it is bound to continue to become even more critical in the future because, according to UNESCO, in the next 30 years, there will be more people graduating than in the whole of human history. Consequently, there will be fierce competition, leading to an escalation in the time people spend studying. But longer studies are no guarantee that you will do better than your colleagues, especially if they are more creative than you. To make this clear, let me tell you a story.

San Francisco, California, 2006. A well-built man, well into his 50s, comes on stage and, after cracking a few jokes, comes to the point of his speech: Why school destroys creativity.

The presentation given by Sir Ken Robinson, a British author and international adviser on educational matters, knighted for his services to education, went viral. The video recording of his TED talk has been viewed by more than 56 million people over the years, more than any other video posted on the site.[41]

Here is a summary of his main points:

Children starting elementary school will be retiring in 60 years, more or less, unless the age of retirement has been raised considerably by then. No one can know what the world will be like in 60 years. Indeed, no one knows what the world will be like in five years, whether some new technological development will have completely

---

40   See for example 'Music Lessons Enhance IQ,' Schellenberg E. G., *Psychological Science*, 2004, and 'Short-Term Music Training Enhances Verbal Intelligence and Executive Function,' Moreno S. et al., *Psychological Science*, 2011.
41   The video 'Do Schools Kill Creativity' is available at http://en.olivier-roland.com/ken-robinson-says-schools-kill-creativity/

revolutionized whole aspects of our society. Yet, schools believe they can prepare us to live in a world of this kind.

Creativity is now as important as knowledge and should be treated as such. To be creative, you need to be prepared to be wrong. Otherwise, you will never produce anything original. Children are often spontaneously creative and original and unafraid of being wrong. However, by adulthood, most of us have lost this capacity because the purpose of school is to turn out obedient pupils who don't make mistakes.

Some subjects are more highly valued at school than others (math rather than dance, for example), but such decisions are made by academics who have their own skills, which don't reflect the skill diversity of all pupils. For instance, academics tend not to have the same relationship with their bodies as many artists or athletes. For them, the purpose of their body is to carry their head to conference halls. The choice and promotion of subjects 'that matter' also derives from the objectives for which schools were conceived in the 19th century: to produce docile and hard-working workers and employees. There was, therefore, little room for music, dance, a spirit of innovation, or creativity.

THE EXAMPLE OF GILLIAN LYNNE

Gillian Lynne was fortunate. Yet, when she was an eight-year-old school pupil in the 1930s, her situation seemed hopeless. She couldn't concentrate and suffered no end of problems: she had trouble learning her lessons, gave in her homework late, and distracted other pupils. Her parents consulted a specialist, who by chance, was competent and open-minded and finally discovered that Gillian loved dance above all else and had a remarkable aptitude for it. He advised her parents to enroll her on a dance course, which they did.

In due course, Gillian became a respected dancer, actress, director, and, above all, choreographer of CATS. She was fortunate not to come across a specialist who prescribed drugs to calm her down!

Whereas, until a few years ago, an academic qualification was virtually a passport to employment, this is no longer the case. In fact, an occupation for which a school-leaving certificate was once adequate now requires a further five years of study and may, in the future, require a doctorate.

What schools now need to do is to fan into flame the spark of creativity that lies dormant in all children and encourage their full range of skills and capacity for adaptation.

GETTING INTO DEBT AS A STUDENT, OR WHY THEY DON'T TELL YOU EVERYTHING

In the USA, the cost of education has exploded in recent years, to the point where some people are speaking of an 'educational bubble,' like a real-estate or stock-market bubble. The average cost of enrolling for one year at a private American university, for instance, was $35,676 in 2019, as compared with just $1,832 in 1971.[42] At a public university, the annual cost is $9,716, as opposed to $500 in 1971.[43]

The cost of studying has, in fact, increased eight times faster than salaries, according to a Forbes study.[44] In the UK, the maximum fees increased from £1,000 in 1998 to £9,250 per annum in 2015. Also, you need to factor in something that is not often mentioned: the opportunity costs of studying. You may remember that we touched on this when discussing learning. The opportunity cost refers to the cost of an activity in terms of what you might have earned by doing something else. In the case of studying, the opportunity costs entail:

1. The salary you would have earned if you had stopped studying earlier and taken up employment.

2. The income you would have earned from investing part of your salary.

3. The income you could have earned if you had taken out a loan to invest rather than pay for your studies.

4. The income you could have earned by investing the money you spent to fund your years of study.

Where the opportunity costs of studying are concerned, the issue is simply never discussed. Research has, however, been done on this subject. And obviously, when these costs are taken into account, the actual return on investment from studying is much lower than you have been led to believe. The most complete study I have discovered was carried out by the OECD, which publishes a detailed

---

42 In dollars at today's values (taking inflation into account).
43 See 'The Average Costs of Attending College in 2018-2019,' *US News College Compass*.
44 'Price Of College Increasing Almost 8 Times Faster Than Wages,' *Forbes*, 2018.

annual report on this subject.[45] The figures from the 2018 report, for instance, are highly instructive:

- Lifetime return on a secondary school leaving certificate:
  - USA
    - $165,954 for men[46]
    - $134,877 for women
  - UK
    - $114,088 for men
    - $69,873 for women
  - Canada
    - $82,753 for men
    - $87,049 for women
  - Australia
    - $123,555 for men
    - $68,999 for women
- Lifetime return on a higher education qualification:
  - USA
    - $311,400 for men
    - $201,246 for women
  - UK
    - $134,800 for men
    - $98,438 for women

---

45   'Perspectives on Education': http://en.olivier-roland.com/ocde-education/
46   Based on the hypothesis of average inflation of 3.75 percent throughout a person's active life, which is closer to the rates chosen by the USA, UK, Canada, and Australia for their calculation of the profitability of education, rather than the rate of 2 percent proposed by the OECD – See page 111 of the report 'Education at a Glance 2018.'

- Canada

    - $152,500 for men

    - $124,876 for women

- Australia

    - $132,300 for men

    - $126,150 for women

Generally speaking, these higher returns, despite the opportunity costs, are due to two factors:

1. The ability to earn a higher salary.

2. The lesser likelihood of being unemployed.

But are these returns really all they are cracked up to be?

Is an academic qualification that earns you an additional $80,000 to $300,000 during your whole lifetime, if you are a man, really worth all the effort and sacrifice involved?[47] What do these additional $80,000 to $300,000 really amount to? A nice car? A slightly bigger house? Will that really make you so much happier?

Note, too, that if you are a woman, the return on an academic qualification is less than for a man. One solution is to set up your own business. As I shall explain in greater detail, it is an excellent way to minimize, if not root out, discrimination.

Unless you work in certain limited sectors, your customers won't inquire about your qualifications, your age, your sex, or your eye color before buying your products. Selling quality products that meet a need using intelligent marketing is what counts most.

But let's assume that this additional return on educational investment really does make a difference. The problem is that, in arriving at these figures, the OECD has based its calculations solely on the salary that students would have earned if they had entered employment rather than continuing their studies, not on the return from investments they might have made with the money saved by not studying. Of course, many of them might not have saved much or invested intelligently in

---

47   For the fact that these returns are calculated for a person's whole lifetime, see 'Education at a Glance:OECD Indicators 2009': https://www.oecd.org/education/skills-beyond-school/43636332.pdf, p.53.

the early years of their working life. But this book is addressed to intelligent rebels, people who break the mold and do things differently.

I'm not saying that all intelligent rebels are past masters in the art of investing. But I do think that most are capable of making their money work better for them than the average person, whether by setting up a successful business or acquiring valuable experience despite failing to make a success of it (something I shall be discussing in more detail in the second part of this book).

Moreover, a higher salary often implies higher expenditure to maintain social status (a need of which the person concerned is generally unaware): a doctor feels greater social pressure than a nurse, for instance, to live in a large house and drive a nice car, even if these things don't really appeal to them, wiping out some of the benefits of his or her superior academic qualification.[48]

Please note: I am not saying that wanting material comforts and paying for them is a problem, merely that having a certain social status leads to social obligations and related expenditures that the OECD study doesn't take into account.

A further point is that the study fails to mention a bias, which I have already referred to, where the relative value of academic qualifications is concerned. Put simply, the most valuable qualifications, those that according to the OECD studies generate the highest returns, are obtained by the students who are the most intelligent and go-getting, the hardest-working, and the most disciplined. So, are the higher salaries they earn due mainly to the fact that they have academic qualifications or intrinsic qualities?

Isn't it possible for an intelligent rebel to secure the skills it takes to get an academic qualification for a fraction of the money, effort, and time usually required, and at the same time, enjoy greater freedom?

I am not trying to discourage you from obtaining a higher education qualification (nor make you regret having one if that is the case). Instead, I am providing you with data on studying that you are unlikely to come by otherwise and inviting you to make a *better-informed* decision. And if you nevertheless decide to continue up the academic route, I am trying to make you aware of its limitations and the need to hack them to succeed.

---

48   *The Millionaire Next Door* by Thomas J. Stanley and William D. Danko.

DIMINISHING RETURNS FROM ACADEMIC QUALIFICATIONS

Another factor is often overlooked: the fierce, rat-race kind of competition to get the best degree, without considering its usefulness relating to your life objectives. This has led to a chronic situation of overqualification and diminishing returns from academic degrees.[49] A degree carries less and less weight, with the result that a person is less and less likely to get and keep the job they covet, which in turn leads to a race for the best degree and a vicious circle very much akin to a stock-market bubble on the point of bursting.

Consequently, many young people may feel that, as things now stand, while a degree may indeed be a *sine qua non* for specific jobs, the real secret of success, not least during the selection and recruitment process, depends more on their personality and aptitude. Moreover, they are overqualified for many jobs, which again points to the futility of what they have learned and the opportunity costs of their qualifications, the return from which is probably minimal. In the USA, for instance, 35 percent of graduates are in jobs for which they are overqualified, and the figure is as high as 46 percent for the younger among them.[50] In the UK, the figure was 31 percent in 2019, as against 22 percent in 1992,[51] and in Canada, 34 percent.[52] Many other Western countries are experiencing the same problem.[53] The evidence, therefore, is not just anecdotal.

In any case, it is clear that, despite all these factors, academic qualification is generally a positive investment, provided you are willing to make a lot of sacrifices to achieve a rather insignificant leg-up in life.

But you are an intelligent rebel. You aspire to something better than a managerial position, the daily grind, and the ultra-competitive rat race I talked about earlier. Studying is fine, but don't let that stop you from wanting to realize your dreams and live out your heart's desires. Especially as there is a roughly 35 percent probability of finding yourself in a situation where you are overqualified and could therefore have invested your time, money, and energy more intelligently.

But hang on a minute, you may be thinking: If I am an intelligent, brave, and hard-working rebel, can't I aim higher and try to get a more prestigious qualification? OK, let's take a look at that...

---

49   'The overeducated generation,' Nader Habibi, 2015.
50   'Are the Job Prospects of Recent College Graduates Improving?' Jaison R. Abel and Richard Deitz, 2014.
51   'One in three graduates overeducated for their current role,' Office for National Statistics, 2019.
52   'Surqualification chez les diplômés des collèges et des universités: comparaison Québec-Canada,' Claude Montmarquette, 2017.
53   'There is a role for EU policy on overeducation among young people,' Henriette Jacobsen, 2015.

WHAT ABOUT PRESTIGIOUS QUALIFICATIONS – AN MBA, FOR EXAMPLE?

Getting a prestigious qualification is the passport to success and a six-figure salary, isn't it?

Possibly. But not in every case. For an honest answer, I asked the opinion of Mariana Zanetti, who has an MBA and has enjoyed an excellent career on the back of it.

First of all, what is an MBA?

The purpose of a Master of Business Administration is to give you the best possible understanding of the world of business. It may take different forms, but generally, it is a two-year course targeting people who already have professional experience and hope to boost their careers to new heights. Unless funded by your employer, such training is generally expensive – $50,000 to $100,000 in total – and is delivered by the most prestigious academic institutions, such as Harvard or Oxford. Obviously, this figure doesn't consider the enormous opportunity costs for young professionals of the two years spent not working when they already have several years' experience of employment behind them.

Mariana is Spanish and was awarded her MBA by a school in Spain that figures among the world's top-10 most prestigious institutions in its field.[54] Leaving aside opportunity costs and related expenses, it cost her precisely €43,200.

Was it a good investment? Ironically, she used the techniques learned during her finance courses to calculate the ROI (return on investment), and it proved to be negative. In her case, as in thousands of others, her MBA lost her money, the exact opposite of the goal most people who take the course are pursuing. And yet, as she shared with me, people place great hopes in this kind of training, to the point of investing all their savings or even borrowing money to pay the fees, as in Mariana's case. The problem, of course, is that of the emperor in the fairy tale whom no one dares say is stark naked, as he is supposed to be wearing a fabric that is invisible only to idiots.

Similarly, you will never hear someone with an MBA say that their studies were not worthwhile, if only because virtually all holders of an MBA are up to their ears in debt and are effectively naked, just like the emperor in the story. Nobody, except a few rebels such as Seth Godin or Peter Thiel, whom we shall be discussing later on... and, of course, Mariana. In an article published on one of my blogs,[55] and in

---

54 According to *The Financial Times*.
55 'Ne vous trompez pas: Pourquoi un MBA n'est pas rentable': https://des-livres-pour-changer-de-vie.com/mba/

a book published in French and Spanish, Mariana sets out the main reasons that convince people to take an MBA and analyzes them with a refreshingly critical eye.

The dream of a six-figure salary

The main argument in favor of an MBA is that it enables you to earn more. So, do holders of an MBA earn a higher salary than others?

On average, yes. Does that mean anything? Not much. Why? Because the selection process for an MBA course is cut-throat: only the best, the most intelligent, courageous, and hard-working are admitted. Depending on the school, between 70 percent and 90 percent of candidates are rejected.

Now let's ask the question: Does having an MBA enable you to earn a higher salary? Or is it just having the intelligence and drive to get an MBA that generally allows you to make more? In other words, if you could obtain an MBA, is it really worth going for one, or would you do better to use your capacities to succeed in your career as a manager or entrepreneur?

According to Mariana, the latter is the better option. She rubs shoulders with many colleagues who don't have an MBA but earn as much as her. They simply used their abilities to add value to their company. They didn't need a diploma to show that they could do so; results speak for themselves.

If you have the talent to obtain an MBA, you have the talent to succeed without one.

Look at most of the world's great entrepreneurs. How many of them have a business school diploma? Or an academic qualification of any kind?

According to a study published in 2015 analyzing the 100 wealthiest entrepreneurs globally,[56] their most common level of academic attainment was... no qualification higher than a high school diploma or leaving certificate (32 percent of cases). This was followed by technical qualifications in engineering (22 percent), then a business qualification (a mere 12 percent).

Quite apart from this, if you are recruited based on your MBA, you can kiss goodbye to a 35-hour week. You may well earn 70 percent more (let's say $60,000 rather than $35,000), but you will have to work 50 percent more (53 hours a week instead of 35). All this time spent working will mean less time for the things that really make life worth living, such as friends, family, hobbies, and so on. You will

---

56   'What Degree Will Make You Rich?': http://en.olivier-roland.com/what-degree-will-make-rich/

probably fill the void with expensive and pointless gadgets, not to mention the need to demonstrate your social status by acquiring possessions that will greatly increase your expenditure.[57]

As Mariana puts it: 'Let me tell you that in the periods when I was earning more than €60,000, I was working many more than 50 hours a week. I was under much greater stress, I was spending much more money without being any happier, and I was paying a lot more tax. What's more, I was on the same salary as all my non-MBA colleagues working the same hours as me in similar positions. An MBA does not guarantee you a higher salary.'

Greater employability, employment security, and long-term prosperity

Holders of MBAs certainly have more chance of finding a job, mainly because they have proved, by getting the qualification, that they can work like stink and accept the way the system works. This, in effect, also makes them willing slaves to be exploited at will. But, of course, getting a good position is by no means guaranteed: many holders of MBAs were laid off during the financial crisis. There are more intelligent ways of making yourself indispensable.

The heart has its reasons, of which reason knows nothing

There is often at least one subconscious reason that drives people to obtain so prestigious a qualification, whether they want to make their parents proud of them or feel important around other people. But buying recognition by obtaining an MBA is a high price to pay for something you can get more intelligently and authentically.

Unique knowledge

An MBA is not good value for money, but it does, of course, have some value. The knowledge acquired is precious. But the student will use 10 or 20 percent of it and forget the rest.

Mariana says she has learned more practical knowledge by reading good books and applying their principles than she learned from the whole of her MBA course. And at infinitely less cost. Books costing $20 or less can bring you into contact with

---

57   Thomas J. Stanley and William D. Danko, *The Millionaire Next Door*, 2010.

the best brains in the world, living and dead. This includes billionaires and highly successful entrepreneurs who have no time to teach academic courses.

Networking

This is the argument put forward by all those who have taken a prestigious MBA course. And, yes, they are right. Paying $100,000 to get a qualification is indeed one way of building a network. But it is certainly not the only way. The truth is that the most interesting people are open to sharing with other interesting people, an activity for which no qualification is required. Once again, if you have the intelligence necessary for an MBA at a prestigious school, you have the intelligence to build yourself a network without doing one.

It is years since Mariana last needed to draw on her MBA network. Her contacts now revolve around her business projects, drawn together by a shared interest.

•••

I will leave the final word to Mariana:

> *I have recently become more aware of the sad situation in which many managers, especially MBAs, find themselves.*
>
> *I still shudder when I remember the expression on the face of my company boss when he confessed to me that he had seen his children only fifty times in the previous year.*
>
> *We happened to be dining together in an award-winning restaurant on an island in Stockholm harbor, following a meeting of European subsidiaries.*
>
> *I felt that the chic menu and the amazing view of the bay hardly made up for it.*
>
> *I also remember the irrational way an American colleague, with an MBA from a very prestigious university in the States, asked me to do the impossible. It was midnight, and, with other colleagues, we were sitting opposite the Sagrada Familia in Barcelona. After two days of nonstop meetings and a business dinner, I thought that, since he had never visited Spain before, he might like to go for a short taxi ride around Barcelona by night.*

'Can you ask them in your language if they'll open the doors for us??? I'll probably never come back here again!!!'

He was like a child who had been made to get off a fairground ride. He had become aware of the wonderful world passing him by while he was at work (almost all of his time!).

The lives of many MBAs are not their own.

They see the best of what life has to offer through a hotel window, from an airplane or a train.

They aren't even aware that, long ago, they accepted the rules of the game.

The saddest thing for me is that many are convinced they have to go on working to pay for the same sort of education for their children.

Well, I have been there, and I have seen the wreckage of people's lives. I plan to change direction, I've books to help me change my lifestyle, and I have a different sort of education in mind for my son.

SUMMARY

For the intelligent rebel who has decided to act

➡ You can't be satisfied with what you learned at school. Since school fails to utilize the discoveries of the neurosciences or doesn't even try, it is up to you to learn how to study.

➡ The present education system derives directly from the 19th-century model, designed to produce docile workers and employees, so we need to stimulate our creativity and independence. We need to learn the essential subjects not taught at school, in particular, to master new technologies, languages, and personal finance.

➡ Intelligent rebels want to avoid the rat race and find a better way of being happy and free. This doesn't mean completely rubbishing school and its benefits, but simply being aware of its limitations and knowing how to get around them to hack your education and way of life.

CHAPTER 3
SCHOOLING, REBEL-STYLE
Hack Your Education and Your Lifestyle – the Basics No One Taught You

Before tackling self-study as a way of overcoming the limitations of the education system (and, as you will see, there are many ways of doing so), let's explore how to hack any form of education, the conventional system, and your own by taking a fresh look at the basics.

Education consists of learning, memorizing, and using our acquired knowledge as best we can in new situations. Success in life consists in reflecting on our objectives, devising an action plan to achieve them, then acting as intelligently as possible.

From elementary school to college, we spend an average of between 15 and 20 years studying. How then do you explain that nobody taught you how to study? Nobody taught you how to memorize, and nobody really taught you to think 'outside the box'?

To be an efficient learner and boost your chances of success, you need to improve several 'universal' capacities:

- **Your long-term memory:** By learning to accurately memorize what you need or want to learn; you will be able to retain the information more easily and for a longer time.

- **Your working memory:** This is the memory into which you 'download' the contents of your long-term memory to process them. Improving your working memory will also develop your intelligence, with which it is directly connected (*see the studies referred to on p.40*).

- **Your powers of concentration:** By boosting your ability to concentrate on what you are doing and avoid distractions, you will improve your productivity and be happier because you will make the most of the present moment.

- **Your willpower:** By strengthening your willpower, you will be better able to resist temptations which might divert you from your goal (for instance, that delicious chocolate cake when you are on a diet, or that video game when you had decided to get some exercise). You will do what you promised yourself you would do, and that will give you an enormous advantage in achieving your goals.

- **Your motivation:** By learning what really motivates you, and learning to feed the flame, you will be more motivated than most other people. This will give you more energy, enthusiasm, and creativity in everything you do, and above all, you will be happier.

The good news is that for each of these basic competencies, there are tools and 80/20 methods to greatly increase your capacities. Let's begin at the beginning. What would you say about enhancing your intelligence?

HOW TO INCREASE YOUR IQ BY SIX POINTS IN 30 DAYS USING A LITTLE-KNOWN BUT SCIENTIFICALLY PROVEN TECHNIQUE

'Parents remember their school experiences and how they survived them, they are often suspicious of educators who 'experiment' with their children. This explains why, in general, schools have not integrated many of the findings of neuroscience and cognitive psychology.'

ELKHONON GOLDBERG, PROFESSOR OF NEUROLOGY

In 2008, an international team of researchers from the University of Bern, Switzerland, and the University of Michigan, USA, dropped a bombshell. Contrary to accepted thinking, it appears to be possible to significantly increase our fluid intelligence.[58]

Since psychologists Raymond Cattel and John L. Horn identified this concept in the early 1970s, most psychologists had accepted that human intelligence subdivides into two main components: fluid intelligence and crystallized intelligence. Fluid intelligence is our 'raw' intelligence, i.e., our ability to think logically and solve new situations. In contrast, crystallized intelligence is the ability to use our skills, knowledge, and experience. What's more, researchers had been unanimous in thinking it was impossible to increase our fluid intelligence: it was innate, whereas crystallized intelligence was acquired.

---

58   'Improving Fluid Intelligence with Training on Working Memory,' Susanne M. Jaeggi et al., *Proceedings of the National Academy of Sciences of the United States of America*, 2008.

At least until this team of researchers led by Dr. Jaeggi developed a software application designed to train the working memory and tested it on 70 people divided into four groups.

The groups used the software for 20 minutes a day for between eight and 19 days. They took an IQ test before and after training, and their results were compared with four other control groups who had not used the software.

The results were amazing. All those who had used the software recorded much better IQ scores. Also, a detailed analysis of the results revealed:

- Their fluid intelligence had increased significantly, by 40 percent on average.

- The level of increase in fluid intelligence correlated directly with the amount of time spent training: those who had trained for 19 consecutive days saw their fluid intelligence increase four times more than those who had trained for eight days.

The researchers had never seen anything like it. It had long been accepted that it was possible to improve on the results of an IQ test... simply by taking lots of IQ tests. But this just improved performance in IQ tests, nothing more. In Dr. Jaeggi's experiment, however, the tasks set by the software application were in no way related to those in IQ tests. The fact that the participants' scores improved, therefore, showed that there had been an enhancement of intellectual abilities. Just as you can develop your strength and general stamina by doing physical exercise, thus improving your performance, it was possible, by training working memory, to become more efficient in all tasks reliant on it: calculating, reading, playing chess, thinking, and so on.

Current research shows a strong correlation between working memory and fluid intelligence: the more efficient your working memory, the greater your intelligence. And research also shows a strong correlation between intelligence and success in all aspects of life.

For example, a test performed on 1,116,442 Swedish people, whose IQ had been measured at the age of 18, showed that, 22 years later, for every 15 IQ points below average, the chances of being killed in an accident or being murdered increased by a third, and the risk of being hospitalized by half.[59] What's more, the higher a country's average IQ, the greater the country's GDP.[60]

---

59 'IQ in Early Adulthood, Socioeconomic Position, and Unintentional Injury Mortality by Middle Age: A Cohort Study of More Than 1 Million Swedish Men,' Batty G. D. et al., *American Journal of Epidemiology*, 2009.
60 'Cognitive capitalism: the effect of cognitive ability on wealth, as mediated through scientific achievement and economic freedom,' Rindermann, and Thompson J.

A meta-analysis of 30 studies on the Dual N-Back (brain-training app) shows an increase in IQ of 6.2 points after six weeks of training.[61] Given that the IQs of 68 percent of the population fall within a range of 30 points,[62] this is very significant. And hardly any scientists now contest that you can boost your working memory with these software tools. In the same meta-analysis, the authors conclude:

> *Our work demonstrates the efficacy of several weeks of N-Back training in improving performance on measures of fluid intelligence. We urge that future studies move beyond attempts to answer the simple question of whether or not there is transfer [from this software application to fluid intelligence] and, instead, seek to explore the nature and extent of how these improved test scores may reflect 'true' improvements in fluid intelligence that can translate into practical, real-world settings.*

A more recent meta-analysis is more critical and shows transfers to general intelligence and cognitive control (the ability to concentrate on a task and ignore distractions and temptations). Other studies,[63] meanwhile, show that this increase in intelligence is long-lasting since it has a long-term effect on the brain's neuroplasticity.

So, are you tempted to try improving your intelligence?

The good news is there are several apps similar to the one used in Dr. Jaeggi's experiment that enable you to work on your own intelligence. I have used the apps developed by IQ Mindware[64] (on a paying basis). There is also a free, open-source version called Brain Workshop.[65]

However, these tools are not for the faint-hearted: the basic principle of Dual N-Back is that it is challenging; these are certainly not fun-to-use video games. You will have to stick at it to get any benefit. Research shows that maximum gains are obtained by practicing for half an hour a day for 19 consecutive days. The gains achieved range from 10 percent after eight days to 44 percent after 19 days. The logical objective for any intelligent rebel, therefore, must be to practice for half an hour a day for 20 or so days.

61   'Improving Fluid Intelligence with Training on Working Memory: A Meta-Analysis,' Jacky Au et al., *Theoretical Review*, 2014.
62   'The Classification of Intelligence Scores. Proposal for an Unambiguous System,' W.C.M. Resing et al., *The Psychologist*, 2002.
63   'Changes in Cortical Dopamine D1 Receptor Binding Associated with Cognitive Training,' Fiona McNab et al., *Science*, 2009, or 'Dopamine, Working Memory, and Training Induced Plasticity: Implications for Developmental Research,' Stina Söderqvist et al., *Developmental Psychology*, 2012, for example.
64   IQ Mindware: http://en.olivier-roland.com/iqmindware/
65   Brain Workshop – a Dual N-Back game: http://en.olivier-roland.com/brain-workshop/

The problem is that, if you don't stay in the course, you are undoubtedly one of the people most likely to benefit from this kind of training. Because, as well as training your working memory, Dual N-Back-type apps also directly improve your attention span and motivation. This is only logical: by improving your powers of concentration and being more motivated, you will build your capacity to use your working memory efficiently, however good its current performance. Using these apps will, therefore, increase your ability to stick at your various projects.

Incredible though it may seem, it has been demonstrated that N-Back training can help alcoholics to reduce alcohol consumption,[66] boost the staying-power of people coming off drugs such as cocaine,[67] be a better indicator of performance at school than an IQ score,[68] help in achieving emotional control,[69] and improve the concentration of children with attention-deficit syndrome.[70]

Do you think becoming more intelligent, focused, disciplined, and motivated will help you in your studies, your business projects, and life generally? If so, and you have given up on it once before, give it another go. It's well worth the effort.

I chickened out on the first occasion after 10 days, just as I was beginning to see the initial benefits. And it took me almost two years to get started again and complete the 20 sessions advocated by i3 Mindware. Don't make the same mistake. Keep at it.

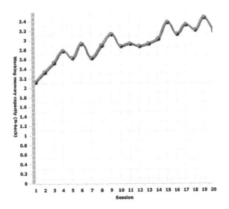

Figure 2: Olivier's 2nd attempt at completing i3 Mindware's 20 sessions.

66   'Getting a Grip on Drinking Behavior: Training Working Memory to Reduce Alcohol Abuse,' Houben K. et al., *Psychological Science*, 2011.

67   'Remember the Future: Working Memory Training Decreases Delay Discounting Among Stimulant Addicts,' Bickel W.K. et al., *Biological Psychiatry*, 2011.

68   'Self-Discipline Outdoes IQ in Predicting Academic Performance of Adolescents,' Duckworth A.L., *Psychological Science*, 2005.

69   'Working Memory Capacity and Spontaneous Emotion Regulation: High Capacity Predicts Self-Enhancement in Response to Negative Feedback,' Schmeichel B.J. et al., *Emotion*, 2010.

70   'Computerized Training of Working Memory in Children with ADHD. A Randomized, Controlled Trial,' Klingberg T. et al., *Journal of the American Academy of Child and Adolescent Psychiatry*, 2005.

Dual N-Back: How it works

Explaining how Dual N-Back works is outside the scope of this book (which is already long enough). I would therefore suggest you do some Internet searches to find out more and learn how to use it, but you can also download the supplement to this chapter by going to http://en.olivier-roland.com/n-back.

HOW TO LEARN WITHOUT EFFORT USING THE FORGOTTEN ART OF MNEMONICS

'Richard of York Gave Battle in Vain.' Does that mean anything to you? It's one of the few mnemonic phrases pupils learn at school to help them remember something. You may well remember this phrase, and you know that the sequence of letters was intended to remind you of something. But what?

Is it coming back to you? Go on, rack your brains.

Yes, of course: the colors of the rainbow.

What then is a mnemonic? It's a way of arranging information to make it easy to recall. And did you know there is a way of using this system to recall everything you learn? In fact, many effective ways have been known since antiquity... and forgotten by today's generation of teachers!

Our brain has evolved in such a way that it retains images more easily than anything else. Words, abstract concepts will evoke images in our minds. For instance, if you say 'dog,' what comes into your mind? The image of a dog, or the word 'dog' and its individual letters, D O G? The image, of course. You'll even be able to tell me what color the dog is!

Now let's see how to use our brainpower to process images and so learn something.

Telling a story as a way of recalling something more effectively

Consider this random sequence of words:

> ice-cream – sheep – general – red – car – tree – house – star – submarine – elephant – rocket – SMS – cap – table

Set the alarm on your smartphone for two minutes, and try to memorize as many of these words as you can.

When the two minutes are up, shut or switch off the book and note down as many of the words as you can. Ready. Steady. Go!

I'm not joking. I really want you to do it. This book is for proactive people. Do you want to be a mover and shaker, or one of those people who are happy to read a book but never apply anything?

OK. Off you go!

How many words have you written down? And have you got them in the right order?

Right. We will do the exercise again, but by telling a story that will string all these words together. For example, here is the story I invented in less than a minute to memorize the same list of words as you (and I can write it down from memory without having to look at them): *I give an* ice-cream *to a* sheep *which is led by a* general *in* red *who is traveling by* car *to a* tree *beside a* house *under the* stars, *to go in a* submarine *alongside an* elephant, *which will take me to a* rocket *to send an* SMS *after I have put on the* cap *which is on the* table.

I memorized this in 90 seconds, which then enabled me to write down all the words in the right order. All very easy. Note that the story doesn't need to be very logical or consistent; you just need to put the words in context in a pictorial way. Now try it yourself with another sequence of words, for example:

> thorn – rails – wall – yellow – clouds – shirt – computer – stripes – concrete – swimming pool – horse – sign – radish – Internet

Set your alarm and allow yourself two minutes to invent a story that includes these words. Then shut or switch off your book and note down the words you can recall. Ready. Steady. Go!

Right. How did you manage? I'm prepared to bet you did much better this time.

Even if you remembered the 14 words in the right order the first time, don't you think the story-telling method enables you to achieve this result more efficiently and economically?[71] And then try to remember the words tomorrow morning. You may be surprised to find that you can recall all, or almost all, the words, and in the right order, thanks to your story.

---

71   If you didn't manage to tell a story, here is an example of what you might have done: I'm looking for a *thorn* between the *rails* near a *wall* that is *yellow*, under the *clouds*, wearing a *shirt* with a *computer* with *stripes*, while *concrete* runs into a *swimming pool* and a *horse* jumps onto a *sign* showing a *radish* for sale on the *Internet*.

TEST YOUR NEW ABILITY TO REMEMBER THINGS WITH YOUR FRIENDS

When you next meet for a drink or two, challenge your friends to a little competition: one of them must write down 14 or more words on a piece of paper and show it to everyone at the same time.

You then have two minutes to memorize the words.

Using the technique you have learned, you are almost certain to beat the uninitiated. Your friends will be asking you how you came to have such a good memory.

This method, based on the association of ideas, was invented in antiquity. It works because the human brain is programmed to retain stories more easily than anything else. In particular, stories we tell ourselves, full of visual elements.

OK, you may be thinking, but how will this help me to learn anything other than sequences of words?

This is where it gets interesting. To find out how to use this technique to learn things more effectively, go to https://en.olivier-roland.com/use-stories.

The method of loci

Here is another technique, forgotten in school, which was immensely popular for over 2,000 years. It is known as loci, and, like the story-telling method, you can use it to recall keywords that will then enable you to remember the essential points of an article, speech, lecture, and so on.

To see how effective it is, let's do a simple exercise. First, read this passage, then close your eyes and imagine a place you know very well, such as your apartment.[72] Go into the hallway and enter the first room. Visualize the contents of this room: the items of furniture, the knick-knacks, the decorative features.

Go on. Close your eyes, and really do it. Don't open them again until you have finished. Are you aware that you have effortlessly recalled dozens and dozens of

---

72   If you're a student living in a 100ft² bedsit, choose a large place you know well, such as your parents' house.

different things: the look of the pieces of furniture, their colors and texture, the appearance and position of the various objects, the color of the walls, and so on?[73]

Congratulations. You have just created your first 'memory palace.'

What is a memory palace? A place you can use to boost your learning. You will be able to remember a list of objects with ease, simply by placing them mentally in the rooms of your apartment.

Let's try with this list:

- Apple

- Banana

- Cup of tea

- Camera

- Computer

- Guitar

- Printer

- Sunglasses

- Paper knife

- Watch

Go into the first room of your home and place the apple on an item of the décor. Then the banana in another place. Then the cup of tea, roses. Place them in separate locations that you can easily identify. When there are no more available locations in the room, imagine moving on to the next room. In the case of items that you already have in your apartment, place them in incongruous places where you would never put them in real life. For example, in my apartment, I start with the kitchen and imagine placing the apple on the kettle (which I would never do in real life), the apple in the sink (ditto), then I move on to the sitting-room and place the cup of tea on a low table. And so on.

---

73   Not only has your brain evolved to remember images very easily, but it is also better at spatial memory – a throwback to the time when we had to have a keen sense of the lie of the land in order to hunt hairy mammoths.

Off you go, then. Study the list of items and, in your mind's eye, place each one in a separate location in your home. Then close your eyes and imagine you are entering your home. Review the items you have placed there. Is it easy to remember them? If you are like me, and like most people, you will undoubtedly find that this method enables you to learn a long list of objects quickly and with a lot less effort.

The loci method is so powerful that you can even recall the list of items in random order, which is much more difficult with the story-telling method we looked at earlier.

Brilliant, you may say, but apart from learning a shopping list, what purpose does it serve? Good question.

The answer is that it enables you to remember not just random lists of items but also objects and symbols associated with key concepts you want to learn. As with the story-telling method, you can use loci to learn the key concepts of a course, an article, a lecture, and so on. For example, Tim Doner, a 16-year-old famous for conversing in 20 languages, uses Union Square in New York as his memory palace for learning a new language.[74]

To find out how to do all this in practice, go to https://en.olivier-roland.com/loci and download the information you will need.

USING IMAGES TO LEARN

Here is another way of using images to help you learn. Have you ever felt like tearing your hair out over the arbitrary genders of nouns in Romance languages? Wondering whether a table in Spanish is masculine or feminine, for example? There is a simple way of solving this problem: imagine each word as stereotypically specific to its gender – or your interpretation of it. For instance, all masculine items surrounded by flames and all feminine ones covered in roses. Hey presto! Problem solved. Once and for all.

OK, I know you might say, 'If this method is so brilliant, why isn't it taught in school?' As is often the case, the answer has to do with a long tradition that no one has thought to challenge. For roughly 2,000 years, from ancient Greece to the 16th century, this method was known and taught. Then, at the end of the 16th century,

---

74   You can see his presentation in the TED talk 'Breaking the language barrier,' where he shares his use of the method of loci on YouTube.

a dispute arose: the Puritans attacked this method as ungodly because, they argued, it evoked absurd and obscene images.[75] Obscene? How so? In the Middle Ages, people who used this method were in the habit of locating erotic scenes in their palaces, to stimulate their memories.[76] Later, during the Renaissance, Catholics and Protestants tried to suppress this method of school teaching, wanting to purify schooling from all pre-Christian 'pagan' influences.[77] It has never reappeared in mainstream public education since then.

But whether or not it is taught in school is of no consequence; all that matters is that this method is effective for our purposes. And there is only one way of knowing whether loci or the story-telling method works for you: be a healthy skeptic and test it out for yourself.

THREE FURTHER WAYS OF BOOSTING YOUR INTELLIGENCE, MOTIVATION, AND POWERS OF CONCENTRATION

1. Cultivate your mind

The practice of meditation is becoming increasingly popular. It can be adopted by anyone and has many benefits:

- It only takes a few minutes each day and doesn't require any bulky or expensive equipment; all you need is a quiet place and some free time; you can easily make it part of your daily routine.

- It can be practiced independently of any religion or as an integral part of one; all religions and spiritual practices include meditation.

- It serves to achieve many different objectives: relax, build self-confidence, find meaning in life, commune with one's god or the universe, etc. So everyone can use it to advantage.

What's more, many scientific studies have confirmed the benefits of practicing meditation[78], which include:

---

75 Frances A. Yates, *The Art of Memory*, 1966.
76 This shocked the Puritans, but nowadays we have no such scruples, so don't hesitate to use this sort of scenario to make the method even more effective!
77 Ioan P. Culianu, *Éros et magie à la Renaissance*: 1484, Flammarion, 1984.
78 See, for instance, the many studies done at Harvard: https://news.harvard.edu/gazette/?s=meditation or the results of 20 years of surveys conducted by the US Ministry of Health: http://en.olivier-roland.com/tm-research-on-meditation/

- Considerable reduction in stress levels

- Reduction in anxiety, feelings of anger, and the tendency to experience depression

- Notable strengthening of the immune system

- Strengthening of positive feelings and the ability to pay attention

- Reduction in blood pressure

- Increase in longevity of 23 percent for people suffering from high blood pressure[79]

And the great thing is that meditating for just five minutes a day is enough to secure many of these benefits, and five minutes a day is better than hour-long sessions at irregular intervals.

But what are the effects of meditation on intelligence, concentration, and motivation? Here are a few of them:

- Increase in capacity to control your feelings[80]

- Increase in your powers of concentration[81]

- Reduction in attention-deficit disorders[82]

- Increase in memory capacity and the ability to process things visually[83]

- Improvement in learning capabilities[84]

- Reduction in the tendency to multitask, i.e., try to do several things at once, thus lowering your productivity[85]

79 'Long-Term Effects of Stress Reduction on Mortality in Persons ≥55 Years of Age with Systemic Hypertension,' Schneider R.H. et al., *American Journal of Cardiology*, 2005.
80 'A Randomized Controlled Trial of Compassion Cultivation Training: Effects on Mindfulness, Affect, and Emotion Regulation,' Jazaieri H. et al., *Motivation and Emotion*, 2014.
81 'Initial Results from a Study of the Effects of Meditation on Multitasking Performance,' Levy D.M. et al., *Conference of Human Factors in Computing Systems – Proceedings*, 2011.
82 'Effects of Mindfulness-based Cognitive Therapy on Neurophysiological Correlates of Performance Monitoring in Adult Attention-Deficit/Hyperactivity Disorder,' Schoenberg P.L. et al., *Clinical Neurophysiology*, 2014.
83 'Mindfulness Meditation Improves Cognition: Evidence of Brief Mental Training,' Zeidan F. et al., *Conscious Cognition*, 2010.
84 'Buddha's Brain: Neuroplasticity and Meditation,' Davidson R.J. et al., *IEEE Signal Processing Magazine*, 2008.
85 'Initial Results from a Study of the Effects of Meditation on Multitasking Performance,' Levy D.M. et al., *Conference of Human Factors in Computing Systems – Proceedings*, 2011.

You can easily learn to meditate by searching online. If you would like to know my approach and a special technique to improve my practice with bio-feedback, go to https://en.olivier-roland.com/bonus-meditation.

2. Use this health hack to triple your energy levels

Countless scientific studies show that exercise improves the performance of the brain, along with many other proven benefits. For example:

- A meta-analysis of 18 surveys conducted between 1966 and 2001 showed that getting elderly people to participate in regular fitness sessions significantly improved their intellectual performance.[86]

- Cardio workouts improve the plasticity of the brain, making it more efficient and better able to adapt to new situations.[87]

- Simply walking 1½ miles a day halves the risk of contracting a brain-related disease such as Alzheimer's in men over 71 years of age compared with those who walk only 440 yards a day.[88]

- Regular exercise significantly increases a person's ability to learn and memorize.[89]

- Taking part in regular exercise sessions for three months increases the blood flow to the area of the brain associated with memory and learning (the hippocampus) by 30 percent.[90]

- Taking part in a sports activity for between 30 minutes and one hour made employees more productive, less stressed, and even less tired.[91]

I could go on and on, but just remember this: exercising regularly is good not only for your health and morale but also for your ability to learn. But avoid sports that

---

86 'Fitness Effects on the Cognitive Function of Older Adults: A Meta-Analytic Study,' Colcombe S. et al., *Psychological Science*, 2004.
87 'Cardiovascular Fitness, Cortical Plasticity, and Aging,' Colcombe S. et al., *Proceedings of the National Academy of Science*, 2004.
88 'Walking and Dementia in Physically Capable Elderly Men,' Abbott R.D. et al., *Journal of the American Medical Association*, 2004.
89 'Exercise and Time-Dependent Benefits to Learning and Memory,' Berchtold N.C. et al., *Neuroscience*, 2010.
90 'An In Vivo Correlate of Exercise-Induced Neurogenesis in the Adult Dentate Gyrus,' Pereira A.C. et al., *Proceedings of the National Academy of Science*, 2007.
91 Coulson, J.C., et al. (2008), 'Exercising at work and self-reported work performance': https://www.researchgate.net/publication/235275530_Exercising_at_work_and_self-reported_work_performance

have a heavy impact on your joints: jogging, tennis, jumping, etc. In the long run, if practiced to excess, they can cause bone and joint conditions. Activities that do not have an equivalent impact, such as cycling or swimming, are preferable.

The seven-minute training session

I know, I know: you are overloaded – doing some Dual N-Back training plus some meditation is already a lot to ask, and now I'm going to suggest you do some exercise! But suppose I told you that you can greatly benefit your health, your mood, and your intellectual performance by doing just seven minutes exercise a day, wherever you are and without any equipment, what would you say to that?

In 2013, two researchers in the physiology of human performance, Brett Klika and Chris Jordan, published a much-read article in the *American College of Sports Medicine's Health & Fitness Journal*.[92] They shared the method they had adopted for their clients – businessmen and women who had little time to devote to exercise but wanted to enjoy the associated benefits – based on high-intensity circuit training.

Several studies have shown that such time-limited but high-intensity training:

- Can be a rapid and effective way of losing weight and body fat[93]

- Effectively reduces subcutaneous fat[94]

- Improves cardiovascular health[95]

- Lowers insulin resistance, thereby reducing the risk of developing diabetes[96]

And all this with sessions as short as four minutes and not requiring any equipment.[97] This is far more motivating for most people: in just a few minutes a day, you can enjoy the essential benefits of practicing a 'conventional' sport for a much longer period.

---

92 'High-Intensity Circuit Training Using Body Weight: Maximum Results with Minimal Investment,' Kilka B. et al., *ACSM's Health & Fitness Journal*, 2013.
93 'Short-term Sprint Interval Versus Traditional Endurance Training: Similar Initial Adaptations in Human Skeletal Muscle and Exercise Performance,' Gibala M.J. et al., *The Journal of Physiology*, 2006.
94 'Dose-Response Studies on the Metabolic Effects of a Growth Hormone Pulse in Humans,' Moller N. et al., *Metabolism*, 1992.
95 In particular a person's VO2max, their maximum consumption of oxygen per minute, which is a classic marker of a healthy heart, 'Effects of Moderate-Intensity Endurance and High-Intensity Intermittent Training on Anaerobic Capacity and VO2max,' Tabata I. et al., *Medicine & Science in Sports & Exercise*, 1996.
96 'Short-Term Sprint Interval Training Increases Insulin Sensitivity in Healthy Adults but does not Affect the Thermogenic Response to Beta-Adrenergic Stimulation,' Richards J.C. et al., *The Journal of Physiology*, 2010.
97 'Just Hit It! A Time-Efficient Exercise Strategy to Improve Muscle Insulin Sensitivity,' Gibala M.J. et al., *The Journal of Physiology*, 2010.

You can do your workout two or three times in a row if you have time, but once a day, five times a week, is effective and sufficient. Surely you can spare seven measly minutes a day to keep fit, stay healthy, boost your intellectual performance, and increase your sense of wellbeing! Search online for '7-minute workout,' and you will find plenty of apps and videos to encourage you.

Five minutes of meditation a day, seven minutes of sport, and 10 minutes of Dual N-Back training is an excellent way of gaining a whole range of benefits very quickly. This is a real 80/20 synergy that will give you an enormous advantage over others in all aspects of life and make you more self-contented.

3. Learn a musical instrument

'An acoustic guitar is a friend for you all your life.'

MARK KNOPFLER,
GUITARIST AND SINGER WITH DIRE STRAITS

Many studies[98] have shown that practicing a musical instrument increases IQ, powers of concentration, and the marks pupils get at school. But above all, learning a musical instrument is an enjoyable experience in its own right and can, eventually, become a useful and impressive skill. Wouldn't you prefer to learn the guitar (or another instrument) rather than swot away for months on end, only to regurgitate what you learned in a stupid multiple-choice examination, then forget more than 80 percent of it once you've got your certificate?

When you have achieved a certain level, there will be many times when you'll be able to play your instrument for others, and that will enhance your social standing. And even if you give it up for a time, you'll forget it much less quickly than all the theoretical knowledge you have merely skated over.

FIGHTING THE FORGETTING CURVE: HOW TO LEARN – AND RETAIN KNOWLEDGE – MORE EASILY

One of the problems with school is that it is still using 19th-century techniques to combat the forgetting curve (*see p.13*). This concept took time to catch on but was eventually analyzed in more detail, and now we are much better at counteracting

---

98   For example (already cited): 'Music Lessons Enhance IQ,' Schellenberg E.G., Psychological Science, 2004, and 'Short-Term Music Training Enhances Verbal Intelligence and Executive Function,' Moreno S. et al., *Psychological Science*, 2011.

it. There is software that can analyze your forgetting curve while you are learning and present you with the knowledge you want to retain when you are in danger of forgetting it, to optimize the storage of information in your long-term memory. This is called 'spaced repetition.'

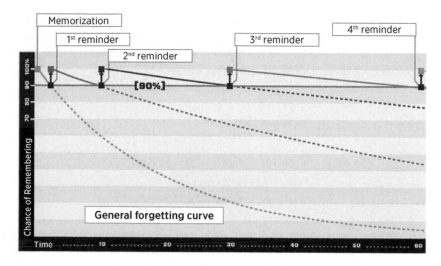

Figure 3: The forgetting curve

The spaced repetition principle[99] is as follows: the more often you are shown the thing you need to learn, the less quickly you forget it, and the more spaced-out the repetitions can become. In 1999, a meta-analysis of 63 separate studies showed that in general, people who practice spaced repetition beat 67 percent of those who do not use the technique when learning something over the same period.[100] In short, its effectiveness is proven beyond doubt. But it has still not been taken up in schools, and this is not about to change. In 1988, an article with the compelling title 'The Spacing Effect: A Case Study in the Failure to Apply the Results of Psychological Research'[101] was already asking why a method whose efficacy 'many researchers regard as one of the most firmly established in the areas of learning and memory' was so little implemented, to the point where 'no class or coursebook seems to be practicing it.'

---

99   Image reproduced from one published in the magazine Wired, based on the work of Piotr Wozniak, author of the first commercial software app for learning by spaced repetition, SuperMemo.
100 'A Meta-Analytic Review of the Distribution of Practice Effect: Now You See It, Now You Don't' Donovan J.J. et al., *Journal of Applied Psychology*, 1999.
101 'The Spacing Effect: A Case Study in the Failure to Apply the Results of Psychological Research,' Dempster F. N., *American Psychologist*, 1988.

Fortunately, as intelligent rebels, we don't need to wait for a technique to be implemented by the Ministry of Education before using it; all that matters is to test it on ourselves and adopt it if it works.

The basic principle is simple: an app frequently presents you with what you are struggling to remember, and less often with what you can remember easily. These apps present what you have to learn in the form of flashcards, which ask you questions on what you have been studying. You answer the question, in your head or on paper, then press a button, and the answer is displayed. You then indicate by clicking on the corresponding icon whether:

A. You have perfectly remembered the answer, in which case the app schedules the next display of this card at a more distant time, which is postponed exponentially as you go on responding correctly to the card concerned.

B. You have remembered the answer fairly well, in which case the app schedules the next appearance of the card rather sooner.

C. You completely fail to remember the answer, in which case the app reinitials the card and will present it to you again after only a very short delay.

Figure 4: Example of a flashcard displayed by the Mosalingua software application for learning Portuguese, with the buttons that enable the app to calculate when the card should be presented again.

What's more, software apps of this kind are designed so you can test your memory. As Francis Bacon pointed out in his *Novum Organum* in 1620:

> *If you read a piece of text through 20 times, you will not learn it by heart so easily as if you read it 10 times while attempting to recite it from time to time and consulting the text when your memory fails.' His theory has since been largely validated by science.*[102]

And the great thing about all this? The most widely used software app is free. And the others are generally very modestly priced.

Anki, or the 80/20 of learning

The first publicly available software app that used spaced repetition to optimize learning was SuperMemo, first marketed in 1985. Since then, though SuperMemo is still available,[103] free apps have appeared and have overtaken it in popularity, the best known of these being Anki.

Although its interface is somewhat sparse, Anki enables you to easily create cards relating to whatever you might want to learn. Hundreds of decks, created and shared free of charge by users, are available on a wide range of subjects.[104] Many of these decks focus on language learning, but plenty of other fields are covered: i.e., anatomy, biology, math, geography, and even ornithology for twitchers.

A touch of gamification, and off we go again!

The main problem with Anki and many other apps isn't that they are ineffective, far from it, but that they are effective only if used regularly for a long enough period.

At first, you may be bursting with enthusiasm, but after a few days, it's another story. This is why the authors of learning apps have drawn inspiration from software, motivating that it turns their users into addicts. I mean, of course, video games.

---

102 See in particular the meta-analyses 'The Power of Testing Memory: Basic Research and Implications for Educational Practice,' Roediger H.L. et al., *Perspectives on Psychological Science*, 2006, and 'Effects of Frequent Classroom Testing,' Bangert-Drowns R.L. et al., *The Journal of Educational Research*, 1991, which analyze respectively 13 and 35 studies of the subject, most of them concluding that regular testing has a positive effect on memory.
103 At http://en.olivier-roland.com/super-memo/
104 http://en.olivier-roland.com/ankiweb-decks/ A Google search for 'decks anki' will also take you to many decks directly available from enthusiasts' websites.

They have therefore begun to include certain features of video games in their learning applications to keep users motivated for the long haul. Such has been their success that it has spawned a new word: gamification.

Typically, gamified apps include such features as:

- A system of visual progression: you earn points, badges, and trophies the further you progress in your studies

- A ranking system comparing you with other participants

- Immediate feedback from the system and proposals for correction

- A system that enables you to compete with your friends

- A story with a narrative, points, and levels to rise through

In short, an effectively gamified system can make the most boring subject far more entertaining, in fact, a lot of fun. Obviously, as with spaced repetition, schools are not about to apply these principles, so it's up to intelligent rebels to roll up their sleeves and search out ingenious apps that will enable them to learn better and faster.

But what are the best apps in the field? One I use every day is Habitica.[105] It turns your whole life into a game, letting you set your own objectives and win points achieving them, and docking points when you fail.

A bit later, I'll be telling you about another app you can use for language learning.

HOW TO LEARN A LANGUAGE WITHOUT TEARS – AND WHY MASTERING AT LEAST ONE FOREIGN LANGUAGE IS A VITAL ASSET FOR THE INTELLIGENT REBEL

As we saw in Chapter 1, learning a language is very important for broadening your horizons, discovering other cultures, and improving your life chances. And yet, the school system makes a very poor fist of it. I am therefore devoting all of this section to the art of learning a language effectively on your own.

---

105 http://en.olivier-roland.com/habitica/

The 80/20 approach to deciding what language to learn

The 80/20 principle applies first of all to your choice of a language: since it takes hundreds of hours to master a foreign language, motivation is essential, and unused knowledge soon rusts away, you'd better choose a language that will be really useful.

But what languages are most widely spoken? There is no general agreement on this, but here is a ranking published by the highly regarded monthly *La Recherche* in 2009[106] with, in brackets, the estimated number of people who speak it, either as their mother tongue or as a second language:

1. Mandarin (1.12 billion)

2. English (480 million)

3. Spanish (320 million)

4. Russian (285 million)

5. French (265 million)

6. Hindi/Urdu (250 million)

7. Arabic (221 million)

8. Portuguese (188 million)

9. Bengali (185 million)

10. Japanese (133 million)

This ranking is far from perfect and is contradicted to some extent by all the others. Some reckon that English is spoken as a mother tongue or foreign language by as many as 1.4 billion people, but at very variable levels of ability.

The researcher George Weber took things a step farther in 1997, ranking the 10 most influential languages based on six criteria:

1. Number of mother-tongue speakers

2. Number of second-language speakers

3. Economic strength of the countries using the language concerned

4. Number of major fields of human activity in which the language is important

---

106   By teachers Louis-Jean and Alain Calvet.

5. Number of countries and population using the language

6. Social and cultural prestige of the language

Here is his ranking, which he still considered valid in 2008:

1. English (37 points)

2. French (23 points)

3. Spanish (20 points)

4. Russian (16 points)

5. Arabic (14 points)

6. Chinese (13 points)

7. German (12 points)

8. Japanese (10 points)

9. Portuguese (10 points)

10. Hindi/Urdu (9 points)

As well as its popularity and usefulness, you also need to consider the degree of difficulty involved in learning a language. The US Foreign Service Institute[107] has measured the time it takes to learn a language well enough to take part effectively in most conversations, taking into account the fact that languages belong to particular 'families,' and that it is easier to learn a language more closely related to your mother tongue.

Here are the different language families, with the FSI's estimates of the number of hours required to achieve an acceptable level.[108] The figure in brackets is the time it would take if you attended 100 hours of lessons a year:

- Group I: 600 hours (six years) – Afrikaans, Catalan, Danish, Dutch, French, Italian, Norwegian, Portuguese, Romanian, Spanish, and Swedish.

- Group II: 750 hours (seven and a half years) – German

---

107 Which researched the subject for the sake of its diplomats.
108 Level 3 of the Interagency Language Roundtable Scale – basically, the level at which you can handle most personal or business-related conversations and be understood most of the time.

- Group III: 900 hours (nine years) – Indonesian, Javan, Jumieka, Malay, and Swahili

- Group IV: 1,100 hours (11 years) – Many languages fall into this group, including Albanian, Bulgarian, Croat, Czech, Estonian,[109] Finnish, Georgian, Greek, Hebrew, Hindi, Hungarian, Icelandic, Persian (Dari, Farsi, Tajik), Polish, Russian, Serbian, Slovak, Thai, Turkish, Ukrainian, and Vietnamese*

- Group V: 2,200 hours (22 years) – Arabic, Cantonese, Japanese, Korean, Mandarin, Mongolian, Taiwanese (Hokkien, Minnan), and Wu

Are these figures completely reliable? No. There are many factors to take into account: your own abilities, of course, and also, for instance, the number of languages you speak already: the more languages you know, the easier it is to learn a new one. But they give a good overall idea of the difficulty involved in learning a language.

Don't you find these figures interesting? How do you explain the fact that such things were never discussed at school?

In Weber's top 10, the only Group I languages closely related to English and fairly easy to learn are:

- French
- Spanish
- Portuguese

German is on the borderline between groups I and II and has the reputation of being difficult for English-speakers to learn – and it is little spoken outside of Germany, Austria, and Switzerland.

The 80/20 choice for Americans is clearly Spanish, given the number of Spanish-speakers in the USA and the importance of this language in the Americas. Not surprisingly, it is the language chosen by 88 percent of Americans wanting to learn a foreign language.[110]

But hang on a moment. The most 80/20 possible choice is the one your parents made for you when they sent you to a bilingual English/Spanish nursery school, which meant you could learn Spanish easily as a child. If this was not what happened in your case, never mind. But consider the possibility for your own children.

---

109   The languages marked with an asterisk are reputed to be more difficult than the others in their group and take longer to learn.
110   'Language Research – FLE – State of Language in the USA.'

The advantages of total immersion

Let's consider the problem from a different angle: you need some basic theoretical teaching of a foreign language to get started. But once you have mastered the basics (let's say after 100 or 200 hours, or a year or two's teaching at college level), what do you think is the best way to go on from there:

- Continue to attend 100 hours of classroom lessons every year for 10 years, while speaking your mother tongue the rest of the time?

- Go to live for six months in a country where the language is spoken?

I think you already know the answer. But let's do a quick bit of arithmetic:

- A hundred hours of lessons a year for 10 years adds up to 1,000 hours spent studying.

- Six months in a foreign country hearing, speaking, and writing the language for about eight hours a day (probably an underestimate) adds up to 1,460 hours of study, in a range of situations totally different from the 10 years spent sitting on a chair. You will be learning the language as it is really spoken and used in daily life – the antithesis of book learning.

Of course, if you spend a year in a foreign country practicing the language for eight hours a day, that adds up to 2,920 hours of practice. And if you practice it 12 hours a day, that makes a total of 4,380 hours.

The figures speak for themselves: after six months of immersion, you will have learned more than in 10 years of conventional school-based lessons. Did anyone ever tell you that at school?

Work it out: how many hours a week, and how many years did you spend practicing your foreign language?[111] Start with the hours of classroom lessons you attend, then add in the hours spent listening (TV series, films, podcasts, etc.), hours of conversational practice with a native speaker, and hours spent reading and writing. I'm prepared to bet that the final figure is lower than you imagined. And definitely insufficient to achieve an acceptable level in a short time.

In short, with languages as with business, getting experience in the field is a faster and more effective way of learning than sitting on a chair listening to

---

111   If you are no longer at school, calculate the number of hours you spent studying a language when you were a student.

a teacher, provided you know the basics and continue to learn the theory as you put it into practice.

So, take a six-month or one-year course in a foreign country, or you may end up like poor Caroline (her again!), who spent 11 years studying German at school and is still incapable of holding a simple conversation. Think of those thousands of hours wasted in the classroom that could have been put to far better use.

Mind you distinguish, though, between just living in a country and being immersed in the local language. Many expatriates live abroad for years without ever learning the language of their place of residence. You really have to make contact with the locals and force yourself to speak to them in their language. So, if you go to Mexico, avoid cultivating a circle of purely 'international' friends you can speak English with.

'OK, that's fine,' you may say, 'but what if I'm now of a more mature age and would still like to perfect my command of a language?'

Here is my straightforward program for achieving your aim without tears. Having a basic level – a year or two's study at college level – is an advantage, but not essential for getting started.

How to learn a language very quickly with Mosalingua

Mosalingua[112] applications are designed to optimize language learning. The principle is simple, based on two concepts we have already come across in this book:

1. The 80/20 principle. The authors worked with teachers of the various languages on offer and asked them to identify the 20 percent of the vocabulary used for 80 percent of the time.

2. The forgetting curve and spaced repetition.

It is easy to use these apps on your smartphone for five minutes a day, while waiting in line, traveling on public transport, etc. In this way, you can very quickly acquire the basic vocabulary of a language, so you can cope when you go abroad, for instance.

You certainly won't become bilingual by using this method, but it will soon get you engaging in conversation and improving your command of the language from that point on.

---

112   http://en.olivier-roland.com/mosalingua/

And the real plus point of all this? At the time of writing, Mosalingua applications are available for less than $5. I don't have shares in Mosalingua, but it seems to be an excellent way of getting started with the language you have always dreamed of mastering or re-activating your rusty knowledge of a language you have neglected for many years.

Personally, I have used this software to learn Portuguese, mastering 5,000 flashcards in five years. Combined with other apps I'm about to mention, and regular practice with Brazilian and Portuguese friends, practicing for just a few minutes a day has got me to the level of being able to deliver a 40-minute lecture in Rio,[113] and a one-hour presentation in Portugal,[114] just three years after I started learning, without ever having lived in a Portuguese-speaking country.

Duolingo, an excellent supplement for beginners... but too easy

Duolingo is completely free of charge, and you can use it to study more than 30 languages, including less common ones such as Esperanto, Hawaiian or Gaelic, and even invented languages like Klingon[115] and High Valyrian.[116]

The application relies on spaced repetition for greater effectiveness and gamification to enhance motivation. However, Duolingo does have one drawback: it is relatively easy, to the point where you can complete one of its courses without really being able to express yourself in the language. The team is aware of this problem and is gradually trying to improve things by introducing more challenging features. In any case, I would still recommend Duolingo as an excellent supplement to Mosalingua.

Developing your understanding of the spoken language as efficiently as possible

There is no short-cut to developing your comprehension of a language as spoken. You need to listen to the language as much as possible, getting someone to explain the words you do not understand.

---

113   I certainly don't consider myself bilingual, but I know enough to make myself understood most of the time. To see an extract from this lecture, view the clip at https://en.olivier-roland.com/conf-portugais/ on my Instagram account.

114   That you can see entirely, with English subtitles, on https://en.olivier-roland.com/webinars-pt

115   A made-up language from the *Star Trek* series.

116   A made-up language from the *Game of Thrones* series.

OK, but what do you do when you don't live in a country where the language is spoken, and you haven't much time to devote to intensive listening exercises?

Simple. How much time do you spend traveling each day? If you live in a big city, you are probably in transit for a good hour a day, whether on foot, on your bike, in the car, or on public transport (or a combination of these). And you probably commute five days a week, 50 weeks a year – 250 hours, the equivalent of more than six 40-hour weeks. Now imagine using just 200 of these 250 hours to practice listening to the language you are trying to master. Wouldn't that make an enormous difference to your understanding? Sure it would.

We have seen that the time devoted to the conventional teaching of a language at secondary school is about 100 hours a year. Listening to a language for 200 hours annually will boost your understanding of the spoken language far more than a year's learning in the classroom. Here are a few examples of how you can use your travel time to listen to a language:

- Listen to podcasts in the language you are studying. You will find thousands in your target language on platforms such as Apple, Spotify, and SoundCloud.

- Listen to audiobooks.

- Watch films in the language you are studying. Most have soundtracks and subtitles in different languages.

- Watch YouTube videos in your target language. Go to the YouTube home page for the language you are studying[117] and watch the videos going viral at any particular time.

- Look for a teacher online, on sites such as Italki.[118]

Quickly developing your reading skills

The ideal way to develop your reading skills is to read books in the foreign language you're learning. That may seem very demanding, but no one is asking you to start with *War and Peace*. Begin with a short book, something simple and easy to read – a comic book, for example. Reading comic strips you have already enjoyed in your own language is a gentle introduction to reading in another language.

---

117 By typing the extension of the country representative of this language in the address, for example http://en.olivier-roland.com/youtube-es/ for Spain, or by choosing the language and country directly in YouTube. At the time of writing, these options can be found at the bottom of the home page.
118 http://en.olivier-roland.com/italki/

Then tackle a real book, again something short and straightforward, for example, a children's story. May I suggest the first volume of Harry Potter? It is relatively simple, and it has been translated into many languages. You might even read the whole series, as I did to improve my English. As the story develops, it increases in volume and complexity in terms of the plot and vocabulary. This is an excellent way of reading more and more complicated books without even realizing it. If you have read the fifth volume of Harry Potter (the weightiest in the series), you can surely claim to be able to read almost *anything* in the language.

At first, you will undoubtedly need a dictionary to translate the words you are not familiar with. This can be frustrating, but if you have chosen a simple book, you will soon be able to manage without the dictionary as you become acquainted with the keywords used by the author. With a little practice, you will quickly be able to set the dictionary aside, guessing the meaning of most of the new words from their context.

And the most ingenious trick of all is to buy the Kindle version of these books and read them on your smartphone or tablet with the app provided by Amazon: just touch a word you don't understand, and up comes a definition and a translation.[119]

But how can I find the time for all this, you may be wondering? Just borrow from your regular reading time[120] and do some reading in the foreign language, rather than in English. Apart from books, you should also start reading newspapers, magazines, websites, and other resources in the language in question. You can access all foreign sites from the comfort of your home thanks to the Internet, and you will find many newspapers and magazines[121] you can read online or on your tablet/phone/computer/integrated artificial retina.[122] This will introduce you to the culture of your target country and open up a new perspective on the world, a new way of connecting with reality, as well as being an enjoyable activity since you will be reading material that interests you.

Additional time required (if you are already in the habit of reading): zero. And if you are not a habitual reader, this will probably be one of the best investments of your time you ever make.

---

119   Another trick I use for making reading easier is to reverse the colors, so I am reading white text on a black background.
120   If you are not currently devoting any time to reading, books in particular, I would urge you to read the section on getting a 'personal MBA' (*see p.117*). But... you are now reading this book, aren't you?
121   I would nevertheless recommend that you go on a 'media diet.' See the passage on this subject in Chapter 3 (*see p.67*).
122   It all depends how far in the future you are reading my book!

And what about writing and speaking skills?

This program of mine doesn't give you any practice in writing and speaking. However, by practicing your reading and listening comprehension, you will inevitably improve in other areas. Not as quickly as if you deliberately practiced them, but remember that one aim of this program is not to take up any more of your precious time.

If you are prepared to devote some additional time to these skills and have some fun, here is what I would advise:

- **To develop your writing skills:** Join a discussion forum on a topic that interests you in the target language. This will enable you to discuss a subject you are passionate about, learn more about it, and build a network of relationships while practicing your writing skills. Ensure that you are not writing in your mother tongue, and you welcome correction from other participants if you use an awkward expression or make mistakes.

- **To develop your speaking abilities without going abroad:** Host people from a country where your target language is spoken through CouchSurfing, Hospitality Club, GlobalFreeloaders, or another free hospitality website. Or just suggest you meet them for a drink and take them on a tour of your town/region. As on eBay, there is a system of comments and references to help you find out who you are dealing with. This is an excellent way of 'traveling without traveling' and practicing your target language, without enormous effort or financial investment. Of course, there is also the highly recommended option of getting a teacher to give you some lessons via Skype.[123]

Accent

If you have a strong English/American accent, you may fear this puts you at a disadvantage. But that's not really the case. On the contrary, try and see it as an advantage. As long as you can make yourself understood without difficulty, a foreign accent is a mark of distinction, making you slightly exotic and automatically interesting. People will ask where you come from, even if you just ask them the time…

Even so, work hard to pronounce the sounds correctly, especially those that could give rise to communication problems.

---

123   Begin by having a look at Italki.

3½ SIMPLE TECHNIQUES FOR USING THE MEDIA MORE INTELLIGENTLY: THE 'MEDIA DIET'

Terrorist attacks. Accidents. Wars. Famines. Natural disasters. Traffic hold-ups. Corrupt politicians. Economic crises. Unemployment. Inflation. Just a few of the subjects the media force down our throats every day. Very encouraging. Just the recipe for optimism and enjoyment of the present moment, don't you think?

Not to mention all the pointless information on a plethora of topics. Information that will take up your time and sap your mental energy when 80 percent of it will be forgotten in a few days and almost all after a few months.

Going on the 'Media Diet' is a way of avoiding this brainwashing, a way of feeding and developing your mind more selectively, rather than stuffing it with junk food.

Going on the Media Diet means replacing this:

with this:

Not convinced? Watch a TV news bulletin on the Internet. What topics are featured? Essential information for living a better, more fulfilled, and more serene life?

Be serious. Which of you, after watching this sort of stuff, has noted an improvement in your way of life?

Does the fact that someone has watched a report on a murder or terrorist attack lead to the matter being dealt with more quickly, or to improvements in their family life or friendships? Maybe in a tiny minority of cases, but not as a general rule. And what if people applied themselves to improving what they could in their immediate circle of influence? Instead of worrying about events on the other side of the world, which they can have no direct effect and interests them only for the few moments when they take a sofa break?

Here are 3½ simple techniques to stop the influx of junk and begin feeding your mind with some healthy, tasty nourishment.

1. Stop reading all generalist information media: Daily newspapers, TV news bulletins, radio news shows, Google news, current affairs websites (Reuters, AFP...), Facebook, etc. These are the source of most of the depressing news that fills and occupies your mind before leaking away over the next few days.

2. Instead, select sources of information directly connected with your occupation and/or that will help you make progress in achieving your objectives: Specialized magazines, blogs, books, etc. Instead of radio news bulletins, listen to some interesting podcasts. Or music. Or listen to audiobooks. Or sing. Or just smile while enjoying what you are doing. Instead of TV news programs, watch videos or TED talks, go and have some fun with friends or do some exercise. Or anything else that will bring some sunshine into your life and help you get where you really want to go.

3. If you are skeptical about going on this sort of diet, fine! Just be a healthy skeptic: Testing it out rather than sticking to your preconceived ideas and doing nothing. Here's a challenge: Go on the Media Diet for just seven days. That should be easy enough. And see if the information you have been imbibing is really so essential. If it is not, try going without it for a whole month. If you can do without it for a month, continue for as long as you can. I bet you will be surprised how long you can 'tolerate' this media diet and the benefits you gain from it!

3½. If you absolutely must stay connected with the world while filtering out 95 percent of the negative stuff, try this: Keep up to date with new scientific discoveries. These will enable you to stay in touch with what is going on and will be mostly positive. And they will give you a better idea of what the future has in store and the countless possibilities the world has to offer.

By trying out the media diet for a week or a month, you will get your own answer to the questions that are probably bothering you: Aren't I going to lose touch with the world? What am I going to talk about with my colleagues/friends/children/pets? How can I be a good citizen? How will I survive?

All these questions will be answered, and you will discover other benefits, too. Just try it.

THE SACRED FLAME

> *'If you don't build your dream, someone else will hire you to help build theirs.'*
>
> TONY A. GASKINS, JR.

Lille, early 2015: While at home preparing to move to a new house, I come across an old folder of handwritten documents. Interesting! Documents from my last year at school, just before I set up my first business. And in there I find a dog-eared green booklet: the old report book that went back and forth between the school, my parents, and myself.

It contained detachable 'coupons,' of which the counterfoils remain: pink for absences, blue for lateness. I'm amused: the coupons for being late have all been used up! None left. And nearly all the coupons for absences had been used, too.

It reminded me of how I spent my last year at school: totally and absolutely lacking in motivation. My first late arrival was just a few days after the start of the academic year. And I was 'off sick' that year more times than in the first 20 years of my career as a businessman.

My marks were catastrophic. I used to fall asleep in class. To the point where the headmaster summoned me at the end of the year and said: 'Several teachers have complained that you drop off to sleep at your desk; they are discouraged by your listless attitude. They don't want to teach you, so we are not going to have you back next year.'

That was it. I was expelled.

This outcome quite suited me because I had decided two months earlier to leave school and set up my business. Then, for a year, I devoted myself to the task, struggling to overcome all the obstacles. My youth. My appearance. My lack of experience, resources, qualifications.

I managed to get €15,000 of funding to start my business. Then I encountered the first serious obstacles: finding customers, putting in place a proper marketing strategy. Fighting to prevent my enterprise from failing after the first six months. Then making a success of it, thanks to some loyal employees and customers.

Then launching into a new web-based project, on a part-time basis, even though I was a complete beginner. Making a brilliant success of it, which gave me freedom and an income I would never have thought possible while helping thousands of other people.

And yet, the demotivated dunce and the successful entrepreneur are one and the same person. The only difference between the two? Motivation. The sacred flame.

Because I had found a purpose in life, a source of joy and desire. With this sacred flame, all the obstacles I had thought of as forbidding mountains became molehills. They might slow me down, but they could not stop me.

Then, after a few years, the sacred flame died down, waiting for a new breath of wind to fan it into life again.

When I discovered the world of blogging, then the philosophy of *The 4-Hour Work Week*, I found a renewed purpose in life, driving me in the same direction as before: greater freedom, even more possibilities. And a challenge both exciting and amusing to throw myself into. The sacred flame was burning again. I started my first blog in total ignorance. I made all the mistakes you can think of. It was a resounding failure.

But no: no one cared a bit.

And so I continued. I started a second blog, then a third, working on them part-time while still managing my existing enterprise. I trained in the best ways to make a blog a proper business. I read loads of books. Recruited a marketing consultant. Launched my first product. And I succeeded, beyond my wildest dreams.

Because, with the sacred flame inside you, all obstacles can be overcome. They may slow us down, but they can't stop us.

You, too, whatever your circumstances, can find the sacred flame.

You may well be a dunce, in a job you hate, have achieved nothing special to date, be telling yourself you are a loser and have messed up.... It doesn't matter.

I was in your position at one time, but that didn't stop me from finding the sacred flame. With it burning inside you, everything is simpler.

You can have it, too, find what you most want from life. For me, it was freedom and independence. For you, it might be love, money, helping others, sex. It doesn't matter. Find out what you want most. Then work out a challenging project to make it yours.

Just do it. It will make everything easier.

SUMMARY

For the intelligent rebel who has decided to act

⇒ You can significantly increase your learning capacity, as well as your autonomy and creativity, by putting the activities described in this chapter into practice.

⇒ Dual N-Back is the only scientifically proven method for improving your IQ, and it also boosts your powers of concentration.

⇒ The story-telling and loci methods are very effective if you still need to learn things by heart – much better, once again, than the methods they teach in school.

⇒ A few minutes exercise and/or meditation and/or practicing a musical instrument each day can significantly improve your intellectual performance, creativity, memory, discipline, attention span and physical performance, and even your longevity.

⇒ Software apps that take the forgetting curve into account are much more effective than all the learning methods used at school, particularly if they are gamified. Do use them. Afterward, you will find that you can no longer do without them when learning something.

⇒ Consider using your daily commute, and any other 'dead' time, to improve your foreign language skills. And use the other techniques mentioned in this chapter to perfect your command of a foreign language.

⇒ The media diet will help you healthily feed your mind rather than stuffing it with 'junk food.' It will save you time and give you more 'available brain time' for creative pursuits.

⇒ Finally, by focusing on what you really want and devising a project to obtain it, you will be lit up by the sacred flame and become unstoppable.

To help you put the activities described in this chapter into practice, go to http://en.olivier-roland.com/hack-education. You will be sent an email with a series of activities and challenges designed to give you the necessary motivation.

CHAPTER 4
BOOST YOUR WILLPOWER
Resisting Chocolate Ice Cream and Three Cheese Pizza

Willpower, closely related to self-control, is undoubtedly the most important of the skills to develop. In recent years, there have been many remarkable scientific discoveries on fostering this trait, masterfully summed up in *The Willpower Instinct* by Kelly McGonigal and *Willpower* by Roy F. Baumeister and John Tierney – though it will no doubt take decades before they trickle down into schools. To save you time, I have summarized the main points and added my experience in this field. Here we go!

Scientific studies show that willpower is a better indicator of performance at university than IQ.[124] Strong-willed students get better marks, are less often ill, and enjoy greater success.[125] A strong will is also advantageous for friendships and marital relationships, stress management, and even longevity.[126] It seems that disciplined people tend to make choices that result in long-term benefits. For example, imagine the positive impact of always making the right choice when faced with deciding between the following:

- Reading a practical book someone has recommended or watching a TV series

- Getting some exercise or indulging in YouTube clips

- Doing a Dual N-Back training session or spending 20 minutes surfing on social media

- Practicing meditation or reading a newspaper

- Eating a healthy meal of vitamin-rich vegetables or wolfing a hamburger high in sugars and bad cholesterol

---

124 'Self-Discipline Outdoes IQ in Predicting Academic Performance of Adolescents,' Duckworth A.L., *Psychological Science*, 2005.
125 'High Self-Control Predicts Good Adjustment, Less Pathology, Better Grades, and Interpersonal Success,' Tangney J. P. et al., *Journal of Personality*, 2004.
126 'Do Conscientious Individuals Live Longer? A Quantitative Review,' Kern M.L. et al., *Health Psychology*, 2008.

- Applying some of the techniques you have learned from this book or playing a video game

I could go on.

Would it make an appreciable difference to your life if you made the 'right' choice just 10 percent or 20 percent more often?

You can be pretty confident the answer is yes. Of course, the idea isn't to turn into a workaholic robot. Just to strengthen your willpower so that you can decide more consciously when to act in pursuit of your objectives or when to relax and enjoy yourself. Instead of continually succumbing to temptations that divert you from what you want to achieve.

WHAT IS WILLPOWER?

There are two systems in our brain constantly fighting to control our behavior:[127]

1. The instinctive fight-or-flight system, shaped by evolution to ensure our survival in an environment that has long since ceased to exist.

2. A more reflective system giving us the strength to resist our instinctive urges, shaped by evolution to enable us to live in society.

If all the human beings on Earth were asked to choose between a green salad and a hamburger with a delicious sugary sauce, most would probably desire the hamburger, even if they were all equally well-nourished.

Our impulsive attraction to the hamburger derives from the fact that, until relatively recently, we lived in an environment where finding a regular source of food was a genuine problem. Consequently, we have an instinct that makes us crave fatty and sweet foods because building up fat reserves is a life insurance policy.

There has since been a complete reversal in most parts of the world. This same instinct now drives us to overeat unhealthy food in an environment where the risk of famine is practically zero, causing many health problems. But our DNA has not had enough time to adapt to the new situation of abundance and retained its original instincts. No luck!

---

127 'The Social Brain: Mind, Language, and Society in Evolutionary Perspective,' Dunbar R.I.M., *Annual Review of Anthropology*, 2003.

From the time humankind began to live in communities, failure to control these basic urges was dangerous. Mating with your neighbor's wife, or keeping the animal you have killed to yourself rather than sharing it with your less fortunate neighbors, ran the risk of upsetting the other members of the community, who might then feel a strong urge to bop you on the head with a club and be done with you... or cast you out of the tribe, which also meant death in the shorter or longer term.

The prefrontal cortex has developed to enable us to control such urges,[128] giving humans an evolutionary advantage in being able to live together and cooperate. So, within ourselves, we do have the capacity to resist temptation.

THE HUMAN WILL IS LIKE A MUSCLE

One of the most astounding scientific discoveries is the 'willpower-as-muscle' model. As with a muscle, the less we exercise our will, the less strength we have to resist temptation. But, counterintuitively, the more we use it, the more we are in danger of exhausting it. Research shows, for instance, that **the more choices we make in a day, the more likely we are not to resist our impulses**.

As a general rule, our will is stronger when we get up in the morning than in the evening, because by then the dozens, or hundreds, of impulses we have more or less successfully resisted during the day will have used up our reserves. Indeed, we spend 25 percent of our waking hours – the equivalent of four hours a day[129] – resisting our desires.

HOW TO BOOST YOUR WILLPOWER: THE ART OF DEFINING OBJECTIVES

'If a man knows not to which port he sails, no wind is favorable.'

SENECA

There is no such thing as willpower in the absence of objectives, so you must list your goals before continuing. Take a pen and a sheet of paper, or open a new file, and write at the top 'My objectives.' Then write down all your personal and professional objectives – short, medium, or long-term, more or less precisely defined. Here are a few examples:

---

128   'Evolution in the Social Brain,' Dunbar R.I. et al., *Science*, 2007.
129   'Everyday Temptations: An Experience Sampling Study of Desire, Conflict, and Self-Control,' Hofmann W. et al., *Journal of Personality and Social Psychology*, 2012.

- Learn to play the guitar

- Pass the level 1 scuba-diving exam

- Score an average of 14/20 this year

- Set up my own business

Some objectives will quickly come to mind; you may then have to rack your brains to come up with the others. When research scientists ask people to list their objectives, most have no difficulty in finding at least 15,[130] so try to at least equal this figure.

There is an even more effective strategy for defining objectives: the SMART method, which I have adapted. To avoid making this book even longer, I have omitted it here, but you can access it at http://en.olivier-roland.com/smart.

When you have written out a full list of objectives, you will have the necessary basis to exercise your will. So let's look at some techniques to help boost your willpower and keep it at the highest possible level.

Slow breathing

Every time you feel an urge to divert from the goal you have set yourself, use this simple and effective technique to give an immediate boost to your willpower.[131]

What do you have to do? Simple: pinch your nose and hop around on one leg for a minute while braying like a zebra.

I'm joking, of course. It's even simpler: take slow, deep breaths. That's all. Inhale and exhale, with each breath lasting 10 to 15 seconds. It will help you relax and increase your self-control while reducing the strength of the urge you are feeling. It's also an excellent technique for keeping your cool in stressful situations, such as making a speech.[132]

Whenever you think of it – even if the chocolate ice-cream or video game threatens to tempt you – practice slow, deep breathing. You can use this simple technique

---

130   Roy F. Baumeister and John Tierney, *Willpower.*
131   'The Effects of Respiratory Sinus Arrhythmia Biofeedback on Heart Rate Variability and Posttraumatic Stress Disorder Symptoms: A Pilot Study,' Zucker T.L. et al., *Applied Psychophysiology and Biofeedback,* 2009.
132   I have often used the technique, when speaking to audiences of up to 1,500 people. It works every time.

in almost any situation. The intelligent rebel, therefore, has every reason to adopt it in all circumstances.

Meditation

The best-documented and most effective way of increasing your willpower is through meditation – another benefit to add to those mentioned earlier[133] and a further reason for taking up the practice (*see also Chapter 3, p.49*). As with the other benefits, there is no need to spend years on a mountaintop to gain better self-control: just three hours are enough to make an appreciable difference, and, after 11 hours, researchers have noted changes sufficiently evident to be picked up by brain scans.[134]

Exercise

As with meditation, there is proof that regular exercise strengthens the will[135] immediately after a session and in the longer term. Performing a physical activity, if only for a few minutes, has beneficial effects, so don't forget your 7-minute workout (*see also Chapter 3, p.52*). A walk around your neighborhood or a nearby park is just what the doctor ordered. Physical activity in a natural environment is even more beneficial.

Establish habits and rituals to avoid running down your reserves

'Sow a thought, reap an action; sow an action, reap a habit;
sow a habit, reap a character; sow a character, reap a destiny.'

STEPHEN R. COVEY

The most surprising aspect of the willpower-as-muscle model, as revealed by scientific research, is that the decisions we make, even the most trivial, eat into our reserves of willpower. Even choosing between muesli and pancakes at breakfast subtly but measurably reduces our capacity to resist future temptations.

---

133 'Meditation, Mindfulness and Cognitive Flexibility,' Moore A. et al., *Conscious and Cognition*, 2009.
134 'Mechanisms of White Matter Changes Induced by Meditation,' Tang Y.Y., *Proceedings of the National Academy of Sciences*, 2012.
135 'Longitudinal Gains in Self-Regulation from Regular Physical Exercise,' Oaten M. et al., *British Journal of Health Psychology*, 2006.

For this reason, it is important to:

1. Establish rituals to ensure that you perform routine daily tasks automatically.
2. Consciously establish good habits that automatically move you toward your objectives.

RITUALS

A ritual is simply a habit that you regularly perform at a particular time of day. You might, for instance, have a morning ritual like this: Get up, meditate for five minutes, do your 7-minute workout, then have a shower.

HOW MATÉO ADOPTED THE DISCIPLINE OF A SHAOLIN MONK, SMALL STEP BY SMALL STEP

Born into a deprived environment in the inner suburbs of Marseille, Matéo soon caught the entrepreneurship bug, setting up his first music business, Only Pro, at the age of 22.[136]

This business was a success, but he had to work very hard and suffered from burnout twice. Then he got interested in personal development. At first, he was skeptical about the benefits of healthy eating, meditation, and even taking up a sport again. But by watching the YouTube videos by a guy called Olivier Roland, he came across the concept of the intelligent skeptic and decided to test it out.

He began by doing a few press-ups, eating fewer kebabs, and meditating for a minute each day.

Astonished by the positive effects of these efforts – more energy, concentration, and contentment, as well as restorative sleep – he decided to increase the time he devoted to each activity gradually.

He now follows a morning ritual worthy of a Shaolin monk: he gets up at 6 a.m. and spends the first half-hour eating a healthy breakfast (a banana, two apples, some ginger, and some almonds) while reading personal development blogs. From 6:30 to 7 a.m., he plans his day, choosing three MPIs,[137] then records and analyzes yesterday's events

---

136   To see my interview with Matéo, go to https://en.olivier-roland.com/mateo/
137   We shall be seeing what MPIs are and how you can use them to become more effective further on in this chapter.

in his diary, highlighting the three best moments and the three things he could have done better. He then meditates for 25–30 minutes and exercises from 7:30–10 a.m.

By gradually establishing this ritual, Matéo lost 44lbs (20kg) and made enormous gains in energy, contentedness, and concentration. And it brought him success, since he was able to work for 10 hours a week on his business and realize a turnover of €2 million a year.

Wow. Brilliant, you may be thinking, but am I supposed to establish a routine like that?

No. I'm giving you this example just to show that if someone with Matéo's background can do it, you should be able to establish at least a two- or three-minute 'mini' ritual of a similar kind to get yourself started. Start small. See the benefits your new routine brings, then decide if you want to take it further.

HABITS

What is a habit? An action we regularly perform, usually *without thinking* and without having to be motivated to do it. It is an action performed by default, mechanically, day after day, the effects of which gradually accumulate and can have an enormous influence on our lives, positive or negative.[138]

Smoking will mean we have less money to spend on more interesting or useful things. It will lead to diminished physical performance, faster aging, and, eventually, cancer and premature death. All on account of a stupid habit generally contracted during adolescence to prove we were adult and 'different,' when, in fact, our friends and we were letting ourselves be manipulated into conformity by companies representing the very worst aspects of capitalism.

On the other hand, doing some physical exercise when we get up in the morning starts the day off on the right foot, gives us a desirable physique, keeps us in good health, slows aging, and prolongs life expectancy.

Two habits, two things we do mechanically, two things we enjoy, two dramatically different results.

---

138 Someone has written an entire book on this subject: *The Compound Effect* by Darren Hardy, Success Books, 2012.

How, then, can we change our bad habits into good ones? I'm not going to share a miracle method for giving up smoking. But I will propose a simple, six-step program that will enable you to review your current habits, identify those that are not doing you any good and replace them with better ones.

1. The first step is to review your habits

Begin by listing 10 habits of which you are conscious. In your mind's eye, go through a typical day and note all the things you do regularly and mechanically without even realizing it. These may be minor things, like eating a chocolate bar at 4 p.m. or having a shower as soon as you get up; entrenched habits, such as watching television when you come in from work or regularly playing video games; or more demanding activities you have established with some effort, like running for half-an-hour every day or spending an hour reading a book.

When you have gone through a typical day, turn your attention to a typical week. The first habits will come to mind quite quickly, but the more you write down, the more difficult it becomes to think of others. Don't stop until you have identified 10.

2. Are they good habits or bad habits?

When you have listed your 10 habits, switch off for a bit, then return to your list and decide whether these habits are good for you or not.

Typically, all the habits that negatively affect your health will go into the 'bad habits' category. And to these, you can probably add all those that don't actively help you in achieving your goals. However, don't be over-strict with yourself. For relaxation purposes, it is normal to allow yourself some minor and, indeed, some more significant pleasures quite unrelated to your objectives.

For activities such as watching television and playing video games, the best thing is to set a daily or weekly limit beyond which the habit shifts into the 'bad habit' category. For instance, half-an-hour of television may be fine, but an hour is too much.

3. Work out the consequences

Once you have identified the bad habits, note them down on a fresh sheet of paper and, against each, write in why it is bad for your health and your various objectives. For example:

- I drink too much beer (or spirits) when I'm out with friends: it's bad for my long-term health and my wallet, and it doesn't convey the image I would like to project – a person who is fulfilled and at ease with themselves.

- I watch television for an hour-and-a-half every day. I'm aware that this is a waste of time and doesn't benefit me, and I'd like to devote the time to more interesting pursuits.

4. What would you like to replace it with?

Then, for each of these bad habits, decide what you would like to do instead. For example:

- I drink too much beer (or spirits) when I'm out with my friends. I'm going to restrict myself to a maximum of two units an evening and consume more soft drinks.

- I watch TV for an hour-and-a-half each day. I'm going to limit my viewing to half-an-hour a day and spend an hour working on my current project.

5. Your action plan

Then devise an action plan to replace the bad habits with good ones.

For each bad habit, decide how you will reduce or replace it, and a deadline for achieving your goal. I would suggest starting modestly and aim to make gradual progress. Above all, focus on only one or two habits at a time.

Start with the habits you think will be easiest to change: you will see some immediate benefits, giving you the confidence to attack the more stubborn ones. Where those entrenched habits are concerned, go at it gradually. Begin with a small step. For example, instead of watching television for an hour-and-a-half when you come home from work, watch for an hour-and-a-quarter. When you feel OK with that, raise the bar a bit more.

6. Monitor yourself

Regularly review your objectives and your habits, let's say once a month. See if you have been successful in achieving your goals. Review your new habits and identify any bad ones that are on the point of becoming established.

If a bad habit seems to be creeping up on you, deal with it immediately. It is much easier to root it out before it has become established. If you are vigilant, you will be able, without expending too much energy, to maintain a set of healthy habits that will bring you many benefits while avoiding destructive forms of behavior.

To conclude this section, let me share a story that appeals to me:

A man is at the bottom of a pit. He's crawling along the ground, close to death. He's been there for a week, trying in vain to find a way out – a week without eating or drinking. He makes one more effort to stretch out his arm, fails, and falls back. On the point of death, he asks, with all his remaining strength: 'My God, why didn't you give me the strength to climb out of this pit?'

And God replies: 'I gave you the strength not to fall into it.'

MAKING PROGRESS WITHOUT ADDITIONAL EFFORT BY EXPLOITING 'UNPRODUCTIVE' TIME

Do you remember the different ways I suggested in Chapter 3 of mastering a language without additional effort? They depend on using time you've already committed to other activities to make progress in your chosen language.

The good news is that you can use this strategy to make progress in any field. The simplest way is to listen to podcasts or audiobooks related to your objectives while doing something else: driving the car, traveling on public transport, exercising, etc. Now think what other activities you could engage in without them taking up any additional time – activities that would be of practical benefit in achieving your goals?

Think about it, make a list, then put your ideas into practice.

CREATING A TEMPTATION-FREE ENVIRONMENT

Given that our reserves of willpower are limited and easily run down with use, it is important to create an environment as free of temptations as possible. For example, if you aim to lose weight and have resolved not to eat fatty or sugary foods or drink fizzy drinks, which of the following would be more appropriate in your kitchen:

- A refrigerator crammed with fatty and sugary foods and fizzy drinks that will be a source of temptation every time you open it?

- A refrigerator containing only foods compatible with your diet?

You are much less likely to abandon your diet in the second case because:

1. You will have fewer temptations to resist and won't be running down your reserves of willpower;

2. If you ever feel the urge to eat something that conflicts with your diet, you will have to go out and buy whatever is tempting you, which is far more complicated than going and taking it from the fridge – complicated enough, probably, to discourage you from doing it.

So do all you can to create an environment free of temptations, which will help you achieve your objectives.

If you aim to start a business and intend to devote two hours to it every evening but are tempted to watch television or play on your games console, banish these devices from the house, at least temporarily. Lend them to someone, sell them on Craigslist or eBay, or just give them away. This may sound radical, but what is more important when all is said and done? Embarking on an amazing adventure that will be a source of pride or slumping in front of the TV watching stuff that will bring no lasting benefit while listening to a still small voice at the back of your mind saying, 'This is not the way it was supposed to be!'

Getting rid of your TV and games console requires far less willpower than resisting the temptation to engage with them each day.

OPPRESSIVE JOBS, OR WHAT TO DO IN AN ENVIRONMENT THAT RESISTS CHANGE

Of course, some environments are difficult to change; this will inevitably be the case from time to time, but these are also opportunities to train your will. But what if this is true of an environment in which you have to spend a lot of time – your workplace, for example? Actually, unless you have the misfortune to be in prison, it is very unlikely that you will find yourself in an environment where it is absolutely impossible to make a few positive changes. If, for example, you want to lose weight by eating well and you are in the habit of eating with your colleagues at a fast-food outlet, this could be a problem. The very fact that they order fat- or sugar-heavy dishes is temptation enough. Once you are aware of this, you can devise solutions to reduce the number of temptations:

- Explain to your colleagues that you want to lose weight and ask them to help you by pointing it out to you if you order a dish that contains too much fat or sugar. You will be surprised by how many people will be supportive if you explain your objective and ask for their help.

- Decide to eat alone at work at least once a week, while reading a book or watching a video, and prepare a simple dish, e.g., a salad, for the occasion.

- Lobby your boss and colleagues about serving organic dishes in your company canteen (this is very much the trend in some enterprises).

There are always ways of reducing temptations, even in environments that are apparently hostile to change. The key is to look for solutions rather than make excuses.

INTRODUCING TEMPTATIONS INTO YOUR ENVIRONMENT

What's that? Haven't I just been saying that you should make your environment as temptation-free as possible?

Well, no. The human will is like a muscle, remember? We don't want to tire it out, but at the same time, we do want to train it. Therefore it is good to make your environment as temptation-free as possible. At the same time, it is also beneficial to introduce one or two temptations, deliberately, to train yourself to resist them.

In *The Willpower Instinct*, Kelly McGonigal gives the example of Jim, who had always been addicted to candy and, aged 38, having discovered the willpower-as-muscle principle, decided to introduce a temptation into his environment. He placed a glass bowl of candies in his office corridor, so he would see them every time he entered or left the office. The rule was as follows: he could eat candy, but *not* from the bowl in the corridor.

At first, Jim found it difficult to resist this temptation, but it gradually became easier, to the point where he would leave his office on purpose to 'do a bit of exercise.' He was really surprised to find he could so easily control impulses that had previously seemed overwhelming.

HOW I OVERCAME TEMPTATION IN THREE STAGES

I bought my favorite chocolate bar, put it in a highly visible position at home, and resisted the temptation for a fortnight, despite seeing the chocolate bar every day. Then I repeated the challenge twice: first for a month, then for three months.

> I have really benefited from this exercise: I am much less tempted to eat sweets and junk food. And I definitely have greater reserves of willpower to draw on throughout the day.

DON'T LET A DEFEAT BECOME A DISASTER

From time to time, you will inevitably succumb to temptation and do something counter to your long-term objectives, despite all the tools and techniques presented in this chapter. *Errare humanum est.*

You just need to recollect yourself and not feel bad about it. The worst thing you can do is to wallow in defeat and think: 'Since I've failed on this occasion, I might as well go the whole hog.' You may have stumbled, but that need not prevent you from making further progress unless you use your defeat as an excuse for bottling out completely.

THE REWARD FOR STANDING STRONG SHOULD NOT BE SELF-INDULGENCE

On the other hand, resisting a temptation or two doesn't give you a license to indulge the next one that comes along because you think you 'deserve' a break.

Unfortunately, research shows that this is all too common. For example, researchers divided people who were following a diet into two groups: the participants in the first group were congratulated on their progress; those in the second received no such encouragement. Then, as a reward, all the participants were offered the choice between a chocolate bar and an apple. The results were instructive:

- Of those who had been congratulated, 85 percent chose the chocolate bar.

- On the other hand, only 58 percent who had not received any congratulations chose the chocolate bar.[139]

Interestingly, researchers at the University of Hong Kong have found a question that works almost like a magic spell in countering this tendency. They first asked

---

139 'Goals as Excuses or Guides: The Liberating Effect of Perceived Goal Progress on Choice': http://en.olivier-roland.com/goals-excuses-or-guides/

the participants to remember the last time they had resisted temptation. This had the effect of opening Pandora's box: 70 percent succumbed to the next temptation that presented itself. But when they asked another question, this figure immediately reversed: 69 percent resisted the temptation.

The magic question was: 'Why did you resist the temptation?'

So next time you are tempted, remind yourself of the last time you resisted the same temptation, and then ask yourself: 'Why did I resist it?' It will remind you of your initial objective, the importance you attach to it, and all the reasons why you successfully resisted it last time.

HOW AN EVERYDAY OBJECT CAN BOOST YOUR WILLPOWER (AND YOUR PRODUCTIVITY)

Halloween, 1978: A group of children disguised for Halloween come into a room where candy had been hidden in various places. The accompanying adult says: 'I shall be away for a few minutes. Meanwhile, you can take one sweet each, but no more. See you soon.' Then the adult leaves them for a quarter of an hour.

What the children don't know is that they are being observed by a team of researchers, who want to see if they will be obedient and take only one sweet or succumb to temptation and take more.

The children in this study were divided into two groups. In the first group, 34 percent of the children ate only one sweet. In the second group, only 9 percent were similarly obedient.[140]

What was the difference between the two groups? The answer is simple and surprising.

A mirror! When there was a mirror in the room, 25 percent fewer children succumbed to temptation.

Why? According to the researchers, a mirror makes us more self-aware, reminding us of our long-term objectives and making us more sensitive to the negative effects of yielding to impulse. And this wasn't the only discovery regarding the surprising effects of mirrors. It is proven that installing a mirror in an office increases managers' productivity,[141] and if you eat in front of a mirror, you will generally eat less.[142]

---

140 'Self-Awareness and Transgression in Children: Two Field Studies,' Beaman A.L. et al., *Journal of Personality and Social Psychology*, 1979.
141 Shelley Duval and Robert A. Wicklund, *A Theory of Objective Self-Awareness*, 1972.
142 'Healthy Reflections: The Influence of Mirror Induced Self-Awareness on Taste Perceptions,' Jami A., *Journal of the Association for Consumer Research*, 2015.

So hang a mirror in your dining room, and have one in your office and in other places where you strive to achieve your objectives.

1 + 1 = 3, OR THE POWER OF FACING A CHALLENGE WITH A FRIEND

Another way of maintaining your reserves of willpower is to find a friend you can face a challenge with, someone who is in the same boat as you and has similar objectives. To illustrate my point, let me tell you a story.

Some years ago, I wanted to do some weight training to improve my muscle tone and general fitness. But I knew it wouldn't be easy to keep it up for the long haul. I had already taken out a year's gym membership but gave it up after only one month.

Then I found a simple way of staying motivated: I asked a friend who also wanted to do some training if we could do it together. We immediately agreed we would meet for a 90-minute session every Sunday. This simple arrangement, which demanded minimal effort, proved enormously beneficial.

Consider for a moment the following scenario: you have undertaken to do at least one weight-training session a week, but this Sunday, you really don't feel like it. You were out partying the night before and are feeling a bit rough. Secondly, it's a nice day, and you would like to be out in the sunshine. What's more, you've done three sessions over the last three weeks and think you deserve a break.

You snuggle back in your armchair, having convinced yourself. Of course, part of you is disappointed (and will later make you feel guilty), but you have made your decision.

Now consider the same scenario, but with your friend in the frame. Yes, you would certainly like to cancel. Except that, to do so, you will have to call your friend Christopher and explain why you are ducking out. You go over the conversation in your head, imagining explaining yourself, and in the end, your arguments don't seem to carry much weight.

In this case, it is no longer a question of missing a training session but letting down a friend who is relying on you. If you back out, not only will you seem weak and lacking in determination, there is also the danger of discouraging your friend, and he might resent it.

You sigh. It's not worth taking the risk. You pick up your backpack, and off you go to the gym. And you'll have no regrets.

The training session will do you good, as will meeting your friend and sharing the latest news. You come back home fit and pleased with yourself, happy you found the strength to keep up your commitment.

That's the power of having a friend to face a challenge with; it creates a mutual bond that will help you resist temptation and make you less sensitive to discouragement, without demanding any more energy than if you had done the activity on your own. The result will be added value for both of you, for very little expenditure of energy and willpower: 1 + 1 = 3!

THE POWER OF FRIENDLY COMPETITION

Another excellent way of reducing the likelihood of succumbing to temptation is to compete with a friend. Set each other regular challenges that will ensure you progress toward your objective. The friendly emulation this creates will motivate you both and make your project a lot more fun.

The challenge should be similar for both of you, but you don't necessarily have to be aiming for the same result: take into account your different strengths and the goals you want to achieve. Take weight training as an example: the 'winner' could be the first to do 20 percent more repetitions or lift 20 percent more weight. If you are both setting up businesses, the winner could be the first to pass an A/B test (*see also p.221*) or to secure their first prospect or first customer.

I used this principle to force myself to begin writing fiction. I had always been a great science fiction fanatic (I told you I'm a former geek) and had always dreamed of writing and publishing something in this genre. As I kept putting things off, I thought some friendly competition might give me the necessary drive. I therefore set up an 'amateur writers' circle' with two like-minded friends and threw down the following challenge:

- We choose a subject for a short story.

- Each of us has a month to write our piece on this theme.

- We send one another the stories we have written and read them.

- Then we meet in a cozy café to talk them over.

It wasn't a question of 'winning.' Rather, emulation resulting from cooperation and friendly competition, and it was the most prolific period of my life where fiction-writing was concerned. I entered one of my stories for a competition, and it was selected, along with five others, for publication in a short story collection published by Éditions L'Harmattan.[143] Though reasonably modest, this success gave me the status of published author. I then decided to devote my energies to establishing my Internet business, but I still treasure my success as a writer, and I may well return to fiction-writing one of these days.

To spice things up, you might decide that the winner gets a prize. Nothing that will break the bank: maybe a meal out, a decent bottle of wine, or a box of chocolates. But be sure to agree the prize before embarking on the challenge!

HOW KATE STRONG BECAME WORLD CHAMPION IN 14 MONTHS AS A RESULT OF FRIENDLY COMPETITION

When a friend told Kate Strong, aged 33, she ought to take up the triathlon, she thought it was a joke. But the idea took root, and when she decided to go for it, Kate didn't do things by halves. She chose to compete in an 'Ironman'-type event: a 2-mile swim, followed by 112 miles on a bicycle, then a 26-mile marathon. Total: 140 miles.

What's more, she decided she would be world champion. Sure enough, 14 months later, she won the gold medal in her category at the world championships in China, beating competitors who had been training for years.

As well as having the right DNA, one of the strategies Kate used during her preparation was friendly competition.[144] When she started, she was all on her own: no one in her friendship group ran, cycled, swam, or even exercised. So she decided to get her friends involved and motivate them to do a bit more exercise each week, not to her level, of course, but each with their own objectives.

They monitored one another regularly and compared results, which helped Kate maintain her motivation during the 14 months of preparation.

---

143 'La Salope de Pavonis,' published in the *Nouvelles du futur, le pire est à venir* collection, l'Harmattan, 2006.
144 See my interview with Kate on my channel to hear the complete story and how she went about it: http://en.olivier-roland.com/interview-kate-strong/

ACCOUNTABILITY AS A SOURCE OF MOTIVATION

As well as friendly competition, another important factor in motivation is the power of accountability. In practical terms, this means undertaking to perform a particular action regularly and asking someone to monitor your progress to ensure that you have, in fact, done it.

So you go and see a friend or colleague, tell them your objective – restricting your pizza intake to once a week, doing three hour-long work-outs each week, or working an hour a day on your business project – and ask them to check up on you and ensure you are sticking to your plan.

To make your accountability partner's task easier, create a spreadsheet or a text document in Google Docs or Dropbox that they can refer to, and fill it in as you go along. This arrangement implies that your partner must be able to call you to order – in a friendly but firm way – when you deviate from the set schedule. But, you may be wondering, how can you get someone, even a friend, to do this for you? By simply offering to do them a service, whether the same task or something else.

This is exactly what happened when I was planning to write this book: one of my business friends, Romain Bastide, suggested I enter into a partnership of this kind. The deal was very straightforward: I was to write a certain number of words each day (recorded on a spreadsheet in Google Docs), while he was to monitor my progress and chase me up if he saw I was falling behind. In return, I gave him regular advice on the positioning and marketing of his business. It was a win–win arrangement, from which the gains were out of all proportion to the limited time we invested in the exercise.

It was very helpful in keeping me up to scratch in writing the book you are now reading, which would undoubtedly have been less comprehensive or wouldn't have come out so soon without the power of accountability.

USING TEACHERS AND COACHES TO SPARE YOUR WILLPOWER

If you can afford it, employing someone to help you progress toward your objectives is one of the most intelligent ways of managing your reserves of willpower: rather than using them up on the activity itself, you select a coach and agree a program with him or her.

For example, after giving up my regular bodybuilding sessions (because my friend had moved), I wanted to take it up again and engaged a sports coach to come round to my house twice a week. Now I didn't have to motivate myself to do a workout; all I needed to do was fix an appointment with him, which required a lot less willpower. Once he arrived at the house, whatever my mood or inclinations, I did the exercise, going further, longer, and harder.

Of course, this is not cost-free, and not everyone can afford it. But if you can, give it a try; it's one of the simplest ways of making rapid progress toward an objective without overdrawing on your reserves of willpower.

I would also recommend having an intentional strategy of using your money for such purposes, as and when the income from your business increases. Invest in good coaching in areas close to your heart, and ideally in practices that will bring you additional benefits. This strategy will enable you to make spectacular progress in a short time, you will feel more at ease with yourself, and you will have more energy and greater powers of concentration. And above all, as you will be paying for something that frees you from temptations, you will be saving your reserves of willpower for other important things, so giving you a definite edge.

VISITING THE WISE MAN ON THE MOUNTAIN TOP

And what about mentors, those inaccessible wise men hidden away on their mountaintops? Go to https://en.olivier-roland.com/sage-montagne/ to receive your supplement for dealing with this strategy :)

THE MIND LIKE WATER: ESTABLISHING A PRODUCTIVITY SYSTEM

'Much of the stress that people feel doesn't come from having too much to do. It comes from not finishing what they've started.'

DAVID ALLEN, PRODUCTIVITY EXPERT

A good way of managing your reserves of willpower is to establish a productivity system. Before I explain what I mean by this, let's take a look at the way the brain works in a typical situation in daily life:

You are at your local supermarket, doing the shopping. While mechanically filling your cart with the items you usually buy, your mind is on many different things. You need to phone your plumber to fix the low water pressure in your shower, and you must give Helen (the boss's PA) the document you should have handed in last week.

You are also thinking that you and your wife might watch the movie you set aside on Netflix a month ago this evening. You really ought to phone your parents, or your mother will be complaining again that you never think of them. Other similar thoughts come to mind, then you go through the checkout, put your shopping bags in the car, and return home.

And that's when it hits you. Back home, you are amazed to find that you forgot to get the milk! Damn, that wasn't very clever. You grumble a bit and make a mental note to buy some at the grocery store on your way home from work.

Then you go to the office and start work on a file that has to be dealt with urgently. You manage to concentrate fairly well but, inevitably, from time to time, other thoughts flash through your mind: call the plumber, give the document to Helen, call your parents, get some milk from the grocer's, watch that film this evening...

Your brain is continually reminding you of all the tasks you have to perform... and often at just the wrong moment. In our example, it reminds you that you need to buy some milk when you see the fridge is empty, then at different times of day while you are doing other things, but not when you are at the supermarket. What an enormous waste of time and energy!

Scientists have studied how the brain is continually reminding us of the things we have left undone, and they have even given it a name: the Zeigarnik effect. They have demonstrated that any unfulfilled task, even the most insignificant, has a negative impact on almost all tasks that are not performed automatically.[145] Secondly, recent experiments[146] have shown that one way of unburdening the mind and stopping it from continually reminding you of the tasks you have to do is to write an action plan.

How so? Let's take a detailed look at one experiment to get a better idea of what happens. The researchers split the participants into three groups:

1. One group in which the participants had to write down the tasks they had recently performed.

2. A second group in which the participants had to write down the tasks they had not yet performed, and that had to be completed soon.

---

145 'Consider It Done! Plan Making Can Eliminate the Cognitive Effects of Unfulfilled Goals,' Masicampo E. J. et al., *Journal of Personality and Social Psychology*, 2011.
146 Ibid.

3. A third group in which the participants had to write down the tasks they had not performed and make specific plans as to how they would accomplish them.

The researchers then asked all three groups to read the first 10 pages of a novel. They regularly questioned the participants to find out if their minds were wandering, asked them if they had been able to concentrate, and finally tested them to check whether they had taken in what they had been reading.

The results were fascinating: the group that performed worst was the second, the one that had to write down the tasks they had not completed. Why? Because their minds were constantly reminding them to finish these tasks, which disturbed their concentration and drained their reserves of willpower.

The most interesting finding was that the group that made an action plan to complete their tasks (group 3) performed even better than the first group.

The Zeigarnik effect, therefore, was canceled out **simply by devising an action plan**.

To give you a simpler example: What is the best way of ensuring that you will buy milk at the supermarket and stopping your mind from constantly reminding you about it at inappropriate moments?

As soon as your mind tells you 'I must buy some milk,' write down 'milk' on a shopping list. If you use this simple method, your brain will stop continually reminding you, thus reducing the risk of forgetting to buy it.

Is this a long and challenging procedure? Of course not. And that is the purpose of a productivity system: To relieve the brain of its burden by systematically noting down all the tasks you have to perform.

Here is an exercise to make this crystal clear: note down in a document the situation or project that is most taxing your mind at the moment. Then write a single sentence saying how you want to resolve it. It might be something like:

- Go for a vacation. Boot up the computer, and search for and select a likely destination.

- Get the car serviced. Call the garage and make a booking.

Done that? Bravo!

How do you feel? If you react like most people, you should feel a little more confident, relaxed, and focused, and be more motivated to deal with the situation. So, what has changed? What is making you see things in a more positive light?

From a practical point of view, there has been little change or improvement in the situation. But you have defined the most favorable outcome and the first step required to making it happen, after just a couple of minutes' thought.

So, what productivity system should you opt for? The best known is David Allen's *Getting Things Done*, also referred to as GTD. It has proved its worth, having been adopted successfully by thousands of managers, artists, authors, and businesspeople since it was first published in 2001.

It does have its faults, though. The first is that it is too all-embracing, a labyrinthine system! I have discussed this with many entrepreneurs who use the system, and none of them use all aspects of it. The second drawback is that it focuses too much on each and every task that comes to mind, merely skimming over the concept of long-term objectives. And yet, becoming productive at something we hate is the surest way of losing our souls.

I tried it out, and I, too, was discouraged by its complexity. So I moved on to a simpler system, Zen To Done (ZTD), a simplified version of GTD created by Leo Babauta, the Zen Habits blogger. Since adopting this system, I have simplified it even more, and have combined it with another, *Master Your Workday Now!* by Michael Linenberger.

Go to https://en.olivier-roland.com/productivity to download my method.

Perform your tasks in uninterrupted blocs of time

It is proven[147] that the slightest interruption when you are working, even the most innocent, significantly increases the time required to complete the task and the risk of your making mistakes.

Why? Because every task we undertake, except for the very shortest, requires a 'warm-up' period, just like in sport.

Imagine you want to work on your business startup project. It will take your brain several minutes to retrieve all the information from your long-term memory, download it to your working memory, and focus completely on the task. Subsequently, every

---

147 'The Cost of Interrupted Work: More Speed and Stress,' Gloria Mark et al., *Proceedings of the SIGCHI Conference on Human Factors in Computing Systems*, 2008.

interruption (an email arriving, a phone call, etc.) will break your concentration. It then takes 64 seconds to recover the threads and return to full productivity.[148]

If during one hour's work, you receive three two-minute phone calls, five text messages, and three Skype notifications, you will lose (3 × 64) + (3 × 2 × 60) + (8 × 64) + (1 × 5 × 60) seconds (for the initial warm-up time), which makes almost 23 minutes in total, not counting the time taken to read the text messages and check out the notifications. So you will have been productive for only 37 minutes in that hour, i.e., 61 percent of the time. Not very good, eh?

Similarly, there is nothing worse for your productivity than keeping a messaging app permanently open, emitting visual and audio signals advising you of incoming communications. As we receive an average of 121 business-related messages each day,[149] one every four minutes over eight hours, this is the virtual equivalent of having a doorbell that rings again and again at random, and each time breaks our train of thought. You would do much better to have set times in the day when you read and answer your emails.

Focusing on one task at a time

Many studies have shown that multitasking is inefficient. The psychologist Glenn Wilson, for example, has found that people who are constantly checking their emails and answering the phone throughout the day suffer the equivalent of a drop in IQ of 10 points,[150] similar to the number of points you lose after a sleepless night. That is even worse than smoking marijuana, which loses you 'only' four IQ points.[151]

David Meyer, doctor in psychology at the University of Michigan, even claims that your productivity can drop by as much as 40 percent when you are multitasking.[152]

To sum up, then: When you intend to perform a task that will take more than a few minutes, eliminate all sources of distraction and focus uniquely on the job in hand. If this isn't possible because you are in an environment you can't completely control (in a company office, for example), try to educate your colleagues/partners by explaining how harmful interruptions are for productivity. Give them the scientific references cited in this book. Or give them the book! Then ask them to interrupt

---

148 Figures from the Observatoire sur la responsabilité sociétale des entreprises (ORSE), cited in an article in *Le Monde*: 'Concentrez-vous!' Belot L., 2011.
149 'Email Statistics Report, 2014–2018,' Radicati, S.
150 Only temporary, of course. See 'Infomania experiment for HP,' Dr Glenn Wilson, 2010.
151 But this loss could be permanent for those who smoke a lot, according to some researchers.
152 'How Multitasking Affects Productivity and Brain Health,' Kendra Cherry, 2015: https://www.verywellmind.com/multitasking-2795003

you between certain hours only if something urgent comes up and cannot wait until the end of your work session.

My secret weapon

My secret weapon for studying more effectively and being more productive: noise-canceling headphones to insulate me from the outside world. Personally, I prefer Bose headphones: these minor technological marvels don't come cheap, but they are incredibly effective. Seeing (or not-hearing) is believing. And I know that if this gadget increases my annual productivity by only 0.1 percent, it's still worth it.

A minimalist environment

Don't forget visual distractions, either.

A University of Illinois study[153] has shown that our eyes are distracted, without our being aware of it, by objects in our field of vision that bear no relation to the current task. We may be distracted for only a fraction of a second each time but, multiplied by the number of times our eyes stray to these objects in a day, the result is significant.

So create a working environment with as few distractions as possible. Ideally, the only things in your field of vision on your (stand-up[154]) desk should be your screen, your keyboard, and a mirror,[155] reflecting your image if you look in that direction.

And of course, your computer desktop should be similarly minimalist: don't use it, like so many people, as a temporary repository for dozens of documents.

As well as increasing your productivity, an environment of this kind will make you feel a lot better, so put this book down and go and make the necessary changes immediately!

---

153 'Human Eye Unknowingly Distracted By Irrelevant Objects,' Arthur F. Kramer, University of Illinois at Urbana-Champaign, 1998.

154 Many studies show that sitting all day long is a killer; it is better to work standing up. For example, Alpa Patel, an epidemiologist with the American Cancer Society, monitored 126,000 Americans for 14 years. During this time, the death rate of those who sat for six hours a day or more was 20 percent higher than for those who sat for less than three hours a day. See 'Leisure Time Spent Sitting in Relation to Total Mortality in a Prospective Cohort of US Adults,' Patel V.A., *American Journal of Epidemiology*, 2010.

155 See my comments on this earlier in the chapter (*p.86*).

SUMMARY

For the intelligent rebel who has decided to act

⇒ Willpower enables us to resist temptations and focus more on the actions that help us achieve our objectives.

⇒ Research shows that willpower is a better indicator of success in life than IQ: the stronger your will, the greater the likelihood that you will be happy in relationships and live to a ripe old age.

⇒ The good news is that willpower is like a muscle and can be trained.

⇒ The bad news is that, again, like a muscle, if you use it too much, it gets tired, making you more likely to succumb to temptation.

Points for action:

⇒ Create a temptation-free environment to avoid using up your reserves of willpower.

⇒ On the other hand, introduce just ONE temptation into your environment – typically your favorite chocolate bar – and make a game of resisting it to build up your willpower.

⇒ Set an hour aside and clearly define your objectives.

⇒ Find someone in a similar situation with whom you can engage in friendly competition.

⇒ Position one or more mirrors in the places where you work, so you can see your reflection when you are working.

⇒ Could you afford to engage a teacher or coach to help you in a particular area, so you can make faster progress and contract out your need for discipline?

⇒ Use a productivity system.

⇒ Establish a minimalist working environment so that you are distracted as little as possible.

➡ When you manage to achieve an objective, don't celebrate it by going off the rails – you risk canceling out the benefits of your self-discipline.

To help you put the activities described in this chapter into practice, go to http://olivierroland.com/self-control to receive an email with a series of activities and challenges that will give you the necessary motivation.

CHAPTER 5
BEYOND THE CLASSROOM
Learn to Learn

'Learning is too important to be left behind in the classroom. Learning to learn is a skill you can master.'

TERRY SEJNOWSKI, NEUROSCIENCE RESEARCHER

So far, we have seen:

- How to boost your intelligence and working memory

- How to store what you have learned more efficiently in your long-term memory using spaced repetition and mnemonics

- How to strengthen your self-discipline, willpower, and motivation

In this chapter, we shall examine the secret weapon of resourceful, rebellious entrepreneurs, a weapon that isn't taught in school but will ensure your success in life beyond the classroom. It's what I call the art of learning to learn. Let's start with a few basic principles before studying some techniques for hacking your learning abilities.

SOUND SLEEP

'I've always envied people who sleep easily. Their brains must be cleaner, the floorboards of the skull well swept, all the little monsters closed up in a steamer trunk at the foot of the bed.'

DAVID BENIOFF, *CITY OF THIEVES*

This may sound like advice your grandmother would give you. Yet it is the most fundamental of all methods for learning efficiently... and undoubtedly the most often ignored by partying students. Sound sleep is essential for:

- Concentrating when you have things to learn in your waking hours

- Consolidating your memory during sleep[156]

- Simply learning more efficiently[157]

SLEEP, A NATURAL NEED

According to current research, one reason we all need to sleep is that our brain gradually accumulates toxins generated by our mental processes during our waking hours.[158] Sleeping triggers a cleaning process that eliminates these toxins. And the brain is unable to carry out this process in parallel with its very energy-consuming waking activities. This accumulation of toxins explains why our mental performance goes into serious decline when short of sleep.

And yet... *very* many of us underestimate the importance of getting sufficient sleep each night mainly because we don't realize the extent to which our performance is degraded when we have a sleep deficit. Let's consider two very enlightening studies.

In the first,[159] the researchers split the volunteer participants into four groups. The members of each group were to sleep the same number of hours each day for a week: three, five, seven, and nine hours respectively, and their performance measured at regular intervals; in particular, their speed in carrying out psycho-motor tasks and their reaction times. The results are fascinating:

- In the group sleeping three hours a night, speed in performing tasks declined. Moreover, their reaction times increased day by day, until the end of the experiment.

- In the five-hours-a-night group, the members' speed also declined during the first few days, and their reaction times increased, then stabilized at a level way below the starting point.

---

156 'Memory Consolidation in Sleep: Dream or Reality,' Vertes R.P., Neuron, 2004, or 'Sleep-Dependent Memory Processing,' Walker M.P., *Harvard Review of Psychiatry*, 2008, for example.
157 This has been shown by countless studies, for example 'Sleep Enhances Category Learning,' Djonlajic I. et al., *Learning & Memory*, 2009, or 'Human Relational Memory Requires Time and Sleep,' Ellenbogen J. M. et al., *Proceedings of the National Academy of Sciences*, 2007.
158 'Sleep Drives Metabolite Clearance from the Adult Brain,' Xie L. et al., *Science*, 2013.
159 'Patterns of Performance Degradation and Restoration During Sleep Restriction and Subsequent Recovery: A Sleep Dose-Response Study,' Belenky G. et al., *Journal of Sleep Research*, 2003.

- Those who slept for seven hours a night experienced an initial decline in their speed in performing tasks, which then stabilized; their reaction times were not affected.

- Those who slept for nine hours a night suffered no decline in performance.

The participants were then given three days to recover, sleeping eight hours a night.

Here again, the results were very instructive:

- Those who had previously slept for three hours a night recovered rapidly, but only to the level of performance of the group that had slept for five hours.

- Those who had slept for five or seven hours made no recovery at all and remained at their reduced performance level.

- The performance of the group that had slept for nine hours remained at a high level.

What this study reveals is that the brain can adapt to a chronic lack of sleep but 1) only if the number of hours sleep doesn't fall below a certain threshold, and 2) at the cost of reduced performance in many tasks. Moreover, three nights of full sleep are not enough to make up for the previous lack of sleep. So what, then? Does this mean we need to sleep for nine hours a night?

Another study[160] analyzed the performance of volunteers who slept respectively for four, six, and eight hours on 14 consecutive nights, and a group which had no sleep for 72 hours. The key findings were as follows:

- Those who slept for four hours a night experienced a significant drop in performance throughout the 14 days, more than the group who slept for six hours and considerably more than those who slept for eight hours.

- Sleeping for six hours a night for 14 consecutive days is equivalent to one sleepless night: brain activity is severely compromised after this period.

- Sleeping for four hours a night for 14 days is equivalent to two consecutive sleepless nights. No comment.

- One of the parameters measured was for a task involving working memory. The participants whose results improved over the 14 days were those who

---

160 'The Cumulative Cost of Additional Wakefulness: Dose-Response Effects on Neurobehavioral Functions and Sleep Physiology from Chronic Sleep Restriction and Total Sleep Deprivation,' Van Dongen H.P. et al., *Sleep*, 2003.

slept for eight hours. The results of the group who slept for six hours were neither better nor worse – no real learning, then – and those who slept for four hours showed an ongoing deterioration in performance[161] (*see diagram below*).

■ Most significant of all: The participants who slept for six or four hours all underestimated the impact of lack of sleep on their performance! They thought they were 'managing' the situation, which was not the case.

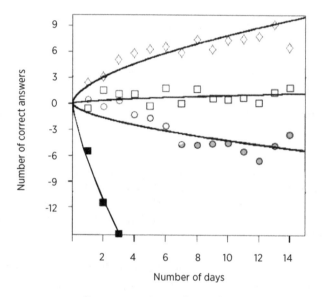

■ Group measurements deprived of sleep for 3 days
○ 4 hours of sleep
▫ 6 hours of sleep
◇ 8 hours of sleep

Figure 5: The impact of lack of sleep on performance.

These two final points are critical. If you look at the diagram, you will see that only those who slept for eight hours a night saw a significant improvement in their performance.

Sleeping less to study more is therefore counterproductive: by so doing, you will considerably diminish your learning capacities.

---

161   As for the group that went without sleep for three nights, no comment. Their results were abysmal.

HOW LONG SHOULD YOU SLEEP TO BE ON TOP FORM?

As you will have guessed from these two studies, most people need to sleep for eight hours a night to function fully. Five percent of people at the very most can sleep for five hours a night and maintain a high level of mental performance in the long term.[162] And a small percentage need to sleep for nine or 10 hours to stay mentally fit. In other words, if you think you need less than eight hours' sleep a night to be in top form, you are probably deceiving yourself.

But, you may say, what if I am one of the 5 percent who need less sleep? There is only one way of finding out if you are one of these fortunate winners of the genetic sleep lottery: be a healthy skeptic, measure the time you sleep, and test your performance.

HAVING A SIESTA

According to several pieces of research, including one funded by NASA to help astronauts perform more efficiently in space,[163] a 15- or 20-minute siesta in the middle of the day boosts working memory and helps you to perform better. Sleeping for longer, however, risks doing more harm than good, giving you the impression of having less energy when you wake up. So set the alarm on your smartphone and try sleeping for between 15 and 20 minutes to find out what suits you best.[164]

However, contrary to certain widely accepted ideas, a nap cannot replace a good night's sleep or make up for the loss of concentration caused by a sleepless night.

If your working environment makes it impossible to have a nap, this is 1) a good reason to launch your own business, so you are free to create a more pleasant environment, and 2) a good opportunity to test the effectiveness of a five-minute catnap. Relax in an office armchair and eliminate distracting influences (smartphone, email, etc.). Just getting a few minutes' shut-eye can have a very beneficial effect.

---

162 According to the study mentioned earlier.
163 'Dynamic Circadian Modulation in a Biomathematical Model for the Effects of Sleep and Sleep Loss on Waking Neurobehavioral Performance,' McCauley P. et al., *Sleep*, 2013.
164 Personally, I have an 18-minute siesta every day, except for perhaps one or two days a year. Why 18 minutes? Simple: at first, I set my alarm for 20 minutes, but I always wake up quite spontaneously two minutes before it rings!

How to get into the siesta habit

If you've never tried having a siesta, it may seem strange to go and lie down in the middle of the day. And you will probably feel frustrated if you can't drop off to sleep. If so, be reassured: 1) it's quite normal, and 2) it doesn't matter two hoots. Whether you fall asleep or not is not the issue. The purpose of a siesta is to enjoy a few minutes' calm by shutting your eyes and being at rest. Take some deep breaths, and still your mind. Whether or not you sleep.

SEVEN AIDS TO SLEEPING LIKE A BUG IN A RUG

This is all wonderful stuff, but how can you fall asleep quicker and sleep better? Here are a few tips to help you get the best possible sleep.

1. Temperature

Research[165] suggests that the ideal temperature for sleeping is between 59 and 66°F (15 and 19°C).

2. Light

Turn the lights down an hour or two before you go to bed. Over-bright lights shortly before bedtime can disturb your body's internal clock,[166] as light is one of the primary stimuli telling the brain whether it is time to rest or wake up and go hunt a mammoth.[167] So opt for subdued lighting in the late evening, rather than sources of bright light.

Blue light is particularly unhelpful, as it prompts the brain to think it is midday with a blue sky. Also, avoid using screens, whether the TV, your computer, or smartphone, for at least one hour or preferably two, before going to bed.

---

165   'Prevention and Treatment of Sleep Disorders Through Regulation of Sleeping Habits,' Onen, S.H. et al., *La presse médicale*, 1994, or the website of the National Sleep Foundation, 'The Bedroom Environment': http://en.olivier-roland.com/sleep-bedroom/

166   'Neurophysiology of Sleep and Wakefulness: Basic Science and Clinical Implications,' Schwartz J.R.L. et al., *Current Neuropharmacology*, 2008.

167   I'm joking, of course, but our genetic programming has been dictated by millions of years of evolution, adapting us to live in a world that for the most part no longer exists, where artificial lighting was a rarity and of poor quality.

3. Sound

Obviously, sounds can disturb your sleep. Less obviously, a sound may not be loud enough to wake you up, but still loud enough to affect your sleep.[168] Sound affects the quality of your sleep by upsetting its rhythms and detracting from its restorative properties. Then you wake up with less energy, feeling more irritable and less cheerful, and with a sense of having slept badly... *without knowing why.*

So try to cut out ambient sounds while you are sleeping. It costs nothing. The simplest solution is to use earplugs. The ones I use are far more effective than the traditional balls of wax or foam. My silicon EarPeace earplugs are shaped to fit snugly in the ear and can be carried around in a small metal case you can attach to your key fob.

4. Physical exercise

Sedentary lifestyles are a curse: a lack of physical exercise reduces your ability to fall asleep and the quality of your sleep itself.[169] So there's yet another reason to get regular exercise!

In addition to sporting activity, don't miss any opportunity to get some exercise: climb the stairs, rather than taking the lift; walk for 10 minutes, rather than taking the car; if you are on an escalator, walk up the steps rather than passively waiting to be carried to the top.

As a general rule, avoid doing exercise in the two hours before going to bed, as this may have the opposite effect and disturb your sleep.

5. A notepad

Nothing spoils our nightly rest so much as having difficulty getting off to sleep. At such times, the brain often throws up dozens of things we ought to do, which go round and round in our heads and prevent us from entering into a state of rest. We remain in 'problem-solving mode,' and this mental churning can go on for hours, producing precisely nothing.

A simple way of stopping this hellish process is to keep a notepad and pencil by your bedside. As soon as you think of something you should do, note it down. This

---

168   'Disturbed Sleep Patterns and Limitation of Noise,' Griefahn, B. et al., *Noise and Health*, 2004.
169   'Effects of Exercise on Sleep,' Youngstedt S.D., *Clinical Journal of Sport Medicine*, 2005.

frees the mind from the burden of thought because you know that, when you wake up, all the things you need to do will be patiently waiting for you.

6. This will not work for everyone, but it may work for you

When none of these techniques work and I still can't get to sleep, there is a trick that works for me, although it seems to contradict my advice in point 4. I get up, leave the bedroom, and do four sets of press-ups. I prolong each set, working as hard as possible on my pecs and back until my muscles are exhausted, then I have a minute or two's break.

I don't know why this works,[170] but nine times out of 10, it breaks my destructive thought pattern and ushers in a state of wellbeing that enables me to fall asleep. There's only one way of finding out if this works for you: be a healthy skeptic and try it out next time you have insomnia. In any case, what have you got to lose?

7. Make your bedroom a sanctuary

Your bedroom is for sleeping and making love, and possibly reading a novel before you go to sleep. Period.

Don't do any work in there, don't watch films while lying in bed, etc. Otherwise, your brain will get used to being active in the bedroom environment and less likely to calm down when evening comes.[171]

HOW TO DOUBLE YOUR LEARNING PERFORMANCE WITH RETRIEVAL

A fascinating experiment took place in 2011. Volunteer students were divided into four groups and asked to read a 276-word text on sea otters, with the aim of learning and remembering information about these creatures:

- Group 1 had five minutes just to read the text.

- Group 2 had four minutes to read the text, with a break of one minute between each reading.

---

170   I suppose that this produces endorphins that relax the brain, and maybe sends signals of physical fatigue that prepare us for sleep.
171   Of course, if you are living in student accommodation, as I was in the early days, this is more complicated! But if you are in that age group, falling asleep is not usually a problem.

- Group 3 spent 25 minutes after the initial reading creating a mind map.

- Group 4 spent 10 minutes after the initial reading writing down all the information they could remember (without looking at the text). Then they spent five minutes rereading the text and again listed the items of information they could remember.

The participants then took a test to find out how much they had retained. Which group do you think performed best? The results were interesting:

- The group that performed least well was not surprisingly group 1, who had read the text just once. They got just 27 percent of their answers correct.

- Next came group 3, who had made the mind map, with 45 percent of answers correct.

- Then came group 2, who had studied the text four times in all, with a score of 49 percent.

- But the best score was achieved by group 4, who used the retrieval technique, with a score of 67 percent.[172]

This result accords with the results of most research studies:[173] the best way of learning effectively is to revise what you have learned at regular intervals.

And yet, the vast majority of students practice the method used in this case by group 2.[174] Why? Easy. Did anyone tell you about this at school? Did anyone teach you how to learn? In your experience, do most teachers take the trouble to go on training throughout their careers to keep abreast of scientific progress?

Of course, you have probably already twigged: this retrieval method with spaced repetitions is the most effective way to combat the forgetting curve.[175]

172   'Retrieval Practice Produces more Learning than Elaborative Studying with Concept Mapping,' Karpicke J.D. et al., *Science*, 2011.
173   'Is Expanded Retrieval Practice a Superior Form of Spaced Retrieval? A Critical Review of the Extant Literature,' Balota D.A. et al., *The Foundations of Remembering*, 2007.
174   'Metacognitive Strategies in Student Learning: Do Students Practise Retrieval When They Study on Their Own?' Karpicke J.D. et al., *Memory*, 2009.
175   'Using Spacing to Enhance Diverse Forms of Learning: Review of Recent Research and Implications for Instruction,' Carpenter S.K. et al., *Educational Psychology Review*, 2012.

HOW TO CHANGE YOUR LIFE IN JUST 30 SECONDS

At the end of a course, a conference, or any event during which you have learned something important, set aside half-a-minute to note down the key points.[176]

Don't take this lightly: selecting the most important points is a difficult exercise. And don't think that, because you have been taking notes throughout the event, this discipline is unnecessary. On the contrary! Devote just 30 seconds to it, no more.

If you make a habit of this, you will develop a vital skill: the ability to pick out and remember essentials. And this will make a huge difference.[177]

Better five minutes a day than an hour once a week

No doubt, it is better to learn little and often rather than engage in intensive study sessions at long intervals.

It is often said, and research confirms it,[178] that when you are studying a subject, whether it is guitar, a language, or anything else, it is better to practice for a few minutes each day than for a whole hour once a week.

Setting yourself challenges

You will make progress by setting yourself regular challenges, rather than staying in your comfort zone and resting on your laurels. So when doing something, ask yourself: Am I learning something new, something that challenges me, or am I just repeating something I have done countless times before?

Between work sessions, I like to relax a bit by playing the guitar because it takes my mind off things and is an enjoyable activity. However, if I want to make progress, perfect my technique, I can't afford to stick to the pieces I know by heart. I need to learn something new, or at least learn new ways of playing what I already know.

So I set myself challenges, playing a slightly more technical piece at greater speed, or trying a different rhythm. I search for these exercises on the Internet, particularly YouTube.

---

176   I would recommend Evernote for this purpose (*see p. 388*).
177   'The 30 Second Habit That Can Have a Big Impact on Your Life,' Robyn Scot, *Huffington Post*, 2014: http://en.olivier-roland.com/30-second-habit/
178   'Spacing as the Friend of Both Memory and Induction in Young and Older Adults,' Wahlheim C.N. et al., *Memory & Cognition*, 2011.

Teaching

One of the best ways to learn a discipline is to teach it. You don't need to become a 'master Jedi' to do this: after a year's practice, you can surely give at least some basic advice to complete beginners.

Teaching forces you to structure your knowledge, present it in a particular order, and eliminate 'gray areas' in your understanding.

You could even begin by practicing with someone who doesn't have a particular interest in the activity in question (but who is interested in you, such as a parent or grandparent). Then see if you can give some informal lessons to friends. Let your enthusiasm infect others.

When I discovered that blogging could be something more than writing a private diary on the web, I was so blown away that I just had to share my discovery with my friends, and so I ran some free sessions for them. I didn't suspect at the time that I would later be teaching blogging professionally as a way of setting up or developing a business. But my 'amateur' teaching helped me structure my knowledge and sharpen my understanding, as well as inspiring a few others. In fact, two of the people who attended my free lessons now make a living from their websites and traveling the world!

THE ULTIMATE SOLUTION: CREATING AN ONLINE PLATFORM

The simplest way is to launch a blog, a YouTube channel, or a podcast, or all three at once.[179]

Share what you have been learning, taking it as read from the outset that you are a beginner, and trying to add value for those who may follow you. It's relatively straightforward: when starting a new activity, you are bound to encounter problems. Each of these problems will have to be faced by other beginners at the same stage. Discuss this and share your solutions, and it will enable you to learn more quickly, for various reasons:

- Your brain will go into 'research' mode for subjects to feature in your articles/podcasts/videos, which will make you much more conscious of the problems ahead, the pitfalls encountered by others, and the solutions.

---

179   You can do this in 80/20 mode to get the best possible results with a minimum of effort: for example, publish a video on YouTube, include a transcription of the text on your blog, and extract the soundtrack and publish it in MP3 format.

- Writing articles or scripts for podcasts/videos will help you to reflect on what you are learning and to structure your knowledge. Writing is like riding a bicycle where the mind is concerned: it carries you farther for the same expenditure of energy, which will give you an advantage over other learners. Ask people you know: 'Do you spend five minutes a day journaling on the things you are learning?' The answer will be 'no' in almost every case.

- Your community will gradually come together, and the questions and challenges people raise will enable you to make much faster progress.

- Finally, it is an excellent way of getting to interview experts. Imagine having half an hour to put your questions to one of the acknowledged leaders in the field you are studying. Wouldn't you like to be able to ask him an interesting question that would help you to go full speed ahead? And who knows? Maybe this blog started from scratch to speed your progress could later become something far more substantial...

Take my student Laurent Breillat. He started his Learning Photography[180] blog using exactly this method. He was a complete beginner, and his slogan was: 'Together step by step.'

Five years later, with a quarter of a million monthly hits, his blog has become one of the most popular blogs on this subject in French. Meanwhile, Laurent, as well as mastering a very steep learning curve, has become a real star. His talks at the national photography show are a sell-out, and he has been commissioned by a well-known publisher to write his first book. Not to mention that he is now running a profitable and efficient business that allows him to travel to all parts of the world.

Even if you don't rise to such heights as Laurent, you will have made great progress in your subject while gaining knowledge of modern publishing tools and establishing a presence on the web.

What have you got to lose?

---

180 Apprendre la Photo in French.

SUMMARY

For the intelligent rebel who has decided to act

➡ You can spend 20 or more years in a classroom and never learn how to study if you go along with the system. Since learning skills are vital for the whole of life, we need to discover them for ourselves.

➡ One essential is to get plenty of sleep: 95 percent of people need eight hours' sleep a night to learn efficiently.

➡ Revise things frequently. When you have attended a course or conference, read a book, or watched an educational video, spend half-a-minute noting down all the points you remember. This simple habit will have a significant impact on your ability to recall essentials.

➡ When you learn something, moderate but regular practice is always better than intense sessions at irregular intervals.

➡ If you have the opportunity, teaching is the best way of learning. And creating a blog is one of the best ways of regularly teaching while building up a community of fans, and maybe even a viable business.

To help you put the activities described in this chapter into practice, go to http://en.olivier-roland.com/apprendre-a-apprendre to receive an email with a series of activities and challenges that will give you the necessary motivation.

CHAPTER 6
REBEL-STYLE SCHOOL
How to Learn What You Want, When You Want, Where You Want

'Self-education is, I firmly believe, the
only kind of education there is.'

Isaac Asimov

As we have seen, the Western education system has its strengths but also suffers from many weaknesses, which is why intelligent rebels cannot be content with the basic education they receive from the system. They must supplement it with self-study and maybe, in some cases, short-circuit it completely. Let's see how.

THE BEST TRAINING IN THE WORLD

'Formal education will make you a living;
self-education will make you a fortune.'

Jim Rohn

As I explained at the beginning of this book, I have no formal academic qualifications, and everything I have learned in developing my business and life, in general, comes from four sources:

- Experience (what I call the university of life)

- Books and other reading material (websites, magazines, etc.)

- Relevant training courses (vocational training, evening classes, online courses, etc.)

- Discussion, especially with people more experienced than myself

But behind these sources lies another, far more fundamental. I am self-taught, a self-made man, and this will inevitably color what I am going to say, as it has colored – in many beautiful hues – my own life.

Like many self-taught people, I have an intense, almost visceral, thirst for learning. I am very curious, and I always want to understand better how the world – indeed, the whole universe (let's not be modest) – actually works. For me, the act of learning is almost more important than the things I learn. I think I would suffer like a junkie going cold turkey if I were deprived of it.

For me, learning to develop wisdom and the relevance of the way we look at the world and, therefore, the relevance of the actions we perform seems to be one of the noblest goals that humankind can give himself, and I made it my quest.

Learning is, therefore, the fuel I burn, my driving force, propelling me toward my objectives. I will be set on my ultimate goal, which is knowledge and understanding, for as long as I live. And that is no bad thing because it has many advantages: by developing my knowledge, I extend my field of action, do more things and do them more effectively.

I draw from a spring of excitement and wonder that is inexhaustible; I am open to horizons whose existence I never even suspected; I meet enthusiastic people and develop the capacity for life-enhancing discussion.

I become aware of the subconscious processes that influence me, and these for me are always 'eureka!' moments, stimulating, and exciting. And this gives me greater freedom as an individual because it makes me more aware of myself and how my mind works, the world, and how I interact with it.

In the final analysis, is there any more exciting and amazing adventure than this hunger to continually extend our boundaries and embrace our imperfections to overcome them? There is a sense of victory when we can say: 'Yes, I have grown; I understand more and act better on the world than I used to, and that's a great thing'? And isn't this sense of satisfaction doubled, or even quadrupled, when we can also say: 'And I have helped my brothers and sisters to understand themselves better, to understand the world and act accordingly. And that too is very good.'

I therefore have a profound admiration for brilliant scientists, inspiring teachers, and innovative entrepreneurs. The scientists have put their quest for knowledge and understanding at the service of humanity, with immeasurable talent and courage. Often, for the sake of truth, they have had to face the wrath of their contemporaries. The teachers have made their discipline accessible, attractive, and exciting due to their talent and desire to pass on knowledge. The entrepreneurs use scientific research and their inspired thinking to bring into the world something that previously didn't exist, bringing value to others.

Such people are extremely rare.

How many inspiring teachers have you had in your life, the kind of teachers who can make even a boring subject interesting and put a smile on your face when you go into their classroom? For my part, I have had a few good teachers, many who were average, and a few who were dreadful. But inspiring teachers who could make their subject enjoyable even for those who detest it – now, *that* really is special. I reckon I had three such teachers during my 15 years of schooling.

Shall I give you an example of one such inspiring teacher? Go and watch the physics lessons of Walter Lewin,[181] a teacher – since retired – at MIT, which are freely available on the web.

Walter Lewin is an Internet phenomenon. In the early 2000s, he agreed to have his legendary lessons at MIT recorded on film, and when the Institute published them online around 2005, they immediately went viral. And that was in the days before YouTube. He was featured in the *New York Times* in 2007, under the headline: 'At 71, a physics teacher is a star of cyberspace.'

The video of his first lesson, first published on YouTube in 2008, has now been viewed more than 200,000 times. Wow! And remember, this is physics we are talking about.

At high school, physics wasn't my cup of tea. And maybe it is not yours. But what would your attitude to this subject have been with a teacher like Walter Lewin, who committed himself body and soul to make it lively, amusing, practical, and relevant?

Though I can say I had three inspiring teachers, none of them measured up to Walter Lewin, and I think most of you would say the same. So, if motivation doesn't come from our teachers, we must go out and find it. And this motivation, born of initial curiosity, can be transformed into a passion that will be your best teacher for as long as you live. And to light the flame, what better than to engage in an exciting and challenging project? Because this was the training or self-training that has had the greatest influence on my life.

181   'For the Love of Physics – Walter Lewin – May 16, 2011': http://en.olivier-roland.com/physics-classical-mechanics-fall-1999/

STARTING MY OWN BUSINESS

When I left school at 18, I was a young man with no frame of reference; lost, unsociable, with few friends, living with my parents, never had a girlfriend, and understanding hardly anything of the world around me.

A year later, I was setting up a business. I was still naïve and inexperienced, but I had left the parental home, had worked for two months as a waiter in a pancake restaurant, which enabled me to rent my first apartment, and had a girlfriend and more friends. Moreover, I had worked for a year on my project, building up a thick dossier, reading books that had been recommended to me, and meeting many interesting people who had acted as mentors, teachers, and guides. I am truly thankful to all these people, without whom I would not be where I am today.

I had engaged with bank managers, juries, naysayers, partners, my parents, and friends, and had persuaded almost all of them of the merits of my approach, the advantages of the market I was targeting, my ability to meet the needs I had identified, and my capacity to develop the enterprise I had in mind.

Progressing from the status of high-school student to business owner was not easy. And the learning curve was ongoing. The new business nearly folded after the first six months due to my mistakes, as I explained earlier. Still, this experience was a rite of passage into the adult world and turned my previous life upside down. An inspiring teacher didn't instigate this, but the spark I had in me: an ardent, overwhelming desire to live life on my terms, to be a creative free agent.

The best forms of training are the mad dreams we put into practice. They teach us more about ourselves and other people than all the courses or books in the world. They are our inner Walter Lewins. Amazing sources of learning and growth, unsuspected until we act on them. You, too, possess these inbuilt resources; these nuggets of gold peeping above the surface, waiting to be picked up.

Given sufficient motivation, it is possible to learn almost in isolation, progressively putting into practice what we have learned, provided we have created an environment to do so. That's exactly what I am suggesting you do in this book: use all the positive aspects of your personality as an intelligent rebel to educate yourself and set up your business. And if that sounds like realizing a mad dream, your motivation will surely be all the stronger.

The Personal MBA, or how to self-educate by reading the best books

'You wasted $150,000 on an education you coulda got for $1.50 in late fees at the public library.'

WILL HUNTING (PLAYED BY MATT DAMON),
GOOD WILL HUNTING

On one day in March 2005, in the USA, the telephone rang for 119 students hoping to be admitted to Harvard for a two-year MBA, a prestigious business qualification costing $150,000, not counting the two years of working for no salary.

In fact, they already knew they had been admitted, having taken advantage of the poor design of the website to find out their results in advance. Except that the authorities, too, had found out what had been going on. And Harvard, deciding that such behavior was unacceptable, was calling them all to tell them their candidatures had been rejected.

This story made headlines in the US press for weeks on end. On his already popular blog, Seth Godin, author of several best-sellers, published a contrary point of view: it was the best thing that could have happened to them. As he pointed out:

An MBA has become a two-part time machine. First, the students are taught everything they need to know to manage a company from 1990, and second, they are taken out of the real world for two years while the rest of us race as fast as we possibly can. [...]

The fact is, though, that unless you want to be a consultant or an i-banker (where a top MBA is nothing but a screen for admission) it's hard for me to understand why this is a better use of time and money than actual experience combined with a dedicated reading of 30 or 40 books.

The message was all the more powerful because Seth Godin holds an MBA from the prestigious Stanford University. An idea was born, and it was immediately taken up by someone who would transform the lives of millions of people.

For Josh Kaufman, then a manager with the giant firm of Proctor and Gamble, it was as if a mental lightbulb had been switched on: of course, Seth Godin was right! Someone needed to take the trouble to compile a list of the world's best business books!

And that someone was going to be him. He wasn't a well-known company boss, nor the holder of a degree in the philosophy of self-education, but he was a real entrepreneur. So he created the Personal MBA, a carefully selected list of the world's best books on business topics.[182]

At the time of writing, this list includes 99 books in 26 different categories covering practically all the fields you can think of for managing a career, a business, and even your private life. More than two million people have visited the personalmba.com website since it first went online; it is enormously influential and a vital resource for shrewd entrepreneurs.

ARE YOU MAKING THIS MONUMENTAL MISTAKE? HOW TO AVOID IT?

'In my whole life, I have known no wise people (over a broad subject matter area) who didn't read all the time – none, zero. You'd be amazed at how much Warren reads – and at how much I read.'

CHARLES MUNGER, BILLIONAIRE AND ASSOCIATE OF WARREN BUFFETT

'Poor people have big TVs. Rich people have big libraries.'

JIM ROHN, LECTURER, AUTHOR, AND SUCCESSFUL BUSINESSMAN

I had been an entrepreneur for 20 years. And during a significant portion of my business career – no less than eight years – I made a mistake of monumental proportions: Not reading books.

Now, of course, I do love reading, so I did, in fact read a lot during those eight years. But almost exclusively fiction. Practical books? An almost complete blank. I was so proud of having set up my business all alone at the age of 19, without experience or qualifications, that for a long time, I considered myself too intelligent to need to educate myself where business was concerned. Not for some years did I realize that I might perhaps be able to acquire useful new knowledge in this way.

So I signed up for evening classes, very much in the guise of a free-thinking maverick, which is why I chose such esoteric topics as the sociology of trade-unionism, as well as subjects that might be of more practical use, such as marketing.

182　See http://en.olivier-roland.com/personal-mba/ for the website.

I love evening classes. There you can meet dozens of people, employees for the most part, who come to study after a full working day, rather than watch television. People who have decided to take charge of their destiny and improve themselves. People who sacrifice several weekends a year to do their homework and revise for exams. They provide a lesson in courage and determination. And this is great for those who want to get a qualification to supplement their academic studies while continuing employment.

On the other hand, it is hardly the ideal solution for shrewd entrepreneurs thirsty for practical knowledge to apply to their business. I learned far more about marketing by reading just one book[183] and applying its principles than by attending six months of evening classes. At evening classes, I certainly learned a great deal about descriptive statistics, central trend indicators, and multivariate analyses, but nothing that helped me in a practical sense. No doubt this is fine for a manager in a big company, but not for a canny entrepreneur.

At this point, I understood that getting some business training could be an asset – and high time, too, after six years – but I hadn't yet found the best way of going about it. Practical books, in particular books on business, were not even on my radar. I don't know why. The idea had never occurred to me.

Revelation came when, quite by chance, I read Tim Ferriss's *The 4-Hour Work Week*. In the space of a weekend, this book completely revolutionized my view of entrepreneurship.

The second book I read, less than two weeks later, *The E-Myth Revisited* by Michael Gerber, also came as a mighty slap in the face. It described exactly the situation I was trapped in, which I naïvely thought was unique to me and did not affect other people.

Two books, one after the other, completely changed my view of what I had been doing for the last eight years. It was the start of a new chapter in my career. I immediately set out on a quest for a list of the best available books on business, which led me to The Personal MBA and then reached a new level when I started my blog: *Books That Can Change Your Life*.

Since that time, I have read hundreds of books on such subjects as personal productivity, negotiation, communication, psychology, health, contentment and wellbeing, history, sales, strategy, philosophy, and, of course, entrepreneurship. Some have been mind-blowing, revolutionizing my understanding of a subject, my

---

183   Jay Abraham, *Getting Everything You Can Out of All You've Got: 21 Ways You Can Out-Think, Out-Perform and Out-Earn the Competition*.

outlook, and behavior; others have quickly faded from memory. But one thing is certain: my life has undergone a radical change.

My business has shifted from being an activity that created a severe work/life imbalance to freeing me up to travel the world. I have increased my hourly income by a factor of 10. I am currently helping more people each month than I could have hoped to do in a year.

These books don't propose miracle cures; it's not just a matter of reading them and waiting for your life to change suddenly.

Inspiring books transform your perspective on a given field, creating a burning desire to achieve your objectives within a totally new framework, and this often gives you the motivation to act – overflowing energy, free fuel you can use to power what you do – for a time.

Books that are good and nothing more can clarify your thinking on a subject, make it sharper, and equip you with the tools and strategies for achieving your ends, but have little or no effect on your motivation. In such cases, it is up to you to maintain your drive and use the new tools you have discovered but of which you have as yet no practical experience.

Consider this: if you read just two practical books a month, that adds up to 24 books a year. After 10 years, you will have read 240 books. Imagine the difference that would make to your knowledge, your intellectual horizons, the tools at your disposal, your ability to reason and discuss, and your personal life, as compared with the person you would be if you spent your time just watching television. There is no comparison.

Reading books is a brilliant way of learning because:

- For a few dollars – or free of charge, if you borrow them – books put you in touch with great minds, in all fields and at all times in history.

- They are far less expensive than most training courses and enable you to learn much more rapidly than by attending a course.

- You can read at your own speed, matching your reading to your objectives.

- You don't need to devote years to them: you can read books at any time in your life while getting on with other activities.

Consider, too, that most courses are written by teachers and based on books: more advanced courses always include a bibliography, don't they? Of course, an excellent teacher can transform a dull book into fascinating subject matter and motivate you to explore a field you would otherwise find boring. But the truth is that outstanding books are, in most cases, more motivating and enable you to gain practical know-how much faster than you would from a mediocre teacher.

And it is easier to find an outstanding book than an outstanding teacher.

If you are skeptical, it is no doubt because you have never read an outstanding book that has permanently changed your way of seeing things.

If this is so, turn to the Resources section (*see p.387*) at the end of this book. Or just continue reading!

HOW ELON MUSK LEARNED TO BUILD SPACE ROCKETS... FROM BOOKS

Elon Musk is the very exemplar of the Rock'n'Roll entrepreneur who seems to crush all others under the steamroller of ambition and success. He was the inspiration for Tony Stark in *Iron Man*. Originally from South Africa, he co-founded PayPal and made a killing of $180 million when the company was sold to eBay.

Instead of swanning around in the world's fleshpots and living the life of a jetsetter, he used almost all of his money to co-found three enterprises in the most competitive and challenging sectors of the economy:

- Automobiles, with Tesla (there had been no successful launch of an automobile business in the USA since Chrysler in 1925)

- Energy, with SolarCity

- Space travel, with SpaceX, a company whose declared purpose is to colonize Mars

Some ambition!

Let's focus on SpaceX. This company has performed a remarkable feat, being the first private enterprise to put a satellite into orbit around the Earth (and only the sixth since the start of human history).

The rocket engine that SpaceX has developed, the *Merlin*, is regarded as the most advanced and efficient in the world,[184] ahead of those produced by government agencies with colossal budgets.

Above all, the company has slashed the cost of launching rockets in a sector that had been stagnating for years, where innovation is concerned. To put a satellite into orbit, the US government pays SpaceX $133 million, against $380 million if it places the order with one of SpaceX's two historic competitors, Boeing and Lockheed Martin. And in the case of launches for private clients, with fewer procedures to comply with, the cost is a mere $60 million. NASA has made no mistake in granting SpaceX a $1.6 billion contract to resupply the international space station.

How has Musk gone about developing an enterprise in a sector as complex as space travel and disrupting it?

Simple. He has become one of the world's leading experts on rocket science.

How? Simple again. He has read dozens of books on the subject.[185]

Yes, Elon Musk educated himself in a field as complex as space rocketry.[186] The very field that many people would think of as demanding long years of study at university level.

Of course, Elon Musk is super-intelligent. But he is also a genius because he has understood, as he says, that 'Books are just another way – and probably more effective than studies – to download information into your brain.'

---

184 It has a thrust/weight ratio of 165, almost twice that of the engine of the first stage of the Saturn V rocket which propelled men to the moon.
185 'Former SpaceX Exec Explains How Elon Musk Taught Himself Rocket Science,' Feloni R., *Business Insider*, 2014.
186 A few of the books he devoured on this subject: *Rocket Propulsion Elements*; *Aerothermodynamics of Gas Turbine and Rocket Propulsion*; *International Reference Guide to Space Launch Systems*.

AN 80/20 TECHNIQUE FOR REALLY GETTING SOMETHING OUT OF BOOKS

'Let no one be deluded that a knowledge of the path can substitute for putting one foot in front of the other.'

M.C. RICHARDS, POET

'The gap between ignorance and knowledge is much less than the gap between knowledge and action.'

CHRIS GUILLEBEAU

If reading is good, getting something practical out of what you read is better.

Have you ever read a book, been inspired by it, and decided to apply some of the principles it advocates? Then did you find you had thousands of things to do, like all of us, and put it all off until tomorrow? And tomorrow came and went, and the next day and the next day? Then, at last, after a few months or even years, you came across the book again, tidied away on your bookshelves or in a cupboard, and you regretfully remembered your enthusiasm and good intentions, and your failure to do anything about them?

If this speaks to you, don't worry; you are not alone. This kind of procrastination is the rule rather than the exception.[187] So here is a simple 80/20 technique that will help you boost the application rate of the inspiring books you read. But let me warn you: it is so extraordinary a technique that it could completely upset your whole worldview. So, before you begin, I suggest you take a deep breath and relax. And sit down.

Ready? Good.

You are going to take some notes.

Wow!

I know. Rather original, don't you think?

After all, it's not as if I was advising you to do something you have been doing since you first learned to write at school, is it? Or maybe it is, but listen carefully: You are not going to take notes any old how. In taking notes, *you are going to focus*

---

187   'Publishing in the Era of Big Data,' Kobo Report 2014.

on actions. In other words, you will take notes not to summarize theoretical ideas but to make a list of practical things you can do in your personal life and business.

So, it's simple: whenever you open a book on practical matters, switch on your practical-action scanner. And note down the things you will do. Nothing else. Big ideas and actions that are not immediately applicable must be shown the door. Then, when you have finished reading the book, reread your notes and choose something you will start putting into practice in the next 48 hours. Ideally, choose a simple 80/20 action that can be implemented quickly, and potentially do you a lot of good.

All good 'practical' books contain at least one brilliant 80/20 action that will bring excellent results for a minimum effort. So if you find and incorporate this action into your daily life and habits, you will get more out of the book than people who have used it simply to broaden their intellectual horizons.

If you don't find a genuine 80/20 action, any other action will serve. The important thing is to act. And to act quickly, before the initial enthusiasm wears off and you slip back into your daily routine.

Sometimes you will realize that the things you have put in place haven't had the anticipated effect. Never mind. There may be many reasons for this:

1. You haven't correctly applied the author's advice. In the absence of feedback from the author, this can be difficult to detect. Here are some ways of getting round the problem:

   - Reread the passage describing the action in question and see if you have omitted some detail, even if seemingly insignificant. Sometimes the difference between success and failure is a mere fraction of an inch and neglecting the smallest detail because it doesn't matter is a sure way of limiting your chances.

   - Try to find someone who has already tested the technique concerned and can share their experience, and possibly give you some feedback on how you are doing it. If you can't find anyone in your circle of acquaintance, join an online forum where people who have read this book are in contact, describe your problem, and ask for advice.

   - Try practicing the action in question for seven, 15, or 30 days (*see p.125*) and see if there is any improvement.

   - Try to contact the author directly, saying you found their book inspiring but, in applying this particular piece of advice, the results have been unsatisfactory. Ask them what, in their opinion, is wrong in the way you are going about things (be diplomatic: question your abilities rather than the author or the quality of the advice). Very important: explain that you have tried everything before getting in touch, to prove that you are not yet another joker who hasn't taken the trouble to read the 'bloody manual.'

- If this doesn't solve the problem, move on to something else. You have experimented and proved that, for the time being, this action doesn't work for you. Well done! You have gone further than the vast majority of people. Now select another action from the same book or move on to another book.

2. The advice is relevant for others, but not for you. It's difficult to be sure of this until you have gone through all the steps described above.

3. The advice is simply not relevant. The author has thought it up off the top of their head, and it has no concrete application. Same again: you can't be sure of this until you have gone through all the steps described above.

Finally, apply this method to any form of practical education, not just the content of books. Obviously, if the teaching is theoretical, it may be difficult to find any practical actions you can apply to your circumstances. Never mind. You can read *A Short History of Time* by Stephen Hawking, knowing it will not have any positive impact on your business, but just for the pleasure of exploring new territory (I have read it). At the same time, adopting this approach of taking notes with a view to action will immediately let you know if too much of what you are learning has no practical application.

THE 30-DAY TRIAL

'The power of the 30-days trial lies in its simplicity.'

Steve Pavlina

The thing you have decided to do is not yet fully implanted in your life, so don't be afraid if it seems rather daunting. You should test it out for a limited period, say 30 days, to see if it benefits you or not. Thinking in this way has many advantages, the first being that putting the action or technique in question into effect seems less daunting: no need to force yourself to do it for the rest of your days! It's just for a limited time, a test that doesn't commit you long term. What a relief!

Even so, you should take it seriously. Commit yourself to thoroughly testing the action/technique for 30 days, even if at first it seems boring or pointless. Sometimes it isn't until the end of the test that you begin to see the benefits, and the pain will diminish when the action becomes a habit.

When you have finished reading this book, choose *one* action to test out in your daily life. You might decide, for instance, to read one chapter of a practical book each day (e.g., one of the books recommended in the final pages), start your business project on a part-time basis, or go on a media diet.

And you don't need to restrict this 30-day-test concept to actions you have taken from books; you can apply it to anything you want to try out in your life. Here are a few examples suggested by Steve Pavlina, the inventor of this concept:

- Turn off the television, possibly recording your favorite shows so you can watch them after the trial period.

- Take a vacation from online forums, YouTube, or Facebook, if you feel you have become addicted to these sites.

- Go out every evening. Go to a different place each time and do something you enjoy – it will be a memorable month.

- Put an item you are no longer using up for sale on eBay every day.

- This is for you if you are single (or bored of your spouse)... Every day for a month, ask a different person out for a date. Unless your 'success rate' is less than 3 percent, you will have at least one date, maybe with your future husband or wife.

- Become an early-riser for 30 days. Have you ever watched the sun come up?

- Every day, call a different member of your family, friend, or business contact.

- Take a long walk every day.

The possibilities are endless. The number of fascinating tests you can do depends entirely on the fertility of your mind.

ANOTHER GOOD PIECE OF NEWS...

Present-day authors often have a platform on which they regularly publish content. These are mostly blogs associated with a YouTube channel, which enable you to dip into what a particular author may have to offer. And sometimes, an author may also provide online training.

If the author is successful in the field you want to break into, this can be worth its weight in gold. School teachers and university lecturers may be competent on a theoretical level, but most haven't achieved anything practical. This is particularly true where business is concerned.

How many teachers of marketing have launched a product? How many teachers of finance are wealthy or at least financially independent? How many teachers of entrepreneurship are themselves successful businesspeople? Not to mention the fields in which it is almost impossible to find teachers in conventional schools: real estate, meditation, wellbeing, the practice of self-study, etc.

And this also applies to people who are not writers: make a list of all the people you admire for their achievements and type in their names plus 'interview' in YouTube.[188] You will be surprised by the number of interesting videos in which these people share their techniques, tactics, and strategies for success. You can also search to find out if they have their own YouTube channel.

Then take advantage of the Internet's amazing ease of access to the world's best brains to track down experts you would never have come across on a conventional course.

HOW TO MAKE THE MOST OF THE MOOC REVOLUTION

Make the most of what? Don't worry. A MOOC is not a new family of intelligence-enhancing drugs or a new space shuttle prototype. A MOOC is a Massive Open Online Course.

Among the best known are:

- The Khan Academy,[189] with thousands of courses in dozens of different categories

- iTunes U, on which many graduate schools have published their courses

- Coursera, whose slogan ('Take the world's best courses, online, for free.') says it all

---

188   As a bonus, try to find the first televised appearance of this person or their first interview; it is often fascinating.
189   http://en.olivier-roland.com/khan-academy-youtube/

- Brilliant, which gamifies the learning of math and science

- Udacity, which offers practical courses that can be used directly by businesses. Such prestigious enterprises as Facebook, Google, Salesforce, Nvidia, Autodesk, and Twitter have designed several courses

- NoRedInk, which helps you to improve your spelling and grammar

And there are plenty more, as you will find if you do some research.

SHOULD I LEAVE SCHOOL?

After all this talk of the deficiencies of conventional schooling and the possible alternatives, am I encouraging you to drop out of school, as I did?

Not really. The purpose of this book is to help intelligent rebels like you set up a business with a minimum of risk and, at the same time, get a world-class education you can go on developing while having fun, experimenting, and putting ideas into practice.

The book is about being daring without taking stupid risks. I first wanted to show some of the limitations of the conventional education system, often regarded as a sacred cow, and demonstrate that there are other ways of educating yourself.

Where starting a business is concerned, as success is never 100 percent guaranteed, however brilliant your ideas, minimizing risk implies having a practical strategy, such as:

1. Covering your back by getting started on a part-time basis while continuing your studies or another job (I shall be giving you a strategy for this in the second part of the book)

2. Making sure any losses are kept to a minimum and having a plan B if things don't turn out as you had hoped

The easiest plan B to implement is simply to ensure that you can continue your studies or find another job if problems arise. This being the case, you would do well to get your high-school diploma, as this is the almost exclusive passport to higher studies.

If you are sufficiently flexible and adventurous, you can manage without it, like thousands of other entrepreneurs and me, but that won't work for everyone.

SUMMARY

For the intelligent rebel who has decided to act

➡ You now know that it is crucial 1) to learn outside the school system while you are still inside it, and 2) to go on learning for your whole lifetime once you have left.

➡ Of all the possible means of educating yourself, the best is to find a project that is ambitious, exciting, and challenging, such as starting a business, and commit yourself to it.

➡ You will automatically learn countless things you can put into practice immediately, adding them to your skills bank.

➡ Nowadays, a wealth of courses delivered by the world's best teachers are available on many platforms, including YouTube. If you want to break into a particular field, take time to search for courses by gifted specialist teachers.

➡ Visit the Personal MBA website, or search the list that accompanies my *Books That Can Change Your Life* blog and select a book to get you going.

➡ It is also vital to continue learning as you grow older: just reading two practical books a month adds up to 240 books over a 10 years. If they are outstanding, this will make a big difference to your culture, broaden your intellectual horizons, and give you tools you can use daily.

➡ Explore the platforms I have mentioned in this chapter and see if any of them grabs you.

➡ Set up a 30-day test. If you are stuck for a subject, select one of those suggested earlier in this chapter.

To help you put the activities described in this chapter into practice, go to http://en.olivier-roland.com/learn-alone to receive an email with a series of activities and challenges that will give you the necessary motivation.

CREATING YOUR OWN BUSINESS AND BREAKING FREE

CHAPTER 7
MEANINGFUL JOB PERKS

The 12½ Reasons Why Being an Entrepreneur Will Benefit You Far More Than Being an Employee

In this chapter, you'll start to see why running your own business will benefit you more at all levels than being an employee.

1. EXPERIENCE

You may be thinking that starting out as an employee will enable you to gain experience. That's not totally untrue, but you forget that setting up a business allows you to build up varied experience at amazing speed, which is gratifying and will stand you in good stead in the future.

When you start a business, you have to be versatile. You have opportunity to meet lots of interesting people and, while learning, you can apply your new knowledge immediately. And this knowledge is quickly translated into useful skills.

Besides, you will be more motivated to learn new things and be more proactive. And when you set up a business, you have the opportunity to invest in a project that is close to your heart. A project to which you commit yourself, body, and soul. Do you remember what I was saying earlier about the 'sacred flame'? Is there any better motivation for learning? And could you say the same about salaried employment?

Often, the main hindrance to learning is a lack of desire. When you are in salaried employment, experience is built up far more slowly and is much more limited. In setting up a business, you will be motivated to succeed, simply because you will have no choice in the matter.

2. ACADEMIC QUALIFICATIONS

Customers never ask about academic qualifications. What interests them is getting the best product or service at the best possible price.

Of course, it isn't possible to start a business in some fields unless the senior personnel have an academic qualification. Good examples would be doctors, lawyers, and accountants. But in most sectors, when setting up a business, your academic qualifications and experience will be far less important than if you were applying for a job. 'All' you have to do is to provide quality products or services at a price your customers are prepared to pay.

Indeed, setting up a business empowers often unlikely people to short-circuit the established hierarchies and elites and create something of their own: a business that is accountable to no one, except the market.

History is rich in people of this kind, people who created giant enterprises even though there was apparently nothing particularly promising about them: Ray Kroc, the milkshake machine salesman who built up the McDonald's empire; Steve Jobs, the hippy high on Indian spirituality, who never washed but revolutionized five industries (IT, the cinema, music, telephony, and retail);[190] Bill Gates, an immature 'daddy's boy' who sold IBM an operating system he didn't even own; Sergey Brin and Larry Page, the two students who founded Google before they were out of college, and so on. The thing all these entrepreneurs have in common is that their academic studies didn't prepare them in any way for what they would go on to create and, above all, that they didn't ask anyone's permission to do what they did. For these reasons, their academic qualifications were of no relevance, and none of their customers ever felt the need to inquire about them.

At a more modest level, this is exactly what I did when I left school at 18 to set up my business a year later. I used my IT skills to embark on an exciting adventure to get around the established system I hated, and this enabled me to leave school and my parents and enter adult life via a wide-open door.

A few years later, I got the IT maintenance contract for several Peugeot dealerships[191] in my region. It was no mean contract: we were responsible for the smooth operation of several hundred workstations. The slightest interruption might cost the business tens or hundreds of thousands of euro.

Had I gone to a recruitment interview for the same job, the first thing they would have asked me about would have been my academic qualifications. But as an entrepreneur, in more than five years of working for them, no one ever asked me the question. For one reason or another, it is a question you never put to an

---

190   With, respectively, Apple and its Macintosh; Pixar and its animated films; Apple and its iPod linked to iTunes; Apple, again, with its iPhone; and Apple, yet again, with its Apple Stores, which are some of the most profitable sales outlets in the world.
191   A famous French automobile marque.

entrepreneur, maybe because the very existence of the business proves that he or she has nothing more to prove.

3. SALARIES AND THE MYTH OF JOB SATISFACTION

As I shared at the start of this book, if you are not bothered about money, if it is not a major concern, and you are in salaried employment, that's fine. Because being an employee is the worst possible way of earning money.

It means exchanging your time for money. But time is the most precious thing you have. And swapping what you value most for money is, therefore, a terrible idea, especially when you relate that to the catastrophic figures I shared at the start of the book regarding the percentage of employees who find satisfaction in their work.

Wow! If you have been immersed in a salaried-employment culture[192] this idea may strike you as revolutionary. Even terrifying. No doubt you are thinking it would turn your world upside down, but let me ask you this question: why is it absolutely necessary to spend time to earn money? Why shouldn't you make money regularly even when you are not working, even if you spend only an hour a month or less on the job, while going on safari in Africa, or skiing in the mountains, without having to work a given number of hours a year in exchange?

This may seem somewhat surreal, but do plants stop growing when you stop watering them? No. You put them in a well-lit place where it is neither too hot nor too cold, i.e., an environment where they can thrive. You then water them from time to time. And they grow all by themselves.

Similarly, it is possible to set up a business you only need to attend from time to time and which will virtually run itself. Earning money without spending your time in exchange is entirely possible and has a long history. One of the classic ways of doing so, of course, is to invest in real estate. Once you have paid off your original loan, the rentals become a passive source of income, i.e., the money you earn bears no relationship to the time you spend managing things. Of course, you will still have to devote some time to it. But so little compared with what you earn that you will have crossed a threshold: you need no longer go out to work every morning to make a living. You can even employ someone to take care of it for you.

It is almost everybody's dream to earn money without working, but the aim isn't to do nothing at all. The objective is to break the relationship between time spent working and income, so you are free to do the things you want to do. If you're

---

192   Or in entrepreneurship seen as a way of creating a job for yourself, rather than a business.

going to work, you can, of course, work, as we shall see, on the things you are passionate about, that give you a sense of fulfillment, that make life worth living.

A word of warning: setting up a business does not necessarily mean being able to dissociate the time you spend on it from the money you earn. Most entrepreneurs work extremely hard, to the point of being the slaves of their business. I shall be dealing with this later in the book (*see p.331*).

4. JOB SECURITY AND THE CHANCE OF UNEMPLOYMENT

Are there still people who believe there is such a thing as a job for life?

Security of employment is nowadays an illusion unless you are a civil servant. Given the economic situation, which is always volatile, you can never be sure of not being out of work at short notice. Clearly, when a business runs into financial difficulties, laying off employees is the most obvious way of cutting costs.

Anyway, who nowadays wants to stay with the same company for 20, 30 or 40 years? Very few people. We prize diversity. Excitement. Something to make the heart swell.

Relying on your company to protect you in hard times and preserve your job in return for your loyalty is, therefore, generally a utopian expectation. I'm not saying this never happens, but enterprises nowadays would find it very difficult to act in such an idealistic way.

If you are made redundant, take it as an opportunity to set up your own business, particularly if you receive a redundancy package. Grasp the opportunity to take the plunge and realize your creative dream!

5. REALIZING SOMEONE ELSE'S DREAM AND THE RESULTING SENSE OF ALIENATION

Here is a somewhat shocking reason why you shouldn't be an employee but should set up your own business: as a salaried employee, you are helping to realize someone else's dream. Of course, some projects are very worthwhile, even if others have conceived them. Being a member of Elon Musk's SpaceX company, for instance, and helping to colonize Mars, is undoubtedly a magnificent project, even within a corporate setting you do not own. And there are advantages in joining an existing organization, in not having to reinvent the wheel, in receiving guidance in a supportive context – and, on the whole, in being seen as conforming to the social norm.

But consider this: an enterprise cannot survive unless it is profitable. For it to make a profit, its employees must put in more than they take out. Where you are concerned, this is really not to your advantage, as you will not get a 100 percent return on the value you bring to the enterprise. That's normal, as you must bring benefits to your company if it is to keep employing you.

When you own a company, you can maximize the added value you bring to others. You can also use the value contributed by the others and transform it into financial revenues.

Over and above this, entrepreneurs are often realizing a personal dream when they set up a business. This may be the dream itself (at last, I am going to be able to change the world by selling revolutionary solar panels), or the means of realizing the dream (this business will, at last, give me the freedom I desire).

In doing an job which doesn't satisfy, you are wasting time by setting your dreams aside all the time you are actually at work.

You can try to realize your dreams in the evening or before you go to work – this is one of the topics I tackle later in this book – but, while you are working for the company, you are helping to realize a dream that belongs to someone else.

6. AS AN EMPLOYEE, YOU ARE A TENANT PAYING OFF THE BUSINESS OWNER'S MORTGAGE

Working for a company you do not own is like being a tenant. It's like renting an apartment where the rent you pay is higher than the owner's mortgage repayments. In other words, someone else is making much more out of it than you.

If you pay $500 in rent and your landlord is making mortgage repayments of $400 a month, they earn $100 a month and still own the apartment when the mortgage is paid off. So you are throwing your money out of the window and helping to grow someone else's wealth.

Moreover, if the landlord falls on hard times and wants to occupy their apartment, they could terminate your lease simply by giving you notice and paying a sum in compensation. Or could sell the apartment to another owner whom you might not get on with.

And that's a very fair comparison with being a company employee. Not only are you sacrificing what you hold most dear for the most inefficient way of earning money, you are also helping to build up something you do not own, in an organization from which you could be ejected from one day to the next, without benefiting from everything you have contributed to the enterprise, apart from the experience you have acquired.

If you own a business, the enterprise you have created belongs to you. All the value you put into it, all the things that make it grow, will eventually pay off. Because if you have built it well, as a real business, not just a self-employed job, when the day comes that you want out, you will be able to sell it, just as you would an apartment to which you hold title.

When my second business began to flourish, I sold my first business, in the form of customer portfolios, to three other businesses, which earned me a tidy sum. And so it should be: after all, I was the one who took all the risks and created the jobs for my employees. But at the same time, my employees contributed to the value of my business and, therefore, to the sale price, didn't they? Yes. Just as the musicians in an orchestra contribute to the success of the conductor.

But the conductor gets more applause than the musicians, as the conductor has carefully selected the musicians and directed them to play together harmoniously. In contrast, without him or her, they would produce a horrible cacophony.

So be the conductor, rather than the musician modestly playing his violin.

7. THE CONCRETE-SLIPPERS TRAP

The longer you continue as an employee, the more normal it will seem. And the more reluctant you will be to undertake a new venture.

It will be more difficult to leave your comfortable cocoon, the illusion of security you have created for yourself. You will settle into a comfort zone, where you are not necessarily a happy bunny, but where life is not too bad, either.

You will be cozily installed, wearing a comfortable pair of concrete slippers, not having to confront your fears or limitations, nor risking failure in the public eye. You will end up traveling this same road, even if you find it less and less congenial. There is a real danger of getting imprisoned in your comfort bubble.

Entrepreneurs are far less likely to get trapped in this sort of routine simply because setting up and managing a business is a daily challenge, far more so than if you are in salaried employment.

8. STARTING YOUR OWN BUSINESS IS A THRILLING ADVENTURE

An adventure in which the journey is as important as the destination.

What can be more exciting than taking risks, facing down your fears, and venturing into the unknown to realize your dreams? There is no finer adventure for a human being and setting up your own business lets you live it to the full.

Do you think it is possible to feel the same excitement, the same enthusiasm, the same deep-rooted desire to take risks when you are a corporate employee? In most cases, definitely not.

9. LOSS OF FREEDOM AND INDEPENDENCE

I have already touched on this point, but I must insist that being an employee means surrendering a degree of freedom and independence.

If you have to work under the orders of a boss you don't like for various reasons, it may cause you considerable suffering. I have seen how such suffering affected some of my customers, employees who were in conflict with their employer but didn't dare resign for many reasons. Mainly the fear of not getting another job. They experienced mental torture day by day as if they were going to the Gulag.

Often it is as if a cage is being slowly constructed around you without your noticing. And yet it has just as bad an effect on your happiness and wellbeing as a physical prison would. Setting up your own business gives you a freedom and independence that is almost tangible.

Obviously, business owners also work under constraints, particularly the demands made by customers. They can't do exactly as they would like, but they enjoy far greater freedom than their employees.

Even if a business can afford to give an employee a raise, it will not necessarily do so. But if the company's situation permits, the owner will most probably increase their own salary, which is quite logical because they are reaping the fruits of their risk-taking, proactive approach, and hard work.

Moreover, if you are successful in creating a business that is automated or semi-automated, you will enjoy far greater freedom than the majority of people. You will have a source of income for which you have to do only a minimum of work or no work at all. The possibilities are endless.

Imagine what you would could do if you no longer needed to work for a living.

10. EMPLOYEES ARE, IN ANY CASE, COMPANY BOSSES

Actually, all the employees in the world are company bosses. Effectively, they are the chief executives of small companies employing just one person. They offer a single service and have only one customer. This means that the only way the enterprise can make a profit is to exchange this single employee's time for money. No leverage effect is possible.

Moreover, do you think it sensible for a business to depend on a single customer? Wouldn't that leave it in a state of dependency at every level, emotional and human, as well as financial?

Imagine what would happen if, for whatever reason, the single employee fell out with the single customer. Would that be a recipe for contentment and job satisfaction?

And yet, this is the situation in which all employees have placed themselves.

11. YOU CAN DO IT BECAUSE A SHY, SPOTTY 19-YEAR-OLD WAS ABLE TO DO IT

The most compelling reason for taking the plunge if you so desire is simply my own example, which shows just how achievable the dream of running your own business is.

I set up my business in July 2000, at the age of 19, without experience or academic qualifications; I like saying I'm two years short of a high-school diploma. When I took the plunge, I was a spotty adolescent, introverted, ill at ease, knowing absolutely nothing about life.

If someone like me can establish a successful business, make a living from it, and develop it sufficiently to sell it 10 years later, what prevents you from doing the same?

I have had opportunities to share my story and ask this question when giving talks in schools and universities. I always say: 'Look, I am living proof that you can create a successful business even when the deck seems to be stacked against you. You, on the other hand, have academic qualifications; you are more mature; you have a much greater chance of succeeding if you set up a business.'

Of course, it's normal to feel frightened because there is no guarantee of success. But if you fail, at least – for all the reasons I have given you – you will have failed for something worth fighting for because you were trying to realize a dream that was close to your heart.

You will have failed while trying to escape from an alienating, conformist system that unfortunately represents the norm in our society. You can call it a worthwhile failure.

Moreover, the experience you will have gained will undoubtedly enable you to bounce back and embark on further adventures. Many successful entrepreneurs began their careers with a resounding setback.

The only obstacles preventing you from taking the plunge are obstacles in your mind, fixed beliefs that are holding you back. This doesn't mean there are no difficulties and setting up a business is a smooth and steady process. But with the right attitude, obstacles become mere constraints. Mountains become hills, taking some effort to climb maybe, but climbable.

Motivate yourself to overcome them for, beyond, the green and pleasant valley of your dreams awaits you.

12. YOUR SKIN COLOR AND SOCIAL BACKGROUND

These may be central issues or minor factors, depending on where you live, but when you run your own company, the color of your skin, your gender, and your social/professional background matter a great deal less.

Obviously, discrimination doesn't disappear as if by magic, but at least you will not face it during the recruitment process. You may encounter prejudice from some of your customers, but in the vast majority of cases, they won't have seen you before placing an order and may never see your face.

Discrimination is barely a factor in businesses operating on the Internet, so this is something you might consider if you suffer from it.

12½. WHEN ALL IS SAID AND DONE, EMPLOYEES WILL ALWAYS OUTNUMBER ENTREPRENEURS

Sometimes, when I share some of the ideas I have been sharing with you, people say: 'Fine, but if everyone acted like that, society would no longer exist. There would be no food, no one to look after children and the pets, and civilization would collapse.'

This always makes me laugh. It's as if a firefighter were giving a motivational presentation to recruit firefighters and people said: 'Hang on a bit, Sir, what would happen if everyone became a firefighter? There would be no farmers, and we would all die of hunger. Nor would there be any television producers or reality television shows, and that would be the end of civilization as we know it.' How ridiculous!

As the startup incubator The Family put it: 'Anyone can become an entrepreneur, but not everyone can be.' What they mean is that not everyone can become an entrepreneur, but that an entrepreneur can come from any location, any social setting, any background.

Of the people who read this book, many will admit that I am right but won't necessarily act on what I say because most people are not proactive. There will always be thousands of opportunities for setting up enterprises and recruiting people to work in these enterprises who will help make your dreams come true.

IN CONCLUSION: DO YOU NEED TO BE AN ENTREPRENEUR TO LIVE A WORTHWHILE LIFE?

My essential point is that it is vital to lead a life that enables you to make the most of your time, without having to do things you don't enjoy simply to put food on the table. A life that allows you to indulge your passions, make a valid contribution to the world around you, and live adventurously. In short, to make the most of the little time granted to us by fulfilling our dreams rather than those of someone else.

Is it possible to do this without setting up a business? Yes, of course.

I think the most essential thing in fulfilling our dreams is to break the connection between the money we earn and the work we do, or to be so passionate about our business that everything else, including private life and family, pales into insignificance. In this case, our chief aspiration becomes to develop the business and raise it to a level of global excellence. An example of this kind of extreme entrepreneur is Steve Jobs. But this is not everyone's idea of happiness: if, for instance, you are a volunteer worker or the employee of an NGO, and passionate about the work you do, setting up your own business or founding another NGO is not necessarily the answer.

There are other ways of breaking the connection between the money you earn and the work you do. For example, you can reduce your needs to reduce the need to work. Take Henry David Thoreau, a celebrated 19th-century American philosopher, who carried out a fascinating experiment. He went to live for two years in a forest, where he built himself a cabin with a minimal but adequate level of comfort, and during this period didn't need to work. He had calculated that farmers worked mainly to pay back the loan on their farm and keep the farm running – a strange paradox, rather like the snake swallowing its own tail. His philosophy was one of simplicity, and, in his view, happiness had nothing to do with material possessions. He told his story in an autobiographical account I would recommend to you: *Walden or Life in the Woods*. It was also a response to the danger of alienation caused by waged employment.

Today some communities seek to be autonomous; they aim to meet their basic needs and live differently from the daily routine of money-grubbing and commuting. However, I think this is far more difficult to achieve in present-day society than setting up a business. Moreover, money brings you much greater freedom and more opportunities, such as traveling the world. We live at a time when it has never been so easy to travel, and I think it would be a pity not to take advantage of so amazing an invention as the airplane to discover the world's many wonders. Be that as it may, money is a useful tool for creating a life of freedom centered around our desires and enthusiasms.

The example of Thoreau and many others demonstrates that accumulating possessions, over and above those we need to enjoy a minimum level of comfort, doesn't make us happy. Many scientific experiments provide evidence of this.[193] We therefore need to use our money better: to buy experiences rather than possessions.

---

193   For example: 'To Do or to Have, That Is the Question,' Van Boven L. et al., *Journal of Personality and Social Psychology*, 2003; 'Pursuing Happiness: The Architecture of Sustainable Change,' Lyubomirsky S. et al., *Review of General Psychology*, 2005; 'Spending Money on Others Promotes Happiness,' Dunn E.W. et al., *Science*, 2008.

SUMMARY

For the intelligent rebel who has decided to act

In short, intelligent rebels who want to become canny entrepreneurs must, in my opinion:

➡ Set up a business (not just become self-employed), making sure they work on it (rather than in it).

➡ Break the connection between the money they earn and the time they work (rather than exchanging money for time).

➡ And above all, of course, avoid the trap of salaried employment.

CHAPTER 8
FOLLOWING YOUR DREAMS
Setting Up Your Own Business, That's Scary!

What you have read so far may have convinced you that being an entrepreneur has many advantages. Even so, the idea of taking such a radical step gives you the shivers: fear has you in its grip. But that's only to be expected. Like all exciting new adventures, setting up your own business is scary. However, a lot of the fear is irrational and has no solid basis. Let's begin by demolishing a few myths.

THE MYTH OF JOB SECURITY

We looked at this in the previous chapter, and anyway, it's no surprise. Unless you're in the public sector, job security is a myth nowadays. The truth is that a company can get rid of you at short notice for any number of reasons, some of them pretty dubious.

An entrepreneur, on the other hand, is in no danger of being dismissed out of hand. You can be fired by the company you set up if you sell more than 50 percent of the equity to other shareholders. But 1) to avoid this happening, you need only hold on to more than 50 percent of the shares,[194] and 2) even if it does happen, you will already have plenty of experience of running a business and will no doubt be able to bounce back.

THE MYTH OF BANKRUPTCY: WHAT IS THE REAL FAILURE RATE OF BUSINESSES IN THE WESTERN WORLD?

But what about the risk of going bust once you have set up a business?

In the USA, the figures produced by the US Bureau of Labor are fairly stable year on year: roughly one-third of businesses are no longer functioning three years after

---

194   Or sell shares without voting rights or with 'diluted' voting rights.

they were established, and roughly half have shut up shop after five years. The picture is much the same in the UK, Canada, and most industrialized countries.[195]

These figures are often interpreted as a failure rate of 33 percent after three years and 50 percent after five years. But this doesn't account for the many other reasons that might cause an enterprise to close down, apart from business failure.

And if a business does fail, what might the consequences be? There is a huge difference between, on the one hand, closing down a business that isn't thriving, but which is debt-free or may have made a small profit, then finding another job, and, on the other, being crushed under a mountain of debt and ending up on the street.

A Small Business Economics survey conducted in 2002 found that one third of the 50 percent of businesses that had closed after five years had done so voluntarily, often with a successful exit strategy.[196]

According to Brian Headd, an economist with the Small Business Administration: 'The significant proportion of businesses that closed while successful calls into question the use of "business closure" as a meaningful measure of business outcome. It appears that many owners may have executed a planned exit strategy, closed a business without excess debt, sold a viable business, or retired from the work force.'

So this leaves us with a 'failure' rate of around 33 percent of businesses after an average of five years. The figures for another country of which I have made a careful study – France – are similar:

- As for the USA, the business closure rate is roughly 33 percent after three years and 50 percent after five years.

- Of these 50 percent:[197]

  - Voluntary closures account for 14 percent.

  - Cessations of activity (in other words, the business has had to close down but has not gone bankrupt) account for 15 percent.

  - Real bankruptcies, leaving the business owner with an average debt of €10,000 to pay back, account for 15 percent.

---

195   'Business Demography Statistics' of the EU, Eurostat: https://en.olivier-roland.com/survival-rate-EU/
196   'Redefining Business Success: Distinguishing Between Closure and Failure': https://en.olivier-roland.com/sbe-study/
197   'Une nouvelle vision de la pérennité des jeunes entreprises.' *Entreprises en bref*, 2005: http://en.olivier-roland.com/entreprises-bref-janv-2015/

That should shatter the myth that half of all businesses end up ruining their founders, wouldn't you agree?

FACE UP TO YOUR FEARS, THEN GIVE THEM THE BOOT

One of the best ways of banishing your fears is to work out a worst-case scenario, then consider the chances of it happening.

The truth is that almost everyone is fearful when setting up a business, even experienced entrepreneurs; there's nothing unusual about that. If you feel no fear, it probably means you are not really aware of what you are getting yourself into.

But there are different kinds of fear: on the one hand, healthy fear, which ensures you adopt a strategy to minimize the risks while maximizing the chances of success; on the other, a paralyzing, all-encompassing fear that stops you from taking action while others take the risks and reap the rewards.

So, if you are afraid of setting up your business, take a few moments, right now, to do this exercise. Get a sheet of paper or open a new document on your computer. At the top, write 'The worst thing that could happen to me.' Then take a few moments to write down what might realistically go wrong, the worst outcome you can imagine.

When I say 'realistically,' I mean it seriously. Don't go imagining improbable scenarios like 'an earthquake might swallow up my business premises, a meteorite might fall on my house, my wife might leave me, and the cat get eaten by the goldfish.'

Just write down what you realistically envisage happening if your business fails. What might your debts amount to? Would you have to mortgage your home? Would you be left without any income? How long would it take you to find a job?

Then assess the probability of these things happening. Are they highly likely? Fairly likely? Not at all likely?

Then, for each problem you have identified, think of solutions to 1) minimize the likelihood of it happening by taking preventive action, and 2) solve the problem once it has arisen.

Then sleep on it for a few days. Your brain will be in 'problem-solving' mode, and will undoubtedly come up with other solutions during this period, solutions you can add to your document.

Then, when you are satisfied you have thought it all through, ask yourself the question again: What is the likelihood of this happening? If you have done a good job, you will now be thinking that your worst-case scenario is much less likely to occur than you first imagined. And if it did happen, it wouldn't be so catastrophic after all. You would survive. You would bounce back. And you would have gained experience that most wage-earners never dream. But once again, what is the likelihood of this worst-case scenario coming to pass?

FAILURE: AN OPPORTUNITY THAT'S BEST AVOIDED

I hope the figures I've shared with you on actual failure rates and their consequences, together with the exercise on facing up to fear, have enabled you to get the measure of the real risks you are taking in setting up a business. And to realize that failure can teach you an amazingly effective, low-cost lesson. However, don't let the knowledge that most failures in setting up a business don't have serious consequences lead you to tempt fate.

The risk here is of adopting a devil-may-care attitude, as if to say 'OK, if I fail it's nothing to worry about, it won't set me back all that much, and it'll look good on my CV, so I can afford to relax.' Paradoxically, this fear-free, casual attitude can lead to a worse situation than if you had been afraid.

Don't take pride in failure; instead, be proud of the fact that you have tried to stack all the card in your favor.

You failed because there was something you had not foreseen, not because of a lack of preparation or tenacity.

Failure is depressing. Failure is to be avoided. The only reason it isn't so catastrophic is that you will get back on your feet, learn from your experience, and try a different approach until you are successful.

SUMMARY

For the intelligent rebel who has decided to act

➡ People are generally very fearful when it comes to setting up a business. Most of their fears are groundless, and, as an intelligent rebel, you are now well aware of the fact.

➡ Only 15.2 percent of new businesses fail. So the risk is much lower than people generally believe.

➡ Does that mean there are no risks at all? Of course not. But it is possible to minimize the already low level of risk and maximize your chances of success.

➡ That's what this book is about.

➡ Now we have dealt with the myths, let's see how you can create the enterprise of your dreams.

CHAPTER 9
LAUNCHPAD
Building an Empire or Having a Business That Works Hard for You – What Business for What Purpose?

In this chapter, you will discover four different options for launching a business and find that the traditional way isn't the only way, which should go a long way to stilling your fears.

People often make the mistake of thinking that going into business must mean setting up something extremely complicated; they need to recruit employees, rent offices, and endure sleepless nights for the rest of their days. It is just not the case. Explore the different options in the following pages and a few chapters further on, and I will tell you exactly how the intelligent rebel goes about creating an enterprise.

WHY DO YOU WANT TO SET UP IN BUSINESS?

There are many possible reasons. Typically, they may include:

- A desire for independence, freedom, not having to work to a boss's orders

- Wanting to earn more money

- Wanting to be self-employed

- Wanting to have more time for yourself and your family

- Wanting to give concrete expression to a vision that inspires you

Some of these motives may seem obvious, others less so, particularly 'wanting to have more time for yourself and your family.' Really? Aren't entrepreneurs supposed to work their socks off trying to develop their business to the nth degree?

Not necessarily. It all depends on what you are aiming for and how you organize your business. Because the good news is that there are as many ways of setting up and running a business as there are motives for doing so. Here are the main ones.

CREATING YOUR OWN JOB

This is the approach of most people who start a business:[198] Unable or unwilling to look for a new job, they set up their own enterprise with the prime and explicit purpose of creating a job for themselves. This is the principal motivation of most artisans and shopkeepers, as well as members of the liberal professions: your local grocer, plumber, baker, even your doctor, all wanted to set up in business to create their own job, their ambition being to live more pleasantly.

It is a perfectly honorable approach and may be all you need to feel free and content if you aspire to be independent.

The problem comes when these 'solopreneurs' are ambitious and want to expand their business. Unaware of the fundamental differences between creating their own job and founding a business, they duplicate the patterns they established when they were on their own in their growing enterprise. Solopreneurs then find themselves trapped in a system that can't function without them and has them working 70 hours a week.

The difference between creating your own job and setting up a business boils down to whether you are working *on* your business or working *in* your business. It's as if a 'one-man (or woman) band' decided to become the conductor of an orchestra. He or she would have to stop focusing on their ability to play all the instruments at once and concentrate instead on their orchestra. In other words, on the capacity of each musician to function to the maximum of their abilities and interact harmoniously with the others to achieve the best possible result.

It is a difficult transition, which few entrepreneurs can make because they are unaware that there are other possible approaches. Most entrepreneurs work extremely hard because they have to be everywhere and have few employees. In any case, they find it very hard to delegate, often because they feel they can do the job better than anyone else.

Most of the time, a large proportion of this work is ineffective: it could profitably be eliminated, delegated, or automated if the entrepreneur did some training and took the trouble to implement the necessary measures. The large amount of work generated by this approach is, therefore, primarily the consequence of a lack of organization. It is, however, possible to establish a business that gives you quality of life if you apply the right methods. Let me explain.

---

198   US Census Bureau.

CREATING A 'QUALITY-OF-LIFE' BUSINESS

An entrepreneur wanting to create a 'quality-of-life' enterprise has just one end in view: to have a business that serves him or her, rather than being a slave to the business. Their objective is, therefore, to establish an enterprise that will demand a minimal amount of work while enabling them to earn enough to live on and achieve their life objectives.

Tim Ferriss has popularized this type of enterprise, which he refers to as a 'muse' in his book *The 4-Hour Work Week*. In brief, to establish a muse, an entrepreneur must:

- Have an idea and test it out, as with all other businesses.

- Identify the 20 percent of its activities that generate 80 percent of its sales, focus on the latter, and discard the rest.

- Achieve the profitability objective he has set to live his 'dreamlines,' i.e., have the means to buy the things he wants to possess and pay for the experiences he desires.

- Eliminate, delegate, or automate all the tasks he doesn't like doing, and perform only those that he alone can do, thus adding value to the enterprise.

- In short, create a business, rather than a job for himself.

- Then find personal activities to fill the void, not falling into the trap of 'work for work's sake.'

- And enjoy life!

There is nothing new about this: canny entrepreneurs have always managed to set up enterprises of this kind. A striking example is how Warren Buffett saved money he then invested on the stock exchange, adopting the method that has made him a mega-wealthy man. In 1950, aged 20, he had earned and saved the equivalent of $96,000 at today's values.[199]

One way he found of doing this was to set up an automated business. As well as *How to Make Friends* and *The Intelligent Investor*, books I mentioned earlier, at the age of 17, Buffett read *One Thousand Ways to Make $1,000*,[200] which gave him a brilliant idea. Noting the long waiting times at the barber, he spent $25 on a secondhand pinball machine and went to see a barber with the following

---

199 $9,800 in 1950.
200 By F.C. Minaker. In 1936, the year the book was published, $1,000 were worth roughly $16,500 in today's values.

proposal: install the machine in the waiting area, in exchange for which Buffett and his partner would come in once a week to collect the money and repair the machine if it broke down.[201] The barber would take half of the profits, Buffett and his partner the other half. The barber agreed, and when Buffett returned a week later and opened the money box, he collected... $50, $25 of which were for him and his partner (worth around $270 at today's values). So he had recouped his investment in a single week, and anything over and above that would be pure profit... for a derisory input of labor. In double-quick time, seven or eight pinball machines were installed at the various barbershops in town, generating serious turnover for Buffett and his partner, at virtually no cost and with minimum effort. This left him time to pursue his studies while delivering newspapers on the side, another profitable activity.

This story illustrates the power of an automated business: it gives you an income out of all proportion to the labor involved, and this frees you from the burden of exchanging your time for money. If it brings in enough for you to live on, you will be free to do as you please. What's more, if you can manage your business entirely via the Internet – or withdraw completely from the organization of a more conventional enterprise – you will have the additional freedom of being able to travel the world. The world is your proverbial oyster. This gives you freedom, which very few millionaires, locked into their businesses, can enjoy.

There is a long history of humans seeking to automate their labor. At first, they delegated it to human slaves and animals, then increasingly found ways of entrusting it to machines while, fortunately, developing a conscience about the wrongness of exploiting living beings.

An early example of an automated machine that performs a back-breaking task is a noria. You don't know what a noria is? It's a wheel fitted with buckets, partially submerged in a stream or river (*see opposite*). The current exerts pressure on the wheel and fills the buckets, which discharge their water into a channel or aqueduct. This, in turn, carries the water to a reservoir, from which it is distributed for irrigation or drinking purposes.

As long as the current flows, a noria will function 24/7, even if the water resources manager is asleep in bed, ill, or on strike. A machine of this kind naturally requires maintenance, but the labor involved is far less than the labor the villagers are now spared. They no longer need to wear themselves out carrying heavy buckets up from the river.

---

201 This story, like others concerning Warren Buffett, is taken from his biography *The Snowball Effect*, Valor éd., 2010.

Figure 6: A noria
(no human being or animal is being exploited in this picture!)

When was the noria invented? A mere 2,300 years ago, by Greek engineers![202] The watermill was invented at roughly the same time and, a few centuries later, the windmill, hundreds of thousands of which were constructed in Europe from classical times to the industrial revolution, freeing millions of people from exhausting labor. In short, entrepreneurs have been trying to transfer onerous tasks to machines for a very long time.

Different types of automated business in the modern era

As far back as 1936, *One Thousand Ways to Make $1,000* listed a wealth of ideas for automated businesses. The one that inspired Warren Buffett was as follows: buying and installing pay-per-go weighing machines in strategic places so that people could weigh themselves. This is one of the possibilities: invest in a machine and install it where people will use it without assistance or almost so, reducing the time spent operating the machine. In fact, we are surrounded by shrewd operators who have set up automated businesses. Once you know how to identify them, you will see them everywhere. Here are a few modern-day examples:

- Bioimpedance meters are scales that monitor body composition (and body fat) by sending a (weak) electrical current through your feet; you will find them in some pharmacies

- Similarly, some pharmacies have machines that take your blood pressure automatically for a small fee

---

202 Bruno Jacomy, *Une histoire des techniques*, Points Sciences, 2015, and the 'Noria' article in Wikipedia.

- Photo-booths

- Vending machines dispensing drinks, condoms, etc. Of course, these machines need restocking at regular intervals, which requires more organization than just collecting the money. However, the amount of work involved is still fairly modest and can be delegated.

- Laundromats

- One of the oldest examples of an automated business is owning properties that bring in more rent than is paid out servicing the mortgage loans (even more, once the loans have been repaid). Managing your tenants and the maintenance work involved, of course, requires time and effort, but these tasks, too, can be delegated.

Does this seem a bit too far-fetched or too good to be true? Here are a few concrete examples of entrepreneurs I have met who have applied the principles of *The 4-Hour Work Week*.

Phil Suslow and his LEDs

Phil Suslow, an American entrepreneur, began selling LEDs when he was still in high school: he had bought some for his automobile, and his friends wanted them, too. He purchased them for a dollar apiece and sold them on for $5, a comfortable margin which enabled him to pay for his studies and have some pocket money left over. He began importing them from Hong Kong, which further bolstered his profits.

He thus earned around $18,000 in the first year alone. Not bad for a student, but still not enough to be able to claim this was a real business. Two years after it all began, Phil suddenly woke up and realized he was on to a good thing...

This might seem obvious, and it was, but for many people, the primary way of earning a living is to have a job and be paid a salary, as this is the only way they have heard of (apart from winning the lottery). Realizing that there are other ways to earn a living sometimes takes time. Even when the solution is staring you in the face, as it was for Phil.

He therefore decided to stop studying, and it then took two years for his business to begin generating a serious turnover. During this time, he lived with his parents and so had few material needs.

From the outset, he emphasized customer relations, ensuring that his customers were literally delighted, and this worked brilliantly: he gained new customers by word-of-mouth, and the business grew at a rapid rate.

He began gradually recruiting staff until he had four employees in the USA and four in Hong Kong, enabling him to delegate more and more of the work and automate the rest.

Having a website had already automated a good part of the 'front end,' the part seen by the customer, who accesses the site, searches the catalog, orders the LEDs they want, and pays up. The system emails a confirmation to the customer and another message to the business team, whose job is to make up and ship the order.

Phil is, therefore, never involved in the process and has also automated and outsourced the 'back end' processes, the things the customer doesn't see, such as ordering in fresh stock from suppliers.

Since automating his business, Phil spends most of his time traveling: by 2011, eight years after establishing his business, he had already visited 40 different countries and undertaken a 45-day crossing of the Atlantic.

The irony is that, on completing the crossing, during which he had had virtually no Internet connection, which would have enabled him to manage his business remotely, he discovered that his business had recorded one of its best-ever months. This is the hallmark of an enterprise that is fully automated: the founder is effectively removed from the daily organization of the work.

In 2011, his business, Oznium, was already making annual sales of $1 million, and a very tidy profit, leaving Phil entirely free to move around and live as he saw fit.[203]

He has since settled in Cape Town (South Africa) with his wife, continuing to make regular trips and generally enjoy life.

J.B. Glossinger, podcaster

Miami, 2007. J.B. Glossinger had just finished writing his book *Get out of Neutral* and was looking for a way to promote it. Employed in the aviation industry and specializing in the purchase and resale of Boeing 747s, holder of an MBA and a doctorate in metaphysics, Glossinger was super-qualified but had absolutely no idea of how to go about this task.

---

203 To see my interview with Phil in video go to https://en.olivier-roland.com/phil/

At this point, a friend came up with a simple idea: present a program on the Internet every morning to give people some positive and motivating input, rather than let them be bombarded with negative news at the start of the day.

So he began recording and publishing a podcast every morning, five days a week. The platform he used was iTunes, which provided JB with a vast potential market, and he continued to create and publish five podcasts a week.

He made many mistakes, and his early podcasts were far from perfect. Still, he gradually improved, keeping in mind his original intention: to produce a podcast created by a human being for human beings, without music, advertising banners, or other special effects. He was quite overwhelmed by the success he achieved: his podcast soon became the leader in the 'personal development' category, then one of the 25 globally most popular podcasts broadcast on iTunes.

He then turned professional by changing his model: the Monday podcast was still available free of charge, but for the other four days, subscribers were asked to pay $20 a month.

Today, JB's business has an annual turnover of around $600,000, mostly profit, deriving solely from these monthly subscriptions. And JB still operates in the way that originally brought him success: he gets up, goes straight to his office, plans his podcast, then records and publishes it. The whole operation never takes more than 30 minutes – very often only 20 minutes – then his working day is over.

After a few years, he decided to launch a second podcast, but, even so, his working day is generally over at eight o'clock in the morning. The rest of the day is his to do as he pleases: spend time with his family, play golf, travel. JB, therefore, lives the '4-Hour Work Week,' thanks to gradual improvements (he aims to improve each podcast by 1 percent, he says) and a determination that has driven him to produce 2,000 daily podcasts without ever missing a day. He is now able to create content very rapidly and reach a large and adoring audience.[204]

DIFFERENT WAYS OF CREATING AN ENTERPRISE THAT SERVES YOU

Dropshipping

Dropshipping is a method of distribution that enables you to automate a business very easily. The concept is simple: you sell products online. When a customer buys

___

204 To see or read my interview with JB, in video and text format, go to https://en.olivier-roland.com/jb/

a product, the order is transmitted directly to the supplier, often a wholesaler, who is responsible for:

- Warehousing the product

- Delivering it to the final customer

- Managing returns and refunds

This greatly alleviates the burden of work, enabling the enterprise to concentrate entirely on marketing and SEO. What's more, whereas the wholesaler is often paid at 30 days or more, the final customer is debited immediately, which results in constant positive cash flow.

Some dropshippers will do even more for you, taking charge of some of the marketing and referencing by including your products in their catalogs and offering them to their customers.

How Amazon can automate your business

The most outstanding example is undoubtedly the 'fulfilled by Amazon (FBA)' service offered by this web giant. The concept is simple: after opening an account with them, you send your products to an Amazon distribution center. Then they will be referenced on the Amazon website, where customers can purchase them in the same way as any other product. And Amazon takes care of everything: warehousing, shipping, invoicing, customer service, and returns management.

The simple fact that they reference your product can generate sales for you, given the enormous number of visitors to their site and the well-oiled machine designed to maximize sales. Still, you would do well also to put in place your own marketing activities to boost sales initially.

When Amazon sees that your product is selling well, the algorithms will feature it more prominently, particularly under the heading 'Customers who bought this article also bought...', which can generate many more sales. And this doesn't stop you from selling your products on your site while delegating the rest to Amazon.

To sum up, I don't have any shares in Amazon, but I must say they provide an excellent service. If you sell products online, there is no reason not to place them with Amazon.

HOW GUILLAUME CAME TO WORK A FIVE-HOUR MONTH

For Guillaume L., reading *The 4-Hour Work Week* was a mind-blowing experience. He saw the creation of a 'muse' as the way to realizing a dream: going to live in India and practicing meditation in a Buddhist monastery.

In searching for a way to create his muse, he discovered Amazon's dropshipping service, and a lightbulb went on: he decided to try it out. He found some products which looked as if they might sell well, found a supplier who could send them directly to Amazon and ordered a few items on a trial basis.

Two months later, he was making around €2,000 a month in turnover and a profit of roughly €1,000... just by working five hours a month.

All Guillaume needs do is monitor the stocks of his products and place a fresh order with his supplier when an item is running out. The supplier sends the items direct to Amazon, which does everything else.

This leaves Guillaume time for many of the things he enjoys: writing blog articles on massage and *Ayurveda*, sport, reading, meeting people... He is also involved in humanitarian activities, giving French lessons free of charge, and doing massage for an NGO.

Obviously, €1,000 a month isn't a princely sum in Europe, but in India, he can live comfortably, and his needs are very simple.

Other dropshippers

Amazon isn't the only company to offer dropshipping. In the new technology field, Techdata and Ingram are two of the bigger names. Alibaba is a well-known site that attracts many Asian manufacturers who are open to the idea of dropshipping.

Many of them can also send the products you order directly to the 'Fulfilled by Amazon' service. To find others, simply type 'dropshipping' and the name of your country into a search engine.

Copyright on books and other intellectual property

Another way to generate an automated source of income is to receive royalties on books and other intellectual property.

If you have written a book and sales continue for 10 years, you will receive royalties during this period. Meanwhile, it is your publisher's task to manage the printing, warehousing, sales, and delivery of the book to intermediaries and final customers.

That, at least, is the theory. In actual fact, most books stop selling three or four months after publication because they are withdrawn from bookshops if they fail to achieve initial sales volumes sufficient to generate long-term demand.

Fortunately, the Internet has changed all this. Nowadays, books, whether in hard copy or digital format, can remain indefinitely in the catalogs of e-commerce sites such as Amazon, and customers can find them by performing keyword searches even years later. Books in paper format can be printed on demand and shipped directly to the final customer thanks to clever systems. In digital books, obviously, the cost of production, warehousing, and distribution are virtually zero. The second piece of good news is that, with these new technologies, you can dispense with intermediaries and earn more in royalties than you would with a traditional publisher.[205]

Let's take a concrete example, again, by examining two services provided by Amazon (I repeat: I don't own any Amazon shares; I just find the services they offer entrepreneurs and authors are first-class). These two services will help you to sell books in paper or digital format without any great effort.

Kindle books

Kindle Direct Publishing[206] enables you to sell books in Kindle digital format on all Amazon sites, which to date means you can easily reach readers throughout Europe, and in the USA, Canada, Mexico, Brazil, Japan, Australia, and India.

Of course, a book written in English will sell less well in Spain or Mexico than a book in Spanish, but you can nevertheless reach English-speakers living in those

---

205 So why did I go through a traditional publisher for the book you are now reading, you may well ask? Because there are objectives other than maximizing royalty income, in this case wanting to reach as many people as possible and have more impact, best achieved by going through the traditional distribution networks. Let me take this opportunity to thank the teams at Éditions Leduc and Hay House for their excellent work and patience during the preparation of this book.
206 http://en.olivier-roland.com/kdp-amazon/

countries. In any case, the additional time and cost required to register your book on the Amazon sites in these countries is minimal. So there is no reason for not doing so.

The second advantage is that if you set the sale price of your book between $2.99 and $9.99, Amazon will pay you 70 percent in royalties. Yes, 70 percent! If you set your price outside this range, the royalties are 35 percent, still much more than the 8–12 percent you can normally expect from a traditional publisher.

Amazon customers can then buy and read your book, even if they don't own a Kindle, since Kindle books can also be read on a computer, smartphone, or tablet using a free app that can be downloaded from Amazon.

And there is nothing to stop you from selling your book on other digital distribution platforms, such as the one managed by Apple.[207]

Paper-format books 100 percent outsourced

It is also possible, using the same electronic file as you used for the Kindle version, to offer your book for sale in paper format. Once again, Amazon will take care of the whole operation: the book is referenced on its e-commerce site and, when a customer makes a purchase, it is printed on demand and shipped direct to the customer.

All you need do is visit the Create-Space website,[208] which belongs to Amazon, and offers many different options for creating a paper-format book to your requirements.

The royalties are naturally less generous than for a Kindle book; they depend on the price you set, the format of your book, the number of pages, whether it is just black and white or in color, and so on.

You can then reference it with just a few clicks on all Amazon websites worldwide. You can even link your Kindle book to the paper-format version (provided they are identical) so that readers wanting the paper-format version can also buy the Kindle version at a reduced price.

---

207 To publish books on iTunes, all you need do is set up an account on iTunes Connect.
208 http://en.olivier-roland.com/createspace/ As I finish writing this second edition, Amazon is in the process of merging CreateSpace with KDP, and all the operations described will therefore be accessible from KDP.

CDs, DVDs, music, and videos

Creating products of this kind obviously requires more advanced technical skills than publishing a straightforward book. Still, it is worth knowing that CDs and DVDs can also be referenced directly with Amazon via Create-Space, which will produce them on demand and ship them to customers. And you can, of course, offer music in MP3 format and DVDs in downloadable video format on Apple, Amazon on Demand, and other online services.

Royalties from inventions

It is possible to earn royalties for an invention exactly the same way as an author or musician. The process is roughly as follows:

1. You design a new product and make a prototype.

2. You submit the design to several major manufacturers in the sector concerned.

3. One of them likes the idea and offers to license your invention.

4. They take care of everything: manufacturing, warehousing, distribution, marketing, aftersales service.

5. And you receive a percentage of the sale price.

That's if everything goes according to plan! In actual fact, at stage 2, inventors often realize that they need to go back to stage 1 and do further work on their idea to ensure it meets market requirements, and sometimes this really means starting all over again.

You needn't be an engineering genius to make a living: you would be surprised at the wide range of people who have had a good idea at the right moment and are now living comfortably off their royalties.

To minimize the risks, and maximize your chances of success, apply the 'lean startup' method (described in detail later) to this process:

- Test out your idea in the harsh light of reality at the earliest opportunity.

- Minimize your expenditure: there is no point embarking on the long and costly process of lodging a patent unless you have a definite order. Meanwhile, use less expensive protection mechanisms, such as getting interested parties to sign an NDA.

- Be flexible: adapt your idea to actual circumstances to have a viable product that can be quickly brought to market by a manufacturer.

If you want to take this further, visit the website of Stephen Key,[209] an American professional inventor who will teach you how you can be like him. His book, *One Simple*, describes the process in detail. You will have to adapt his ideas slightly if you live outside the USA, but what he says is on the whole universally applicable.

AUTOMATING A CONVENTIONAL BUSINESS

The methods we have been discussing generate a passive income stream by their very nature, but it is also possible to automate even the most conventional business. It then becomes a question of mindset and strategy. Here are two concrete examples.

How Matéo progressed from burnout to working 10 hours a week

Matéo, whom I have already mentioned in the section on habits and rituals (*see p.78*), quickly made a success of his agency managing urban music artists, Only Pro,[210] in particular promoting the French rapper Soprano.

But he also experienced what is all too common with a flourishing business: a lot of hard work and stress, which eventually led to burnout. Twice over.

He then read *The 4-Hour Work Week*, which revolutionized his thinking. He decided to gradually reduce his working hours by 1) conducting an 80/20 analysis to cut out anything superfluous, 2) delegating the remainder, and 3) finding other activities to fill the vacuum and avoid the trap of work for work's sake.

At the same time, by establishing the rituals I mentioned in Chapter 4 and putting in place all these measures, he has to date reduced his working time to roughly 10 hours a week (two hours a day, five days a week) while generating a turnover of €2 million per annum.

Thanks to the teams and delegation mechanisms he has introduced, he can now manage his business entirely via the Internet, which allows him to spend his time partly in Barcelona, New York, and Rio, partly in his home-town of Marseille.

---

209 http://en.olivier-roland.com/inventright/
210 http://en.olivier-roland.com/onlypro-agency/

Thanks to meditation, daily exercise, and the freedom he has carved out for himself, he is in top form, in the prime of life, liberated and content, and he devotes himself only to what he enjoys about his profession.

If an overworked, overweight entrepreneur from a disadvantaged background has achieved all this, what is there to prevent you from emulating him?[211]

How Olivier was able to live in a little paradise on the other side of the world

When he founded Eurojob Consulting,[212] specializing in recruiting French and German professionals, Olivier Jacquemond was not necessarily thinking of living on a dream island on the other side of the world. However, he quickly integrated the new technologies into his business set-up and has never needed a physical office; everyone works remotely.

For several years he lived in France and Germany, and it wasn't until he discovered and fell in love with the Philippines in the early 2010s that an idea was born: since he was already working remotely from home in Europe, why not do the same from the Philippines? He therefore got himself organized and left for the magnificent island of Palawan, where he lives in a luxuriant natural setting with deserted beaches of white sand while continuing to manage his business online.

At first, he kept to his established pattern, working some 60 hours a week. He then put a simple but radical mechanism in place that immediately enabled him to reduce his weekly online working time to just 15 hours: he discontinued his home Internet subscription! Obliged to travel 13 miles to log on in the nearest town, he was forced to rationalize his work, eliminate everything superfluous, and enjoy a non-connected life in his little corner of paradise.

WORKAHOLICS OR WORK-LOVERS?

Please note, I'm not saying that you absolutely must create an automated business. Some entrepreneurs are perfectly happy to work like crazy because it is their passion and greatest pleasure in life. What I am saying is that creating an automated business can be very much a fun undertaking and, once you taste the freedom it

---

211   To watch my interview with Matéo, in which he talks in depth about his life and career, visit https://en.olivier-roland.com/mateo/
212   http://en.olivier-roland.com/eurojob-consulting/

brings, you might rather like it and think that those who spend so much time at the workplace are, in fact, workaholics.

Here we have two contradictory world-views. Let's take the example of Jean, a shrewd entrepreneur who is making a great success of his business. He delegates effectively and uses the various procedures intelligently. He has entrusted to others the tasks he dislikes or isn't particularly good at, sticking to those he enjoys and to which he can bring real added value. He works hard – more than 50 hours a week – because he loves his work and is ambitious. His business has grown exponentially, and he wants to take it to the next level because he can't resist a challenge, is curious, and enjoys what he is doing. There isn't much room in his life for other interests, apart from his wife and children, although he doesn't see them as much as they would like.

So is Jean a joyful entrepreneur or a workaholic? To decide the issue, an in-depth analysis is required. In *The 4-Hour Work Week*, Tim Ferriss criticizes entrepreneurs who work too intensely, claiming that many of them perform tasks for reasons that have nothing to do with efficiency, in particular, because:

1. The tasks concerned haven't been subjected to 80/20 analysis and could probably be eliminated or delegated as non-essential.

2. The tasks are being performed to fill a vacuum. We intensely dislike having nothing to do and getting bored. If we organize our business efficiently, it saves us time – and if we fail to fill this time with interesting activities, we fall into the trap of work for work's sake, where efficiency is no longer an objective. The aim of work is then simply to keep us occupied, to counteract our *horror vacui*, and give us the impression we are doing something useful.

We have already established that Jean has organized his enterprise efficiently, but he still works more than 50 hours a week. The question, therefore, is as follows: Has Jean filled the vacuum by engaging in activities he is passionate about in his business? Or has he fallen into the trap of work for work's sake because he is afraid of being bored, isn't making sufficient effort to explore extra-professional activities, and/or is driven by excessive ambition when he already has all he needs to make him content?

This question is difficult to answer. My perspective is as follows: It is very easy for an entrepreneur, even if they are very efficient and intelligent, to become a workaholic because they are afraid of exploring non-work-related options. Once your business is up and running on an automated basis, you can take the opportunity to explore the world and the dozens of possible activities it offers, or you can take your business to a new level because the challenge of doing so is stimulating and fulfilling. The only way of being really sure is to explore both options. Set up your business, develop it, automate it as best you can, then go away for six months on a world tour (for example). When you return, decide what you want to do. And this isn't necessarily a binary choice. There is nothing to prevent you from developing your business by working like crazy every other month and going away for surfing lessons to Miami Beach or trekking in Nepal for the rest of the time.

In conclusion: The basic idea is to imagine your business as the prototype of a franchise that could be duplicated anywhere in the world. This means analyzing the business, documenting the way it operates, then exiting from the system to check that it can work in your absence. Which brings us to...

CREATING A BUSINESS IN THE TRUE SENSE

The ambition of entrepreneurs who create 'true' businesses is more than just wanting to have their own job: they want to set up a structure that will fulfill a vision or 'bright idea' of theirs, and they generally have big plans. A nationwide chain of stores, or even the continent, franchised or directly owned by the enterprise. A website used by millions of people. An application that disrupts an entire sector, an innovative technology destined to create a whole new market. These are a few examples of projects set up by entrepreneurs wanting to create a true business.

Such businesses may sometimes be set up initially without a grand vision and take off subsequently, after a change in ownership or because the owner becomes aware of unexploited potential. But always, behind all of these giant enterprises, there comes a time when a powerful vision emerges, carried forward by one or more founding partners. Let's take a look at a few enterprises of this type, all of which had modest beginnings.

A chain of stores established all over a country, or even a continent: McDonald's

The story of McDonald's is a perfect illustration of the invention of an outstandingly effective method that generates a whole load of money and of the difference in strategy between an entrepreneur whose priority is his quality of life and an entrepreneur with a big vision who aims to create a business in the true sense.

The fact is that these two worldviews were in opposition to each other when McDonald's was born, which is why the business has two distinct birth dates: 1940 and 1961. 1940 was when the first 'McDonald's' was opened by the McDonald brothers in

California, a fast-food restaurant serving hamburgers. 1961 was when the enterprise was taken over by Ray Kroc, a 52-year-old businessman, a milkshake-machine salesman, who built it up into the empire we know today.

In 1948, the McDonald brothers had rationalized the operation of their restaurant by introducing a production-line system for preparing hamburgers: the 'Speedee Service System.' This enabled them to make their hamburgers much more quickly, reducing customer waiting times while maintaining the same level of quality. The McDonald brothers continued to rationalize all aspects of their restaurant, turning it into a highly efficient and reliable money-making machine. They then opened several more restaurants based on the same principles, each of which enjoyed considerable success.

This brings us to 1954 when Ray Kroc made a discovery. The sales of the company he worked for were in freefall because a competitor was making less expensive machines. During this slump, he received a larger-than-normal order: eight milkshake machines for the McDonald brothers' restaurants. Many salesmen would have sent round a little present to thank the customer, or maybe wouldn't have done anything at all. Still, Ray Kroc, intrigued by the exceptionally large order, took it upon himself to visit them and discover the cause of their apparent prosperity.

When he visited the main restaurant in this modest chain, he was astonished to find a method of organization that was clearly superior to that of other restaurants – and much more profitable. 'Astonished' is putting it mildly: as he said later, he 'felt like Newton when the apple dropped on his head.' Here was an extremely efficient method that could be duplicated anywhere. This was plain as plain could be.

In discussing matters with the two brothers, he learned that they were looking for a new agent to develop their franchise. Ray Kroc grasped the opportunity and opened his first McDonald's restaurant in Illinois, which was immediately and immensely successful. So he went on opening restaurants.

Meanwhile, the McDonald brothers' priority was their way of life. They thought they were earning enough already, so were in no hurry to transform their business into an empire, lest they collapse under the stress.

Ray Kroc, on the other hand, had a grand vision, foreseeing a McDonald's restaurant in every corner of the USA, and then the world, and was becoming increasingly frustrated by the lack of ambition of the two founders. In 1961, he, therefore, made them a proposal that respected their concern to put their lifestyle first: he would purchase the business and pay them royalties. The brothers agreed to sell the business for $2.7 million[213] and be paid a 1.9 percent share of the profits.

---

213   The equivalent of $23 million in today's values.

Everyone was satisfied with this arrangement: Ray Kroc because he was at last free to build the empire he dreamed of; the McDonald brothers because they could now enjoy themselves while earning a comfortable living, without ever having to work again. The rest is history.

In 2018, McDonald's posted a turnover of $22.8 billion and was employing 235,000 people worldwide. As an advocate of healthy eating and a balanced organic diet, I can't say I have any great affection for McDonald's. But you can't but applaud the intelligence with which this method of organization was invented and the brilliance and self-sacrifice of this milkshake salesman in spreading it around the world.

It is an excellent example of a down-to-earth business – this is a hamburger restaurant when all is said and done! – which has become:

- A 'quality-of-life' business for its founders, following rationalization.

- Then a business empire, thanks to the ambition and vision – not to mention the sheer hard work and persistence – of Ray Kroc.[214]

THE KEY POINTS: WHY MCDONALD'S HAS BEEN SUCH A RESOUNDING SUCCESS

- Scientific analysis of the business processes and their continuous improvement.

- Documentation of these procedures.

- Duplication of the system elsewhere.

- It wouldn't have been possible without a grand ambition – the establishment of McDonald's worldwide – as envisioned by Ray Kroc.

A STARTUP

A startup is, to put it simply, an enterprise that aims to change the world by growing very rapidly and thus reaching large numbers of customers. Obviously,

---

214 Since the first edition of this book was published, a film has been made about Ray Kroc: John Lee Hancock's *The Founder*. I would warmly recommend you see it, particularly the part on how the McDonald brothers rationalized the organization of their restaurant.

such ultra-rapid growth isn't possible without 1) adding considerable value to what is currently on offer, often with the aid of new technology, and 2) effective advertising and marketing.

Successful startups often add such value to existing arrangements – and with such sudden effect, they disrupt the established market. In other words, they upset the applecart, directly threatening vested interests, often long-established companies that haven't anticipated the development of new technologies and whose very existence is thereby under threat.

Examples are legion: Amazon has disrupted Barnes & Noble and the publishing industry as a whole with its Kindle; Apple the music, telephony, and tablet sectors, in that order; Airbnb the hospitality industry; Uber the taxi business, and so on.

Let's take a look at some of these disruptive giants and how they began without great pretensions...

Amazon

Seattle, 1994: A young American, aged 30, lays down a list he has just compiled. He has recently read a report predicting that e-commerce will grow by 2,300 percent per annum. Flabbergasted, he imagines what his life will be like if he continues to work as an advisor for a large finance company and realizes he will forever regret his inertia if he fails to take advantage of what the report calls 'the new gold rush.'

He, therefore, puts in place what he calls a 'regret minimization framework,' which sets out all the efforts he needs to make to avoid having any regrets at a later stage. The list he has just compiled fits into this framework: 20 products he can sell online. After some reflection, he reduces the list to the five most promising products:

- Audio CDs

- IT equipment

- Software applications

- Video cassettes[215]

- Books

---

215   Yes indeed, this was before DVD took over!

Finally, this young entrepreneur – Jeff Bezos, by name – decides to focus primarily on book sales because there is a worldwide demand for books, they are inexpensive, and there are many titles available.

This is how Amazon was born in Jeff's garage in Washington State. Despite its modest beginnings, Jeff's vision was of an online enterprise which would sell hundreds of thousands of books and other items throughout the USA then the whole world, operating with reduced costs compared to conventional companies (no physical stores) and a more extensive catalog than that of its competitors. As the books didn't need to be displayed on shelves but simply printed on-demand or shipped on request by publishers, Amazon could list even the most obscure titles.

Having no experience of book-selling, Jeff Bezos decided to take a four-day training course on setting up a bookshop. The teacher, himself a bookshop owner, was fanatical about customer service and this so impressed Jeff that he decided to make it the cornerstone of his business. 'We know that if we can get our competitors to focus on us, while we focus on the customers, then ultimately, Amazon will come out ahead,' he said later.

After only two months, Amazon was selling in all 50 states of the USA and in 25 foreign countries, posting sales of $20,000 each week. The company's growth was also fueled by using what was then an innovative online mechanism: affiliation, which Amazon put in place in July 1996.

The principle was simple: anyone could register with the Amazon partners program and get affiliated links for any of the products sold on Amazon, then include them on their websites, in emails, and so on. After that, if a customer clicked on one of these links and purchased the product, the affiliate would earn a commission without this increasing the price of the product.[216]

Even so, due to the tiny margins, Amazon wasn't making a profit and wasn't likely to do so soon. The business plan forecasts a deficit for the first four or five years because of these small margins and the investments that had to be made. This generated a lot of criticism from commentators who couldn't see how the business would attract investors and survive in the long term.

But Jeff Bezos was confident in his vision and believed that, once the business began to earn money, a giant enterprise would be born and was bound to grow and overturn the established ways of doing things.

---

216 This program still exists and, in particular, I use the French version of *Books That Can Change Your Life*, which automatically brings me in several thousand euros a year.

History has proved him right because, having survived the bursting of the Internet bubble in 2000, Amazon posted its first profits in 2001, which, though modest ($5 million for a turnover of $1 billion), were sufficient to demonstrate the viability of the business model.

The rest is history. In 2018, Amazon's turnover was $232 billion, its net profit was $10 billion, and the company was employing 600,000 people worldwide.

THE KEY POINTS: WHY AMAZON HAS BEEN SUCH A RESOUNDING SUCCESS

- Identification of a rapidly growing sector.

- Rational analysis to determine what products and services might benefit from this growth.

- Resulting in the right idea at the right moment.

- The founder's clear understanding of his strengths and weaknesses (Jeff Bezos attended a course on running a bookshop).

- Intense focus on the quality of the customer experience from the word go.

- Use of innovative marketing methods, such as an affiliation program.

Airbnb

San Francisco, 2007. Brian Chesky and Joe Gebbia are unable to pay the rent of their large apartment. They have the bright idea of converting their loft into a B&B, installing three blow-up mattresses, and promising to serve breakfast.

They create a Mickey-Mouse website, and three people hire their mattresses for $80, solving their rent problem.

A mental light-bulb is switched on as they consider the potential: they decide to create a proper website to enable people to rent their spare accommodation. They get help from a previous flat-mate, Nathan Blecharczyk, a brilliant engineer.

So they launch their new site, AirBed & Breakfast, during the summer of 2008, hoping to benefit from major events such as the Democratic Party Convention, when rooms are often in short supply.

Lacking funds, they hit on an original way of making some money: taking advantage of the presidential election campaign, which is in full swing, they buy a ton of breakfast cereals, and design a packet for each of the two leading candidates.

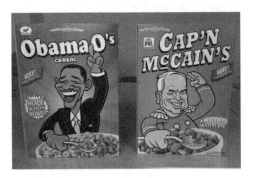

Figure 7: The packets of cereals that enabled AirBed & Breakfast to get off the ground. Proof that a modicum of creativity can overcome a host of problems.

They order 500 of each packet and sell them as a numbered limited edition for $40 apiece: the 'Obama O's' is a sell-out; the 'Cap'n McCain's' do rather less well. But they earn $30,000. Enough to launch AirBed & Breakfast and attract media attention.[217]

A well-known business angel, Fred Wilson, keeps a packet of Obama O's as a souvenir in his conference room

A souvenir of what? Of an enormous mistake he made: not investing in Airbnb when the founders came to see him in 2009. And yet, they had explained to him how they had used these boxes of cereals to raise the money they needed to start their business. And Fred just loved the team. But he decided to give it a miss. Though not before asking them for the packet of Obama O cereals they had brought with them.

Since then, this box has served as a reminder of his mistake. But he also keeps it for another reason: each time an entrepreneur comes to see him and complains

---

217 The founders had the idea of sending their packets of cereals to major hi-tech media enterprises, which resulted in a number of articles, such as this one by TechCrunch: http://en.olivier-roland.com/whats-for-breakfast/

they haven't enough money to launch their business, he gets up, takes the box, and tells this story.

Then he asks: 'If three guys without any money were able to make $30,000 with some packets of cereals, what can you do to earn the money you need to set up your business?'

And what about you? What can you do?

Despite this bright start, their business struggled to get airborne. The three founders were reduced to eating the contents of the unsold Cap'n McCain's packets to save money.

They joined the Y Combinator[218] startup ecosystem in early 2009 and persuaded one of its founders, Paul Graham, to invest $20,000. They used the money to go to New York and promote the site and extend their service to virtually all kinds of accommodation, going way beyond the airbed offer they had previously advertised.

They also changed the name of the site to Airbnb. They then obtained a further $600,000 from investors and were at last able to stop eating cereal. The staff increased to 15, and Brian Chesky spent several months each year living in places rented via Airbnb, garnering valuable information about the service and what needed to be improved.

At last, the business began to grow, but not as fast as they had hoped. So they tried a different approach, getting professional photographers to take shots of some of the apartments. The results were mind-blowing: the apartments featured in professional photographs attracted two or three times more clients than the others!

So Airbnb introduced a new service: every owner renting an apartment on their platform could benefit from a free appointment with a professional photographer. Growth then rocketed, reaching 800 percent in 2011, which also brought a further $7.2 million from new investors.

In 2012, Airbnb overtook the Hilton hotel chain in terms of annual overnight stays... obviously without owning any hotels.

The rest is history. In 2018, Airbnb's annual turnover was more than $2.6 billion, and the business was valued at more than $38 billion.

---

218   The equivalent in Europe is The Family.

Uber

Paris, December 2008, LeWeb Conference. Travis Kalanick and Loïc Le Meur, creator of LeWeb, are walking the snow-covered streets searching for a taxi.

There are none to be found. Travis exclaims: 'Wouldn't it be good if I could order a taxi with a single click from my smartphone!' An idea was born. An idea that many people had had before, no doubt, but Travis was the first to see it as a business opportunity.

Back in the USA, he began work with his partner Garret Camp on the famous application that was to cause such controversy. Garret Camp was an experienced entrepreneur, creator of StumbleUpon, which he had sold on to eBay for $75 million. Nor was Travis Kalanick a raw beginner: he had already created a peer-to-peer sharing app, Red Swoosh, which he had sold on for $19 million.

But this was a very different kind of challenge: revolutionizing the urban transport sector, no less. They spent several months considering and then developing the application, as a part-time project, alongside their 'real' jobs. Then, when the prototype was ready, they conducted a limited trial in New York, with positive results, and launched the service officially in San Francisco on May 31, 2010.

In 2018, eight years after its official launch, Uber was operating in more than 60 countries and 400 cities and was worth more than $120 million. Uber has revolutionized cab travel by offering a user-friendly application; rapid, high-quality rides; a service much better than that of a standard cab; and the convenience of payment by credit or debit card.[219]

THE KEY POINTS: WHY UBER HAS BEEN SUCH A RESOUNDING SUCCESS

- The right idea at the right time, triggered by a personal problem troubling the founders.

- Excellent teamwork.

- Immediate focus on the quality of service.

SELLING A BUSINESS ON AT THE EARLIEST OPPORTUNITY TO GENERATE A LARGE CASH RETURN

Some entrepreneurs set up a business in the hope of being able to sell it on to a larger enterprise for millions or tens of millions, thus securing the freedom to live the rest of their lives as they please.

PayPal

Palo Alto, California, July 1998. Three partners have just created Confinity, a startup whose aim is to enable Palm-Pilot[220] users to send one another money remotely using their device.

For the launch, they recruited James Doohan, the actor who played the engineer Scotty in Star Trek, to announce to the press: 'I've been beaming people up to my

---

219   Parisian taxi drivers were notorious for refusing to take your card, but being very willing to wait (with the meter running, of course!) while you got some cash at an ATM. With Uber, you register your card once with the system, then it is debited automatically every time you hire a ride. Fortunately (and inevitably!), things have now changed where traditional taxis are concerned, and drivers are now obliged to accept payment by bank card.
220   Pocket-sized electronic diaries, ancestors of the smartphone and the tablet.

whole career, but this is the first time I've ever been able to beam money!' This initial service was a fiasco, simply because Palm Pilots were not very widely used.

Fortunately, this didn't discourage the team, who then had an idea that would change everything. They had already developed the technology to send money electronically. But what was the electronic technology in most general use?

The answer was obvious: email.[221] They, therefore, decided to offer a service that would make it possible to exchange money simply via email. PayPal was born.

At first, PayPal had only 24 users: the company's founders and employees. To develop their customer base, they had a simple idea: give $10 to everyone who signed up, and pay them a further $10 if they could involve a friend, plus $10 to the friend in question. A customer, therefore, cost them an average of $20, but the customer base doubled every seven days. After a few months, PayPal had hundreds of thousands of active users. Then the service became associated with eBay, used by most buyers and sellers to settle their transactions.

The rest is history: in 2002, PayPal was sold to eBay for $1.3 billion.

> **THE KEY POINTS: WHY PAYPAL HAS BEEN SUCH A RESOUNDING SUCCESS**
>
> - Perseverance against the odds: the initial idea failed, so they changed their strategy.
>
> - An original marketing idea to encourage growth by word of mouth.
>
> - Merging with their closest competitor, rather than competing.
>
> - An exceptional team.

And the enterprise became the stuff of legend thanks to the culture it developed. Almost all the co-founders of PayPal and many of the first employees went on to found startups which then became giant enterprises or were sold on for hundreds of millions of dollars.

---

221   This has not changed: in 2019, there were more than 3.8 billion users of email (Radicati group), as against 'only' 2.2 billion Facebook users.

- Max Levchin created Slide, a sharing site, which he sold to Google for $182 million in 2010, and co-created Yelp.

- Luke Nosek co-created Founders Fund, a risk-capital company managing a billion-dollar fund.

- Peter Thiel was Facebook's first external investor, and co-created Palantir, a software development and data analysis company, which posted a turnover of almost $1 billion in 2018.

- Elon Musk created SpaceX, a 100 percent private space travel company, which I have already covered in this book, and Tesla Motors.

- Reid Hoffman co-founded LinkedIn, which was taken over by Microsoft for $26.2 billion.

- Chad Hurley, Steve Chen, and Jawed Karim created YouTube, which was one of the fastest and most lucrative re-sales in history.

Which brings us to...

YouTube

January 2005, San Francisco. Chad Hurley and Steve Chen are at a party and shoot some video clips. They would like to send them to a friend but realize that this is impossible: the files are too large to be sent by email, and there is no satisfactory solution for sharing them via a website.

Being flush with money after the sale of PayPal, they decide to roll up their sleeves... and solve the problem themselves. They contact a friend who also worked at PayPal, Jawed Karim, and get busy.

The Youtube.com domain name was registered February 14, 2005 – Valentine's Day.[222] At the time, they still had no clear idea of what their platform might become. The idea that the content of their site could be supplied by the people using it was new, and many were skeptical. At first, they imagined YouTube as a kind of video dating site.[223] When they saw that this wasn't catching on, they tried another idea: people could share their videos within a restricted circle of friends and family.

---

222 Karim later said: 'That's one of the things about being a computer geek. Valentine's Day is just one of many days.'
223 Yep!

The platform was launched on April 23, 2005, and the first video was posted by Karim.[224] At first, it was a struggle: the platform was rudimentary, not even allowing users landing on the home page to search for videos. The only way to view them was to watch those that were displayed at random, and since there were very few of them, it was always the same videos that appeared.

The founders were so desperate at this point that they advertised on Craigslist, offering women $20 for each video they published. They didn't receive a single response.

Then came a turning point. Karim was at a barbecue, also attended by Keith Rabois, a business angel and another former PayPal employee. He was convinced that web-based videos had a bright future and was looking for a startup to popularize the concept. When Karim showed him YouTube, Keith was persuaded and, for the first time in his life, decided to invest directly in a startup.

Keith then spoke about YouTube to an investor, who immediately saw its potential and helped the enterprise obtain $500,000, enabling it to get its head above water and focus on growth.

Six months after it was founded, YouTube was employing 10 people, most of them former PayPal staff. Jawed Karim had gone off to do a master's degree in IT. Not until this time, in September 2005, after days of brainstorming with Julie Supan, the new marketing director, did the co-founder, at last, adopt the positioning that would ensure the platform's success: as a means for ordinary people to share their videos with the whole world. Sustained growth followed, aided by the extreme simplicity of publishing a video online: a simple 'upload video' button was sufficient, whereas competitors were asking for complicated information such as 'What is the codec used for the video?' or 'What is the resolution?'

Another function that ensured YouTube's popularity was the ability to post its videos on any other site, thus enabling people to share videos on their blog or on social media such as MySpace.

At roughly the same time, Google launched Google Video, clearly a serious competitor. But it suffered from the same lack of simplicity as the other players.

In November 2005, YouTube secured the sum of $3 million from Sequoia to boost its growth, and it was around this time that the first brand – Nike – used the platform to publish an advertisement. Then came the first videos that went viral, notably a rap

---

224 An interesting video clip shot at the San Diego zoo, in which Jawed Karim comments on the elephants in the background, noting that they have long trunks! The video is still available online: http://en.olivier-roland.com/zoo-youtube/

music parody that registered 1.2 million hits in 10 days. This was unprecedented. The press coverage further fueled YouTube's growth, to the point when, in mid-2006, the site accounted for 60 percent of the online video market in the USA. The market share of its nearest competitor, Google, was a mere 17 percent.

The platform's growth was phenomenal, and several enterprises began to court YouTube: Microsoft, Yahoo!, New Corporation, and, of course, Google.

The rest is history. Google acquired YouTube by buying shares worth $1.6 billion, 18 months after it was founded. The team then consisted of 55 people.

Many voices were raised denouncing the deal Google had agreed to as 'ridiculous,' but 10 years later, it looks as if it was one of the best deals Google ever made. In 2017, the site received 1.5 billion individual visits a month.

THE KEY POINTS: WHY YOUTUBE HAS BEEN SUCH A RESOUNDING SUCCESS

- The right idea at the right time.

- Born of the founders' personal frustration: how to overcome the difficulty in sharing videos online?

- A motivated team is deeply involved in the project.

- Perseverance, through several changes of direction.

- The right connections at the right time.

- An excellent interface making it very easy to post videos online.

SUMMARY

For the intelligent rebel who has decided to act

➡ Before launching your business, take time to reflect on your ultimate objective. You may wish to build a business empire or just an enterprise that will give you the quality of life you desire. In any case, you can do it. Whatever your objective, whatever your reason, it is possible.

➡ Does that mean it's easy? Certainly not. It's difficult. But it is possible. Many people have achieved even greater things from a starting position below yours. Even more, have failed in wanting to do the same.

So what?

➡ By taking a calculated risk, you will have gained no end of experience, even in the worst-case scenario. And you will be able to bounce back. And of course, it is also quite possible that you will pull it off.

CHAPTER 10
HEAD START: THE RIGHT MINDSET
How to Start a Business Despite Your Fears and Imperfections

You may have the best idea in the world, but if you haven't the right mindset – that of an entrepreneur – it will be like the seed of a wonderful fruit tree falling to the ground in a desert.

What, then, is the entrepreneurial mindset? Over and above the three principles stated at the beginning of this book, let me share a few essential aspects I have identified in my career and when meeting thousands of entrepreneurs in many countries.[225]

PROACTIVITY

Stephen R. Covey gives a wonderful explanation of proactivity in his book on entrepreneurship and personal development, *The 7 Habits of Highly Effective People*, a modern-day classic. Take a few moments to reflect on the concerns that most often exercise your mind. Are you worried about getting good marks at school, finding your soulmate or strengthening your marriage, establishing your business and making it profitable, keeping slim and fit, taxation, your country's foreign policy, a war going on somewhere, an epidemic, or something else? It's quite natural. We all have our worries and concerns. Now I want you to separate these concerns into two categories:

- Those over which you can have some concrete influence, e.g., you can improve your marks at school, find your soulmate or establish your business by making sufficient efforts.

- Those over which you can have no direct influence, e.g., the level of taxation in your country, foreign policy, a war.

---

225 In particular, at conferences I have spoken at in countries as diverse as France, the UK, the USA, Canada (Quebec), Russia and Brazil, and also in the course of my frequent travels.

Suppose we were to draw a circle representing your concerns and, within it, another circle symbolizing the things you can influence directly.

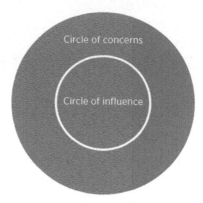

Figure 8: Circles of influence and concern

The more proactive you are, the more you will concentrate on your circle of influence and the things you can act on directly, rather than dwelling on circumstances outside your control that you can do little or nothing about. And, paradoxically, the more you concentrate on your circle of influence, the larger it will become, enabling you to have more impact on the world.

Why? Because the simple fact of having objectives, of making an effort to achieve them, sets you apart from most people. You stand out from the crowd. Secondly, being proactive mathematically increases your chances of achieving your objectives. For instance, if you want to climb Everest, are you more likely to succeed by making concrete efforts to do so or by sitting around and watching *Game of Thrones* on television? Thirdly, when you achieve your objectives, you often gain additional advantages: more money, more skills, more experience, and a wider audience. Yes, indeed. Suddenly you are influencing other people, who, in turn, become movers and shakers. This enlarges your circle of influence and reduces the scope for concern.

For example, if you were concerned about the lack of entrepreneurial spirit in a given country, you might shake things up by setting an example and establishing your own business. This would be far more positive than just moaning about the country's economic backwardness and waiting for someone else to solve the problem for you. It might encourage others to take the plunge and set up a business, which in turn will inspire imitators, and gradually the economic state of the country will improve. And, at the very least, if you fail to inspire others, you will have made an effort to achieve your own objectives, gaining valuable experience in the process (see Chapter 7). And, who knows? You might well succeed, improving your financial situation and that of your family and country while providing products and services of value to society. That's a good example of a proactive mindset, the mindset of someone who makes an effort to achieve their objectives, whatever the circumstances.

The opposite of this state of mind is reactive: constantly reacting to external events, generally in words, but powerless to do anything about them.

Now let's look at some situations through a proactive/reactive prism, aware of course that for all of us, there are times when we are reactive and times when we are proactive.

Subject	Reactive response	Proactive response
Taxation	'Taxes are too high in my country. They're a real pain in the neck!' I do nothing about it, just moan and groan.	I use all legal methods to reduce the amount of tax I pay. I leave the country for a lower-tax environment. I decide I'm going to earn twice as much to make up for the high tax rate.
The economy	'We're in the middle of a recession, the situation is catastrophic, and the whole economy is depressed. I can't possibly set up a business in this environment!' I do nothing and I wait for 'better days.'	'What opportunities have arisen as a result of the recession?' 'What sectors of the economy are not affected (or only slightly affected) by the recession?'
Love life	'I can't find the right partner. It's because I'm so useless; I'll never make it!' I do nothing and wait for the right person to come along.	'I'm going to get a grip and make something of myself one step at a time.' I'm taking a course to boost my self-confidence. I go out more to spread my net as widely as possible.

Subject	Reactive response	Proactive response
Health	'I don't need to bother about my health; I prefer to take things as they come. The health system will take care of me if I fall ill. And if it's an incurable disease, that's just hard luck.' I do nothing and, if I fall ill, I realize too late that I could have taken steps to prevent it or reduce the risk.	I understand that one can enjoy life and care for one's health – the two things go together; one does not preclude the other. I research health issues so that I understand the basics of a healthy lifestyle. I understand that the risks of contracting many diseases can be very much reduced if I adopt the right habits. I learn to eat healthily and well. I look out for a sport that appeals to me, then practice it regularly.
Money	'I'm always hard up. The wealthy are to blame; they should be taxed more heavily so that I can benefit. In any case, money is filthy and corrupting.'	I understand that money is neither good nor bad in itself, and the amount I earn depends directly on: 1. The value I add to the world; 2. My ability to sell this value to people. Therefore, I set myself an earnings target and work to improve my skills so that I can add more value and be a better salesman.
Philosophy	'You are born with a certain set of genes, talents, and skills; there's nothing you can do to change things.' Lulled by this way of thinking, I do nothing to improve myself in the areas I consider important.	I understand that we are all born with greater or lesser potential, but it is up to each one of us to maximize our natural endowment. I want to succeed, and equip myself to do so by learning and being active rather than standing on the sidelines and waiting for someone to do something for me. I explore new areas. I do things that seem scary and take me out of my comfort zone, so as to discover my hidden potential.
Method	'If there was an effective method for doing X, it would already be public knowledge.' I don't look beyond the end of my nose and sit around twiddling my thumbs, not checking the truth of this statement.	'What are the most effective methods used by the people with most expertise in this field?' 'How can I learn and apply them to my own situation?'

But what is your natural tendency? Clearly, it's not possible to be an entrepreneur without being proactive: the very fact of starting a business is a good example of proactivity. And by being proactive, the mind is always searching for solutions, albeit imperfect ones, rather than continually rehearsing problems that seem insoluble.

In your opinion, which attitude is more likely to produce a solution? Proactivity is, therefore, an essential component of an entrepreneur's mindset.

NO ONE EXPECTS YOU TO BE GOOD WHEN YOU START OUT

Navegantes, a small town on the coast of Brazil. Erico Rocha, a friend and exceptional entrepreneur, is teaching me to surf, a new activity for me. The first stage is to climb onto the board while pushing it in front of you, in the hope of being able to ride a wave – a difficult maneuver for an outright beginner like me.

Finally, after several failed attempts, I manage to kneel on the board while keeping it stable. It's hard to keep my balance, but I do just enough to stay on the board and steer it to the right and avoid some swimmers. Still kneeling. Then, as the wave slowly dies and approaches the shore, I overbalance and flop into the water. When I get to my feet, a young girl is laughing her head off, and everyone around her is smiling. I suddenly feel annoyed. Hang on a minute. Am I going to take it badly? At last, I too break into a smile. At least I have made a little girl's day while learning something myself. And obviously, there is no malice involved: I'm just an amusing curiosity in a world of experienced surfers. And that's OK.

No one expects you to be brilliant when you are learning a new activity. Falling flat on your face is a normal part of the learning process, as is the laughter of the idle bystanders who have nothing personal against you. You just have to accept that you may appear funny or pathetic while learning and not get upset. It's the same for everyone.

When you start educating yourself, when you begin planning your business, initially, you will expend a lot of energy for minimal result, like me, with my surfboard. You may even make people laugh, or frighten them, or even be an object of pity. It's all par for the course.

So I retrieved my surfboard and went back into the sea for another attempt. The sun was shining, the temperature ideal, the sea, and the landscape magnificent, and I was having my first surfing lesson. Uninspiring though the initial results may have been, I loved this learning process, just as I love the experience of traveling, even before reaching my destination. I climbed back onto my board and fell off again.

Then, after a few attempts, I, at last, managed to stay upright for a few seconds, before again coming a cropper.

Brilliant! I was on my way!

JUST DOING IT, DESPITE YOUR IMPERFECTIONS

Scottsdale, Arizona, a few weeks earlier. Although I have overcome the pathological shyness of my youth, I am still nervous about speaking to groups of people, and there I was facing an audience of 70 entrepreneurs from all over the world – a daunting prospect.

So I began my talk, sharing my current project: the book you are now reading. I have a strong French accent, which was accentuated by my nervousness. Seated in front of me was an audience of world-class entrepreneurs, and I took the opportunity to ask them about a subject closely related to this book: their education. I committed a few howlers with my English (e.g., saying 'teached' instead of 'taught'), but I got some interesting answers, for instance, the fact that, for two-thirds of them, their current occupation bore no relation to what they learned at school.

Then Jeff Walker, my mentor, a brilliant entrepreneur who had recently been the subject of a lengthy article in *Forbes Magazine*, had this to say: 'Olivier, I think we should stop these questions and talk about the thing you don't want to talk about.' Gulp. Not what I had been expecting. Seventy pairs of eyes shifted from Jeff to me, then back again, waiting for developments.

'You began work on this book one month ago. How many pages have you written? How much time do you spend on it each day? Have you a plan, and do you know how many pages you have to write each day to finish on time?'

Ouch! Jeff had touched a sensitive nerve. Very sensitive. I held my breath, then confessed I had written only six pages in the first month and that, though I had an overall plan for the book, I had no idea how many pages I had to write each day to finish in time. I had just admitted in front of all these entrepreneurs that I was procrastinating, intimidated by the magnitude of the task. Jeff and the others gave me some advice on how to increase my productivity, and so finish the book on time. They asked some pointed questions, which were very humbling.

Then I realized that my fly was open! That really did it. Strong foreign accent, nervousness, pointed questions, and the revelation to this audience of first-rate entrepreneurs that I was struggling to get my project off the ground. And my fly.

You couldn't say my presentation was perfect. You couldn't say my project was perfect. Nor could you say that I was perfect, far from it!

But I went through with it nonetheless, and the advice I received has helped me write the book, right up to this decisive moment, as you are in the process of reading these lines. I would never have reached this point if, rather than embracing my imperfections, I had waited for the 'right moment,' if I had waited for everything to be perfect, if I had let fear paralyze me.

The fact is that all the projects I have carried out have been imperfect – start, middle, and finish – with countless mistakes of every kind. And when I completed them, I was still just as imperfect as I am today.

When I left school at 18, I was shy, sickly, and worse-looking than Woody Allen. When I set up my first business, I had no professional experience, no network, no strategy for winning customers. When I recruited my first employee, I was lucky in my choice, but I made every possible mistake in managing him, with the result that he left after six weeks. The person I hired to replace him almost got me taken to court.

When I created my first blog, I had no real experience of writing and no idea what subjects would interest my readers or how to promote my articles. When I produced my first online video, the webcam image and sound quality were atrocious, the lighting a foggy yellow, and the camera angle didn't exactly show me to advantage. But at least my haircut was OK, unlike when I shot my first marketing video. When I was first interviewed on the radio, I couldn't get to the studio due to a train strike and had to do the whole thing over the phone. I was as nervous as could be and had the horrible impression that I was making a fool of myself before thousands of people each time I stammered an answer. (In fact, the broadcast was a success, and no one wrote a nasty letter advising me never to go on air again.)

We are all far from perfect. We all make countless mistakes and, when you start a business, when you set about educating yourself, you will be no exception. In the end, we shall always be imperfect. But you will have done something that matters, something praiseworthy, something that adds value, for you and for others. Don't let your imperfections prevent you from embarking on projects, pursuing your dreams. No one expects you to be perfect.

BURN YOUR BOATS OR MINIMIZE RISK?

Carthage, 310 BCE: Agathocles, the tyrant of Syracuse and the King of Sicily, landed on the shores of powerful Carthage on a punitive expedition.

He had just lost an important battle against the North African Carthaginians, who were masters of half of Sicily, losing the support of several major towns that had previously been his allies... and was besieged in his own city.

Desperate, he put everything on the line: he took the elite of his army, put them aboard ship, and sailed to attack Carthage on its home soil. It was a bold move – as if Cuba, besieged by the USA, had raised the siege by attacking Washington. Not to mention that the Carthaginians were masters of the Mediterranean, and Agathocles knew he couldn't hope to defeat their fleet.

But he also knew this was the thing his enemies were least expecting; they were not used to fighting on home territory. So it was do or die.

When they landed in Carthage, he wanted to make an impression on his men and show them they had no other choice. He made them burn their boats. All of them. Then it was simple: either he and his troops would be victorious, or they would perish. There was no alternative. This was the origin of the expression 'to burn one's boats,' meaning to throw oneself into a project with no possibility of going back.

Many people think this is the most common, or indeed the only way, to act as an entrepreneur. To set up a business, you'd do best to quit your job and put yourself in the most desperate position to succeed.

I'm glad I can tell you that this is a myth. It is one possible approach, among others, and is adopted by very few successful entrepreneurs. The approach I recommend and have adopted is simply to minimize the risks involved. This means:

- Limiting your financial exposure as much as possible
- Thoroughly testing your initial hypothesis, committing a bare minimum of money, time, and energy
- Starting your project on a part-time basis, alongside your existing job or your studies
- Or at least arranging for a negotiated departure, so you can receive unemployment benefits while pursuing your project
- Making the most of any financial assistance or subsidies you are entitled to

Shrewd entrepreneurs adopt Lean Startup strategies and other less well-known techniques to gain experience that will enable them to test out their planned product/service in the real world, with a minimum expenditure of time, money, and energy. In fact, the aim of the second part of this book is precisely to teach you these techniques.

PERSEVERING IS GOOD; PERSEVERING AGAINST ALL THE ODDS IS EVEN BETTER!

If you go to any beach where there are cliffs, you will see just how much they have been sculpted by the waves.

If you tried to do the same with your hand, you would hurt yourself badly: rock is harder than human flesh. And yet, if you strike water with your hand, it goes in more easily than a knife through butter. How is it possible that an element less resistant than your body can sculpt an element that is so much harder? Simple: it is the tireless action of water on the rock over a very long period that shapes the cliff, atom by atom. Such is the power of persistence.

But there is persistence, and there is obstinacy. If your objective is to sculpt the cliff with your head, and you persist until you achieve your goal, not only will you be unconscious and have the most enormous lump on your head, but you will also most likely be awarded the Oscar for the stupidest human undertaking of the year.[226] Because this is obviously not the right method.

There are, on the other hand, hundreds of different ways you might effectively sculpt this cliff. It all depends on what you mean by 'sculpt.' If it means 'create a work of art,' then maybe you should learn the art of carving. That would entail finding a visual arts teacher and following his or her instructions, and if you find you are not achieving the desired results quickly enough, changing teachers, changing methods, or, better still, taking some trial lessons with three different teachers, and choosing the best. Because, in the final analysis, the art of persevering is really the art of persevering intelligently, i.e., 'meta-persisting.' Rather than hitting your head against a brick wall, recognize that you have taken a wrong turn and change method without losing sight of your final objective.

But I see that many of you are asking: 'Okay, but how do you know if you should persevere on your present trajectory, and when to change method?' It's a good question, and I won't lie to you: there is no blanket answer.

In my fields of expertise, I often see people who give up when they are within a whisker of success; if they had persisted just a little longer, they would have begun to enjoy the fruits of their labors. For example, a blogger in the field of financial independence had done excellent work and was close to achieving the respectable figure of 50,000 visits a month. He had many fans, and all the signs were that

---

226   On the other hand, a video of you hitting your head against the cliff would no doubt attract millions of visits on YouTube, so if you are looking for celebrity at any price, go for it!

he would create his first product and begin to turn his blog into a real business. Instead, he decided it wasn't worth the effort and dropped out.

On the other hand, I see people who insist on following a method that clearly doesn't work for them. So, how do you know when you should persevere and when you have been persevering long enough? The bad news is that it all depends. But the good news is that some basic rules will help you to decide.

Go find Yoda

Here is the first basic rule: go and consult more experienced people who have achieved the objective you have set yourself. Quickly explain your situation and ask: 'What would you do in my place? Try something else or persist in my present course?'

Even experts can't predict with 100 percent certainty whether a person will succeed using such and such a method (otherwise, publishing houses and literary agents would all be mega-rich), but consulting several may remove some of the unknowns and steer you in the right direction.

When you are about to give up...

Here is another simple rule: when you lose motivation because you are not getting results, try something else rather than giving up completely.

Maybe a fresh approach will increase your motivation, and you won't be starting from scratch because you have acquired experience from the first method. Secondly, because you lost motivation the first time, you will be more likely to put in place actions, habits, reminders, etc. to avoid getting demotivated again.

Cherry-picking

If you have reached a plateau, whereas previously you were making good progress and were quite satisfied with your mentor, maybe you can clear the blockage by doing some exploration elsewhere.

First, discuss the situation with your mentor and ask his or her advice on moving forward. If that doesn't work, go on a tour of other schools and ask people more experienced than yourself for their opinions. Note all the ideas that come your way and try out those that seem most interesting.

The power of introspection

Before dropping a method or a project, perform an analysis: over a whole day (or all the time you are engaged in your activity), note what you are doing and how long it takes. At the end of the day, ask yourself the following questions for each activity:

- Why am I doing this?

- Is it really necessary?

- Is this one of the 20 percent of actions that achieve 80 percent of results?

- What results has this brought me in the last two months?

- And since I began doing it?

- Is there an activity or action I could do that would achieve better results?

The ideal, of course, is to spend a whole week analyzing your activities – if your work lends itself to such analysis.

In conclusion: How I almost went bankrupt after six months

Six months after setting up my first business, it was on the verge of going bust. It was a disaster. I had left school 18 months earlier and had thrown myself body and soul into the project. But, because of my inexperience, I had failed to implement an effective strategy for getting customers. In my naïvety, I had shelled out a lot for advertising in rubbish magazines. Result: the cupboard was bare and, even though I paid myself only €200 a month, the money wasn't coming in quick enough.

So what should I do? If I went on like this, my business would soon be in the red, which was a problem because the bank had required me to stand security for my own debts. So I had to make a decision: stop immediately and cut my losses, or analyze my mistakes, decide how to rectify them and find the money to continue.

The principal requirement of a business owner at such times is that he can't afford to bury his head in the sand; he has to take the bull by the horns.

The truth is that anything can happen to an entrepreneur. Despite all precautions, his business might be destroyed by an earthquake, his flagship product might be rendered obsolete, or an employee might leave and steal a large part of his clientele. But an entrepreneur can never afford to bury his head in the sand when his business is threatened. Never.

Despite my inexperience, I was well aware of this, so I analyzed the situation: I was beginning to gain some regular customers, the grapevine was working, and, finally, but for my poor advertising strategy, I would have had enough money to carry on for several months. Obviously, I wouldn't make the same mistakes again, and I was confident that within a few months, I could reach the break-even point when the income from the business would cover all the expenses.

However, I still had to find the money I needed to tide me over for the next few months. I had borrowed a total of €15,000 to set up my business, €3,750 of which had been lent by family members. I had just repaid the €600 lent me by my maternal grandparents, having temporarily buried my head in the sand. So, sick at heart and with a real feeling of shame, I picked up the phone to call and ask them if they could lend me the same amount again – temporarily. Fortunately, they agreed without any fuss, which was a great relief. Then I went to the bank, from which I had borrowed €3,750, and asked for an additional loan of the same amount – the amount I reckoned I would need before I reached the profitability threshold. The bank manager refused and even tried to flog me some insurance... What a nice guy!

I then contacted a business mentoring organization, which had previously lent me €7,500. I explained everything in detail: the mistakes I had made, my analysis of the situation, why I needed more capital, how this would solve the problem – rather than see the money disappear as with previous loans. They considered the situation carefully and arrived at the same conclusion as I had: the business model was viable; the problem was simply one of cash flow. They mentioned a business startup loan that had just been introduced by the government, which enabled me to borrow a further €3,750, precisely the amount I needed. Wow!

Obviously, neither they nor I was 100 percent sure things would work out. But they believed in me, mainly because I had demonstrated that my head was screwed on, and I faced my problems. And, in the end, this insignificant little sum was just what I needed to get my head above water. My business, which might have lasted for only six months and been a resounding failure, in fact, survived (and thrived) for ten years and only ceased trading because I eventually sold it on so I could embark on further adventures.

The moral of the story: persevering against all the odds also means taking the bull by the horns and not burying your head in the sand. This is undoubtedly the essential quality that no entrepreneur can do without.

CHOOSING THE RIGHT FRIENDS

In 2007, an article[227] published in the serious *New England Journal of Medicine* caused a tremendous stir. Researchers had analyzed a database of 12,067 people, who had been monitored for 32 years as part of a celebrated study on heart disease in the town of Framingham.

This was a complete database, containing precise information about relationships among the participants (who was friends with whom, who was whose neighbor, who were blood relations and how closely related) and the body mass index of each person and how it had changed over the 32 years.

The original feature of this survey was that the researchers had asked themselves this question: do people who are overweight influence others and so cause them to be overweight too?

The answer was a massive yes: the simple fact of having a friend who became obese increased a person's own risk of becoming obese by 57 percent! And if you had a close friend who became obese, the risk of becoming obese yourself increased by 171 percent. Yes, indeed, 171 percent! Nor did it stop there: the researchers also found that having an obese neighbor had no influence, and family members had less influence than friends. And the most interesting thing? Even if your obese friend lived hundreds of miles away, the influence was still strong.

Don't choose your friends based on their waistline but influence them to cultivate a healthy lifestyle which will be good for them and for you. And surround yourself with proactive people who drive you forward, rather than friends who are constantly complaining and doing nothing.

HOW TO GET LUCKY

'Luck is not only a skill but a skill you need to work at.'

PHILIPPE GABILLIET

*'Luck is what happens
when preparation meets opportunity.'*

OPRAH WINFREY

---

227 'The Spread of Obesity in a Large Social Network over 32 Years,' Christakis N.A. et al., *The New England Journal of Medicine*, 2007.

Richard Wiseman, as well as being a magician, having a doctorate in psychology, writing several best-sellers, and creating a very popular YouTube channel with several million subscribers,[228] has also found the time to study the phenomenon of luck from a scientific point of view.

He studied more than 400 people who described themselves either as particularly lucky or as particularly unlucky. The conclusions of his research are clear: although most unlucky people have no idea why they are out of luck, their bad luck is caused above all by their behavior and state of mind.

One of his experiments was to give volunteers a newspaper, asking them to count how many photographs it contained. On average, the unlucky people took two minutes to count the photographs, while it took the lucky people just a few seconds. Why? On page 2, he had inserted a message taking up half the page in (very) large letters: 'Stop counting. There are 43 photographs in this newspaper.'

Everyone should have seen it, but the people who described themselves as unlucky were much more likely to miss it than the others. Why? Because they were far too busy counting the photographs to notice the message.

Just for fun, Richard Wiseman added another enormous message half-way through the paper: 'Stop counting. Tell the person conducting the experiment you have seen this message and earn £250.' And again, the people who described themselves as unlucky were too busy counting the photos to notice it.

Another of his discoveries was that unlucky people are more tense and anxious than others. Now the fact is that anxious people have difficulty in concentrating on what they are doing, occupied as they are in thinking of their problems, which might well explain why they are more accident-prone. Also, anxiety may reduce the efficacy of the immune system and increase the risk of falling ill.

OK, but how do you get lucky, then? Good question. The conclusion of all Wiseman's research is that lucky people generate their own luck as a result of four basic principles:

- They are skilled in creating opportunities for themselves – and being aware of them.

- They take 'lucky' decisions by trusting their intuition.

- They engender positive 'self-fulfilling prophecies' by having positive expectations about their future.

---

228 Quirkology.

- They have a resilient attitude, which makes them see the good side of life by regularly imagining what would have happened in worse cases.

On the strength of this discovery, Wiseman founded a 'school of good luck' to teach these skills and determine if it made a difference in people's lives. The results were impressive: a month after enrolling, 80 percent of the volunteers said they felt happier and luckier. So here are the three easiest and most 80/20 techniques for increasing your luck, according to Richard Wiseman.[229]

1. Listen to your intuition

This doesn't mean transforming yourself into a hippy and trying to foresee the future wreathed in marijuana smoke, but simply listening to your intelligence and your gut instincts.

According to Wiseman, lucky people are those who are also able to discern their emotions because emotions often serve as an alarm bell, and this leads them to examine certain decisions more carefully.

So, the next time you have a slightly tricky decision to make, listen to what both your intelligence and your emotions are prompting you to do.

2. Break with routine

Routine is the enemy of luck. Unlucky people tend to do the same thing: taking the same route, performing the same activities, or speaking to the same people at parties and events.

Try to introduce more variety into your life and make a game of it. For example, try to perform as many tasks as you can with your non-dominant hand for a day, explore five new routes for getting to work over five days, or speak to everyone wearing a certain color at a party.

3. Count your blessings

Lucky people always tend to compare their situation with a worse scenario that might have happened.

---

229 If you want to take this further, I warmly recommend his book *The Luck Factor.*

Practice this simple and effective exercise: regularly imagine a much worse situation that you might be in. It might be a realistic situation (what would have happened if I hadn't avoided that car at the last moment?) or an unrealistic one (where might life be like for me now if I had been born in one of the poorest countries in Africa?). Begin by doing this once a day for seven days, like the healthy skeptic you are, and see to what extent this peps up your life.

This apparently silly but amazingly effective exercise has been known to Buddhists for thousands of years and practiced by Stoics since classical times. You try it, too, and tell me what you make of it.

SUMMARY

For the intelligent rebel who has decided to act

➡ Your mind needs to be fertile ground for ideas and opportunities to germinate in.

➡ Distinguish between things you can influence and things you can't and concentrate on the former.

➡ Understand that it is better to act despite your imperfections than to wait forever for things to be perfect, especially since no one expects you to be perfect, especially when you are just beginning.

➡ Take calculated risks, and understand the difference between obstinacy and true perseverance, which is perseverance against all the odds: retain your objective but change the method.

➡ Surround yourself with people who are going in the same direction and share your mindset.

➡ Learn to get lucky: this is a skill and an important one for an entrepreneur.

CHAPTER 11
DIGGING THE FOUNDATIONS
Finding the Idea on Which to Base Your Business

This stage is the downfall of most aspiring entrepreneurs: they have a burning desire to start a business but have no concrete idea on which to base it. If this is your situation, here is some practical advice. But if you already have an idea for your business, you can go straight on to the next chapter.

THE WINNING TRIAD: EXPERTISE, PASSION, AND MARKET

Let's begin by stimulating your creativity. Take a sheet of paper or open a file on your computer. Go on, do it now!

Brilliant. Now, at the top of this document, write 'Things I'm passionate about.' Now write down 10 things that really excite you. You will find that the first three or four come easily, then things get a bit more complicated. Don't stop until you have listed at least 10. If you really can't think of 10, write down some activities or areas you are keen on, rather than really passionate about.

Done it? Good! Now let's do the same exercise for your talents and areas of expertise. Take another sheet, or open a new document, then write at the top 'My talents and areas of expertise.' Then write down 10 of your talents, areas in which you are gifted, and have experience. Once again, don't stop until you have listed 10. And if you can't think of 10 talents or areas of expertise, write down fields in which you are competent or have experience, but without being especially gifted. Stop reading this chapter and do it now. This will really help you in finding your business idea.

Done that? Good! These two documents will serve as a basis for thinking about your business idea. Now go on reading. (If you haven't done the exercise, are about to go on reading, and feel guilty about it, stop; continuing will be pointless. You would do better to close the book, get on with your current tasks, and re-read this chapter when you are in a more receptive state of mind).

There are two main ways you can proceed: adopt a 'conventional' business idea, one that is tried and tested, that may have been around for a long time, or try something innovative.

Finding a conventional business idea

The fact that there are already millions of bakers' shops doesn't mean there is no place for yours. The same is true for thousands of businesses with a tried-and-tested model that, in many cases, has proved successful; no need to reinvent the wheel when becoming an entrepreneur.

Start with yourself. Take a careful look at your list of passions and talents. Do they include a field in which you could start a conventional-type business and which you would find satisfying? And better – in fact, ideal – is there a business idea that spontaneously enthuses you, and for which you have a talent or a skill?

Coming up with an idea based on your passions, your skills, or the two together has both advantages and disadvantages.

Coming up with an idea based on your passions

Advantages:

- You will be motivated by the nature of the field in which you are starting out.

- You will have a better chance of developing expertise, possibly exceptional expertise, in a field you love (fields you are enthusiastic about but in which you haven't yet developed any skills are simply fields you haven't yet experienced).

- You might possibly realize one of your dreams by becoming skilled in a field you love while earning a living as a by-product.

Disadvantages:

- You will nevertheless have to develop your skills from scratch, or nearly so, which may take time, or you will have to recruit or go into partnership with someone who has the necessary technical skills (which increases the risk because you will have additional outgoings each month).

- Being enthusiastic about the field concerned and acquiring the necessary technical competence yourself or recruiting someone should not obscure that managing a business also demands other skills.

- Sometimes, in the long term, working in a field you love results in associating unpleasant feelings with your work (due to awkward customers, stress, financial problems, etc.). So you will be less and less keen on the field concerned, to the point where it is no longer something you love. This doesn't always happen, but it is a possibility. And there is also a question of time: maybe you are mad about surfing, but not for more than 10 hours a week, and doing it for 20 hours might transform a very agreeable activity into hell on earth.

Coming up with an idea in a field in which you have expertise

Advantages:

- You already have the technical skills needed to work in your chosen field, which will free you up to prospect for your first customers and deal with other aspects of the business (finance, recruitment, management, etc.).

- Experience may bring you several initial assets: an existing customer base, a network of suppliers and partners, greater credibility, etc. If you have previously earned your living as an employee on the strength of this expertise, the creation of a business in the same field may be a natural next step, reducing your fear of taking the plunge and spurring you to action.

Disadvantages:

- If you are not passionate about the field you have chosen, once the initial enthusiasm of setting up the business has passed, you run the risk of being bored to death and feeling you are not doing something really worthwhile.

- Being technically competent in the field should not blind you because managing a business also demands other skills.

Coming up with an idea in an area of expertise that you are also passionate about (or vice-versa)

Advantages:

- This is the ideal scenario: you are passionate about the idea and competent in the field concerned. You will, therefore, have the necessary experience, competence, and motivation, which will boost your chances of success.

- As you have already practiced this activity and are still passionate about it, you are less likely to be ground down and discouraged than if you were starting out with great enthusiasm in an area in which you had no expertise. It will be even better if you have already practiced this activity professionally, as you will have endured the associated stress and kept your passion intact. The initial enthusiasm is then likely to be maintained after you have established the business.

Disadvantages:

- Starting out on this basis could blind you to the fact that running a business also demands other competencies.

Don't forget that however you set up your business, you will also have to learn to manage it financially, find new customers and persuade them to buy your products and services, possibly recruit and manage staff, and so on. Fortunately, there are many books and training courses to help you develop these areas of expertise. The book you are now reading is a good starting point!

EXPLOITING EXISTING IDEAS BY TAKING ON A FRANCHISE

Imagine you wanted to open a fast-food outlet and sell hamburgers. You have a choice between opening your own restaurant, 'Chez Gaston,' or opening a McDonald's. Which solution do you think will enable you to reach many people and achieve profitability more quickly?

You are no doubt familiar with the idea of franchises: networks of enterprises you can join to run your own business. Generally, you pay an entrance fee and commit to paying a percentage of your turnover to the franchise.

In return, you are trained by the network in methods of operation that have proved effective, and you benefit from various other advantages related to the size of the franchise: group purchasing at more competitive prices, legal and technical support, mass advertising of the brand, etc. For many people just starting out, it is a good way of learning to manage a business, following a tried-and-tested method, and benefiting from the support of a group.

However, not all franchises are born equal. And there is a lack of transparency about the way many of them operate. For example, their websites often state that 90 percent of businesses are still going strong after five years (sometimes the figure is 80 percent). The problem is that no source is given to back up these figures.

In fact, some authoritative sources indicate that the success rate for franchises is much the same as for conventional businesses. In a letter written in 2005, Matthew

Shay, president of the International Franchise Association (IFA), called his members to order as follows:

> *It has come to our attention that some IFA-member companies may be providing information about franchising that is long out of date and no longer presents an accurate picture of the sector.*
>
> *Of particular concern is information claiming that the success rate of franchised establishments is much greater than that of independent small businesses.*
>
> *Many years ago, the US Department of Commerce conducted studies about franchising, which presented such statistics. This information is no longer valid. The agency stopped conducting such studies in 1987.*
>
> *We strongly urge you to remove any information from your Web site and published materials that make such a claim. The use of such data, in the absence of current research, could mislead prospective franchisees who are attempting to conduct responsible investigations.*[230]

The studies mentioned by Matthew Shay were, in fact, surveys carried out by the US Department of Commerce from 1984 to 1986, to which barely 2,000 franchisees voluntarily responded, and which indicated a failure rate of 5 percent after five years of business activity.[231]

This figure can be easily explained by the fact that, for obvious reasons, many of the failed franchises didn't receive the questionnaire, and those that did were not strongly motivated to reply. And yet, even now, most people continue to read and believe that setting up a franchise is less risky than trying to establish a conventional business.

Now you know the true picture. It is also clear that serious franchises offer real advantages to aspiring entrepreneurs, but this doesn't necessarily mean you will have greater success than if you adopt your own approach... or indeed that you will succeed at all.

But this doesn't necessarily mean that you will have more success than if you were to open a conventional restaurant or develop your own approach – or even that you

---

230 http://en.olivier-roland.com/outdated-franchising-statistics/
231 'Franchising in the Economy 1984–1986,' US Department of Commerce.

will succeed at all. Moreover, some agencies will investigate the franchise network you are thinking of joining.

FROM LOCAL TO NATIONAL

Rather than join a franchise scheme, you might try to create your own. The basic idea is:

1. To have a business that works very well, with all processes carefully thought out, calibrated, and improved.

2. To duplicate this efficient business in all places where the thinking and testing behind the better procedures will give it an edge over competitors.

It's a bit like taking modern chemists armed with the scientific method to a town where there are still alchemists using medieval formulae. Not a level playing field!

Do you remember the story of McDonald's? How Ray Kroc felt like Newton when the apple dropped on his head? He immediately understood that their way of running a restaurant was infinitely superior to any he had come across previously. And that it could be duplicated.

Sometimes a discovery is made locally, and no one thinks of duplicating it in other places. This could be a stroke of luck for an entrepreneur who takes hold of the idea. Let me tell you another real-life story that illustrates this very clearly.

HOW NESTLÉ MADE A FORTUNE WITH ITS COOKIES

The early 1930s, in the USA. Nestlé managers, seeing the poor sales figures for their Semi-Sweet chocolate, are thinking of stopping production. But they notice that the chocolate is selling very well in a small town in Massachusetts. They might have overlooked this detail but decide to send someone to investigate.

They discover that an innkeeper had invented a new cake recipe that has taken the town by storm, and she is using Nestlé chocolate as an ingredient. Taking stock of this, the Nestlé people offer Ruth Wakefield, the innkeeper, a deal: Nestlé gets the right to print her recipe on all boxes of Semi-Sweet chocolate, and to own the recipe, in exchange for a free lifetime supply of chocolate. The 'cakes' in question were cookies,

> a truly original concept because previously chocolate chips were not mixed in with the dough during the cooking process.
>
> Sales of the chocolate took off, and Nestlé made a fortune selling cookies throughout the USA, then worldwide.
>
> This would never have happened if the company managers hadn't decided to investigate the exceptional sales in that one small town.

THE TIME MACHINE, ONE OF THE BEST SOURCES OF IDEAS

The easiest way to get business ideas is to do some time-traveling. If you could travel into the future and see what works, and then return to the present, it would be easy to know what business to start up, wouldn't it? Or, if you could travel into the past, you would easily find out what type of business to establish there based on what works at the present time.

Very well, then. Great. That's all you need to do!

Probably a lot of you are now thinking a) that I must have taken some strong, probably illegal, substance, and b) that the editor must have lost concentration at this point! But really, my point is simple. The concept I am about to enlarge on is perfectly summarized by a quotation from the cyberpunk writer William Gibson:[232]

The future is already here. It's just not evenly distributed yet.

Time travel in the future

If you live in the USA, you have an advantage because the States is far ahead in many areas, though they are often too focused on the domestic market when they first start a business. Look around you: there are many ideas that a curious and open-minded entrepreneur could take up and implement elsewhere. For example, the German Samwer brothers have become experts in identifying startups that work well in the USA and creating enterprises with an identical concept in Europe and elsewhere. Rocket Internet (including subsidiaries) currently employs 30,000 people, has a turnover of €2.2 billion, and heads up hundreds of startups,

---

232 Who I am particularly fond of, as you will already have deduced, since this is the third time I have mentioned him.

all clones of concepts that originated elsewhere and, in many cases, dominate the market in the countries where they were first established.

Maybe you don't feel comfortable with the idea of 'copying' formulae that have worked elsewhere. But there is no harm in implementing a concept that works in another country but would take years to reach your own (or might never arrive) because going international isn't a priority for the business that first developed it.

In entrepreneurship, innovation is an overvalued concept. We are talking here about business, not about writing poetry or music. Most new businesses rely on ideas that have existed for centuries: bakeries, hotels, restaurants, hairdressers' and so on. And all businesses without exception, even the most innovative, rely on something that already exists.

Once the wheel was invented, it was invented. There is no point in trying to invent a 'square wheel,' which wouldn't be a wheel, just for the pleasure of having created something original. On the contrary, the entrepreneur who introduces the wheel to their country for the first time performs an immense service, paving the way for hundreds of new applications. Just don't claim to have invented it and be honest that it is an imported concept.

This is why, when a company innovates and opens up a new market, creates a new product or service that proves profitable, it often gives the signal for hundreds of new enterprises to rush into the breach. Sometimes it pays to be the innovator; at others, it is the followers that turn out to be the winners.

The added value contributed by the Samwer brothers doesn't consist in the invention of an original concept, but in the perfect execution of an existing idea and in their expertise in implementing these ideas in many countries. They have, for example, created startups in countries often cold-shouldered by Western entrepreneurs, such as Nigeria.

Moreover, some of the companies that have been copied have greatly benefited from the arrangement. When Groupon wanted to set up in Germany, they acquired the 'copy' Citydeals and recruited the three brothers to help them with their international strategy (as I write this, they own 6 percent of Groupon, worth the equivalent of $1 billion). As they put it: 'Groupon taught us the business, and we taught them about internationalization.'

So, if you are American, the good news is that traveling to almost any other country is like 'coming back from the future.' And if you are not, you can study what is going on 'over there' to find business ideas to apply back home.

Time travel in the past

The best way of traveling back into the past is to leave your own country and visit a less developed one. A trip to India or the Philippines, for example, would show you that they still lack many products and services that are commonplace elsewhere, particularly on the Internet.

FINDING NEW IDEAS: THE CREATIVE ENTREPRENEUR

Are you aware that modern man made his appearance roughly 200,000 years ago and that:

1. The domestication of animals began roughly 15,000 years ago, starting with dogs? For 185,000 years, nobody had realized that animals could be of use for anything other than being hunted and eaten.

2. Agriculture was invented only 12,000 years or so ago? It took 188,000 years, or 1,880 centuries, for people to discover that they could, to some extent, control the growth of plants rather than just harvesting wild ones.

3. The wheel was invented only 5,500 years or so ago? For almost 195,000 years, not a single person had the idea of constructing wheels to facilitate the transportation of heavy loads.

4. Writing was invented at roughly the same time as the wheel? Previously, no one had thought of communicating the spoken word with written signs.

5. And – most importantly, I think – ice cream was invented around 4,000 years ago? But it was not until 3,900 years later that someone had the idea of the cornet.

These examples show that, all around us, there are always ideas that can be exploited – ideas so simple that, while they enrich their inventor, other people are left wondering: 'Why on earth didn't I think of that myself?'

Reread the stories about how certain businesses were created in Chapter 9, and identify those born of their founders' frustrations. How many was it? Adopt an attitude that will inspire such ideas in you. Listen in particular for statements containing sentiments such as these:

- It's useless.

- It's not much use.

- That really annoys me.

- It would be good if...

- That's not very clever.

Whenever someone says something like this when speaking of a product or service, whether free or paid, you know they are pointing out some failing. Offering a solution minus this failing could make you a fortune. Meanwhile, this is an initial idea that you can compare with the data from the market study (*see p.223*), and you can have dozens of ideas of this kind every week.

One piece of advice: note your idea down as soon as it comes to mind, in a notebook you keep in your pocket or on your phone. Have you ever had an idea that was so brilliant you were sure you would remember it your whole life long, then the next day you vaguely remembered you had had an idea...? If your answer is yes, note down your ideas as soon as they come to mind.

SUMMARY

For the intelligent rebel who has decided to act

➡ Make a list of the things you are passionate about. Then make a list of your areas of expertise. See if some of the former match some of the latter.

➡ Analyze the economic/financial potential of each of your interests and areas of expertise.

➡ The ideal is to start your business in a field you are passionate about and already have some expertise. Financial potential is essential if you want to create a viable business.

➡ A franchise can be a good way of getting started in business without having to start from scratch. But it isn't a miracle solution, and there are also risks and disadvantages.

➡ As a general rule, be attentive to your surroundings, putting your brain in 'ideas search engine' mode.

➡ Take note of what works particularly well, as well as things that people complain about. Can you be the person who offers a service or product that solves the problem concerned?

➡ Going abroad is a great way of time traveling: some countries are ahead in certain fields, and you can harvest ideas to bring back home with you; others are behind the times, and you can bring new ideas that have become commonplace where you usually live.

To help you put the activities described in this chapter into practice, go to http://en.olivier-roland.com/idea to receive an email with a series of activities and challenges that will give you the necessary motivation.

CHAPTER 12
THE LEAN REVOLUTION
How the Intelligent Rebel Establishes a Business

'Before your business makes its first sale, it is nothing more than a set of unproven ideas that you are spending money on.'
MICHAEL MASTERSON, READY, FIRE, AIM

THE LEAN STARTUP METHOD, A REVOLUTION IN THE APPROACH TO STARTING A BUSINESS

May 1999. The moment when a friend and I had a simple idea: since we could easily and quickly put the right problems that seemed insoluble to our mates, why not offer a home computer repair service for members of the public? Would they be prepared to pay:

- For a rapid home-based service to deal with urgent problems, even if their computer was eligible for after-sales service (which meant taking it to the dealer's and maybe having to wait a week)?

- Or simply for having the same service for a computer no longer under warranty?

It was a perfectly viable proposition, and we thought it was a good enough basis to establish a business. And this is what most entrepreneurs would have done: take the necessary steps to create their business, draw up a budget for equipment, office supplies, and advertising, get a loan from the bank, and off you go (short version).

Long version: work on the project for between six months and a year with the help of a startup mentoring agency, draw up a three-year business plan, apply for various freebies and subsidies in addition to a bank loan, and off you go.

The problem with this approach, whether you choose the short or the long version, is that if the initial hypothesis is unworkable, all this energy, time, and money will be a dead loss.

Fearful of leaving school at such a young age and for nothing, we therefore decided to test out, in the most realistic conditions, whether or not people would be prepared to pay for our services.

And we found a good solution: publish an advert offering our services in a local free newspaper and see what response we would get. In the end, we invested 60 francs, offering our services at 100 francs an hour. A month later, we had recorded sales of 5,000 francs (including sales of equipment), at a time when:

- We didn't own a vehicle

- We had to attend school and do our homework

- Our advert was completely lost in a welter of other advertising material

- I was getting 50 francs (around 8 euros) in pocket money each week

Let's just say we were over the moon! This experience gave me the confidence I needed to realize my dream of independence, to leave school at 18, and establish my business. My friend decided to continue studying, so I took the project forward on my own. Without knowing it, I had put into practice a concept – or at least a rudimentary version of this concept – that would take the world by storm in the 2010s: The Lean Startup.

The Lean Startup concept is simple: you test the hypothesis on which your business is based as simply, as economically (in time, money, and energy), and as realistically as possible... rather than committing astronomical resources to an unproven idea. And if the result is negative, you change your initial hypothesis, taking the feedback from your experiment into account. Or you start again with a completely fresh hypothesis (known as 'pivoting' in Lean Startup terminology).

Now, the experiment on which I had based all my hopes, which gave me the confidence, at the age of 18, to do what many 45-year-old managers only dream of doing, was far from perfect. It was unrealistic in many ways:

- The hourly rate I had decided on was ridiculously low compared with market rates. It was fine for a young person without a care in the world, but not appropriate for a real business that has to pay the owner's salary, as well as expenses, taxes, rent, and equipment.

- It wasn't protected by any legal framework. Indeed, it was a black-market enterprise. Consequently, there were no income taxes or VAT to pay, which obviously distorted the results.

- And yet, my rate was appropriate for the free newspaper I had been advertising in... So, once I had set up the real business, this newspaper would no longer be an adequate marketing vehicle.

- Nor had I split tested the advertisement to assess its effectiveness; I had absolutely no knowledge of the concept of split testing (I'll explain this in detail later).

In short, several parameters were unrealistic, as I was to discover. But at least I was not starting with a madcap idea: customers were willing to pay for a home computer repair service. I had therefore completed the first phase of the Lean Startup strategy, carrying out an imperfect but instructive trial.

The fact is that adopting an experimental approach to your business ideas will ensure you avoid the mistakes I made (and some I didn't!) and may be the difference between success and failure. So let's take a look at the Lean Startup method and how you can apply it to your project.

THE GENESIS OF THE LEAN STARTUP METHOD

San Francisco, Silicon Valley, 2004. Eric Ries and his friend have just established a new startup for which they have great hopes. It has to be said that, up to this point, their careers as entrepreneurs had hardly been error-free. And yet, Eric Ries definitely had a touch of genius. He created his very first startup, Catalyst Recruiting, in the late 1990s, working from his student lodgings, with a brilliant idea: enable students to post their CVs online and so connect them with recruitment agents. Up to this point, it was very much like the Facebook success story. Except that his business failed. Just when they had run out of funds and Eric and his friend were trying to persuade investors to put more money into their project, the dotcom bubble exploded in March 2000. It wasn't so much a cold shower for the investors and founders as a tsunami of icy water.

Nevertheless, many of the parameters were promising: the timing was perfect, the idea good, and the need real. But Eric Ries and his friend had no effective method to guide them, and, like thousands of other startups at that time, they wasted what resources they had. So the enterprise was bound to fold. Eric Ries resumed his studies and, once qualified, was recruited in 2001 by another promising startup, There.com... which went under two years later.

So, in 2004, when he set up IMVU, he had everything to prove, including himself. Fortunately, IMVU was a more successful venture. In 2011, this online gaming site had three million active users, the business generated a turnover of $40 million and was employing 120 people.

What was the difference between the first two ventures, which ended in failure, and this later one? Simply the method he adopted. At IMVU, Eric Ries gradually developed a method which he subsequently baptized 'Lean Startup,' drawing inspiration from the lean management method pioneered by Toyota and from Steve Blank's customer development method.[233]

This method makes it possible to minimize the chief uncertainty felt by every entrepreneur: 'Will my product or service really be of interest to customers?' In other words: 'Is it really worthwhile investing so much time, energy, and money in this business?'

The idea is to deploy the product or service as quickly as possible and get real feedback, rather than spend years in an ivory tower creating something no one gives a damn about.

This method has been used successfully by well-known businesses such as Dropbox, Airbnb, Instagram, and Intuit, and by others that are less well known but no less successful, for instance, Grockit, Votizen, and Aardvark.[234] All very well, you may be thinking, but what is this Lean Startup method exactly? I'm glad you've asked me the question. It is simply a scientific way of starting a business.

ESTABLISHING A BUSINESS AS A SCIENTIFIC EXPERIMENT

'Virtually everything that differentiates the modern world from previous centuries can be attributed to science.'

BERTRAND RUSSELL, MATHEMATICIAN AND PHILOSOPHER

By envisaging your business startup as a scientific experiment and minimizing your costs, you will be doing yourself a favor in several ways:

- You will be going much farther than the standard pre-startup approach, which consists essentially of doing some market research and extrapolating from the results.

- If the experiment works out well, you will have a list of customers and maybe even some money, even though things will still be at the prototype stage, and you may not yet have a product or service!

If, on the other hand, the experiment is a failure, you won't have lost much money, maybe none at all, thus limiting the damage.

---

233 Author of *The Four Steps to the Epiphany*, 2013.
234 See http://en.olivier-roland.com/lean-startup-case-studies/

After this initial setback, you will be able to use all the data and feedback you have gathered to design a new experiment, either going back to square one or identifying which parameters need changing and adopting a variant of the initial experiment.

The very fact that you envisage it as an experiment can take a huge weight off your shoulders. An experiment is fun and requires far less commitment than a traditional business startup, which is burdensome and can involve high costs.

Lean Startup 101

And fortunately, that is precisely the approach of the Lean Startup strategy:

- Gather data

- Consider possibilities

- Define what you are offering

- Create an initial version of the product/service ('the minimum viable product'), inevitably imperfect

- Make your first sale

- Attract your first customers ('beta testers')

- Use their feedback to improve your product

- Or change it completely (the famous 'pivot')

- Begin again

The idea, then, is to test your hypotheses in the light of real-life experience. A little further on, I will share how to do this with a minimum of time and money, but first, let's look at some important concepts. There are three levels of risk when you start a business:

Technological risk

You might think of this in terms of: 'Is it really possible to do that?'

If you discover a remedy for cancer, you run absolutely zero risk of people not being interested... Much riskier is: will I manage to discover a remedy, or will I spend a fortune and waste years of my life in vain?

Market risk

In other words: 'If I manage to do that, will people buy it?'

This is the most obvious risk in business. History abounds in brave and enterprising people who were convinced their idea was so brilliant that everyone would come running... only to discover, often after years of hard work, that people couldn't care less about it. All entrepreneurs are guilty of behaving in this way, even the most brilliant... (After all, if we want to set up a business, it is because we believe in our project, isn't it?)

Let's examine a case study as evidence of this.

WEBVAN, THE ANTITHESIS OF A LEAN STARTUP

Webvan was founded in 1996 by an experienced entrepreneur, Louis Borders, backed by such companies and risk-capital providers as Yahoo!, Sequoia, and Goldman Sachs, which invested almost $400 million in the venture.

What was Webvan's objective? To become an 'online supermarket.' The idea was that, on their website, you could order almost as many products as you could buy in a conventional supermarket and have them delivered to your home without delay.

A good idea in theory... but untested and therefore short of hard data.

Convinced that everyone would rush to their site to do their shopping in the comfort of their own home, the team worked flat out to build a gigantic infrastructure to meet the demand.

Ultramodern warehouses were constructed in 10 US cities (a billion-dollar order for the main contractor), served by fleets of new-generation trucks, and an enormous budget was devoted to advertising.

In November 1999, the enterprise was floated on the stock exchange to raise the cash required for its development, drawing in $375 million, which gave the company a valuation of $4.8 billion. At this point, the business had made nothing but... losses, to the tune of $50 million. This was maybe not as bad as it sounds: many businesses take a long time to turn a profit, often because they prioritize growth over short-term profitability (Amazon is a good example).

But the real problem was that Webvan's business model was untested. The company preferred to invest in massive infrastructure, paying out astronomical sums that far exceeded its income from sales, rather than develop slowly and learn from the results of its early experience in the field.

Thanks to a series of well-orchestrated advertisements, sales began to grow, and the brand achieved visibility. Still, it was too late: the initial investment had been so over the top that the enterprise went bust in 2001.

Here you have the very opposite of a Lean Startup, and a story that should serve as a warning if you are tempted to invest a lot of money in an untested idea which, you are convinced, is bound to change the world.

Almost in parallel, Ocado, a company with a very similar business model, was founded in the UK in 2000. Unlike Webvan, Ocado has gone for slow, cautious growth, is still in business, and, in 2019, achieved a turnover of almost £1 billion and profits of £15 million without any physical sales outlets.

Business model risk

In other words: 'Will we find a way of earning money with this idea even if we implement it perfectly?'

This is the risk run, especially for startups offering a service that is innovative but which may not be profitable even if it is a roaring success. For example, when Google was launched, it was outstandingly successful thanks to the quality of its search algorithm. Still, it wasn't apparent that this, and the associated advertising, would make it into a financial giant because, at the time, no one could be sure that companies would switch their advertising budgets to the Internet.

To sum up

To manage the three risks facing any new business, the Lean Startup will:

1. Define its idea and what it has to offer

2. Conduct an on-the-ground survey

3. Create a minimum viable product

4. Measure

5. Pivot

6. Repeat

Brilliant, you may be thinking, but how do I do all that in practical terms? Let's look at the method that has worked for me, which borrows heavily from this Lean Startup philosophy.

TEST THE IDEA QUICKLY AND CHEAPLY

The first thing to accept is that it is impossible to be 100 percent sure that a new business will work, whatever the sector. There will always be a degree of uncertainty, and this can't be eliminated, even with all the prior market research in the world.

But the uncertainty can be greatly reduced. The classic way of doing this is by doing market research. This consists of studying several factors to discover whether there is interest in your product/service and potential customers for the business. It is obligatory if you have to seek funding to persuade investors and lenders. But many people promoting a project rely too heavily on such research, which is useful but only one tool, among others.

Generally, the more you want to reduce the uncertainty, the more data you will try to gather to make as informed a decision as possible, except that this can lead to procrastination and paralysis. In my method, once your market research is completed, it is time to set up a small-scale experiment to check that there is a demand for your product/service, giving you the green light to go ahead.

The right legal vehicle for your experiment

In most countries, you are legally obliged to declare all income, starting with the first euro/dollar/rupee you earn. This also means that, as long as you are not earning money, you are not obliged to create a vehicle to carry out your experiments.

In any case, try to use the least cumbersome vehicle possible. You can develop it later, if necessary (a good problem to have!).

Depending on where you live and your circumstances, it may be possible to declare the income deriving from your experiment simply as 'additional income' on your personal income tax return. Consult a qualified accountant to find out if this is possible. Or contact your tax office directly by mail. In most cases, a written reply from the tax authorities is binding. In other words, even if they tell you a load of nonsense, which can happen, they won't be able to reprimand you if you have followed their instructions.

The A/B or 'split' test, the spearhead of your experiment

We shall be using several tools to obtain and measure feedback from our experiment. One of the most important is the A/B test.

It consists of showing two variants of the same page or advert to a given audience and measuring which variant performs more effectively. For example, let's suppose you are thinking of publishing an advertisement on AdWords, Google's advertising agency, promoting an anti-flea collar for dogs. A text-format AdWords advert on Google is limited in terms of space, consisting of a title, a URL (which appears underneath), and two lines of text.

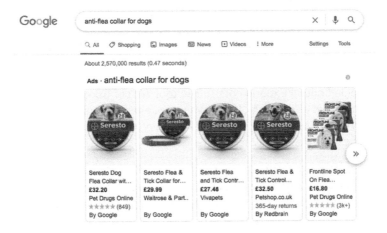

Figure 9: In this case, what can you do to optimize the performance of the advertisement and find out whether certain words have more impact on surfers than others? It is all the more important to have this information as there is often fierce competition around certain keywords, as you can see in this advert for flea collars.

You therefore need to carry out an A/B test. So, for example, you publish two competing adverts:

Smart flea collar	Smart flea collar
www.smart-flea-collar.com	www.smart-flea-collar.com
The first flea collar	Eco-friendly and organic
Organic and Fair Trade!	For better respect of your dog

Subsequently, AdWords will tell you which advert attracted the highest number of hits, i.e., the percentage of visitors who clicked on the advert. To be sure you have found a winner, the tool should indicate a statistical confidence level of least 95 percent... which means that you accept a margin of error of 5 percent... which means that for every 20 tests carried out, an average of one will be wrong. You can wait to have a confidence level of 97, 98, or even 99, but this will take much longer and considerably reduce the number of tests you can perform.

And, of course, there is nothing to prevent you from testing three or four variants at a time... but the more you test in one go, the greater the volume of traffic required.

Google AdWords includes all the tools needed to perform these calculations automatically, but how do you go about it if you want to test a web page or even a blog or a complete e-commerce site? Don't worry. There are many tools, some free, some not, which will take care of all the tricky aspects of these tests. I would recommend in particular:

1. Google Content Experiments: a free tool, part of Google Analytics, which is also free. Its location often changes, as the tool is evolving all the time. Carry out a search via the Help function or via Google if you can't find it in the interface.

2. Visual Website Optimizer[235]: a simple 'plug and play' tool. You can install a plug-in on your WordPress blog, or copy-and-paste the code given on the page, then you can test absolutely anything you want with just a few clicks. You will have to pay for this tool.

3. Optimizely[236]: an interesting alternative. Also available on a paying basis.

4. To learn to perform split tests, search for 'split tests experiments,' and you will come across some real gems.

---

235 http://en.olivier-roland.com/vwo/
236 http://en.olivier-roland.com/optimizely/

STAGE 1: MARKET RESEARCH ON STEROIDS

Getting an initial idea of the reality of your market

The mentoring organization you choose later on will help you to complete your market research. Still, it is vital to prove that your idea has financial potential before visiting them. Obviously, it will be easier to do this if you want to start a tried-and-tested kind of business, like a bakery, but even so, you will need to perform a market study. The study won't be concerned with the financial potential of your flagship product as such (everyone knows that bread and cakes sell well), but rather on the potential of the location you have in mind, the number and proximity of competitors, the turnover and level of profitability you can expect.

This will also enable you to sort through your ideas if you have several and work out:

- The kind of market you are selling into: will you be more geared to individual customers (B2C), businesses (B2B), or both (and in what proportions?)?

- Who your product or service will attract. Determining your type of customer (age, educational level, occupation, leisure activities, place of residence, civil status, etc.) and knowing why he/she would be interested will be useful for marketing your product or service.

- Who your competitors are: how many, size of the business, the products, and services they offer, and at what price?

However, at this stage, you don't want to spend too much time and money, so I would suggest you do your market research online. Via the Internet, you can easily access data free of charge, data that would have taken you a lot of time and energy to obtain thirty years ago. And when I say a lot, I mean a lot. Here, then, are some tools you can use:

- Amazon isn't only an amazingly successful e-commerce site but also a great place to carry out market research. You will find not only books on all subjects, but also a huge number of products advertised. So how will that help me, you ask? In two ways:

    - Amazon gives you a sales ranking for all its products.[237] A precious tool for finding out what is selling best in many sectors. How much time, energy, and money would you have had to spend to obtain the same information in the past?

---

237   In the product information sheet. Look for 'best seller rankings' on the product page.

- Amazon allows its customers to express an opinion – positive or negative – about its products. Customers' negative comments are an excellent source of ideas and clues to what ideas will work.

- Similarly, eBay is an excellent site for finding out what is selling and what is not, and for testing a product you have an idea for, as we shall see later.

- The Google keyword tool.[238] This free tool, designed for advertisers, is accessible to all and sundry. It tells you the number of monthly searches on Google for all the keywords you can possibly imagine, in every country where Google is active. Moreover, this tool will help you to find out:

  - What exactly surfers are looking for in your field of interest.

  - The level of competition among advertisers for specific keywords and how much they are prepared to pay for a hit: a very interesting indicator of your competitors' profitability in this sector (generally speaking, the more they are prepared to pay per hit, the more profitable the products or services they are selling).

  - The seasonality of a sector, product, or service.

- Similarly, Google Trends[239] enables you to find out what is in fashion and how trends are changing, and to compare trends one with another.

- The Facebook advertising system can provide you with excellent demographic data free of charge. For example, would you like to know how many women aged 30–45 in Missouri love chihuahuas? Facebook will give you a reliable estimate in just a few seconds – and it's free.

- Discussion forums. Search for relevant forums by typing in 'forum' and the name of your sector, and possibly sub-domain names. For example, if you want to start a business in the field of skiing, you will type 'forum skiing' and, if you want to specialize, maybe 'forum cross-country skiing' or 'forum snowboarding.' Then explore these forums in search of different pieces of information:

  - The number of people registered on the forums, and the number of active members

  - The number of messages posted

---

238 http://en.olivier-roland.com/adwords-keyword-tool/ You now need to conduct a paying campaign to get exact figures, so you might instead use the free Uber Suggest tool.
239 http://en.olivier-roland.com/google-trends/

- The different forum headings, and which attract most activity

- What the members are talking about, their concerns and problems

This will give you an incomparable insight into the interests of consumers in your field, their problems, and the things they are discussing. Again, how much time, energy, and money would it have cost you to get all this information as recently as twenty years ago?

■ Facebook discussion groups have the same advantages as forums; to find them, simply type the name of your sector into the Facebook search engine.

■ Magazines. There are specialized magazines in many fields and, by studying them, you will be able to glean a great deal of information on the burning issues in your market. Nowadays, you can access many magazines online without going out to the news-stand on Zinio and Magzter, for example. In particular, study the advertisements published in these magazines. Note which ones are published regularly. If they continue for some time, you can be sure it is because they are effective, and the products they are promoting are profitable. What products are most visible? What adverts are the most attention-grabbing? What products are the most expensive? Least expensive? Are there any products or services that, at first glance, don't seem to mesh with the subject matter of the magazine but appear, nevertheless? This could indicate a trend in your target market that you haven't noticed.

■ All other forms of advertising. As in magazines, the fact that an advert persists for a certain time clearly indicates that it is effective and that the product it promotes is profitable. This will give you some important clues concerning trends in your market, and what will sell and what won't.

- Observe television commercials. In particular, is there a cable or satellite channel that specializes in your field of interest? Study the programs and the commercials that are broadcast during them.

- Type keywords relating to the field you are studying into your favorite search engine. What advertisements are displayed in response to these keywords?

A thorough exploration of these resources will provide you with incomparable quantitative and qualitative data, all in the comfort of your own home! If you want to supplement it, you can purchase existing online market studies by various bodies at relatively affordable prices.

A magic wand: The survey

Online market research will enable you to define the chief features of your market. This is the point at which most businesses call a halt. For intelligent rebels, it is just the first stage. In particular, you will need sufficiently accurate data to:

- Identify the characteristics of your core customer: age, sex, occupation, etc.

- Determine his or her ability and desire to buy your product or service

- Determine the price he or she is willing to pay for it

And for this purpose, we are going to carry out a survey. Yes, a survey. And don't worry, it's not as boring as it sounds.

How do you obtain the answers?

You can, of course, conduct a survey in the street. But this takes a lot of time and energy, and the area you can cover is limited. Not 80/20 enough for the intelligent rebel. There is an exception to this principle: you can conduct 'physical' surveys by targeting places where you are sure that there really are potential customers. This will enable you to determine whether there is a genuine need for your product or service.

Then there is the telephone, which is much quicker and enables you to cover a much larger geographical area, but still requires a lot of time and energy.

The most effective method is undoubtedly to use the Internet. It's free, or the cost is derisory. It also saves a lot of time: you draft a questionnaire, you receive emailed replies, and the software processes the statistics automatically.

To conduct your survey via the Internet, you need to:

1. Have a list of email addresses of people potentially interested in your product or service

2. Draft a questionnaire using the online survey software

3. Send them a link to this questionnaire in an email

4. Analyze the answers

That's it!

But how do you get a list of email addresses when you are starting from scratch? I'll tell you about that presently. But first of all: why email addresses?

It's simply a question of time spent, competition, and habit. Most people access their electronic mailbox more frequently than any other function on the Internet, morning, afternoon, and evening. Sometimes more often. And although there may be many emails competing for their attention in their mailbox, when they decide to open an email, they generally concentrate on it exclusively during the time it takes to read. Compare that with a tweet or a Facebook notification, drowned among thousands of other such communications: they are much less effective in reaching prospective customers than an email, except in a few rare cases.

So, at first, you need a shortlist of the email addresses of qualified leads. This is how you can go about it: start by asking friends and family members interested in your idea if you can include them in a list of email addresses and keep them informed from time to time of how your project is progressing. Then send them a link to the questionnaire or ask them the questions directly. But won't your family and friends be biased in your favor?

Yes, but that is just the point: if you can't persuade them to answer your questions or let you include them in your list when they claim to be interested in your product/service, it could be a first indication that it isn't such a good idea after all.

To go up a gear and begin to obtain qualified prospects who are not your nearest and dearest, you will need...

A customer magnet

This is a tool you will use throughout the testing phase, first to compile a list of the qualified prospects to whom you are going to address your survey.

A 'customer magnet' is simply a free resource you can give in exchange for your prospects' email addresses. You create it in such a way as to attract only qualified prospects who will definitely be interested in your product or service. The free resource is typically a PDF guide or report that will help your prospects to solve a current, significant problem relating to your product or service.

For example, if you have invented a revolutionary anti-flea collar for dogs, you will need to compile a list of dog owners. You know their recurrent problem is that they want to teach their dogs to obey several basic commands: sit, lie down, come here, and so on.

So you draft a report entitled, for example: 'How to teach your dog the five basic commands – and ensure it obeys your every glance and gesture!' To do this, you draw on your experience in the field or adopt a journalistic approach and simply do an online search, gathering and summarizing the best available information clearly and practically. You can also be more specific and target dog owners suffering from problems with fleas, say with a report entitled: 'Three easy ways to rid your dog of fleas.'

Although it is advantageous to target your market as accurately as possible, be careful not to over-restrict your audience. In your case, writing a report to help dog owners rid their dogs of fleas may sound like a good idea, given that you then aim to sell your revolutionary anti-flea collar. Indeed, you will then have prospects already concerned with this problem. But fleas don't stay on a dog forever, and when the dog in question is 'cured,' the owner will no longer need an anti-flea collar. Moreover, a dog owner may not have a flea problem at the time when he becomes aware of your free resource, and his dog may well catch fleas some days later. So in this case, it is preferable to devise a more general resource that will interest the majority of dog owners (it will then be easy to filter the responses by including a question in the survey: 'Is your dog suffering from fleas at the present time?')

Here are some other examples of the resources that creators of well-known businesses might have written to compile a list of qualified prospects before launching their flagship product/service:

- 'Five tips for quicker Internet searches' – Google
- 'The seven best historical novels of all time' – Amazon
- 'The easy way to share your videos on the Internet' – YouTube
- 'How to meet your soulmate on the Internet (in five stages) – Meetic
- 'Six ways of earning money by selling the contents of your loft' – eBay

This resource doesn't need to be a masterpiece. After all, you are giving it away free. Five or six pages with a royalty-free[240] photo on the cover should do the trick. Yes, I know. You are afraid your prospects will be horrified by the crassness of such a document; they will be so annoyed that they will put you on their blacklist; they will contact the *New York Times* to demand you be exposed, and they will curse

---

240 http://en.olivier-roland.com/flickr/ to find photographs that are free of charge and in the public domain (not all of them are, please check). http://en.olivier-roland.com/fotolia/ for photos often of excellent quality. You will have to pay for them (but they are affordable) and they are in the public domain.

you and your descendants to the seventh generation for having dared send them so useless a report.

Calm down. You will come across prospects of this kind, who want something for nothing and will start moaning even if they haven't paid a cent, but most people will be happy to receive helpful information free of charge, or at worst, won't care either way. When you start out, imperfection is the usual state of affairs. Remember, it's a trial. You don't yet know if your idea is viable or not, so the main thing is to find out as quickly as possible whether there is a market for it. You can refine your idea later.

Next, you need to create a squeeze page. This is a web page offering your resource free of charge in exchange for the email addresses of visitors. Here are some user-friendly tools for creating squeeze pages:

- Optimize Press: http://en.olivier-roland.com/optimizepress/

- The 'Landing Page' plugin for WordPress, free, and effective: http://en.olivier-roland.com/landing-pages/ For other plugins of the same type: http://en.olivier-roland.com/squeeze-page/

- Unbounce: Create a squeeze page with just a few clicks. Again requires payment, but with a free 30-day trial period: http://en.olivier-roland.com/unbounce/

- LeadPages: A rival to Unbounce, another tool you will have to pay for, very simple to use: http://en.olivier-roland.com/leadpages/

You then need to attract people to this page. Useful tools for this are:

- Google AdWords and/or Facebook. You have to pay for the traffic, but $100 spent on Facebook will enable you to display your advert to 10,000 people or more. Not bad! What's more, you can easily get coupons worth $50 or $75 that allow you to test AdWords. Type 'Google AdWords vouchers' into a search engine to find them. An excellent way to build up a list of prospects quickly and free of charge.

- Comments on other blogs. Search for blogs devoted to the same topic as your resource and publish comments on them. However, be careful not to wade in with hobnail boots and make dozens of cryptic comments containing a link to your squeeze page. This is the best way to get a reputation as an obnoxious spammer. Think, instead, of 'adding value' and 'long-term relationships.' Many blogs have a field in the comments form for 'your website address,' which is then linked to your name. If you post thoughtful comments, some of the blog's readers will be intrigued and click on your link, thus landing on your squeeze page.

- You can adopt the same strategy on Facebook forums and discussion groups devoted to your topic. Here again, no hobnail boots! Reputations are established slowly in communities of this kind. Make sure you add value when responding to published content.

- You can also use Q&A sites such as Yahoo Answers[241] or Quora. Pick out questions that relate to your niche area and answer them. You can be rather more aggressive on these sites, so don't hesitate to include a link to your guidance doc, making clear that it is free and provides additional information.

- Publishing articles on blogs by invitation. You can contact the authors of blogs and offer to write an article in an area closely related to your product/service. The article must add value, for example, by suggesting solutions to current problems in the sector concerned. Make a 250 percent effort: your host must receive an article of exceptional quality and not have to clear up after you by correcting spelling mistakes. Include a sentence at the end of the article along the lines of: 'For further information, please refer to my free guide *Five mistakes not to make with your hamster*; click here to download it free of charge.' With the host blogger's agreement, of course. If your article is top quality, publishing it on a popular blog will have many benefits:

  - It will enable you to raise your profile in the relevant field.

  - You will immediately get a high volume of traffic from well-qualified visitors, some of whom will sign up to your email list to receive your free guide. Subsequently, your article will continue to be read (particularly by readers who encounter it via search engines), bringing you a regular flow of qualified traffic.

  - As far as the host blogger is concerned, you will be giving them a quality article on a silver platter, which will bring them additional traffic free of charge for years to come.

  - This will help you develop your relationship with him or her, a great benefit when you eventually bring out your product/service and want blogs in your sector to feature it.

  - Where readers of the hosting blog are concerned, you will be providing them with quality content, an interesting resource, and the good fortune of becoming your first prospects! Who knows, your first delighted customers may result from this article?

---

241 http://en.olivier-roland.com/answers-yahoo/

But be careful:

- – The more effort you have made to develop a good relationship with the blogger beforehand (particularly by publishing quality comments), the greater the chances of them agreeing to your request.

- – Be careful not to write too 'promotional' an article boasting of your 'brilliant idea.' Your first goal is to add plenty of value. Only then should you mention your free bonus, as discreetly as possible.

- – As a general rule, the more popular the blog, the more difficult it will be to get articles accepted, but that doesn't mean you should give up trying. You may be pleasantly surprised, and sometimes the authors of these blogs are glad to have a bit of breathing space and will appreciate the respite of being able to publish an article they haven't written themselves.

- Syndication with sales outlets. If you intend to produce this anti-flea dog collar and want to compile a list of dog owners, why not visit local pet stores and offer them a good old win-win deal? Print and bind your guide, then visit the outlets, telling them you are prepared to offer it to all their customers via email, an arrangement that will boost their sales. All they need do is announce an exceptional promotion: 'With each purchase worth more than $10, a free digital guide, *How to teach your dog the five basic commands – and ensure it obeys your every glance and gesture!*' All the customers need to do is fill in a form (hard copy or on their computer) to receive your bonus free of charge by email. You can also approach voluntary organizations, dog-training firms, and so on with a similar offer.

To manage a list of emails and prepare the registration forms, you can use such tools as:

- Mailchimp:[242] Free for up to 2,000 contacts

- Active Campaign:[243] 14-day trial for $1, then $19 a month for up to 500 contacts (the sector leader, which I use myself)

- Système IO:[244] powerful and user-friendly

These three tools are online applications designed to manage email lists several thousand (if not tens of thousands) strong. I would recommend them rather than

---

242 http://en.olivier-roland.com/mailchimp/
243 http://en.olivier-roland.com/activecampaign/
244 http://en.olivier-roland.com/systeme.io/

plugins or free tools that claim to help you manage email lists. However, at first, and only during the survey stage (when you have only a few hundred prospects), you can use some of these free tools. But, again, I wouldn't recommend it.

For the survey, you can use:

- A public form created using Google Surveys: You will have to make the calculations yourself in Excel
- SurveyMonkey[245] (free for up to 100 responses): Far and away, my favorite tool – all the calculations are performed automatically, which saves you no end of time

Creating your survey

In the survey, try to find out whether people think they will be interested in your product/service and, if so, what they would want it to be like. You will also want to know:

- What price they are prepared to pay
- What reservations they have about your product/service
- The classic issues of their socio-professional category, age, etc.

Be careful not to ask these demographic questions straight away: they are irritating and could well put your prospects off. Ask them on page 2 of the form. End the survey by thanking all those who have taken part. When I did this survey, the main things my readers told me were that:

- Their principal objective was to establish their business
- The greatest difficulty or frustration that prevented them from achieving this was that they procrastinated too much over their projects
- They would like me to help them with their projects in the form of monthly courses in MP3 format (audio seminars they could listen to)
- They were prepared to pay between €20 and €50 per month for this service, but everyone else should pay between €50 and €100!

Beforehand, I had no idea what product would interest my readers. Afterward, all I had to do was what they were asking of me: share my experience as an entrepreneur and advisor in the business startup world through the medium of an

---

245 http://en.olivier-roland.com/surveymonkey/

audio course. That was how I started Agir et Réussir (Act and Succeed), which has helped hundreds of creative people with their projects and enabled me to become a professional blogger and establish my second, entirely Internet-based business.

Of course, you need a sufficiently representative sample of responses to be really useful. A hundred responses is a good figure and not too difficult to achieve if you are starting from scratch.

Here is a handy technique for increasing the response rate: find an excellent video on YouTube or TED.com relating to the field of your product/service, and in your email say: 'I found this brilliant video, which I would like to share with you. To receive it, all you need do is complete this short survey.'

The paying version of SurveyMonkey allows you to redirect everyone who has completed the questionnaire to the URL of your choice. So create a page on a WordPress blog that includes the YouTube video, and redirect your prospects to it, or send them directly to the YouTube video.

The limitations of surveys

> *'If I had asked my customers what they wanted, they would have said a faster horse, not a car.'*
>
> HENRY FORD

> *'A lot of times, people don't know what they want until you show it to them.'*
>
> STEVE JOBS

A survey is an excellent way to start a conversation with your prospects and find out what they have in mind, but it has its limitations.

If your product or service is innovative, your prospects may well have no idea what they really want. Clearly, if Steve Jobs had done a survey at the time of CDs and the Walkman, asking his customers what they wanted, they certainly wouldn't have envisioned the iPod, but may have said something like: 'Yes, definitely, a Walkman featuring the Apple logo would be really nice!' or 'Seriously, guys, concentrate on computers; that's what you do best...'

But you also have to consider that:

1. You are not Steve Jobs.

2. You are almost certainly operating in a less innovative sector than Apple.

And even when innovation is involved, customers may well have something to contribute. A study carried out by Eric Von Hippel, a researcher in technological innovation at MIT, revealed that of the 1,193 commercially successful innovations he studied, 60 percent had originated from ideas put forward by customers.

So you can see that, though the responses to your survey should be treated with a pinch of salt, they can tell you a lot about the desires and frustrations of your prospects and maybe even give you new ideas for products/services.

Also, bear in mind that you are dealing with prospects, not customers, and you may have completely missed the mark in generating your list of email addresses. However, it is likely that you will find your first customers in this list of prospects, provided the first version of your product/service corresponds at least to some degree to their needs.

STAGE 2: FORMULATING YOUR HYPOTHESIS

Once in possession of this data, you can formulate your business hypothesis. This is the stage at which you feed your idea through the 'data-mill' to develop a real business project. This exercise will enable you to create a dossier you can use to contact mentoring organizations if you need this sort of support. You will need to decide:

- The name you envisage for your business

- Its sector of activity

- In just a few lines, your business objective and what makes it different from others

- A slogan which sums up this positioning in a few words

- The results of your market research:

  - The overall size of the market (national or international, depending on your objectives): Do some intensive Internet searches to arrive at these figures.

  - The qualitative and quantitative results of your research among customers and prospects in this sector (this is where the survey results will be useful)

  - The qualitative and quantitative results of your research among competitors in this sector

- The avatar(s) of your customer

- Your flagship product or service (this is clearly the most critical point, the thing you are going to test with the list of prospects you have compiled)

- An estimate, albeit vague, of your turnover in the first year and possibly the first three

- What you need in terms of support and funding

Let's go through the most important points together.

The name

Quickly note down on a sheet of paper or in a Word document the names that come into your mind. First, work in isolation as you think up as many names as possible. If there are a number of you in partnership, each should do this exercise on their own. Many studies over several decades have shown that brainstorming is ineffective for generating more and better ideas as compared with individuals working in isolation.[246] Only when each person has made their own list should you share and compare your ideas.

Then set these names aside for a week or two. If the idea for a name suddenly comes to mind, note it down immediately on your cellphone and add it to your list when you get back home.

When you have drawn up your list, consult the people close to you to see if they prefer one name over another. You can also – why not? – send a further survey to your list of prospects: people love choosing names for businesses, products, and books, as they love voting for product designs. But don't propose more than 10 alternatives. You could also publish an advert on AdWords or Facebook, conducting A/B tests to see which name gets the most clicks. This will give you a good idea of the level of interest aroused in your prospects by one name or another.

Your slogan

The slogan you choose for your business is important. It is its Unique Selling Proposition (USP) which enables your prospects to see immediately what your business is offering (and ideally why it is better than anything else on the market) and what distinguishes you from your competitors. Some well-crafted slogans

---

246 See, for example: 'Productivity Loss in Brainstorming Groups: Toward the Solution of a Riddle' by Diehl, M. et al., *Journal of Personality and Social Psychology*, 1987, or 'Productivity Loss in Brainstorming Groups: A Meta-Analytic Integration,' Mullen B. et al., *Basic and Applied Social Psychology*, 1991.

have been instrumental in ensuring the success of the business or product they were promoting, for instance:

- Domino's Pizza in the 1960s: '30 minutes or it's free.' Observe how this slogan sums up very neatly the advantage of using the services of Domino's rather than a competitor.

- FedEx: 'When it absolutely, positively has to be there overnight.' Here again, everyone immediately understands what the business exists for and when it is useful to call upon its services.

- M&M's: 'The chocolate that melts in your mouth, not in your hand.' An excellent slogan that immediately communicates a key advantage of M&M's while evoking the feeling of a sweet melting in the mouth… and no doubt arousing the desire to purchase a box.

- L'Oréal: 'Because you're worth it.' Perfectly conveys the idea that L'Oréal's products are expensive but of the highest quality, and that the customer (especially if female) deserves them.

- Apple: 'Think Different.' Capitalizing on Apple fans' feeling that there is something of the rebel about them if they use a Mac.

On the other hand, some slogans are rather less inspiring, even hackneyed:

- IBM: 'Let's build a smarter planet.'

- Microsoft: 'Your potential, our passion.'

- Nestlé: 'Good food, good life.'

These latter companies are proof that you can succeed even with a slightly iffy slogan. But a good slogan can improve perceptions of your business and its products/services and convince prospects of the advantages you are offering.

So spend time thinking up a good one. Your business slogan may allude directly to your flagship product or service, or indirectly, as in the cases of Domino's Pizza and FedEx. Or it may suggest a state of mind, a way of seeing things, as in the cases of Apple and L'Oréal. You will have noticed that the M&M's slogan promotes a product (M&M's is a brand belonging to the Mars group) so, later on, you too can create slogans for some of your key products.

But for the time being, let's keep it simple and practical. Try to find a slogan for your business. This slogan should ideally highlight a benefit rather than a function.

The difference between functions and benefits

A function is a logical, objective description of a product's capacities. A benefit is the practical advantage the product confers. Let's take two very simple examples to illustrate the difference.

A horseshoe is a U-shaped metal object affixed like a shoe to a horse's hoof. Its function is to protect the hoof from wear and tear. But what benefits does it confer? The one that comes immediately to mind is 'to protect the horse's hooves.' That's fine as far as it goes. But by delving deeper, we can think of others:

- To nip problems in the bud

- To spare the horse unnecessary suffering when going over rough ground

- To enable the horse to trot or gallop for longer periods

- To avoid having to rest the horse while the hoof regrows

- All in all, to save time and money

What your customers are interested in are the benefits, not the functions, so this is what you need to highlight.

An example of the functions and benefits of a lead pencil:

Functions	Benefits
Is made of wood	Easy to sharpen
Has a specific diameter	Easy to hold
Contains a graphite lead	Creates impressive marks
Has an eraser at its end	Makes corrections easy

The importance of scientific experiments and setting one up to find a name and a slogan that will 'stick'

Testing is the basis of your success in marketing and sales: you should never put your trust in preconceived ideas. Even the greatest marketing experts always carry out tests: their expertise and intuition may take them a long way in finding an effective solution, but they rarely come up with the most effective strategy for selling a product straight away.

A slight change in the price or other parameters in an advertisement or in their sales method can make a huge difference in profitability. And just a few words can make all the difference between an enterprise that fails and one that enjoys great success, as we shall see a little later.

To ensure the success of your business, the name and slogan are the two first things to put to the test, and there is a scientific way of finding out if one particular name or slogan appeals more than another. All you need do is use a technique we have already covered in this chapter. Can you guess?

Yes, the good old A/B Test.

It also works for book titles...Tim Ferriss is the first author I know of who used AdWords to find the right title for his book. He tried out six titles, including *Broadband and White Sand* and *The Chameleon Millionaire*. No real consensus had emerged from the traditional survey of his friends and family, his agent, his publisher, and so on. Tim, therefore, spent $200 on AdWords, and *The 4-Hour Work Week* received by far and away the most clicks. In hindsight, it is difficult to imagine that the book would have had such enormous success (2.1 million copies sold in 35 languages) with the title *Broadband and White Sand*.

So test your ideas for names and slogans on AdWords or Facebook. It can make all the difference!

Creating an avatar

As well as your flagship product, the survey results will enable you to define your typical prospect. This is an important step, which many entrepreneurs unfortunately overlook or neglect. There is nothing worse than a message that doesn't address anyone in particular. Imagine, on the other hand, a marketing message so precise, so clear that when you hear it, you get the impression it is addressed to you and no one else while reaching a mass audience. Impossible?

Not as impossible as you think with avatars.

What is an avatar? Simply a model, a fictitious character who combines the most common characteristics of your typical prospect.

This is very much akin to the concept of the 'ideal type' invented by the sociologist Max Weber for studying a group of individuals, which consists of creating a fictitious individual embodying their general characteristics. Except that we will use this technique with the practical aim of communicating more effectively with our prospects. And simply producing this definition of the typical prospect sets you apart from the majority of entrepreneurs. This exercise is also known as defining an avatar or an ideal type.

The responses to your survey will have provided you with demographic data and a good general knowledge of your prospects' desires and frustrations. Use this data first of all to determine your avatar's:

- Sex
- First name
- Age
- Level of educational attainment
- Occupation
- Marital situation (married, cohabiting, divorced, etc.)
- Number of dependents

As far as possible, use the survey data. Use your intuition only for questions you didn't ask in the survey (e.g., number of children). Then answer these questions:

What is your avatar's strongest desire where your business is concerned? This will be the desire your prospect expressed in the survey, the goal he or she is aiming for, and that your product or service will help to achieve. For example:

- 'I want to be able to run a marathon.'
- 'I want my dog to be free of fleas.'
- 'I want to lose weight.'

What is your avatar's strongest 'hidden' desire? This is the desire underlying the one expressed, the real final goal. Often prospects are less clearly aware of this than of the desire they openly express. For example (concerning the three desires expressed above):

- 'I want to prove myself and prove to those around me that I can take up a difficult challenge and make a success of it.'
- 'I want to feel happier and more at peace with my dog.'
- 'I want to feel more at ease with myself and be more attractive.'

Imagine your prospect is saying: 'If only...' and try to complete the sentence.

What is their strongest unsatisfied desire at the present time about the scope of your business? There must be a desire somewhere that will drive them to buy the product. And, generally, it will be a frustrated desire. The survey partly covers this with the question: 'What is your greatest frustration?' But you need to take it further. For example, with my Agir et Réussir (Act and Succeed) product, my customers told me both their desire and the obstacle to it: 'I want to start a business, but I'm always putting it off until tomorrow.' Their strongest unsatisfied desire was certainly to start a business but, if we take it further, we find it was also not to have a boss, to be financially independent, and to be free to arrange their own timetable.

What steps will bring your customer to the point of satisfying his or her desire? You need to identify these steps, then work out at what stages your product or service will help them and how. When you know this, you will have a plan of attack for communicating with your customers.

If you can point out these stages to them, and exactly how you can help them straight away, they will no longer see you as a 'salesman' but as someone who has understood their wishes and can help realize them.

Define your avatar as accurately as possible. What do they look like? What clothes do they wear? What are they like? Are they physically fit? And so on.

How about their lifestyle? What are their work-related and leisure activities? Do they go to a gym or sports club? Does their job entail anything special? Do they beaver away from 7 a.m. to 8 p.m., or are they content to work minimum hours? Are they happy with life?

STAGE 3: HOW TO LOOK INTO THE FUTURE AND TEST YOUR HYPOTHESIS

The purpose of this stage is to check that your product or service is of sufficient interest to persuade your prospects to buy it.

At this point, you still won't have an official structure or have spent any money, or very little: for the survey and emailing software and possibly a minimum of advertising (normally less than $200). However, you will have:

- A market study

- A list of prospects

- A survey that tells you:

  - Your potential customers' greatest problem and greatest frustration… the thing they most want you to resolve for them

  - A range of prices they say they are willing to pay for this

  - Socio-demographic data that enables you to accurately define an avatar of your prospects

  - One or more avatars of your potential customers

So now it's time to check whether people are interested in your product or service. For this purpose, I suggest you adopt a method beyond the Minimum Viable Product proposed by Lean Startup.

The idea is to look into the future to know with absolute certainty before you have created your product or even invested one hour in its manufacture if it will really sell. How can you do such a thing? Is it really possible?

Yes, it's very straightforward. It just involves offering your product for sale… even though it doesn't yet exist – and in a completely legal way, which is also ethical.

How, then? Simply by inviting your prospects to pre-order. Such mega-enterprises as Amazon and Fnac do it, so why shouldn't you? All you have to do is design your product on paper, just the main features: if your aim is to sell a book, produce a table of contents; if a training course, the program; if a physical product, a description. Then you give your list of prospects the opportunity to pre-order.

Be honest and open about it: explain that the product isn't yet available but will be on such and such a date, and offer a substantial discount (between 30 percent and 50 percent, if possible) to thank the early birds who have shown confidence in you. I would also suggest you offer a 30-day guarantee – satisfaction or your money back – starting from the date of receipt, to reassure them and show that you are shouldering all the risks.

Subsequently, there are two possible scenarios:

- The product doesn't sell in sufficient quantities: in this case, simply reimburse the few customers who have made a purchase and move on to something else, grateful to have discovered the truth now rather than later.

- If your product sells well: bingo! You can go ahead and produce it and set up your business on the strength of it if you haven't already done so.

A method that will revolutionize your business

Have you any idea of the time, energy, and money you can save by adopting this method? While your competitors are working their socks off making products that will inevitably gather dust on the shelves, you can be sure of developing only products that will sell, with 100 percent certainty.

Moreover, having sold the product to your customers, you will be highly motivated to finish making it and deliver in good time. No more procrastination! Just think how much that could shorten the product creation cycle and increase your profitability.

Now, this method won't work for everything. I have successfully tested it with information-related products: digital books and online training courses, to which it is particularly well suited. And I'm certainly not the first person to have grasped this point: way back in the 1970s, an American author of practical guides named Malvin Powers found his own unique way of writing books he was sure would sell.

When he had an idea for a book, he would produce the contents page, plus an advert promoting the book, which he would then publish in relevant magazines, together with an order form to be mailed back with a check. Then it was simple:

- If the 'book' sold fairly well, he would write it.

- Otherwise, he would return the money to the customers who had replied and move on to his next project.

Fine, you are probably thinking. This method applies perfectly to information-related products, but does it apply to physical ones? Definitely, yes!

San Francisco, 2013. Josh Gustin is fed up. A designer of top-of-the-range garments, he is sick and tired of the fashion sector's traditional model:

> *When I started designing jeans and selling them to high-end stores in 2011, I began to hate the structure of this industry. I was selling at high-end prices; I couldn't talk directly to the customer; I had to guess a year in advance what people would want to wear, and the cash flow was erratic.*

Then he had an idea that was to change everything: create only garments he was sure of selling. How did he go about it? By launching a new version of his website, organized around a simple concept: propose new models to clients and manufacture only those pre-ordered in sufficient quantities. He launched this new concept with a lot of razzmatazz on the participatory launch site Kickstarter, raking in $449,654 when he had been looking to raise $20,000.

A new business model was born.

As he told the prestigious Forbes Magazine a few months later: 'My jeans used to cost $205 in the store, now they cost $100, and I still make the same margin. The company's revenue has gone up 40 percent.'

Looking into the future with crowdfunding

The most emblematic of products sold before even being designed are, of course, those funded through participatory funding platforms or crowdfunding. These websites enable companies to offer products on a pre-order basis to anyone interested. This also works well for musicians who want to produce an album, authors who want to write a book, film-makers, and creators of video games.

Those seeking funding indicate how much money they need to create their product. If this amount is achieved, manufacture begins. Otherwise, the product is shelved. The people who have paid are reimbursed (or their accounts are not even debited), and the designers move on to another project or try to sell their product differently.

There are different levels at which potential customers can make a financial commitment to these projects: from a minimal donation with nothing in return to the pre-ordering of one or more products, sometimes with prestige options such as numbered or signed editions. If the sum initially sought is exceeded, the company may decide to add functionalities to its product or do so at a later stage.

Anybody is permitted to offer a product on these platforms and so reach their audience. However, I would recommend that you contact the people on your list and encourage your prospects to buy your product to achieve additional leverage.

At present, the leading crowdfunding platforms are Indiegogo and Kickstarter, but there are also plenty of others.

How to engage in crowdfunding

Of course, many projects have failed to reach their target or haven't raised any money at all![247] This is instructive in itself.

So go and have a look at these two platforms and explore the various projects. Find out what was a great success, what just made it, and what failed. This is a possible indicator for your market research.

---

247 Ulule found that, in 2014, 66 percent of published projects secured funding, while KissKissBankBank gives a figure of 55 percent.

But what if you have tried crowdfunding and it didn't work for you? Should you just give up the idea? Not necessarily. Because crowdfunding is just one way among others of looking into the future.

How to sell your product before it has been made without crowdfunding

By following the method advocated in this book, you have compiled a list of prospects – a list you can also use to sell your product on a pre-order basis.

The simplest option, in this case, is to:

- Create a PayPal or Stripe account if you haven't got one already

- Create a sale page or a sales video for your product, being sure to explain that you are offering your product on a pre-order basis

- Send an email to your list of prospects, directing them to your sales page

In my experience, though, there is a better way to improve your conversion rate and boost your chances of success:

1. Email the prospects on your list roughly a week before you begin your promotion, sending them some free quality content related to your product. For instance, if you are a dog trainer and you want to sell a book on this topic, you could send them a link to a YouTube video showing a dog that is good with children, a dog that has rescued someone, or simply a dog that is amusing and affectionate. It is preferable that you create the content, but not obligatory. The aim is to 'warm-up' your prospects by sending them a useful or fun item without trying to sell them something.

2. A week later, send them an email saying essentially: 'Hello [first name], I'm writing to thank you for responding to my recent survey. [XXX] people replied, which was heart-warming. A big THANK YOU! Your answers have shown me how I can best help you. I have therefore decided to organize an online seminar entitled [name of seminar], in which I shall share [X number of benefits]. Registration is on a paying basis, but you can take part for free when it is broadcast on [date] at [time]. You can follow it on your computer and ask me any questions you like. It will be a pleasure to have a discussion and get to know you a bit better. [Your first name]'

3. Conduct the webinar (see p.245) and sell your product on a pre-order basis.

4. After the webinar, sell the right to view the recorded version (to record it, use Camtasia or Screenflow).

5. Then send out an email offering your product for sale, with a link to PayPal or Stripe, to all those who haven't yet purchased it (in this case, it is your email, and everything you have sent out previously, that serves as the sales page).

6. Then send an email with a link to your video or sales page.

By following this sequence, you will achieve a better conversion rate and so a more realistic idea of how interested your prospects are in your product. But hang on a minute, what is a webinar?

How to use webinars for sales

Have you ever seen someone make a PowerPoint presentation?

Figure 10: Powerpoint presentation

OK, there is no doubt some you are happy to have forgotten, but unless you have been living in a remote part of the world for the last 30 years, there is a strong chance you have been present at one, at least. A webinar is a PowerPoint presentation that, instead of being delivered in a physical room, is done on your computer and shared via the Internet so that potentially hundreds of people can be present in the comfort of their own homes.

This has many advantages over a conventional presentation:

- No need to hire a room and manage the logistics of a physical presentation.

- You can make the presentation from your own home, with a regular computer and a standard high-speed broadband connection.

- Your audience can also follow you from home with a basic computer or almost anywhere with a smartphone.

- Potentially, then, you can reach customers all around the world. When I organize webinars, I regularly connect with people from 40 different countries.

- No need to be good at face-to-face sales for it to work: personally, I'm not very good in this department, yet I have made sales worth hundreds of millions of euros through webinars.

- You don't need to be an extrovert, either. You don't even need to show your face! Personally, I don't have a problem showing my face in a video – I do so regularly on my YouTube channel – but I don't show it in webinars; it's entirely optional.

- Your audience can ask you questions live, without interrupting you, if you use chat software. This means you will receive objections and questions from your prospects while on air, a great help in identifying any significant blockages you were unaware of. You can choose to answer these questions as you go along or hold a Q&A session at the end of the presentation. Or both.

OK, you may be saying, but how exactly does one organize a webinar? How do you get people to log in, and how do you sell enough products on a pre-order basis?

How to organize a webinar that generates sales

First of all, don't be daunted by the technical aspects: the software involved is very simple, you can use your existing computer, and there's no need to make an ultra-design PowerPoint presentation. I have made sales worth more than €250,000 via webinars using just a bullet-pointed list with some text. But that didn't stop the webinar from being very effective.

The only extra equipment I would advise you to get is perhaps a second screen because with two screens you can take advantage of PowerPoint's 'presenter' mode, which displays on one screen what your audience is seeing, and, on the other, the next bullet point on your list.

How does that help? Simple: as the speaker's notes appear in advance on your screen, you can read them, then display them on the screen seen by your audience. This means you don't have to learn your presentation by heart. And is there anything more boring than following the presentation of someone who merely reads the text that is already displayed? As we read faster than we speak, we have often finished reading before the speaker has finished what he has to say, and that's (deadly) boring. The effect is quite different if the speaker speaks first, then displays a bullet point summing up what he or she has just said.

This is the benefit of PowerPoint's 'presenter' mode. On the left, you have what your audience is currently seeing. And on the right, under 'Next slide,' you have what will come up next when you press the right-hand arrow on your keyboard or click the mouse. So you can read the speaker's note before it is displayed for your audience.

So, to sum up: by organizing a webinar, you can make a live presentation to thousands of people without seeing them (and therefore without the stress generally associated with public speaking). And you can do it in your own home with a cup of tea beside you, reading your presentation without having to learn it by heart.

I'm sure that sounds less stressful than having to address a thousand people in a conference hall, doesn't it?

A structure which sells on your behalf: ICOS

As I gained experience with webinars, I invented a way of structuring them so that:

- They add value, even for people who don't purchase.

- They generate sales effectively because of the way they are structured.

I then refined my method so I could teach it as part of an online training course.[248] Here, then, is the result of years of experiments that have generated hundreds of thousands of euros of online sales over periods of several months: my ICOS structure. ICOS stands for the four main parts of a webinar:

- Introduction

- Content and value

- An irresistible offer

- Sale

But before we go into this in more detail, it is necessary to decide on the overall topic of your webinar.

---

248 Webinar Pro. You can view a series of three videos explaining the process at https://en.olivier-roland. com/webinars

Deciding on the subject of your webinar

To decide on a subject, your point of departure should be the survey you conducted, particularly the all-important 'magic question': 'What is the main difficulty or frustration, or the main problem, you are faced with at present?' (i.e., what is preventing you from achieving your goals, and how do you feel as a result?).

Because, in answering this question, your prospects are telling you exactly what urgent problem they want your help with. The problem your product is supposed to solve or help to solve... And that should be the subject of your webinar!

After all, what is more, likely to motivate someone to follow a presentation than the prospect of being able to solve, or at least mitigate, a frustrating and urgent problem?

So your webinar should offer free advice that will directly help your prospects to solve their chief problem.

Let's return for a moment to the (fictitious) example of the dog trainer... As a result of a survey, he discovers that his customers' order of priorities is as follows:

1. To get their dog to obey simple commands.

2. To get their dog not to bark when barking is unwelcome.

3. To toilet train their dog.

So he will organize his webinar around these three problems, offering suggestions on how to solve them. He will make up a title that clearly indicates to his prospects that they will find solutions to their problems. Here are some examples of possible titles:

- 'Five secrets for getting your dog to obey you.'

- 'How to train your dog quickly and easily.'

- 'How to ensure your dog is affectionate, obedient, and contented.'

In short, the title should be a slogan... Or the name of your product (or brand), provided it is accompanied by an explicit slogan.

Put yourself in your prospect's shoes: you are in a hurry, with loads of things to do; you pay only scant attention to the emails and videos people send you. But you have a problem that is causing you frustration and that you would dearly love to solve. What better way to capture your attention than a slogan that immediately suggests there is help available?

So:

1. Analyze the results of your survey.

2. Note the answers to the all-important question.

3. Decide what your prospect's main problems are.

4. Decide on the solution you are going to propose in your webinar.

5. Based on this information, devise a title and a slogan for your webinar.

To learn more about the ICOS structure, go to https://en.olivier-roland.com/webinars.

Software for organizing webinars

There is a whole host of apps for conducting webinars. Have a look at Gotowebinar (expensive but reliable), Webinar Jam, or simply some webinars on YouTube or Facebook Live.[249]

Selling a product that doesn't yet exist

On eBay or Craigslist

Do you remember the technique I shared at the beginning of this book to determine if people might want to hire a parking space? The idea is to put it up for hire on Craigslist or another advertising site and buy it only if enough people call to hire it. You tell them that the space is definitely for hire but isn't available now, and you will call them back when it is.

You can do exactly the same to test whether there is interest in your product or service. Put it up for auction on eBay, see how many potential buyers there are and how much they are prepared to pay than cancel the auction at the last moment. On Craigslist, see how many people contact you in response to your advert. Then repeat the process several times, making changes to some of the parameters.

---

249 The interfaces of these last two platforms are such that participants are much more easily distracted. Consequently, a webinar I organized for testing purposes on Facebook Live attracted only half as many sales as on Gotowebinar.

You can also advertise on the Internet and send prospects directly to a pre-ordering page. However, the conversion rate using this method is generally very low, and placing the ad may be expensive, so I would advise against it in most cases.

STAGE 3B: IF YOU CAN'T LOOK INTO THE FUTURE, OFFER A PROTOTYPE OF YOUR PRODUCT

Unfortunately, it is not always possible to look into the future by crowdfunding or selling on a pre-order basis. For example, can you imagine Sergey Brin and Larry Page, the founders of Google, staging webinars to sell their search engine on a pre-order basis? Impossible, given that use of the search engine itself is free. The source of the company's profits is paying advertisers. Could they have funded their project by crowdfunding, had such platforms existed in 1998? Maybe, but by no means certain. The same reservations would apply to other web giants, such as Amazon, Uber, and Airbnb.

If your enterprise is similarly constituted, you will have to use the Lean Startup method: create an initial functional version of your product based on your market research. And get it into the hands of real-life users as quickly as possible.

Then improve it, if the product sells. Or pivot, if it doesn't.

STAGE 4: CREATING THE PRODUCT

Once you have secured your first customers using the 'sale by pre-order' method, you will obviously have to create your product as quickly as possible. The great thing is that, with customers who have already paid and been promised delivery by a certain date, procrastination is not an option. The sense of urgency is likely to give you wings.

Moreover, if your product permits, you can deliver it in stages to keep your customers happy. For example, my principle online products are video-based training courses extending over several months. Each time I launch a new course, I am in the habit of:

- Conducting a survey of my audience to determine their main problem/ frustration about the idea I have in mind.

- Programming the course to help them resolve this problem.

- Preparing the first two or three lessons.

- Staging a webinar in which I give concrete suggestions for solving the problem, make a presentation of the training program, and invite them to register on an early-bird basis.

- If sales have been satisfactory, I continue to create the lessons and send them out to the students at regular intervals. Not only is this practical because it enables the students to start the course immediately, even though I haven't completed it; this approach is also better from a teaching perspective because receiving all the content in one go virtually guarantees that the student won't apply any of it. Can you imagine what would have happened if you had been given the entire content of what you were supposed to learn in a year on the first day back at school, even with a staged plan?

- Then, once roughly 10 percent of the course has been written, I ask for initial feedback from my first customers to find out if there are any obvious weaknesses in the program and make improvements based on their suggestions if necessary.

- Then I go ahead with a large-scale public launch of the course, making it an online event using the orchestrated launch method.

In this way, I have the assurance, when I commit significant resources to the orchestrated launch, that the product is going to sell. And of course, I am highly motivated to complete the course in good time – my customers expect it.

You can adopt a similar strategy with a book. As soon as you have finished a chapter, you send it to the customers who have bought it on a pre-order basis. For them, this is one of the benefits of having purchased it in this way.

STAGE 5: IMPROVING YOUR PRODUCT/SERVICE BY APPLYING THE FEEDBACK FROM YOUR FIRST CUSTOMERS

Once you have created the first version of your product, carry out another survey, in this case, of your customers. Ask them questions such as: 'In your opinion, what is the greatest improvement that could be made to [name of product]?' and 'Have you found anything absurd in the way that [name of product] works? If so, how should it work, in your opinion?'

Identify the additional functions that would be most useful or the key improvements required. And make them.

STARTING A BUSINESS WITH NO MONEY: ARE YOU JOKING?

It is quite possible to start a business on an extremely limited budget, say around $100. To convince you, this is how I started my second business.

Lille, 2008. I was an entrepreneur accustomed to working a 70- or 80-hour week. In the early years, this was fine with me, as I was 'all fire and enthusiasm,' passionate about what I was doing.

As the years went by, I began to find the imbalance between work and private life increasingly wearing. But what could I do? My business was my only source of income. I couldn't see a way to sell it, and, as a business owner in France, I couldn't claim unemployment benefits. I looked for a solution for some years, without result.

Then, in 2007, I came across an absolutely brilliant personal development blog.[250] The first thing I realized: a blog is not just a personal online diary; it can be a great way of expressing ideas and adding value. Ah, I see. Second realization: it was possible to earn business-like sums of money from running a blog. The author had published an article on his earnings, explaining how fruitful an occupation this could be: he wrote roughly one article per week, on a subject he was enthusiastic about, and did not need to manufacture any products, nor carry out the marketing or provide the after-sales service associated with them... and he was earning around $40,000 a month. How could that be? To some extent, thanks to advertising, but mainly by promoting affiliated products. He found a product he liked and wrote an article about it with a 'magic' affiliated link: every time someone clicked on this link and purchased the product, he received a commission. Moreover, since he could manage his business entirely online, he wasn't tied down to any physical place and was free to travel.

I was amazed that it was possible to earn a living in this way. And I had a feeling that this was the solution I had been looking for: I loved writing and dreamed of enjoying the same sort of freedom. So, I decided to try blogging, starting with my area of competence (IT): the right (digital) tools for clever people. I called my blog 'Technosmart.'

You don't understand what that means? You think it's something to do with techno music? Don't worry, you're not the only one. This blog was one of the most monumental failures of my entrepreneurial career! From the title to the

---

250 This was a blog by Steve Pavlina http://en.olivier-roland.com/steve-pavlina/. You can read an interview I did with him, in which he shares his views on free love and other fascinating subjects at https://en.olivier-roland.com/itw-steve/

positioning, not to mention the SEO and monetization strategies, I got it wrong all down the line.[251]

I still remember an article that took me hours to write, that seemed to me so brilliant that I expected everyone to be reading it. Only to discover that my mother, and a few stray visitors, were the only people who viewed it.[252] Not surprising, given the time I had spent promoting it: zero minutes.

The result: six months after launching the blog, I had earned the staggering sum of €16.38 thanks to advertising – hardly an encouragement to make it a full-time business. A failure, then? Yes, but a miraculous failure, as it was a part-time failure. Part-time. And above all, it had cost me a mere €30... (the cost of hosting the site for one year).

I subsequently launched two other blogs, which, thanks to that first experience, were destined to do better: *Habitudes Zen* (Zen Habits) and, above all, the French version of *Books That Can Change Your Life*, which really set me on my way to becoming an Internet entrepreneur.

And the best thing about all this? These two blogs were also started part-time, alongside my first business, which was still demanding a great deal of my time. I have calculated exactly how much time *Books That Can Change Your Life* required in the first year, including the work of reading and summarizing the books concerned: less than 10 hours a week on average. And the cost was derisory: roughly €60 a year for hosting the two blogs.

Obviously, these two blogs did not earn me large sums straight away: after a year, they were together generating sales of about €300 a month, deriving from advertising and Amazon affiliation commissions. But, two months later, I made my first really significant killing with a product created for the audience of the blog and sold through it: €3,000 per month.[253]

A few months later, turnover was up to €14,000 per month, then increased to an average of €28,843.75 net of tax in the first year of my business.[254] The profit margin was also impressive since I had no employees, and I was selling virtual products. A respectable turnover for a VSE (Very Small Enterprise), enabling me to validate my business model, establish my second business without qualms, and sell my first business in 2010.

251 I have left this blog online to show people how not to do things: http://www.technosmart.net
252 The article entitled 'Mr Vieille école et Mr Efficace' can be read at http://www.technosmart.net/mr-vieilleecole-et-mr-efficace-1ere-partie/
253 For seven months, the duration of the training course.
254 Roland Publishing, which I founded a little more than a year after launching my books blog. Previously, the small amount generated by this blog went into the coffers of my first business.

I've told you what came next at the start of this book: I was able to start living the life I had dreamed of, traveling the world. In September 2010, a month in the Pacific, on Wallis and Futuna, and Fiji, whereas before, I had never taken more than a week's holiday. In short, I was enjoying the taste of freedom. Break out the bubbly! And it was also something I saw as quite an achievement: establishing a profitable business without needing a loan or any other investment. Similarly, I had already tested the business model in real conditions, with no investment apart from spending €10 on an advert in a free newspaper.

So, if you have no money, and no one can lend you any, ask yourself the question: can I launch my project part-time and with minimal investment? Can I test the concept practically on the ground to generate some income that will enable me to develop the business and/or have some credibility when seeking funding?

There's nothing wrong with your business getting off to a slower start. At least it will be starting, and you will have a much better chance of success than if you did nothing. And even if you fail, you will have gained valuable experience at little expense, something you can turn to advantage for your next project.

STARTING PART-TIME

The ideal way of testing your idea practically and as rapidly as possible, with costs and risks kept to a minimum, is, therefore, to start up your project on a part-time basis.

How to find time to start your business part-time

But how do you free up the time you need? Here is a simple technique. Begin by listing all your activities, both 'public,' such as going to your judo club for two hours twice a week, and 'private,' such as playing video games or watching television for roughly eight hours a week. Include your work time, the time you spend asleep, and time spent traveling.

Typical example:

- Total number of hours in a week: 168

- Number of hours spent sleeping: between 49–60 hours[255]

---

255 Don't forget the point made in Chapter 5 (*see p.99*): don't try to make time by cutting down on your sleep, which would be completely counterproductive. The vast majority of people need eight hours' sleep a night to maintain top performance.

- Number of hours spent washing/grooming and eating: 14 on average

- Number of hours spent working + traveling: 40–50 hours (if you are unemployed, all this time is free – a real opportunity!)

- The remainder: 44–65 hours, a large part of which is taken up by other commitments, such as family, friends, and various other activities

To start a business on a part-time basis, 10 hours a week would seem to be the minimum. The more time you can devote to it, the better. Then answer the following questions, writing your answers on a sheet of paper or in a Word file:

- Can I fit my business startup project into my present timetable?

- Can I perform some tasks in 'dead' time during other activities? For example, follow audio lessons on entrepreneurship while driving or work on my strategy on the train?

- What activities could I give up or suspend to make the time required to start my business? Begin by cutting down on all non-essential 'private' activities, such as watching TV and playing video games. If you spend an hour a day watching YouTube, you will gain three hours a week (78 hours after six months) if you reduce your viewing time by 30 minutes. Even five minutes saved each day will add up to 30 hours in a year. This will make a significant difference to your project.

Some case studies

You are a student

The time you have available will depend on your studies: if you are cramming for university entrance or studying for medicine, law, or an MBA, you may have much less time than if you are taking an arts degree or studying psychology. However, generally speaking, you will be able to take some time out from your studies, and this time can be used for testing your idea.

For example, one of my pupils, Laurent Breillat, conceived the idea of starting his blog Apprendre la Photo in 2010, when he was 22 and studying biodiversity management. He worked for about ten hours a week on his project from his 100ft^2 student room. His studies took up roughly 20 hours, leaving him plenty of time to enjoy himself. In 2019, his blog was receiving some 200,000 visits a month, and his business was making more than €500,000 per annum... without his having to take on any employees.

Another of my pupils, Sylvain Jeuland, was studying for a doctorate in IT when he got fed up with being an eternal student. He had the idea of creating a business tutoring math students, alongside his studies, to find out if entrepreneurship would suit him. Sylvain realized he had embarked on his studies 'by default' to keep him occupied until he discovered what he really wanted to do: be his own boss and work at his own pace, with clients he enjoyed interacting with. In short, he wanted to be an entrepreneur after his own fashion. When his business began to take off, he abandoned his studies and is now much happier than before.

You are an employee

If you are employed and want to set up a business, you will come into one of two broad categories:

1. Your job is of the 'normal' kind, i.e., you work a maximum of 40 hours a week.

2. You are an overworked manager, i.e., you work 50–60 hours a week.

And is your job very exhausting, or just slightly exhausting? If you come into the first category and work is not too exhausting, you are in much the same boat as the student who decides to devote some of their time to a business project.

If you are in the second category, and your company pressures you to stay at the office until 8 p.m. to demonstrate your zeal, and you also spend Saturdays working then Sundays on the couch recovering, it will inevitably be more complicated. In this case, it would be wise to find a way of escaping this situation.

Can you take a sabbatical? Or negotiate a teleworking arrangement, even for one day a week, which would save you the time spent on public transport and spare you endless meetings that lower your productivity? Or take a less well-paid but more relaxing job?

HOW EMMA AUTOMATED HER WORK

One of my friends (let's call her Emma) was recruited to a high-flying position in a major German company in London. After three months of 'normal' work, learning the ropes, she began analyzing her tasks and identifying repetitive actions, particularly those of an administrative nature. Then she began optimizing one task a week following the 80/20 principle.

For example, she had to coordinate communications between people in 90 different countries and was the main point of contact for many of them, which led to inefficiency. She, therefore, introduced a process that centralized information in a Google Docs table, accessible to all and regularly updated by members of the team. She programmed an automatic email, sent it out once a fortnight, reminding everyone to update the file.

Then she created an FAQ page with answers to the questions most commonly posed by her colleagues, gave more responsibility to her team members, and merged many of their regular meetings. This and other improvements reduced the time she needed to work to three hours a day.

At the same time, her boss was extremely pleased with her productivity gains, making it easy for Emma to negotiate working from home on Wednesdays. A month later, figures in hand, she proved to her boss that she was more productive working from home and negotiated first Tuesdays, then the whole week, at home!

She was helped in this by the ingenious process she had put in place, and also by the fact that her company wanted to develop a remote-working culture, mainly because office rents in London were so high.

So now she works an average of three hours a day, from home... or from anywhere, as long as she is in a time zone compatible with her work, which means she still has plenty of places and activities to explore.

She is still adding enormous value to her company, with the result that everyone is more than happy with this arrangement. If you can make yourself indispensable in an intelligent way, there is nothing to say that you absolutely must spend eight hours a day in an office.

So, what process could you put in place to automate part of your work and negotiate at least one day a week at home?

You are unemployed

If you are unemployed, no problem: use all the free time at your disposal to throw yourself into your project. There are many supported startup schemes for the unemployed, which you should investigate.

Identifying your strong points

Take time to think of all the things that might be to your advantage where your project is concerned. And the things that might hold you back.

Your plus points might include:

- Your skills in your project area

- Your network

- The time you have free

- Your financial resources

- Your motivation: Do you have the sacred flame,[256] every obstacle is a challenge, and nothing will get in your way?

What might hold you back? The very same things. It all depends on your circumstances. For example, when I left school at 18, these were some of my strong points and my weak points:

Strong points:

- The sacred flame – motivation that drove me on

- A good knowledge of IT

- My youth, which significantly reduced my material needs

- My powers of persuasion

Weak points:

- No experience in business

- No financial assets

- Very few customers

- Very few relationships

---

256 Not everyone has the sacred flame. It is a powerful, invincible source of motivation that comes from within and makes you know you must succeed, or else you will die – not necessarily in a physical sense, but at least spiritually.

- My youth and the naivety that went with it

- My appearance

Take a pen and paper, or open a computer file, and list your strong and weak points when it comes to starting your project.

Take the time to do this exercise properly.

Then answer the following questions:

- Can I take greater advantage of my strong points? How?

- Can I identify other strengths that would be of benefit? How?

- Can I find a way of ensuring that some or all of my weak points don't count so much against me or are eliminated? How?

HOW ROMAIN COLLIGNON FOUNDED HIS 'LIFESTYLE' BUSINESS IN TANDEM WITH HIS REGULAR JOB

Romain had a very well-paid job as a senior manager in an agency dependent on the French Ministry of Scientific Research. In 2011, while undertaking my Blogeur Pro training course, he launched his own Décodeur du Non-Verbal blog, sharing methods and techniques for decoding body language.

He started his business following the principles taught in this book: online market research, testing in real-life conditions using his blog... all on a part-time basis, in tandem with his regular job and spending very little.

But it also involved sacrifice, as he explained: 'It took a real effort in the beginning to develop my Décodeur du Non-Verbal business. I would get up every day at five o'clock to work on it, and every weekend. I would spend my eight hours at the agency, then in the evening, go back to working on the blog.

I worked to make it a money-earner for 18 months, then I resigned from my day job to further develop the Décodeur business.

By the end of 2015, the business was automated and required only half a day of real work each week.'

Today his business is generating sales worth €120,000 per annum for half a day's work each week. This enabled him to engage in a new activity he is passionate about.

In short, launching a part-time business alongside your regular job definitely demands sacrifices. But it is possible. Just as it is possible to turn a business into a largely automated 'lifestyle' business in the long term.

TURNING A PROFIT AS QUICKLY AS POSSIBLE

One of the most common strategic errors made by entrepreneurs immediately after founding their business is a tendency to neglect two fundamental activities:

1. Finding prospects who are potentially interested in their products and services.

2. Persuading them to buy these products and services.

The priority objective of a newly founded business is to reach the profitability threshold, i.e., to break even, with income balancing expenditure. Unless it comes to this point quickly, the embryo business is doomed to fail once the initial cash reserve has been used up. The founder of any business must, therefore:

- Have estimated how long he or she can survive without breaking even, assuming a) a low level of sales, b) an average level of sales, and c) a high level of sales (e.g., just 40 percent of the break-even point reached after X months for the lower level, 60 percent for the average level and 80 percent for the higher level).

- Spend at least 80 percent of their time finding prospects and persuading them to buy the product or service concerned.

Unfortunately, however, most new business owners do just the opposite: they spend 80 percent of their time focusing on secondary issues, like choosing their office décor, the design of their business cards, the graphics of their website or the configuration of their computers, and just 20 percent on generating sales. This is a drastic error.

Your superb mahogany-colored Ikea desk, the magnificent 1960s armchair you hunted down in a junk shop, the business cards painstakingly designed during endless evenings staring at your computer screen, all of these things are pointless if you fail to reach your break-even point in time.

In the beginning, just make it 'cheap and cheerful.' Avoid gadgets, which may reassure you, but whose main effect will be to make you put off the critical things, the things you would prefer to avoid from a sense of fear.

The three most important things when you begin are, therefore, sales, sales, and sales.

Obviously, the lower your expenditure and the greater your initial funding, the longer you will have to reach the break-even point.

SELLING MUST BE YOUR GREAT OBSESSION, EVEN IF YOUR INVESTMENT IS NIL

If you start your business part-time and organize things to minimize your expenditure, which you can cover from your salary, or have no expenditure at all, it may be that you reach the profitability threshold from the very outset.

In this case, your objective should be to get your business off the ground as quickly as possible, so you should still spend 80 percent of your time focused on sales.

WHY THE 'WHY' IS IMPORTANT

Your customers will be much more likely to forgive your errors, follow your lead, and be enthusiastic about your products if you explain to them why you do what you do. In other words, why you founded your business and what mission you seek to accomplish through it.

This is the argument made by Simon Sinek, author of the best-selling *Start with Why*,[257] whose TED-talk video has registered more than 43 million views,[258] placing it among the top ten on this site.

---

257 Éditions Performance, 2015.
258 Simon Sinek, 'How great leaders inspire action': http://en.olivier-roland.com/ted-great-leaders/

According to Simon Sinek, the thing that characterizes such innovative enterprises as Apple – which always outscore their rivals, despite having access to the same resources, talents, and means of communication – and leaders such as Martin Luther King, is that they know why they are doing things, rather than just how. And they let people know about it.

The example of Apple

So, let's take Apple. If Apple was like any other company, this is how it would communicate: 'We make great computers. They are magnificently designed and user-friendly. Would you like one?'

Whereas this is how Apple communicates: 'In everything we do, we believe in challenging the status quo. We believe in a different way of thinking. We challenge the status quo by making products that are magnificently designed and user-friendly. The result is that we make great computers. Would you like one?'

You see the difference? On the one hand, you have a conventional sales pitch, which everyone filters out without thinking about it. On the other, you again have a sales pitch, but one which connects much more powerfully in emotional terms with people who believe in similar principles. The difference is fundamental.

People don't buy what you make; they buy why you make it.

The example of the Wright brothers and the invention of the airplane

Simon Sinek gives another edifying example of entrepreneurs motivated by the why, who have easily beaten rivals who were better resourced but motivated solely by money and fame. And this was during the glorious days of the aviation pioneers in the early years of the 20th century.

To read about their exploits in more detail, go to https://en.olivier-roland.com/freres-wright/.

Why I wrote this book

Reread the paragraph right at the beginning of this book (*see p.xv*), where I explain my big WHY.

And how about you? What is your big WHY?

Take a few moments to think about this. What is the mission that drives you? What do you want to contribute to the common good? Sum this up in a sentence. It could well become your slogan. In my case, it is: 'I teach the way of freedom to Intelligent Rebels.'

SUMMARY

For the intelligent rebel who has decided to act

➡ Imagine creating your business as a scientific experiment: you must prove, to yourself and to the world, that your business model is viable and with minimum expenditure of money, time, and energy.

➡ Carry out a market study on the Internet to reduce uncertainties and gather information that will be valuable subsequently.

➡ Use the information to create your 'customer magnet' and build up a list of qualified prospects interested in your offering.

➡ Define your business by giving it a name and describing its unique selling point (slogan), if possible, focusing on its benefits. Possibly by conducting a survey and several A/B tests to decide which are most powerful.

➡ Create one or more avatars representative of your customers. It is this/these avatar(s) you will be targeting when you communicate with your prospective customers.

➡ At this stage, you will be able to test out your product and discover its real sales potential... by selling it before it has been produced. There are many tools you can use for this purpose. The webinar is one of the most effective. Choose one of the tools presented in this chapter and use it.

➡ If your sales are satisfactory, go ahead with the product or service, taking into account feedback from your first users so you can gradually improve it. Or pivot and offer a different version using another approach.

➡ If it is not possible to sell your product on a pre-order basis, create a simple prototype that meets your customers' basic needs, and sell it.

➡ If you are in employment, take time to analyze your timetable and identify activities you can cut down on.

➡ Above all, take time to think about the WHY of your business and your product. And make that your starting point. It will make an enormous difference where successful communication is concerned and your ability to attract fans, not just customers.

To help you put the activities described in this chapter into practice, go to http://en.olivier-roland.com/creer/ to receive an email with a series of activities and challenges that will give you the necessary motivation.

CHAPTER 13
BUSINESS BASICS
How to Make Your Business Sustainable

SHOULD YOU GO IT ALONE OR IN A PARTNERSHIP?

This question very often arises when starting a business. And, as with many difficult questions, there is no definitive answer: In either case, there are advantages and disadvantages. Let's begin with starting a business on your own.

Setting up on your own: advantages and disadvantages

The most obvious advantage is straightforward enough: you will always agree with yourself (unless you are schizoid). This may seem trivial, but as so many businesses have folded or failed to grow due to deep disagreement between founders who believed they were lifelong buddies, it would be dangerous to underestimate this advantage.

For example, one of my friends, whom I shall refer to as John, seeing how well my blogs were doing, decided to start one of his own and turn it into a dynamic little business. He went into partnership with a close friend, whom I shall refer to as Bertrand, and they decided on their objective: to create a personal development blog for men. After a year, they were making good progress: traffic was increasing, with several thousand visits a month; they had several thousand subscribers on their mailing list, and they were making a monthly profit of around €2,000. Not bad for a part-time project started while the two partners were finishing their studies. All was set for the profits to at least triple during their second year, allowing John and Bertrand to live their dream and setting them free to travel the world.

Unfortunately, however, growing tensions due to differences of opinion over working methods undermined their relationship. Bertrand was inclined to work like mad on the business, fussing over even the smallest details, willing to sacrifice his evenings and weekends. He also wanted to experiment with new methods rather than sticking to tried-and-tested formulae. John favored an 80/20 approach, not spending too much time on minor details such as the hyper-precise positioning of the navigation bar. He wanted to stick to what had hitherto proved successful and simply keep up the good work.

Bertrand persuaded John to test a new promotional method he had invented for the launch of a new version of a product that had worked well in the past (an online training course on self-confidence). The new method turned out to be much less effective, which only increased John's resentment toward his partner. Bertrand, for his part, took the setback very personally and lapsed into a depression that sapped his motivation.

The pair eventually ended their joint venture and, discouraged by the experience, went off in quite separate directions: John became a nuclear engineer (the career he had trained for originally). At the same time, Bertrand moved to another area and started a new project in a totally different field. No need to add that their friendship didn't survive this unhappy episode.

The saddest aspect of all this is that, if each of them had undertaken the project independently, I am convinced that at least one of them would have been successful. But who was right? Bertrand, who aimed for perfection in every detail and was prepared to work long hours, or John, who was content with an 80/20 approach? I would tend to vote for John, whose approach is closer to my own, but I can't deny that many successful entrepreneurs are more like Bertrand – Steve Jobs, for example. The real problem was that their working methods were incompatible.

It is easy to be wise with hindsight. The truth is that, in starting a business together, John and Bertrand had only the vaguest idea of their respective styles, which they developed as time went on. So it would have been very difficult for them to foresee their incompatibility. But this is precisely the issue: it is impossible to know what will occur between the partners in an enterprise, and you must always envisage the worst outcome – a total divorce – and make provision for what you would do in that case. In writing.

When a couple marries, they generally do so in good faith, thinking their marriage will last and making every effort to ensure that it does. But, given that the divorce rate is nevertheless high, how can you believe that nothing could cause two childhood friends to fall out after working together for a year to develop a business.

Liking another person doesn't necessarily mean you agree on everything. Of course, a falling-out of this kind isn't inevitable – you may be able to work together in total harmony – but at least starting a business on your own eliminates this risk.

Another advantage is that you won't have to pay two salaries, buy two computers, and so on. Depending on your initial budget, that could make a huge difference.

On the other hand, you will, of course, have fewer resources. Which brings us to...

Starting with a partner/partners, advantages and disadvantages

The main advantage of starting a business with a partner is that you can do twice as much work, provided the tasks are fairly shared and have complementary skills. But that means you really must complement each other.

When I was on the jury of a business funding organization in Lille, I remember dealing with two individuals who wanted to start an IT services enterprise. Given the similarity between their activity and my own, I abstained when it came to the vote. But I remember the hesitations of the other members of the jury, who homed in on one particular point: Why on earth were they starting this business together? They had the same skills, whereas one needed to be strong on the commercial side, the other on the technical. The fact that both were IT technicians implied that:

- They would need twice as many customers to keep them both occupied full time and to cover two salaries and the related charges.

- It therefore would take them longer to reach the break-even point... with the risk that they would run out of cash before then...

- ... And all of this without having the skills to quickly acquire enough customers. The jury, therefore, decided not to grant the loan. But this didn't stop them, who by pure chance set up their business in the same building as mine.

So I was able to follow their progress. I can give you both good and bad news. The good news is that 15 years on, the business is still trading. I even sold them part of my client portfolio from my first business when I changed direction. The bad news is that their business has never really got off the ground and has experienced many difficulties that could well have put a stop to it all. The jury's doubts were well-founded: from the outset, the enterprise has lacked the commercial nous to put in place a real client acquisition strategy.

Even a simplified version of such a strategy would have been more effective than the situation that has prevailed: the total absence of any strategy for acquiring customers. I'm not going to condemn them: I have made the same mistake myself, as have many millions of other business owners.

Moreover, their duplication of skills meant that they were effectively overmanned during the early years, but the time that was freed up wasn't efficiently applied to finding new customers.

How did they manage to keep going? By leveraging the chief advantage of starting up as partners rather than with employees: they believed in their project and were prepared to make sacrifices. In particular, they were ready to:

1. Spend much more time on their business than an employee

2. Go without a decent salary, or any salary at all, while the business was getting off the ground

3. Invest money in the business

If you are thinking of starting up with a partner who doesn't agree with even one of these three points, I strongly recommend that you look for someone else.

The business has therefore survived because its founders were prepared to go without a decent salary and be paid less than the few employees they did take on. This super-motivation is an asset when you first begin but can become a liability in the long run, as it conceals a built-in weakness. An enterprise can survive for a long time 'on life support,' whereas if the partners were paying themselves an average salary or taking on an employee to free one of them up, it would soon be deep in the red. Consequently, a poor strategy and inefficient organization can persist for a long time, preventing the managers, if they hide their heads in the sand or get used to mediocre performance, from really facing up to their problems and seeking to improve.

Clear enough, then. If starting a business with a partner (or partners) is to work, you need to complement one another and share the various tasks intelligently according to your strengths.

If this is the case, it can really boost your business. If you consider the giants of the new technologies, Apple, Microsoft, Google, etc., you will find that they all started from scratch and with partners with complementary skills.

The textbook case is obviously Steve Jobs, the brilliant visionary and entrepreneur, in partnership with Steve Wozniak, the IT genius; the way they complemented each other was the foundation of Apple's success. What would the pair of them have achieved left to themselves? Probably, not much. Steve Jobs lacked the technical skills to design computers and would have been hard put to persuade 'normal' partners to join him, given the unkempt-hippy and the way-out-Hindu-disciple image he was cultivating at the time. Steve Wozniak was an IT genius, but also the prototype of the introverted geek. Left to himself, he was no doubt capable of designing a groundbreaking computer, but how would he have sold it, let alone made it the flagship of a great multinational company? Maybe he would have given his computers away or sold them at way below their value.

Of course, your objective isn't necessarily to found the next Apple or the next Google, so deciding whether to work with a partner/partners is also a matter of ambition. If your aim is to create a 'quality of life' business, going it alone is undoubtedly a good option and will save you many headaches. If you are very ambitious and prepared to sacrifice evenings and weekends to launch the 'next big thing,' going into a partnership is almost a *sine qua non*. Just be aware of the dangers to which this can lead and the need to get things right at the outset – in particular, avoiding a 50/50 shareholding.

HOW TO MINIMIZE RISK AND MAXIMIZE YOUR CHANCES OF SUCCESS

I'm all in favor of trying to minimize risk and maximize your chances of success. When setting up a business, the way to do this is:

- Ensure that, even if you fail, you won't suffer any significant loss but will be able to bounce back unburdened by a great mountain of debt.

- Have a plan B so that you still have a source of income if you fail.

The essence of this approach is to test your idea by engaging with the market at the earliest opportunity and with the least possible investment, i.e., to get started part-time alongside your current job studies.

If you already have a saleable product or just a website receiving thousands of monthly visits, you are starting with a considerable advantage. But that's not enough: there are measures you can take to further reduce the element of risk.

Look for support

The myth of the lone-ranger entrepreneur who does everything off their own back is just that: a myth. You would be surprised how many organizations can help you with your business project free of charge and provide you with invaluable resources: oversight, help in drafting a business plan, networking, getting funding, introductions to banks, and so on. These organizations may be public or semi-private, but all have the aim of encouraging business startups and are very much aware of the importance of fostering economic dynamism.

Seek out these support networks in your nearest administrative center. Explain your project and ask if they can give you support and, if so, how they can best help you.

Of course, you don't want to be involved with too many different organizations, but meet them all, choose one that can provide the bulk of the support you need, and maybe two or three others that can offer complementary services. No more than that.

N.B. Most of these organizations will be good at supporting you in setting up a 'conventional' business, market research, loans, and so on. Still, they may not be familiar with the Lean Startup approach. All you need to tell them is that it involves a grass-roots experiment that takes the market research a stage further and helps reduce uncertainty. Anyone will understand this and see the advantages.

Is mentoring obligatory if you don't need financial support?

The straight answer is no... but it is nonetheless helpful. If you have perfectly executed the Lean Startup strategy, are already cash-flow positive, and don't need additional finance, congratulations! But even if you are so fortunate, having support may still be advantageous for several reasons. It can help you:

- Learn about the resources that could be made available to you. You might be surprised.

- Find out what assistance and funding you are eligible for.

- Make yourself better known and develop your network. Your success won't go unnoticed, and this might open doors for you.

Get as much support as possible in the form of 'honor loans,' guarantees, and grants

The more you can obtain grants, keep receiving unemployment benefits, be exempted from making social security contributions, get interest-free and 'honor' loans (government loans free of obligations if your business fails), the fewer debts you will have if it all goes pear-shaped. So try and get as much of this kind of support as possible.

Request all the financial assistance you are entitled to through the startup support organizations you are registered with to help you: some specialize in this field. In some cases, they are themselves the agencies that decide whether or not to grant funding.

Find out if you can set up your business in a free zone, i.e., a port or other area in your country where companies are taxed very lightly.

Fund your project adequately

You remember the story of how my first business almost went belly up in the first six months? It was undoubtedly due to my naivety and lack of experience when it came to acquiring customers. But also due to inadequate funding: in those dire circumstances, the measly sum of €3,800 was enough to get my head above water and transform a bankrupt business into one that thrived for the next 10 years.

The problem is that it is much easier to secure loans and other forms of financial assistance when you first set up your business than six months or a year later when it is on the skids. In the first case, you can give the impression that you have a clear vision and are prepared for all eventualities; in the second, you are bailing out a sinking ship. So budget generously, and add a safety margin for your peace of mind.

Keep your personal and business assets separate: choose the right legal vehicle

This is the least you can do to minimize risk. If you have to sue for bankruptcy and your business is incapable of repaying its debts, this will prevent creditors from getting their hands on your personal assets.

So if, for instance, your business is bankrupt and has debts of $100,000 it can't repay, no one, not even the state, can seize your house or your car to get their money back because your business is deemed to be a legal entity in its own right, distinct from you as an individual.

All developed countries provide legal vehicles that give you this basic protection, but most also have structures that make no distinction between enterprise and owner.

As a general rule, there is no advantage in going for a structure that doesn't afford protection. Still, if at first, you have to make a choice between protection and simplicity, in most cases, I would advise opting for simplicity (as you are not even sure your business will get off the ground).

Once you have reached a certain threshold (a turnover of $50,000 or $100,000, for example), you can change your structure for one that affords greater protection and be in a position to pay an accountant to advise you.

Sign here on the dotted line, Sir

Many aspiring entrepreneurs don't realize that such protection doesn't extend to the bank.

When a bank grants you a loan to start a business, it will either lend you the money personally or ask you to act as a guarantor, which means you will be obliged to repay the loan if the business can't. Similarly, banks will generally demand that you provide surety for any over-drawing on your business account. Of course, everything is subject to negotiation, but when you are setting up a business, you are hardly in a position of strength. Even so, you should visit several banks because, in any negotiation, the more options you have, the stronger your position. You should also consider renegotiating these points when your business is beginning to make money; bankers tend to be more helpful in such conditions.

Meanwhile, remember one thing: when you stop trading, you are 'entitled' to owe money to all and sundry, but not to the bank. In practical terms, this means it would be better not to pay your suppliers or even the state than to have an overdraft with the bank. This is because if you have adopted the right legal vehicle, not even the state can take away your personal assets in most cases. Whereas the bank has only to brandish your personal guarantee to enable it to seize almost all your belongings.

Protect your main place of residence

In your country, there are undoubtedly mechanisms for protecting your home so that it can't be taken away from you: investigate the options.

Darling, who are those men in black knocking at the door?

If you are married, go for a nuptial arrangement that enables each partner to keep their own share of the property. Otherwise, creditors can seize all of a couple's assets.

A salary? What salary?

Until you reach the break-even point, don't pay yourself a salary. Begin by working part-time following the Lean Startup principles. Seek to remain on unemployment benefit. Continue to live with your parents a bit longer than planned. Reduce your personal expenditure as much as possible. If you really have to, draw the strict minimum to keep you going.

In my first year, I hardly paid myself anything at all – €228 a month. I was 19, I had just left home, and living in a 140ft^2 studio held no terrors for me; in fact, it was a significant improvement, as now I was free and independent! But neither was it a bed of roses: I did my shopping in a discount supermarket; I could hardly afford a drink if I went out with friends; in my apartment block, my room was located between the toilets and the shower room. As for sound insulation, I'll leave it to your imagination. I didn't care. I was burning with the sacred flame, and such details were of secondary importance. The main thing was to ensure that my business made a profit. That was all that counted.

Of course, if you are older, perhaps married with children, it will be impossible for you to live like that, and I'm not expecting you to. But do ask yourself: can I live a bit more simply? Are there things I can cut down on or do without for a while? Examine your bank statement and make a list of your monthly items of expenditure. Then reduce or eliminate as many as you can.

In a few months, it may be that every dollar will count and be the difference between the success and failure of your project. And if your business takes off, you will be able to enjoy all the things you deprived yourself of a hundred times over.

Minimize pointless expenditure

You should, of course, minimize pointless expenditure on your business. It is easy enough to justify excessive spending with arguments such as: 'I need a large office as that helps me to have a big vision.' But be pragmatic. Ask yourself: Is this really an investment that will earn money, or is it a vanity trip?

When my business almost went bust, I analyzed all my expenses with a fellow entrepreneur. We soon realized that the office I was renting was larger than necessary: 388ft^2 just for me because I had a very optimistic business plan and was expecting to take on additional staff in my first year. So I moved to a 312ft^2 office, which saved the business several thousand a year, at a time when this was vitally important.

A few years later, I was proud to move to an office larger than the one I had left and accommodate two full-time employees.

In a word, keep a careful check on your spending: every three months, take a look at your bank statement and analyze your expenditure. What can you cut down on? What can you cut out completely?

Smooth your income by getting paid regularly

One of the tricks that most helped me to make my business profitable I learned from one of my first business customers, an old hand who had managed a business with 200 employees. He said: 'Olivier, some people are happy when they make a killing, but a real businessman knows that serious money is earned from repeat sales.' This permanently changed my philosophy. I began offering my business customers regular maintenance contracts rather than just emergency repair services. And it worked! By adopting this method, I quickly acquired sufficient maintenance contracts to cover my business expenditure and break even every month, without having to find new customers. Everything else was a bonus.

So ask yourself: How can I transform my one-off products and services into repeat business? If you can find a way of doing this, it will lead to a complete change of outlook, and the profitability of your business will be assured. Just imagine the serenity that would come from knowing your expenses are covered each month without having to find new customers or sell more. Wouldn't that be wonderful? It's within your reach.

SUMMARY

For the intelligent rebel who has decided to act

➡ Setting up on your own has advantages and disadvantages, as has starting a business in partnership.

➡ If you are hesitating over whether or not to establish a business with one or more partners, rereading the first part of this chapter will be helpful.

➡ Always try to minimize risk, particularly the risks associated with financing.

➡ With this in mind, accept all the financial assistance, grants, exemptions, and honor loans available to you. They may make the difference between success and failure.

➡ At the same time, choose the legal vehicle that will afford you the most protection, possibly after testing your model with a flexible micro-enterprise structure.

➡ Be aware that debts of all kinds are excusable, except with the bank.

➡ Until you have reached the break-even point, pay yourself only the absolute minimum you need to survive and, in the early days, focus above all on three things: sales, sales, sales. Nothing else matters. And this is an excellent point to conclude, as in the next chapter we shall consider how to sell effectively.

To help you put the activities described in this chapter into practice, go to http://en.olivier-roland.com/creer/ to receive an email with a series of activities and challenges that will give you the necessary motivation.

CHAPTER 14
MONEYMAKING
How to Sell Effectively – The Art of Marketing

*'I have always been struck that some of the greatest, from
Michelangelo to Van Gogh, never sold much because
they didn't know how to do it. Too many actors, writers
and artists think that marketing is beneath them. But
no matter what you do in life, selling is part of it.'*

ARNOLD SCHWARZENEGGER

Ah, marketing! If ever there was a word that divides opinion, this is it. Some people detest the word, and all it implies. 'It's pure manipulation'; 'It creates needs that don't exist'; or 'An excellent product needs no marketing, so it serves only products of no value,' they argue. Others understand its power and importance. If you are in the former camp and think that marketing is bad and/or unnecessary, I've news for you: almost everyone who has ever succeeded in any field was 1) good at what they did and 2) good at selling themselves.

Consider the great artists of the 20th century: do you think that Picasso, Paolo Coelho, Madonna, or James Cameron, to name but a few, were not good at selling themselves? And did their commercial savvy detract from their artistic talents?

Some people think so: they are convinced that, once you begin marketing yourself, you are selling your soul to the devil or some other disgusting monster, and this permanently corrupts what you create. These are the same people who complain that the world isn't interested in them, no doubt because it is too ungrateful, too stupid, or too ignorant to appreciate their worth. The fact is that creating the best product in the world, whatever your field, isn't enough.

The second truth is that refusing to use marketing often betrays a sense of superiority, of disdain for people, as it implies that those with 'intelligence' and 'education' will immediately understand the product's qualities. But things are not so simple. How can you expect people to know that your product is great if they've never heard of it? If they've never had a chance to test it? How do you expect the news to get around on the grapevine? And even if the word does get around that your product is excellent, is it better that the information is spread by 100 people who came across it by chance or by 10,000 who were reached by a marketing campaign and decided to try it?

The purpose of any marketing campaign is to capture your prospects' attention and, ultimately, motivate them to buy your product. Here are the five key stages to moving your prospects from attention to action:

1. Attention

2. Understanding and memorization

3. Conviction

4. Involvement

5. Readiness to act

The aim of all the activities we shall be examining in this chapter is to maximize the number of prospects who move from one stage to the next.

THE UNIVERSAL MECHANISMS OF INFLUENCE

To engage in effective marketing, the canny entrepreneur needs to know the universal principles of influencing people. Why 'universal'? Aren't human beings all different, and don't cultures vary enormously from county to country? This is true. But we also have many things in common. In particular, those things that distinguish us from other animal species: we are bipeds, we have opposable thumbs, and we can communicate through language, for example. All these things are determined by our human nature, in other words, by our genes.

Let's do a mental experiment. Imagine for a few moments that you had been born with the genes of a chimpanzee. How would you be behaving at this very moment? Go on, think about it (mime the actions if you can!). Your behavior would be very different from the way you behave with human genes, wouldn't it? You certainly wouldn't be reading this book. You can read it because you have learned the language in which it is written. And the ability to learn a language derives directly from our genes; this is a characteristic shared by all humans. The fact is that many influencing mechanisms are shared by all human beings, and they transcend cultures.[259]

---

259 Robert Cialdini, *Influence: The Psychology of Persuasion*, Pocket, 2014.

But what is influence? The power to persuade someone, either on a theoretical level, by getting them to adopt a concept, or on a practical level, by motivating them to act, or both. And the action of selling is, of course, dependent on the power to persuade someone to buy one of your products. In business, as in life, there is a foundational principle: it is impossible to go against human psychology. And we are influenced by both reason (ideas) and emotion (feelings). In some cases, more by one than the other, depending on our personality, our mood, circumstances, and so on.

To sell something, we must appeal to both the reasoning faculties and the emotions of our prospects. This is quite logical. Let's take a simple example. You are in a shop buying an item. Would you prefer to buy from:

- An ill-humored salesperson who barely makes an effort to greet you and communicates gloom and doom; or

- A smiling salesperson who greets you with a hearty 'Good morning!' cracks a couple of jokes and gives you some tips on making the best use of the product in question?

Obviously, most of us would much prefer to buy the article from the second salesperson. From a purely rational point of view, however, the product is exactly the same, whoever you buy it from. But it is only human to want to please the friendly salesman who cheered you up a bit than buying from the grumpy one.

Similarly, your prospects will be more strongly motivated to buy your product or service if you come across as pleasant and friendly rather than disagreeable or indifferent. It is therefore natural that you will want to create an agreeable online image of yourself, as you do in everyday life.

And being pleasant and agreeable is only one of the many factors that enhance your influence. As with the Force in *Star Wars*, these factors can be used for good or for ill. To sell quality products or to sell garbage. The canny entrepreneur will use them to sell products that add value because he or she knows that, in the long run, this is the only way of creating value for him/herself, his/her business, and his/her family.

Clearly, being pleasant and friendly on its own isn't enough: human beings are also influenced by their intelligence. We address their intelligence by offering them a product that precisely meets their needs, as identified in surveys, and by making them an 'Irresistible Offer,' as detailed later in this chapter.

But first of all, what are these factors of influence? Here they are, taken from two books – *Influence: The Psychology of Persuasion*, by Robert Cialdini, and *Made to*

Stick, by Chip and Dan Heath[260] – with concrete examples that show how to apply them as part of your communication/advertising strategy.

Influence factor 1: Reason

In his book *Influence: The Psychology of Persuasion*, researcher and psychologist Robert Cialdini reports on an instructive experiment showing that being able to give a reason for what you are doing is surprisingly influential. In this experiment, someone makes a request to people queuing to use a photocopier, with three different variants:

Variant 1: 'Excuse me, I've only got five pages. Could I use the machine first, because I'm in a hurry?'

Variant 2: 'Excuse me, I've only got five pages. Could I use the machine first?'

In the first case, 94 percent of people agreed to let this person jump the queue; in the second, 60 percent. We might deduce that people are more inclined to say yes if we tell them we are in a hurry.

But now let's look at variant 3: 'Excuse me, I've only got five pages. Could I use the machine first, because I have to make some photocopies?'

What do you think the 'agreement rate' was in this case? After all, if you want to use a photocopier, it's obviously to make photocopies, not to make a strawberry milkshake. Even so, it was 93 percent!

Robert Cialdini explains that the way our brain is wired makes us more likely to agree to a request if it is backed by a reason. No matter what the reason may be.

So, whenever you ask your prospects to do something, be sure to give them a reason. But it must be plausible, and above all, true. For example, if you are doing a promotion, say that you want to do your customers a favor and offload your stock. Or tell them bluntly that you have to pay your taxes. This is the tactic adopted by the American entrepreneur Jeff Walker, whom I spoke about earlier (*see p.188*). He received an unexpected tax demand and decided to do a promotion to raise the money he needed... so he sent an email to his whole list of prospects, telling them about it. His prospects could easily identify with his problem – who has never been caught out by the inland revenue? And the promotion was a success. You are

---

260 Pearson, 2016.

not obliged to be as frank as that but be sure always to give a reason – the words 'as' and 'because' are surprisingly powerful.

Influence factor 2: Reciprocity

Reciprocity is simply the need we feel, when given something, to give something back in return. Whether consciously or not, the fact of being given something creates a debt of equivalent value. This rule applies to all human societies and is the glue of social bonding, even in so-called primitive societies.[261]

Imagine your embarrassment, for example, if at Christmas a family member who earns roughly the same as you were to give you a far more expensive present than the one you have got for them. Maybe a rare item they know you are going to love, discovered by spending weekends rummaging through old junk shops, while you give them a nondescript bottle of wine you bought at the last minute... You might be so embarrassed, in fact, that you tell the person that the bottle of wine is a stop-gap because their real present hasn't arrived yet, and you will let them have it as soon as it is delivered. Or again, imagine you are moving to a new address, and one of your neighbors comes round quite spontaneously to say hello, then offers to give you a hand moving the furniture. Gratefully, you accept. Then he comes round a few months later to ask you for a hand with something. Does the fact that he has previously helped you influence your response? Can you and would you want to refuse after the help he has given you?

Each of us knows the rule and is familiar with the social disapproval heaped on those who fail to observe it: they are labeled ungrateful, opportunistic, selfish, mercenary.

How can you use the rule of reciprocity to your advantage in business? Give free gifts to your prospects and customers. Handy samples, for example, which will also enable you to familiarize them with your products. Or simply provide some content: whatever product or service you are selling, you can give them a guide or a video on the lines of: 'The X mistakes to avoid making when doing [*Action Y*]' or 'Five tips (or secrets) for making a success of [*Action Y*].'

For example, if you run a pet shop: 'Seven mistakes to avoid to ensure your pet thrives' or 'Seven tips to keep your pet happy and healthy.' If you are a plumber: 'Five fatal errors to avoid if you want to reduce your water bill,' or 'Five trade secrets for reducing your water bill.' If you are running a startup in the online healthcare field: 'Six scientifically proven tips for living longer and maintaining your health.'

---

261 See in particular *Essai sur le don. Forme et raison de l'échange dans les sociétés archaïques*, by the anthropologist Marcel Mauss, PUF, 2012.

If you own an organic food store: 'Eight mistakes to avoid when buying organic food.' And so on and so forth.

This requires very little time or investment and is what I would recommend you do in the beginning. You can then provide these resources in hard-copy format, or as PDF files or private videos online, with the advantage that both media cost absolutely nothing.

Giving away this kind of content has many advantages: it reinforces your authority, gives your prospects and customers something they can share with others, and will help them practically if your advice is sound and they put it into practice. It will create reciprocity even stronger than being given a small present.

Moreover, you can ask the people who come to your store or visit your website to let you have their names and email addresses – and possibly further details – so they can receive your freebie, which will boost your list of qualified prospects.

Influence factor 3: Consistency and commitment

We have an almost obsessive desire to appear consistent, as in most cases, consistency is regarded as a strength. By the same token, inconsistency is generally frowned upon: anyone who constantly changes their mind may be seen as capricious or unreliable. Moreover, someone whose opinions, words, and actions don't add up may be regarded as hypocritical or even unbalanced. In contrast, consistency in word and deed tends to be associated with intelligence and strength of character. It is seen as the basis for logic, rationality, stability, and honesty.

There comes a moment when it is crucial to ask prospects and customers to commit themselves to your products. To this end, simply ask if they value the product or service you have sold them. This straightforward question will make them aware that they like your product (assuming they do) and will encourage them to affirm the fact. Of course, your product had better be high quality if you want most of your customers to answer 'Yes!' However, this simple affirmation increases the chances that your customer will speak well of your products to others since they will have expressed a commitment.

At the start of my first business venture, I used to go into company offices to carry out emergency maintenance on computers. Sometimes, customers would phone me back a few days later to complain that the problem wasn't resolved. When I returned, I would often discover that it wasn't the same problem that had re-emerged, but a new one. It was useless to explain that because a car's brakes had been repaired, there was no guarantee that something wouldn't go wrong with the starter motor. And it was often tricky to invoice these additional hours, as the customers would refuse to admit I was right.

So, following a maintenance operation, I began asking the user of the computer to check that everything was working properly. They would sit down, carry out a check, then tell me that, yes, everything was working just fine. This simple confirmation on their part committed them to accept that my work was duly completed and drastically reduced the number of subsequent complaints.

Always try to get your prospects and customers to be aware of the reality of a situation and commit to it, whether by saying that a service has been performed satisfactorily, that a product exactly meets their needs, or simply that they are pleased with you.

Influence factor 4: Social proof

Social proof is the fact that we feel better doing something when others are doing it with us. And if enough people are doing something, it can trigger in us the desire to do it too.

Imagine arriving in a town you don't know. It's late, you are hungry, and your smartphone is dead: no chance of consulting Yelp or TripAdvisor. Two restaurants are open, one empty, the other crowded. In which of the two will you feel more comfortable? Most people will tend to choose the more popular restaurant. Deep down, they think: 'The locals must know something about these two restaurants that we don't.' And, of course, if your smartphone is working and you compare the two restaurants, one with an average score of 4.5/5 and 60 comments and the other with 2.5/5 and six comments, which are you going to choose?

When choosing between your product and that of a rival, your prospects will always go for the one with the better marks, the higher number of likes, the more positive comments, and so on. So it is imperative to get your prospects and customers to give an opinion, leave comments, share, like your posts, and so on. You must ensure that a prospect who discovers you for the first time knows that they are not the only person interested in what you are offering and that plenty of satisfied customers have been there before them. This will provide reassurance and encourage the hesitant.

Of all the social proofs you can get, the most powerful and persuasive are video testimonials from your customers. I shall be sharing a detailed method of how to get them later in this chapter.

Influence factor 5: Authority

We are far more likely to obey people we see as having authority: doctors, judges, policemen, politicians, and so on.

Your prospects and customers will be more willing to listen to you if they regard you as an expert, a recognized authority in your field, not just any Tom, Dick, or Harry. Nothing surprising about that. If you wake up one morning with a horrible stomachache, would you listen to the advice of your mechanic or your doctor? And if one morning your car won't start, will you take advice from your mechanic or your doctor? Or from your mother, whom you love, but who has no competence in either of these two areas? The answer is obvious.

There are two sources of authority:

- Intrinsic expertise, which is your real competence in a given field

- Perceived expertise, which is competence as perceived by your audience

You need to develop both to the highest possible degree, taking care that one is always in step with the other.

The problem with most experts is that they are no good at selling: their intrinsic expertise is much greater than their perceived expertise. You must also avoid the opposite problem: if you have plenty of perceived expertise, but your intrinsic expertise isn't up to scratch, you are quite simply an old windbag. And windbags have a limited shelf life. Pointed criticism causes them to explode, or they deflate very quickly.

Influence factor 6: Friendliness

I already mentioned this factor at the start of the chapter: people prefer to buy from pleasant and friendly salespeople. The Tupperware brand built its success because people were buying from a friend, not an unknown salesperson.[262]

The final goal of any product or service is to make the customer happier. This won't be the case if you are sullen, depressive, and unsmiling! This is a principle as old as commerce itself, so respect it: be pleasant. Make sure that your company and your products are user-friendly.

---

262 Tupperware plastic containers were invented in 1938, but it was not until the 'demonstration selling' method, better known as 'Tupperware parties,' were adopted in the 1950s that sales began to take off.

If you are gifted with a naturally friendly, charismatic personality, make good use of it. Make your presence felt on YouTube, on social media, on your blog.

Even if you are dull as ditchwater (which is very unlikely, given that you are one of my readers), you must nevertheless have learned to be polite at some stage in your life and have acquired a minimum of social graces. Use them when you communicate.

Influence factor 7: Rarity value

Scientists have conducted a simple experiment to illustrate the influence of rarity value. They invited students to sample some cookies, then asked them to note down their impressions.[263] The students were divided into two groups:

- One group was presented with a box containing 10 cookies.

- The other group was given a box containing two cookies.

(The cookies in the two boxes were exactly the same.)

In your opinion, which group expressed a greater appreciation of the cookies? Yes, you're right: the second group! The result was even more evident when the researchers first handed out a box of 10 cookies, then said they had made a mistake and replaced it with a box containing only two. This was when the participants gave the cookies the highest average mark.

Something rare is desirable. So always highlight the rarity of your products. Insist, for example, on the end date of a promotional campaign: you will be surprised to find a spike in demand on the day the offer closes.

If your product is available only in limited quantities, whether a limited edition, a training course, or seats for an event, keep your customers regularly informed that there are now just X items/places/days remaining.

The combination of rarity value and social proof is compelling. If your audience sees that one of your products is very much sought after and available only in limited quantity, there may well be an explosion in demand. This is why some artists limit the numbers of people at their concerts, why there are long lines outside Apple stores when a new product is launched, and limited editions sell out in a flash.

---

263 'Effects of Supply and Demand on Ratings of Object Value,' Worchel S., *Journal of Personality and Social Psychology*, 1975.

Influence factor 8: Simplicity

As one lawyer put it: 'If you advance 10 arguments, even if they are all relevant, the jury will have forgotten them all by the time they withdraw to decide on their verdict.'

It's the same with your prospects. And this is why you must make sure your message is simple and crystal clear. The simpler it is, the greater its power to persuade.

Influence factor 9: The unexpected

Do you remember my point about the importance of grabbing people's attention before trying to persuade them to buy? Well, one of the best ways to do this is to take them by surprise. Because surprise 'acts as a kind of emergency override when we confront something unexpected and our guessing machines fail. [...] Ongoing activities are interrupted; our attention focuses involuntarily on the event that surprised us.'[264]

How do you go about it? The best way is to send your prospects a counterintuitive message that flies in the face of common sense. You need to identify the message you wish to communicate, work out what aspects are counterintuitive, and express it in such a way as to foil your prospects' 'guessing mechanisms,' thus taking them by surprise.

For example, when people ask about my occupation, I reply, 'I teach freedom.' This is entirely in line with my BIG WHY. It takes people aback and makes them want to know more.

Influence factor 10: The concrete

'Concrete' also means 'specific.'

When you have a figure to communicate, be precise. This boosts your credibility. For example, it's better to say that following your method will improve your prospects' performance by 18.67 percent in 21 days than to say 20 percent in 30 days.

Being concrete also means speaking in plain language and, above all, avoiding corporate jargon, such as 'customer-orientated visionary paradigm' or 'cost-based reciprocal re-engineering.' Remember, you're speaking to human beings! Your audience will be glad to connect with your company more directly than is possible with many of the major brands!

---

264 Chip and Dan Heath, *Made to Stick*, Pearson, 2016.

Influence factor 11: Credibility

Credibility is very similar to authority in that it, too, depends on perceived expertise. The main difference is that authority makes prospects more likely to listen when you communicate with them, whereas credibility has to do with your prospects believing what you communicate.

The fact is that your prospects are being constantly bombarded with advertisements that promise the Earth... So they have a 'bullshit filter' in place the moment they realize they are being 'got at.' You need to be credible for your message to get through this filter. Therefore:

- Your message needs to be simple and specific.

- The figures and studies you present must be accurate and verifiable.

- It helps if you are pleasant and friendly.

- The more social proof, the better.

Influence factor 12: Emotion

If you can manage to arouse strong feelings in your prospects, they will be more taken by your message and more likely to act. This is by no means easy to do unless you can make a Hollywood-style film. But some brands have tried producing short videos that take their cue from Hollywood by creating real-life stories. I'll give you a couple of examples in the next section.

Influence factor 13: Storytelling

As human beings, we are very sensitive to storytelling. The same message communicated in the style of an 'official report' will be far less compelling than if it were expressed in the form of a story. Here are two examples of adverts that tell a story and thereby arouse strong emotions.

Beats headphones by Dre

The American football star Colin Kaepernick is on a bus. Suddenly, a man appears, emerging from the open roof of an automobile traveling alongside the bus. He brandishes a banner saying, 'You are a turd, Kaepernick,' while shouting 'You're shit! You're shit!' The bus stops near a stadium, greeted by a crowd waving placards, shouting insults at the footballer, and throwing garbage at the bus.

At this point, Kaepernick puts on a set of headphones, and the noise made by the crowd suddenly fades away, replaced by the sounds of Aloe Blacc's *The Man*, a very moving piece of music. He then gets off the bus, protected by bodyguards as he moves through the still demented crowd. As he enters the stadium, he breaks into a smile.

Next, we see him in the dressing-room, concentrating before going out onto the field. A slogan appears: *Hear what you want*. This is followed by an image of two sets of Beats by Dre headphones, accompanied by the wording 'with adaptive noise canceling.'[265]

CD Baby

CD Baby has been selling music online, particularly the work of independent musicians, since 2000. Here is the email each customer used to receive as soon as they made a payment for a CD:

Your CDs have been gently taken from our CD Baby shelves with sterilized contamination-free gloves and placed onto a satin pillow.

A team of 50 employees inspected your CDs and polished them to make sure they were in the best possible condition before mailing.

Our packing specialist from Japan lit a candle and a hush fell over the crowd as he put your CDs into the finest gold-lined box that money can buy.

We all had a wonderful celebration afterward, and the whole party marched down the street to the post office where the entire town of Portland waved 'Bon Voyage!' to your package, on its way to you, in our private CD Baby jet.

I hope you had a wonderful time shopping at CD Baby. Your picture is on our wall as 'Customer of the Year.' We're all exhausted but can't wait for you to come back to CDBABY.COM!!

Thank you once again!

---

265 This video can be viewed at http://en.olivier-roland.com/hear-what-you-want/

In conclusion

The common ground in these two stories is that neither is true, nor do they try to hide the fact. No one believes that Colin Kaepernick really purchased a set of Beats headphones to avoid hearing angry supporters; no one believes that the CD Baby email is recounting actual events.

They are simply good stories that arouse strong feelings in us. And these feelings urge us to do something. Because what matters in a story isn't so much truth as transparency and the emotion it stimulates. So if your story is fiction, you have to be sufficiently transparent for everyone to understand its true nature. You can even play around with untruthfulness in a humorous way, as CD Baby does.

And if you use a good story based on truth, you can touch your audience at an even deeper level. For example, I have produced several training courses for entrepreneurs. In the related sales videos, I don't hesitate to share my story of how I left school at 18 and set up a business when I was 19, the difficulties I experienced, and the mistakes I made. Not only is this story true, but I know my audience can identify with it because they have experienced the same things in one way or another. At the same time, they know that I have been in business for a long time, and so have a wealth of experience and that I have overcome the obstacles they are facing.

What aspect of your career could be the subject of an interesting story to share with your audience – and would help you increase your sales? How did you begin? Was it easy? What obstacles did you face? Can you help your audience to avoid them by using your product? How did you get involved in this venture? What drives you, and what might motivate your audience? A sense of mission? A goal? Sheer rebellion? Try to find common ground between your own story and that of your prospects, and you will be able to connect with them more easily.

THE IRRESISTIBLE OFFER

I've already touched on the concept of the Irresistible Offer in the webinar section (*see p.247*), and I'm going to insist on its fundamental importance once again.

To persuade your prospects to buy your product, you need to appeal to both their intellect and their emotions. You have already addressed their intellect by creating the product they say they need (based on replies to your survey)... then their emotions, relying on the appropriate influence factors. Now you are going to appeal again to their intellect by making an irresistible offer... an offer so compelling that they would feel they were crazy to turn it down: the perceived value of your product must be much greater than its price tag.

Entrepreneurs often think that all they need to do is lower prices. But this isn't true; they need to make sure that the value of their product is greater than the price. All you need do is:

- Ensure that your product contains the exciting element your prospects are looking for.

- Possibly add one or two functionalities or a bonus to make the offer even more attractive.

This enables you to offer extraordinary value at a high price. And this is where profits are made. Let's see how you can do this in practice.

INFORMATION: THE UNDEREXPLOITED RESOURCE OF THE WEB

One crucial factor often neglected by online businesses is the value of information.

Imagine you are lost in the desert, and you have run out of water. You have only a few hours to live. How much would you be prepared to pay to know the location of the nearest oasis?

Closer to home, imagine you are a young bachelor. You want to be smartly dressed but going to a men's outfitters is a real pain because you don't know what suits you, and you don't trust salespeople. Wouldn't you value regular, high-quality information that helped you decide what garments were stylish and suited to your particular needs? Information that would transform others' opinions of you and prevent you from making costly mistakes when choosing your clothes? Such information would be very valuable, especially if, as a singleton, you thought that being well dressed would help you in attracting a soul mate!

Now imagine you follow a blog that regularly publishes articles on the art of choosing suitable clothing, with excellent content that teaches you lots of interesting and exciting things and dramatically improves your wardrobe. Farewell to the 1980s-style coat that seemed just the thing when you tried it on, especially when the salesman expressed a favorable opinion, and the oversized shirts with sloping shoulders!

Consider for a moment 1) the degree of expertise you accord to bloggers in the clothing field, and 2) how trusting of them you are and how grateful for their advice. How does this compare, let's say, with the degree of expertise you ascribe to a conventional e-commerce site and the trust you place in it? The bloggers win hands down, don't they? All thanks to the information they provide.

This explains the success of Bonne Gueule, a French men's fashion blog that has attracted an enormous number of fans. Besides online books and training courses, they market a whole range of clothing items that sell like hotcakes, online and instore.

Each product, be it a shirt, a jacket, shoes, or a pair of jeans, is described in detail and at length on a separate page. Not only the materials from which it is made but also advice on how to wear and care for it with photographs.

What's more, the information and other ingredients you provide enable you, quite literally, to create a tribe around you and/or your brand. That's right, a tribe.

Creating your tribe

As Seth Godin says in his book *Tribes: We Need You to Lead Us*:

> *A tribe is a group of people connected together, connected to their leader, connected to an idea. For millions of years, human beings have been part of one tribe or another. A group needs only two things to become a tribe: a common interest and a means of communication.*

A common interest and a means of communication. Can you provide these things, and at the same time quality content, to gather an audience and create a tribe? If you can, you will be a leader in your field and have an enormous advantage over your competitors. One of the great strengths of Bonne Gueule is that they have formed just such a community of fans, who are grateful for the valuable advice they receive.

If the idea of being a tribal leader frightens you, let me end with another quotation from Seth Godin: 'Most people think you have to be charismatic to be a leader. They're wrong. The very fact of being a leader makes you charismatic.'

THREE PILLARS FOR USING INFORMATION WHEN SELLING ON THE WEB

To sell on the web using content, you need to construct three solid pillars to base your success:

- Traffic
- Authority
- Relationships of trust

Developing one of these pillars will enable you to develop the others; neglecting one will weaken the others. Each of these pillars needs to be worked on independently if you are to create an ecosystem that ensures success.

First pillar: Traffic

This is undoubtedly the most important of the three. Traffic is like the ratings for a TV program, an indicator of your success in the Internet context and of the likelihood of your making money.

If you have plenty of traffic, you might even be able to afford to neglect the two other pillars. Even if you forego a lot of money by doing this, you should still generate a reasonable income.

On the contrary, if you have no traffic, all the authority and trust in the world won't earn you a brass cent.

There are two basic principles for generating traffic:

Principle 1: Create and promote the best possible content

Don't make the mistake of thinking that creating excellent content is sufficient. Even if it goes viral and is widely shared, it will always have less effect than if you had actively promoted it.

Principle 2: Don't remain in splendid isolation

Make contact with other players, both in and outside your field. Enter into partnerships, support one another.

Second pillar: Authority

Your authority is a mixture of your real and perceived expertise.

It is difficult (and dangerous) to try and pass for an expert in a particular field when you are not; the least one can say is that it isn't very ethical. But it is also easy not to be perceived as an expert when you really are one. The more you develop your authority, the more attentive your audience will be, and the more disposed to change their habits and perceptions because they will think: 'On this subject, this person or this business knows a lot more than I do. I'd better try out what they are offering because there's a good chance it will work for me.' And so your influence will increase.

How do you find out if someone really is an expert?

Generally, you note what he or she says, writes, or teaches and their results, and you compare these things 1) with your own skills/expertise, 2) with what other experts write and teach and their results, and 3) what the person's customers say about them. As we have seen, there are two types of expertise:

- **Intrinsic expertise:** Your real skills and competencies (or those of your business) in a particular field. Obviously, these develop over time.

- **Perceived expertise:** What your audience, prospects, and customers perceive to be the case. This tends to be the weak point of many experts. They are incredibly good technically but poor at selling themselves, so their audience sees them as less competent than they really are. How then do you boost your perceived expertise or that of your business?

Create quality content

This can really give you an edge over your competitors. Try your hand at blogging, podcasting, and producing videos. I would suggest creating at least one item of content each week (whatever the format), and at least once a month, you should create a Pillar Content item, i.e., an extraordinary item that will teach your readers something useful and interesting and will impress them. You will recognize such items from the number and quality of the comments they provoke and the number of links and mentions they get from other sites and bloggers. Sometimes you will think that such and such an item should be pillar content, but your readers will judge otherwise.

Some people are better at writing articles, others at producing podcasts, or videos. Experiment with the different media and see which you get on best with.

Post your results

In your blog, publish details of your results, even if you experience difficulties in the early days. You will gradually improve, and your improving results will be seen by your readers as evidence of your expertise.

If you suffer setbacks, even serious ones, but come bouncing back, this will boost your status as an expert and the relationship of trust with your audience. Don't just baldly state your results; explain how you achieved them and give your readers/ listeners tips on how they can emulate you.

Make a point of showing that you have followers. Post the numbers for your Facebook fans, followers on Instagram, and YouTube channel subscribers once they total more than 50. This shows that what you have to say interests many people, and your followers are in good company. It generates social proof, which, as explained earlier, is a decisive influence factor because we feel comfortable when others are doing the same as us.

Moreover, your ratings will regularly increase, boosting your perceived expertise: 'If more and more people are showing appreciation, it must mean it's a good thing.'

The number and quality of comments may be helpful and encourage audience members to make their own comments at the end of an article or video.

Interview or show yourself with experts or star performers in your market

An excellent way of generating authority is to interview acknowledged experts. Not only will you develop your intrinsic expertise by learning from such people in the course of the relationship and subsequent discussions, but you will also increase your perceived expertise by being associated in the minds of your audience with the expertise of your interviewees. If you interview an acknowledged expert and ask pertinent questions, you will emerge as having greater expertise yourself.

Third pillar: Relationship of trust

Nowadays, the last thing your customers want is to be treated anonymously, to be dealing with a big 'soulless corporation.' People prefer to deal with real human beings who can interact more personally, even via a computer screen.

Publishing content is an excellent way of developing a relationship with your audience. Why, after all, do people read a blog rather than a magazine on the same subject? For the quality of the content, certainly, but that's not all. Most are looking for something different from the impersonally formatted writing you find in the vast majority of newspapers. They want openness, honesty, style, and all in all, a human relationship between the blogger and themselves.

Imagine you are a writer, keeping your readers on tenterhooks with the thrilling story, not of your life, but of your thoughts and results were the subject of the blog is concerned.

So, in a nutshell, if you want to create a blog and an 'ecosystem' that ensures success, you need to establish a relationship with your readers and inspire them with trust in you. How, then, do you do that?

Show who you are

Don't hide behind a pseudonym; use your first and family names. Your readers want to engage with a human being, not a screen, and with a blog, nothing is more humanizing than a photograph of the author. So publish a smiling picture of yourself on your home page, on your 'about' page, and, if possible, every page on your website.

Tell who you are

Write an 'about' page that describes you and summarizes your life and career, why you started your blog, and, if possible, your BIG WHY.

Once your blog has a few readers and has been going for a few months, I would also recommend writing one or more articles describing your life in more detail, trying to gear it to the subject of your blog, and the successes and failures you have experienced along the way.

Adopt a friendly tone of voice

Usually, this comes naturally but, if you find it difficult, try writing your articles in a conversational tone. Also, use humor, as this creates a more human relationship with readers.

Produce some podcasts

Despite all your efforts to convey your personality and style in your writing, the written word is, by definition, rather cold and impersonal. In contrast, the spoken voice transmits a range of emotions via the subtlety of intonation and the energy you put into it.

Interact with your readers and get to know them

The great advantage of the Internet is that it allows for close interaction in real-time with people worldwide. Respond to comments and emails, carry out surveys to find out more about your readers, aspirations, and problems. When your platform has achieved a degree of success, you will sadly not answer every comment, in which case you must be selective or delegate this task.

In a video, you are communicating via all the usual channels (except maybe smell!), and this is amazingly effective in generating a relationship of trust. You could begin by making a short video presentation of your blog or YouTube channel and what it offers for publication on your home page.

Interviewing experts in video format will further increase your perceived expertise. Moreover, you could shoot some of your videos in an attractive landscape when you on vacation, for example, thus combining business with pleasure. If you are successful in creating a relationship of trust, your audience will be more indulgent when you make mistakes and more helpful. People are more likely to interact with you, mention your platform to their friends, and participate in your success.

COPYWRITING, OR THE ART OF COMMUNICATING IN WRITING

Have you ever heard that words count for only 7 percent in communication, whereas the voice counts for 38 percent and body language 55 percent? You've probably come across it: these figures are trotted out in many training courses in all parts of the world by people who haven't taken the trouble to dig deeper.

Do you know their origin? They derive from a survey carried out in the 1970s by psychologist Albert Mehrabian. And the problem is that they have been taken out of context.

On his website,[266] Mehrabian explains: 'Please note that [these numbers] were derived from experiments dealing with communications of feelings and attitudes (i.e., like-dislike). Unless a communicator is talking about their feelings or attitudes, these equations are not applicable.'

Other specialists in non-verbal language[267] have also shown that these percentages depend on context. One study,[268] for instance, has demonstrated that, in the case of a formal presentation at a conference, words are more important than anything

---

266 http://en.olivier-roland.com/smorder/
267 In particular, Judee Burgoon, David Buller and Gill Woodall.
268 Quoted in the document 'L'impact de la communication non verbale sur la relation commerciale.'

else: they counted for 53 percent in convincing the audience, as against 32 percent for body language and 15 percent for the tone of voice.

Similarly, some slogans are more effective than others. For example, during the debate on gay marriage in France in 2012, which of these two questions do you think received the more affirmative answers:

- Are you in favor of gay marriage?

- Are you in favor of marriage for all?

The slogan 'marriage for all' was invented precisely because it attracts more support than 'same-sex marriage.'

Fine, you are thinking, but what is this leading to? Simply the fact that words matter, particularly in commercial communication. When it comes to copywriting, thousands of scientific tests[269] have explored which words are most effective in sales literature.

A famous example is a mailshot for a correspondence course in piano-playing, which generated a spectacular increase in sales. It was produced by John Caples, who, when he started working as a copywriter in 1925, was presented for training purposes with two piles of advertisements: one consisting of ads that had proved effective and the other, by far the larger, of adverts that hadn't worked.

Two months later, Caples invented the heading that was to make him famous and earned a lot of money for his clients (and himself):

'They laughed when I sat down at the piano – But when I started to play!'

The remainder of the advertisement tells the story of Jack, an aspiring pianist who takes his place at the piano after one of his friends has played a virtuoso piece. His friends laugh, thinking he is joking, but then Jack begins to play. The laughing stops abruptly, replaced by a silence that is the best homage to pay a musician. Then he is asked who his teacher is and how he acquired such ability. He replies that he doesn't have a teacher but took a correspondence course, and all you need do is post off the advertising coupon to receive the first lesson free.

Almost a 100 years after it first appeared, this advertisement is regularly cited as an example of an ad that, without copywriting, would never have achieved such success and persuaded so many people to take music lessons by correspondence.

---

269 I give details of the procedure in Chapter 16 on 'The scientific business.'

It was also copywriting and its underlying principle – scientific advertising – that enabled Claude Hopkins to popularize tooth-brushing in an America where it hadn't yet been adopted as standard practice. I'll examine this story in more detail in the next chapter.

What you need to remember is that choice of words is of crucial importance in your advertising, and the beauty of the Internet is that you can make use of simple tools that calculate everything for you and tell you which words are really persuasive. And in copywriting, the most important thing is always the heading or title because this is what incites people to read, listen to or look at the rest of your sales page.

Here are a couple of examples, taken from emails, that virtually guarantee a higher opening rate than more conventional headings:

'Bad news'

This heading is undoubtedly one of the simplest and most effective and will get you a much higher than average opening rate. Obviously, it plays on people's curiosity and natural tendency to want to know about accidents and disasters. To be used sparingly, and only if you can link it to a real event, for instance, the end of a promotion.

'Two'

Or another figure that corresponds to something in your email. Just stating a figure without any explanation again stimulates people's curiosity and makes them want to open the email to determine what it refers to.

Use special characters

Using special characters before the heading of your email generally increases the opening rate.

Use the recipient's first name

Including the recipient's first name in the heading of the email is another guaranteed way of increasing the opening rate. You could, of course, combine this with all the headers seen previously, for example: 'Bad news, [*first name*].'

Another effective heading: 'This is brilliant, [*first name*]!' This heading significantly increased the opening rate in all the tests I ran. In the same category, 'Wow, [*first name*]!' also works well but was a little less effective in my tests.

In conclusion: uses these techniques sparingly, as overuse will inevitably reduce their effectiveness. Similarly, the heading of your emails should always relate to their content. Don't head an email 'Bad news' if you are going to talk about something totally different in the email itself.

SPIN SELLING FOR BETTER RESULTS

Most of the sales advice and techniques found in books is based directly on salespeople's experience. Some of it is good, some bad, though most of it has never really been tested by scientific experiments, even by simple split tests.

Instead, what do you think of the idea of using a scientific sales method, based on an extensive survey that analyzed 116 factors that might play a part in sales performance? Its hypotheses have been rigorously tested in 35,000 sales interviews in 27 countries, and it was funded by major companies investing several million dollars.

Does that sound better than the advice of Joe, the photocopier salesman? Let's go, then!

These studies were carried out by Neil Rackham, inventor of the SPIN Selling method and author of a book of the same name. What is generally taught in training courses is that the three most essential factors in making a sale are the art of using conclusions, the management of objections, and the detection of needs by asking open questions.

Conclusions are a great classic of sales strategy. The best-known include:

- **Assumed conclusion:** Assuming that the sale has already been made, by saying, for example: 'Where would you like it delivered?' before the customer has even agreed to purchase.

- **Alternative conclusion:** Asking, for example, 'Would you prefer to have it delivered on Tuesday or on Thursday?' Again before the customer has agreed to purchase.

- **The now-or-never conclusion:** 'If you can't decide now, I shall offer it to another customer who will be only too pleased to buy.'

These, of course, are just a few examples; there are hundreds of types of conclusions. All the great gurus said there was a strong correlation between the number of findings and your chance of making a sale. What Neil Rackham discovered was totally different:

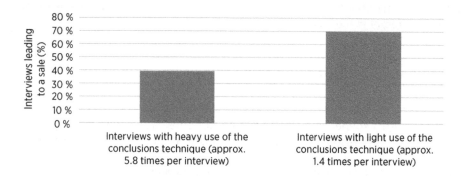

Figure 11: Effectiveness of the conclusions technique (1)

Which doesn't mean you should absolutely never use this technique:

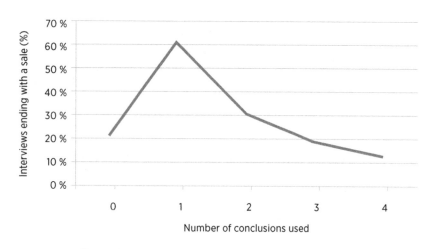

Figure 12: Effectiveness of the conclusions technique (2)

But, as you can see, using two conclusion techniques is almost as effective as using none at all!

According to Neil Rackham's research, the key to increasing sales is to transform customers' implicit needs into explicit needs.

- Implicit needs: the customer speaks about their dissatisfaction, problems, and difficulties. Typical examples might be: 'We are not happy with the speed of our present process' or 'I'm not happy with our discard rate.'

- Explicit needs: the customer speaks explicitly of their needs and desires. Typical examples might be: 'We need a faster system' or 'We need a more reliable machine.'

This works because anyone taking a decision about a purchase has to balance two factors:

1. The seriousness of the problems the purchase would solve

2. The cost of the solution

If the customer perceives that the problem is more serious than the cost of solving it, they will decide to buy it. On the other hand, if they perceive that the problem is relatively minor and the expense is significant, there is little chance of concluding a purchase. The SPIN strategy, therefore, consists of revealing the implicit needs, then developing them into explicit needs. SPIN is an acronym standing for:

- Situation

- Problem

- Implication

- Need-payoff

'But you do like sauerkraut?' – SPIN-type questions

Situation-related questions

These are the questions you ask at the beginning of an interview, especially with a new customer or prospect. They might be: 'What is your position in the company?' 'Do you take the purchasing decisions?' 'What is your annual sales volume?' and so on.

Research carried out by the British Huthwaite training center shows that:

- Situation-related questions are not positively connected with success.

- Inexperienced salespeople ask more of these types of questions than their experienced colleagues.

- They form an essential part of the interview but should be used with caution.

- Potential buyers become bored or impatient if you ask too many of them.

Problem-related questions

Experienced salespeople are more likely to ask questions such as 'Are you satisfied with the equipment you are using at present?' 'What are the disadvantages in the way you are currently managing things?' 'Does this old machine have reliability problems?' And so on.

What do these questions have in common? Each of them probes the customer to detect problems, difficulties, and sources of dissatisfaction, inviting them to talk about his/her implicit needs? Huthwaite's research shows that:

- Problem-related questions are more closely linked with sales success than those relating to the situation.

- Where minor sales are concerned, this is a very strong link: the more problem-related questions the salesman poses, the greater the chances of making a sale.

- Where major sales are concerned, however, there is no strong link.

- Experienced salespeople ask a larger percentage of problem-related questions.

Implication-related questions

Most experienced salespeople, when meeting a customer, do a good job of asking situation-related and problem-related questions. Unfortunately, most people stop at this point, which isn't very effective for major sales. It is implication-related questions that enable the customer to explicitly express their implicit needs and become aware of them in the process.

The SPIN model, then, can be summed up as follows:

1. The salesman asks situation-related questions to establish the context.

2. This leads to problem-related questions, getting the customer to reveal his/her implicit needs.

3. The implicit needs are developed using implication-related questions, getting the potential buyer to experience the problem more clearly and pertinently.

4. This leads to questions about the needs to be met, enabling the buyer to speak about his/her explicit needs.

5. The salesman can then say how the product would benefit the buyer, which is strongly linked to sales success.

80/20 SPIN Selling online

That's all very nice, you may be thinking, but how do you do this in practice online?

Your survey replaces some of the dialogue between salesman and purchaser, enabling you to identify some of your prospects' characteristics, as well as their implicit and explicit needs. But this leaves out an important part of the SPIN Selling method: asking implication-related questions to make customers more acutely aware of the nature and extent of their problems and see the advantages of your solution.

How can you put these questions to your online prospects? The advantage of the web is that it not only enables you to reach a mass audience with virtually zero financial outlay, it also makes it possible to interact with this audience. You can, therefore, simply ask your prospects questions by asking them to respond in the comments box during a sales process. This works particularly well with webinars, which I have already discussed with you, and with product launches, which I shall tackle later.

OK, fine, but what questions do you ask exactly? We shall focus on the 80/20, or even the 1/99, by asking just a couple of questions. That's quite enough.

First: Make your prospect aware of their problem

This question is simple and breaks down into two parts. Firstly, ask: 'What is the biggest obstacle to you achieving your objective today?' Then: 'And where will you be in six months, or a year, if you can't overcome this obstacle? How will you feel about it?'

Thanks to your survey, you have already identified their most serious problem or frustration but ask the question again: the aim is to make your prospect aware of his/her problems with greater clarity.

Examples:

- If you sell men's clothing, like Bonne Gueule: 'What is the biggest obstacle to your being dressed as you would like to be? And where will you be in six months, or a year, if you still can't find clothes that suit you and your budget? How will you feel about that?'

- If you are a dog trainer and you are selling a training course: 'What is the biggest obstacle to your having a contented and obedient dog today? And where will you be in six months, or a year, if you can't get him to obey you? How will you feel about that?'

Next: Help your prospect to visualize the solution

Then ask simply: 'And if you manage to overcome this obstacle and achieve your objective, how will you feel then? And what will you do?'

Answering these two questions will enable your prospect to visualize the suffering caused by their problem more clearly, and why they want to achieve their objective. Once they have become more precisely aware of this, your job is to convince them that your product will help to solve the problem or, better, will solve it completely (if such is the case).

Choose the right moment

Practically, when is the right moment to ask these questions online?

In a webinar, you can take advantage of a five-minute interval to allow people to get a drink and go to the loo. Or buy the *SPIN Selling* book or even follow a course on the subject (and/or send it to your salespeople on it), which could completely change your company's results.

CUSTOMER TESTIMONIALS, THE FAST TRACK TO SELLING YOUR PRODUCTS

In your opinion, who is most likely to persuade you to buy a product:

- The company selling the product and claiming it is the best on the market, or

- A satisfied customer who tells you he or she has bought the product and has found it to be the best on the market?

The satisfied customer, of course. After all, almost all companies claim their product is the best in the world. But how many businesses have really delighted customers who take the time and trouble to broadcast the merits of their products? We all know the answer.

Clearly, the problem with customer testimonials is that they generally reach only a few people. To add insult to injury, several surveys[270] have shown that a person who is dissatisfied with a product will advertise the fact more widely than a person who is satisfied. Wouldn't it be great if we could reverse the tendency so that the testimony of a satisfied customer could reach thousands or even millions of people? Ah, if only we had a tool that enabled us to reach such an extensive audience worldwide, without it costing too much...

But hang on a bit! I was forgetting... the Internet. Ever heard of it? Yes, of course, here we have a tool that enables us to reach a worldwide audience, without it costing an arm and a leg!

Using the Internet, you can magnify the power of your customer testimonials, featuring the best and using them for years to reach thousands or even millions of prospects. Brilliant, don't you think? Much better than them serving just once for a few people. So you must have a system for collecting customer testimonials.

How to gather testimonials

Fine, you are thinking, but how exactly do you go about gathering testimonials? It's as simple as sending customers an email and asking them what they think of the product they have purchased!

Another strategy that works well is to send out a questionnaire to get your customers' opinions on your product. A survey of this kind isn't only useful for

---

270   See, for example, the '2011 American Express Customer Service Barometer.'

collecting testimonials but also for gathering a large amount of information that can help you to refine your communication/advertising. This is the sort of thing I would recommend:

Thank you for buying [*name of product*]! Your answers to these few short questions will help me to make further improvements.

Have you used [*name of product*]:

- Almost every day since you bought it?

- Frequently?

- Fairly often?

- Not very much?

- Just a few times?

- Not at all?

Then possibly, a few specific questions asking your customers how they have used the product:

- Some possible questions for an anti-flea collar:

  - On what sort of pet do you use it?

  - Do you put the collar on all the time or at specific times?

  - Is the color important for you or a secondary matter?

- For a surfboard:

  - Do you find it light enough?

  - What do you think of its stability?

  - And what about its design?

- For an online meditation course:

  - Have you followed the lessons in module 1?

  - And are you applying them?

  - How have you coped with the challenge of meditating for 10 minutes a day for seven days?

Then some demographic questions, such as:[271]

- Age

- Gender

- Occupation

- Level of educational attainment

- Possibly level of income

Then some 'magic' questions in terms of the amount of valuable information they will bring you:

- What do you like most about [name of product]?

- What, in your opinion, most needs improving where [name of product] is concerned?

The first question will elicit many comments, straight from the horse's mouth (as it were), that you then use in your commercial advertising. The second will simply draw out a lot of constructive feedback on how you can improve your product. And then comes the question that will really provide you with testimonials:

Is there any comment you would like to make? How has [name of product] benefited you?

Here is an example you can give:

'Hi there [your first name].

Thank you once again for [name of product]. Previously, I had [problem no. 1] and [problem no. 2], which caused me a great deal of stress. These problems are now resolved, and I have even managed to [benefit no. 1] and [benefit no. 2]. Incredible to think that, just a few months ago, I thought I would never be rid of these problems, and now they are in the past! Thank you again.

George, aged 34, Bristol.'

---

271 Don't ask them at the beginning, as everyone finds these questions irksome and many people won't be motivated to respond. Asking them at the halfway stage is less problematic, thanks to the Zeigarnik effect.

Why include an example of a testimonial in the question? Simply to show your customers what a good testimonial consists of. Of course, they are free to write whatever they want, but the example will be inspirational and ensure you get a greater proportion of good and excellent testimonials.

What if you haven't yet had any customer testimonials and so have no example to show them? Simple. Since this is just an example of what you are looking for, you can invent it. Of course, you should *never* invent testimonials and claim they were written by real customers. But I think it's quite ethical to invent an *example* for illustrative purposes to get your customers to make comments. It is understood that you will never use this example in your commercial advertising.

Then, when you look at the answers to your survey, you will not only have feedback of inestimable value but also some golden testimonials.

To use them commercially, all you need do is contact the people who made these positive comments and ask for permission to quote them. Don't forget to ask for their email addresses and possibly phone numbers, so you can contact them again. If a person is willing to be quoted, try to 'upgrade' their testimonial by transforming it into a better one. Because not all testimonials are of equal value.

The best types of testimonials

In your opinion, what would be most convincing for a prospect who comes across your product, for example, in a brochure or a video:

1. A sentence in inverted commas, backed up by a person's first name?

2. A sentence in inverted commas, backed up by a person's first name, age, and place of residence?

3. All of the above, plus a photograph of the customer?

4. A video of the customer expressing their satisfaction?

Obviously, a video is the best possible form of testimonial. In all the other cases, the prospect may still harbor doubts about the veracity of the testimonial. The more details you give of the person making the comments, the greater their credibility, but there will still be a lingering doubt in the prospect's mind. With a video, doubts usually evaporate. The prospect sees that the person is real and is aware of their enthusiasm and sincerity, which changes everything. A video is, in fact, the closest thing to a person-to-person communication... but with the advantage that it is possible to reach thousands, tens of thousands, or even millions of prospects thanks to the magic of the Internet.

But whatever you do, there will always be skeptics. On two occasions, people have made comments beneath customers' videoed testimonials on my YouTube channel, saying in one case that the customer 'is a good actor,' and in the other that 'he is using a green screen.'[272]

So, when one of your customers gives you permission to use a testimonial obtained through a survey, always try to upgrade it. Thank them warmly and ask if they would be willing to make a short and quick video using readily available means. Emphasize that it involves no more than using their webcam or smartphone, that it will take only two or three minutes, and the video doesn't need to be perfect.

Once, I received an email from someone called Stéphanie, confessing that she had accessed one of my training courses via a friend's subscription. She said she was really impressed by the training, and rather ashamed she hadn't paid me for my fabulous work and asked me how she could settle the bill.

As you can imagine, I was delighted to receive her email. What better testimonial to the quality of your work than to have a 'pirate' write to you, confess her 'crime' and offer to make amends? So I explained how she could pay for the course... and asked if she would make a video telling me exactly what she had written.

My instructions were simply: 'No need to rehearse or do anything sophisticated, just switch on your webcam and talk normally, as if you were talking to a friend in a café. It doesn't matter if you stumble or make mistakes. It will seem all the more natural!' She agreed, and thus supplied me with the very first testimonial for my training course, which had begun a few months earlier. And what a 'fresh' and spontaneous testimonial it was![273]

You'll be surprised how many of your customers will agree to make a video. And with those who are not keen to do so, ask if you can use their first and family names and/or a photograph. Always try to upgrade your testimonials.

How to use your testimonials

Ideally, post them on YouTube, Dailymotion, Vimeo, Facebook, your own website, your sales page – anywhere you can think of where prospects might view them. Someone is bound to come across them.

---

272 Don't let these idiots upset you; there'll always be a few to contend with.
273 Go to http://en.olivier-roland.com/stephanie/ to view Stéphanie's testimonial.

Give the videos headings such as '[*name of product*] review' or '[*name of your company*] review,' and use keywords in the descriptions so that prospects who type these terms into a search engine, and are probably looking to make a purchase, will come across them. Don't forget to include links to your products in the descriptions of the videos or to superimpose them on the videos, as you can still do with YouTube.

As well as these online strategies, if your company has salespeople who go out to meet prospects, you can equip them with iPads featuring videoed testimonials.

Two advanced selling techniques using testimonials

You can go even further in your use of customer testimonials for sales purposes. Here are two possible techniques.

Technique 1: Case studies

When you receive a positive review, ask your customer if they are willing to feature in a case study, i.e., a longer and more detailed interview. You can produce the interview by meeting your customer or simply via Skype, which from a logistical point of view, is easier for both parties.

You can record the interview in audio[274] or video format (which I would recommend), using software such as Camtasia Studio or ScreenFlow (make sure that your own and your customer's webcams are both on so that your faces are visible!).

You can also ask your customer to use a smartphone or camera to film themselves during the Skype interview, which will give you a much better-quality image. Then ask your customer to send you the file from their camera. In this case, I would suggest you nevertheless record at least the audio material at your end. Also, ask your customer to activate their webcam (as well as their smartphone or camera) and record the screen at your end. This will ensure that you have a back-up if there is a problem with the main video. Given that your customer probably isn't a specialist in making video recordings don't be surprised if they experience some issues, e.g., their camera's memory may be almost full, or they may have difficulty with the framing.

Once the case study interview has been recorded:

- Edit it, or rather find someone on Upwork to edit it for you. (*See Chapter 15 for how to outsource tasks effectively.*)

---

274   With a software application such as MP3 Skype Recorder, which is free.

- Publish the edited video on YouTube, Dailymotion, Facebook, Vimeo, and any other sites you can think of that accept videos.

- Extract the audio material and publish it on Apple, SoundCloud, and other audio platforms.

- Get the interview transcribed (again, you can outsource this task) and publish it on your blog.

- If appropriate, extract especially interesting sections from the interview and use them to make shorter videos.

- Take care in each instance to use headings and keywords to ensure that people looking for comments on your product will be directed to the case study.

Technique 2: Responding to objections

Every time you receive a testimonial or record a case study, enter into a dedicated Excel file a link to the video, the title, the name of the customer concerned, and, above all, the main objection the video counters.

As we have seen, all prospects put forward objections that need to be countered if you are to conclude a sale. Now, which is the more effective way of countering an objection: a response on your part or a response from one of your delighted customers? The answer is obvious.

In some testimonials (but not all), your customers will quite naturally express objections they may have had, how an objection was overcome, and, ideally, how pleased they are that it didn't prevent them from making their purchase. For example, a customer might say to you: 'At first, I was hesitant to buy [*name of product*] frankly because it was more expensive than rival products of the same type. But, fortunately, a neighbor of mine had bought one and lent it to me so I could try it out, and I found the [*super-new function*] to be superb. That's how I realized that this function made it well worth the higher price. Consequently, I purchased one, and I'm delighted. I would do the same again.'

This is an almost ideal testimonial. Not all will be so explicit. When you are recording case studies, trigger such moments by asking two 'magic' questions:

1. 'Did you hesitate before deciding to buy?'

2. And if the person says yes: 'What was the deciding factor?'

These two questions invite the customer to say what objections they may have had and how they were overcome. This isn't only a very important piece of information for you but also an amazing way of convincing hesitant prospects who are entertaining the same objections. So, when you or someone in your company meets a prospect who is hesitating because of an objection already covered in a testimonial or case study, simply send them the link to the video concerned, whether in the form of a comment, an email, or a reply on social media.

CREATING MORE REALISTIC CUSTOMER AVATARS

In Chapter 12, we discussed the importance of creating an avatar of your prospects using your survey data to make your communication/advertising more personal. As soon as you have a large enough pool of customers, it is time to compare the avatar you first created with your actual customer avatar.

You remember the questionnaire designed to elicit testimonials? Well, it's useful not only for getting testimonials or feedback about your product but also for getting a more accurate picture of your customers' demographics. Use this data to create a new 'ideal customer' based this time on real customers, not just on your imagination and aspirations. For example, you may have thought that your product would interest mainly managers holding a specialized degree, tired of working for a big company. Now you realize that, yes, some of your customers fall into this category. Still, you have also attracted a significant percentage of entrepreneurs, a result you hadn't anticipated at all. So you will have to recalibrate your communication/advertising accordingly.

Once you have created this first new avatar... go on and create a second. The truth is that your product will be of interest to more than one type of customer. Using your survey data, identify the top five, or even all, of your customer categories, and create avatars for each of them.

You won't necessarily communicate with each of these avatars, especially if some of them are very few in number, but nevertheless, review each one. Is it possible that there is concealed potential in some of them, which would be well worth developing? For example, by performing a targeted advertising test for prospects in a particular category, publishing an advertisement in a magazine, they are likely to read, or targeting them on Facebook or Google AdWords. When carrying out your test, use the words your avatar uses by adopting verbatim words and expressions used by your customers.

UP-SELLING, CROSS-SELLING AND DOWN-SELLING, OR EASY WAYS TO INCREASE YOUR SALES

'Would you like fries with that?'

A McDONALD'S EMPLOYEE, SPEAKING TO SOMEONE
WHO HAS JUST ORDERED A HAMBURGER

Up-selling and cross-selling, two ways of increasing your customers' average shopping cart

Here is a method that can be very effective if your business is already selling products and is very simple to put in place. So I hope I have your full attention!

It consists quite simply of offering a second product to a customer engaged in making a purchase. This could be a more expensive version of the product or one with more upmarket options. This is known as an up-sell. Or the second product could be an accessory or addition to the first. This is known as a cross-sell.

Let's take some well-known examples in the automotive field: offering a package with more options (up-sell) or with additional individual options (cross-sells) to someone buying a vehicle.

This method is very effective for two reasons:

1. The customer has already got his payment card at the ready; there is no better moment to offer them an additional product than when they are in the process of making a purchase.

2. Up-sells/cross-sells are precisely targeted as, in ordering this product, the customer has made plain that they like it enough to want to buy it. From this purchase, you can deduce many aspects of the customer's tastes, especially if you have a system of assessment that enables you to identify trends.[275]

Brilliant, don't you think? Amazon is the champion of this method and doesn't hesitate to use and abuse it with their famous:

- 'Products frequently purchased together,' in the product information sheet, just under the description

---

275 This is, for example, the case of Amazon, which systematically presents linked items when you place an item in your basket under the mention 'Often bought with [name of the product you have just put in the basket].'

- 'Customers who bought this article also bought,' just below

- 'What other articles did customers buy after looking at this article?' again below

- 'Often bought with' once the product has been added to the basket

And so on, at every stage of the purchasing process.

Why does Amazon use this technique so much? Because it works! Amazon is undoubtedly the world's most split-tested website (*see Chapter 16 on the scientific business, p.359*), and you can be sure that, if something is on their site, it's because it enables them to sell more.

And that's not all. There are two other enormous advantages to up-selling and cross-selling, so useful that it would be criminal not to exploit them.

- Up-sells and cross-sells can be products you show only to your customers. Take advantage of this to offer them more specific, more varied, and more extravagant products, obviously with a price-tag to match. Use this method to test your new product ideas; if your customers aren't interested in them, who will be?

- You don't need to create up-sells/cross-sells that then fail to sell. Do you remember the section of this book where I explained how to go beyond the Lean Startup method and take a look into the future by selling products you haven't yet created? Here, the same applies. By proposing up-sells that are not in the catalog, you can look into the future. You will subsequently produce only the up-sells for which there is a strong demand and drop those that arouse little or no interest, reimbursing the few customers who did want to buy.

Down-selling, or how to sell even to hesitant customers

Down-sells are simply products you offer to prospects who haven't purchased a product you offered them initially. You then offer them a less expensive version of the same product.

A typical example would be a prospect who goes into a car showroom and asks to see a sedan that has caught their eye, but then realizes they can't afford it. The salesman then steers the prospect toward a less expensive automobile so as not to lose the sale.

If you use an autoresponder to send emails to your prospects, it is very easy to offer down-sells: following an email sales campaign featuring a certain product, send an email to all those who haven't made a purchase.

All you need do is transfer the email addresses of customers for this product to a specific list, then exclude this list when you send an email to your audience. All decent autoresponders have this function. This ensures that only people who haven't purchased your product will see the down-sell offer, and so you will avoid irritating your paid-up customers.

You can also install an exit pop-up on your sales or ordering page, i.e., a window displayed when a visitor tries to close down the page, offering them a less expensive product. (They were about to leave in any case.) And you can also install mechanisms that detect cart abandonments, i.e., when a prospect puts items in their shopping cart but then fails to complete the purchase, not only so you can contact them again in the future but also to offer down-sells.

Top-of-the-range up-sells

A stout man, hair graying at the temples, full of confidence, is speaking in a firm but gentle voice, as if everything he is saying were gospel truth. The audience holds its collective breath, hanging on his every word.

'Who here knows the price of a loaf of bread?'

Only four or five hands are raised. There are a hundred or so of us entrepreneurs attending this conference in an air-conditioned hotel room in Arizona. Andrei Parabellum, a Russian-Canadian entrepreneur of genius, initiator of a biotechnology startup in Toronto, and owner of a media empire in Russia, points to the few hands raised and exclaims: 'Exactly! Who gives a damn?'

'And there are people for whom anything costing less than $10,000 is like a loaf of bread. They don't even look at the price-tag. Whether you price your product at $50 or $8,000 would make no difference.'

Silence. He pauses for a few moments to let his words sink in.

'Or, in any case, they are prepared to pay $8,000 for a product priced at $50, if in exchange they get a service that really benefits them. If you sell only inexpensive products, you give them no opportunity to spend more and to receive more services and products from you – even if they love what you do/make. So at least be sure to offer them some top-of-the-range up-sells!'

I think that says it all. Always offer up-market up-sells with the products and services you are selling. Ensure that these products or services are of the highest quality and make clear that you can offer them only to a small percentage of customers, at a premium price. The price need not be $10,000, but Andrei's theory holds true for most people – only the amount of money differs. Apart from the very poorest members of society, we all have a sum – it could be 10 cents for a minimum wage earner or $1 million for Bill Gates – below which we pay little attention to the actual price.

The higher the price you ask, the lower the percentage of people for whom price is no object. But consider this: if you sell a $100 product with an up-sell to $1,000, only 10 percent of your customers need to buy this up-sell for you to double your turnover – with the same number of customers.

So what have you to offer in the upmarket category? It could be:

- Individual mentoring to accompany a product intended for many people (e.g., individual tutoring to go with an online training course)

- A deluxe or customized version of your product (e.g., one that is numbered and signed)

- A luxury accessory

- A specific service related to the product

Don't forget that it is often easier to sell to existing customers than to find new ones. So ask yourself this question: what upmarket super-product can I offer the small fraction of customers who have the means and are willing to give me more of their money?

RECOVERING CART ABANDONMENTS

I mentioned this briefly in the preceding section: recovering abandoned carts is one of the most under-used techniques on the web, yet one of the most effective for boosting sales.

The cart abandonment rate is reckoned to be around 68 percent![276] Yes, that's right. On average, more than two-thirds of visitors to a site who have initiated a purchase don't make it through to completion. Isn't that amazing?

---

276   According to a Baymard Institute meta-analysis of 22 surveys, January 2016: http://en.olivier-roland. com/cart-abandonment-rate/

That doesn't mean that the sales concerned are necessarily lost: for one thing, you can put preventive measures in place to reduce the abandonment rate. Secondly, three-quarters of people say they intend to complete their purchase later, online or in a physical store.[277] Obviously, this is no more than a statement of intent; as you well know, 'later' often means 'never.' But a stated intention to buy the product means you can adopt several tactics to try to recover a sale.

To keep the length of this book within bounds, I explain specific methods for reducing your cart abandonment rate in a separate PDF booklet. Please go to http://en.olivier-roland.com/abandon-panier.

EXTENDING YOUR CLIENTELE THROUGH PARTNERSHIPS

Lille, 2011. Benoît, my customer, has just made the journey from Paris for an hour of individual tutoring with me. He is a personal trainer and is having difficulty getting his business off the ground: How can he find customers quickly and effectively?

After analyzing his customer-acquisition strategy, I propose a new approach, simple but very powerful. Rather than finding new customers all on his own, why not recruit other people's customers? Legally and with their agreement, of course!

How? It begins with the avatar and the answer to a very simple question. What non-rival businesses have the same customer avatar as yours? Go on. List them – not necessarily by name, but by type.

In Benoît's case, his ideal customer was a 30-year-old woman, a senior manager with a specialized degree, wanting to take care of her body. The non-rival businesses of which she was also a customer were easy to identify: beauty parlors and spas.

The second question you need to ask is: 'What form of partnership would they be reluctant to turn down?' Let's consider for a moment the case of 'Super-Co.,' a conventional business.

As we shall see in Chapter 16, Super-Co. has a clientele consisting of X customers who purchase X times a year and spend an average of X dollars. The aim of a business isn't only to expand its clientele but also to get existing customers to buy its products more frequently and spend more each time... while ensuring that they are delighted. But the fact is that Super-Co. customers are constantly buying products and services elsewhere, which is quite normal because Super-Co. can't sell everything its customers want or need.

---

277   According to a survey conducted by Hybris Marketing: http://en.olivier-roland.com/see-why/

Wait a minute, though... What would happen if Super-Co. steered its customers toward non-rival businesses that sold products or services those customers were looking for – businesses whose reliability and quality had been carefully vetted by Super-Co.? In return, obviously, for a commission on any sale concluded with a customer referred by Super-Co.?

Do you see the truly staggering growth this could lead to? Let's return to the real-life example of Benoît. Once we had identified beauty parlors/spas as having clienteles very similar to his own, I suggested the following action plan: go and visit all businesses of this type in his town (or neighborhood, given that he lived in Paris), and offer a partnership arrangement. This could take different forms:

- Asking permission to leave brochures advertising his services as a sports coach. Given the absence of competition between the companies concerned, this wouldn't present any particular difficulties, just cultivate good relations. Offering to do the same in return would greatly facilitate the process.

- Suggesting they promote his services as a sports coach on a commission basis. This could be done in various ways: handing out flyers, offering Benoît's services every time Super-Co. make a sale (cross-selling, as described earlier). Where the monitoring of referred customers is concerned, the company could either trust the coach (and ask its customers how they rated his services from time to time) or get their customers to contact him to request his services, possibly via a common email address.

- Suggesting they include his coaching services in their catalog. For example, in their 'body-care and wellbeing' packages. Or simply in their catalog of services.

- Suggesting offering a free gift to their customers in return for permission to send them a promotional email.

This latter strategy brings together many of the ideas I have been sharing in this chapter. The concept is simple: Benoît tells the company he will send all their customers a free PDF booklet with a title such as 'Happier and fitter in 7 minutes a day,' sharing the benefits of the '7-minute workout' I mentioned at the beginning of this book (see p.52). In the booklet and email, Benoît includes a home-coaching offer for those who want to take things further. The company undertakes to send this email to its customers, and of course, receives a commission on any subsequent sales.

This method is excellent because it enables the host company to add value for its customers without any effort while promoting a new service without its customers feeling 'got at.' It also enables Benoît to add value while generating authority, friendliness, credibility, reciprocity, and even social proof if he includes customer testimonials in his brochure (which he should, of course, do). The customers are given good advice free of charge and can decide on an informed basis whether or not to take things further. In short, everybody is happy.

A few weeks after this consultation, Benoît got back to me to say that I had changed his life: he had found a beauty parlor that was keen on a partnership, and he had already seen a large increase in his clientele – all with unprecedented speed.

Moreover, plenty of other businesses were likely to have the same types of customers and be willing to enter into a partnership – for example, yoga centers. The future looked bright, the opportunities endless.

So what about you? What companies have the same sort of customers as you and are not in competition with you? What could you offer them?

SUCCESSFUL PRODUCT LAUNCHES

Jeff Walker is still a humble man; living in that small town in Colorado and driving a Ford pickup truck -- but he's sold $20 million of his product called Product Launch Formula which has been directly responsible for helping other business owners rake in a cool $400 million of their own cash.

The laudatory description in the prestigious *Forbes Magazine*[278] isn't fortuitous: Jeff Walker has completely transformed how products are sold online, in thousands of different sectors: guitars, cookery, artwork, photography, blogging, dating advice, marriage preparation, cruise ship recruitment, selling games relating to medicinal herbs,[279] teaching Photoshop, learning Spanish, and so on.

How has he had such influence? By inventing a way of launching products that brings the combined marketing power of Hollywood and Apple to small businesses.

Take a classic big-budget Hollywood film: are the studios content to pay hundreds of millions of dollars to produce it, then say 'Oh, by the way, we've made a great film, it's out now, why not go and see it?' Of course not. They put in place a ruthlessly efficient promotional plan. You are going quietly about your daily business when, suddenly, it's as if everyone is talking about this film: you hear about it on the

---

278 'Why Jeff Walker Is The 400 Million Dollar Man – And 7 Lessons You Can Learn from Him.' *Forbes*, 2012.
279 http://en.olivier-roland.com/learning-herbs/

radio; you see the advertising banner on television and on YouTube; your friends and colleagues are all talking about it. Does that ring a bell?

Similarly, consider Apple: do they just bring out a product saying: 'Hey, this is great; we've just brought out a new product, you'll love it.'? Obviously not. You'll be hearing about it for months in advance. First, rumors begin to circulate, then it is mentioned on Keynote, then it is taken up by all the news media, then people are falling over themselves in a rush to buy it.

Here you can see two factors that make all the difference between a product launch and the mere issue of a new product:

- Anticipation/suspense is created before the product becomes available
- The actual launch is a staged event

Jeff Walker's Product Launch Formula does precisely the same thing, adapting it to the resources of small and very small enterprises and drawing, to some extent, on all the techniques described in this chapter. And it is amazingly effective. Over the last eight years, operating online, I have used it to make €5,450,303 net of tax and refunds. It is the strategy on which my success as a professional blogger has been based.

The concept is as follows: once you have conducted your survey, defined your avatar, and confirmed that there is interest in your product, use a webinar to:

1. Create an event (on- or off-line)

2. Give out free samples

3. Use the universal mechanisms of influence described in this chapter

4. Make an irresistible offer

Creating an event

Put yourself for a moment in the shoes of one of your prospects: they are excessively busy, tend to put things off, and have difficulty finding time for the activities you are concerned with. They are assailed on every side by advertising, television, websites, emails, and the newspapers. Everyone wants them to fork out money. What can be done to break the hold of this prospect's habits, the daily grind, the constant bombardment of information, and interest them in the product you are offering?

You need to create an event. Something exciting that will arouse their enthusiasm and motivate them to devote time and attention to your message. Fine, you will be thinking, but how exactly do you create an online event?

Simple, all you need do is offer some free content. Yes, free content. It may be in the form of an article, an email, or even a podcast, but generally, it will be a video clip. And this content will:

- Use the universal mechanisms of influence described in this chapter
- Give a clear idea of what you are offering (free sample)
- Make an irresistible offer

Giving out free samples

One of the key points of the event is to give prospects a clear idea of your expertise without making them feel they are being 'sold something.'

A launch is also a golden opportunity to give a glimpse of your expertise, your product, and how it will benefit your prospective customers. It will enable them to appreciate your expertise (your authority) and your friendliness (your ability to relate to them). While motivating them to become more involved in your field of activity.

The right sequence: how best to structure a product launch

The sequence is how your launch is structured. There are many possible sequences. One of the most widely adopted is as follows:

- Video 1: Your story + some great content
- Video 2: Some great content + first part of your offer
- Video 3: Answers to questions, final part of your offer (the price)

This is the 'pre-launch,' staged over four and 20 days (typically a week).

The launch itself begins with video 4, a sales video presenting all aspects of your irresistible offer. From this time on (and not before):

- Either your product will be available for sale if it is a new product or a new series of a product that has sold out; or

- Your promotional offer will begin (a 20 percent reduction in price or, better, the addition of a bonus to create a value-added package).

In practice: How to make sales when launching a product

Let's take the Bonne Gueule male fashion blog as an example and imagine they intend to launch a new range of clothing. They will first conduct a survey, enabling them to work toward an irresistible offer for their new range.

They may possibly skip this stage, given the strength of their community and their sales experience. However, 1) it won't cost them much, and 2) it lets their community know that something is brewing, and therefore begins to create the sense of anticipation required for the actual launch.

Let's say their survey reveals that their avatar is called Philip, aged 29, a company manager with a master's degree. Philip earns a decent salary but has difficulty knowing what clothes suit him, and he doesn't like shopping. The Bonne Gueule team will therefore create some content that both helps Philip and positions Bonne Gueule as consultants and experts, rather than just salespeople. Here is the plan Bonne Gueule might put in place:

- Video 1: Four fatal mistakes beginners make when buying clothes

- Video 2: Five tips for choosing clothes that suit you (including an initial presentation of the new range)

- Video 3: The six characteristics of quality clothing (with a full presentation of the range)

- Video 4: Answers to questions (ending with a presentation of the irresistible offer)

- Video 5: Sales video (summing up the new range and the irresistible offer)

Before making the videos, the team at Bonne Gueule will write a script, then produce a simplified version: a PowerPoint presentation, to serve as an aid for the webinar. By staging the webinar, they will be able to:

- Test the impact of the content they are offering

- See if they have forgotten any important points that would be of interest to their audience, as viewers are sure to ask pertinent questions

- Above all, test out their irresistible offer by offering the products for sale, possibly on a pre-order basis if they are not yet available

Following the webinar, they will fine-tune the video scripts, then shoot the videos. You may think that shooting videos is very technical, but in actual fact, the most important thing, even more, important than the quality of the camera, is good lighting. You can buy serviceable lighting kits for $100 or less.[280]

Then, having 'looked into the future,' and being confident that its audience will be attracted by its content and irresistible offer, the Bonne Gueule team will do all they can to make the launch an event, following the formula to the letter and promoting the launch in all possible ways. And you can, of course, conduct the whole launch using emails and articles, with no video at all. That's how I managed my own first launch.

How to do a no-cost launch: The example of my first attempt

November 2009. My 'Books That Can Change Your Life' blog was doing very well. In one year, it had attracted a community of devotees, and traffic on my site was showing a steady increase. I was wondering about monetization. One of my objectives in creating this blog had been to turn it into a money-making proposition and, with a mere €300 a month deriving from advertising and Amazon affiliation, I couldn't claim to have achieved my goal.

So I had to create a product. With the help of Sébastien Night, a marketing consultant specializing in product launches, I, therefore, devised a strategy that can serve as an excellent example of how to do a launch with limited resources. This is how it went.

Two months before the launch

October 2009. My assets: my blog was receiving roughly 500 visits a day, and I had gathered a small community of enthusiastic fans. Small but nonetheless significant: a seed that had only to germinate. My challenges: I hadn't got a list of email addresses (you should see the progress I've made since then!), and I had no idea what product might interest my readers.

One month before the launch

November 2009: On the 27th, I published an article announcing my new project and asking my readers to kindly complete a questionnaire. This was a survey designed on the lines described in Chapter 12 (see p.213), asking them essentially what sort of product would help them most.

---

280   You can easily find some on Amazon by entering 'light kits.'

The replies were very instructive. They enabled me to create an avatar of my typical reader (a manager with a master's degree, earning a good salary but bored by their work and hoping to break free), and above all, to find out what my audience wanted. The answers to the famous 'magic question' were quite clear: many intended to set up their own businesses but were having difficulty knowing how to go about it practically. They were procrastinating, constantly putting off the vital decisions, telling themselves that tomorrow they would really get stuck in. And tomorrow was always a repeat of today. One of them described the situation in terms that I often refer to: 'It feels as if I'm wearing concrete slippers.' Sound familiar? This is very common: many people would like to set up a business but never get started, but I was unaware of this at the time.

The survey revealed what my audience was expecting of me: they wanted me to help them get off their backsides and take the plunge and to support them throughout the creative process. For my part, I already had 10 years' experience as an entrepreneur. For eight years, I had been on the jury of a startup funding organization, assessing hundreds of applications in many different fields. I was involved in business creation mentoring circles in Lille and had read dozens of the best available books on business and productivity as part of a challenge I had taken up when I launched my blog.[281] So I felt qualified to help.

The survey showed that most of my readers would prefer to have lessons in MP3 format (easier to listen to on the go), at a rate of one lesson a week. So I set about creating exactly what they wanted: a training course to help them set up their own business, in the form of weekly lessons in MP3 format.

A few days before the launch

December 2009. The problem was that I didn't have a list of email addresses, which is the most effective way of selling online. I therefore had to compile one before the product launch. And not any old list! It had to be specifically created for this product, i.e., consisting of qualified prospects.

In return for registering on my new list, I offered something that would interest only people likely to purchase the intended product: an MP3 presentation entitled '7 steps to overcoming procrastination and staying motivated to create or manage a business.' Creating this content was also a good exercise for me, given that the course would be in the same format, and the feedback received from my listeners would be valuable in preparing the subsequent lessons.

---

281   'My crazy project to read 52 of the best business/entrepreneur books in 52 weeks and post a weekly review' on *Books That Can Change Your Life.*

I published a short article on December 3, in which I thanked my readers for the many replies I had received to the survey and shared my project with them. I also offered the podcast in exchange for registering for my newsletter: interested readers only had to leave their first name and email address to receive it – approximately 200 people registered in the days following the publication of this article.

To reach readers interested in another format, I made a short video, which I posted on my YouTube channel (creating it especially for the occasion). I offered a longer video, '7 essential books for setting up a business,' to readers prepared to give me their email addresses.

Thanks to these two content items, I was able to gather some 450 email addresses. Not many, you may say, but these were highly qualified prospects, and a good proportion of those who registered were longstanding readers of my blog, some of them fans. As it turned out, these 450 addresses were to make all the difference.

The launch itself

I sent an email to my new list on December 9, announcing that I was working hard on the project, I would publish the program on the December 11, and the course would start on the 17th, all of which contributed to the sense of anticipation and helped create suspense.

On December 11, as agreed, I published the program on my blog,[282] together with the title of the course: Agir et Réussir (Act and Succeed). The course was to last seven months, at a rate of one lesson a week, together with exercises and, above all, practical activities to progress the students' various projects.

The article ended with a call to arms and the following question to my readers: 'What do you think of this Agir et Réussir program? Does it seem to cover everything? Have you any additional questions that ought to be answered as part of the course?' This enabled me to get initial feedback on how to improve the product and also to generate social proof and commitment from my audience. I also sent an email to those on my new list, asking for their opinion of the program. Forty or so comments were posted (with mine), which was excellent for my blog at the time, and showed a real interest on the part of my audience.

The price hadn't yet been announced (with a launch, it is announced at the very last moment to maintain the suspense), and almost all the comments included a question on this subject. This was a particularly good sign. When prospects ask

---

282 https://des-livres-pour-changer-de-vie.com/creer-votre-entreprise/

you how much your product will cost, it means they are interested in buying, or why would they take the trouble?

I sent out a further email on December 15 with news of the course and, on the 16th (the day before registration), the link they would need, indicating the exact start time. The registration page was displaying only one thing: a countdown clock. Everything was designed to increase the tension and anticipation. Then, on December 17, I announced the opening, again providing the link to the registration page, which was now functional.

This was the first time the price had been stated: €47 a month for the standard version; €97 a month for the premium version. This was a special launch price (set to double for the full-scale launch three months later). I made roughly 25 sales on the first day, having set myself a target of 50 sales in total.

Then, during the first week of registration, I sent out several email reminders, and, by the end of the campaign, I had achieved my objective of 50 sales. At a stroke, I had increased the turnover from my blog from €300 to €3,000 net per month.[283] Still short of the figure you would expect from a real business, but very encouraging given the rapid implementation of the launch and the extremely simple technical methods I had adopted.

And it effectively paved the way for the second launch three months later, undertaken with state-of-the-art techniques, including three videos and partnerships with other businesses promoting the course to their customers.

With this second launch, my project at last achieved turnover worthy of a 'real' business: €14,000 a month, obviously with a large profit margin, as the costs of production, warehousing, and distribution of this online course were virtually zero.

THE STRUCTURE OF MY FIRST PRODUCT LAUNCH

- First item of free content: podcast '7 steps for overcoming procrastination and staying motivated to start or manage a business.'

- Second item of free content: video '7 essential books for setting up a business' (very simple, shot with a webcam, unfortunately with poor sound quality!).

---

283 Over seven months, the duration of the course.

- No third item of free content (contrary to the strict canon), but publication of the course program with a request for feedback from readers of the blog + persons on my list.

- Final email reminder.

- Opening of registration for one week.

- Total turnover: €18,000 net (taking into account refunds, as I offered a 60-day customer-satisfaction-or-money-back guarantee), i.e., €40 net per prospect, an excellent figure.

Though not performed strictly according to the rules, this launch followed them closely enough. The resources committed were minimal/rudimentary: some audio recordings, a video shot with a webcam, and some written articles/emails. True, I had established a (small) community beforehand, but there was nothing here you couldn't do yourself.

Launches, a magic formula?

After all that, you may be wondering whether there is something 'magical' about this product launch formula. No, of course not. It is quite possible to make a complete mess of a launch: however good the formula may be, if you use it to sell ice to Innuits or sand to Tuaregs, it won't work. This is why the survey is a vital component, as is making a really irresistible offer, and I strongly recommend you test your offer with a webinar before undertaking a launch.[284] All these stages can reassure you that the product you are offering is of real interest to your prospects.

But do you remember the three vital principles of entrepreneurship presented at the beginning of this book? The product launch is an 80/20 method of selling online, more effective than others. In fact, it is the most powerful method I know. But if you are skeptical, at least be an intelligent skeptic: test it to see if it works for you.

---

284 Because a webinar can be organized much more quickly than a full-scale product launch.

SUMMARY

For the intelligent rebel who has decided to act

➡ The intelligent rebel knows that marketing is essential if you want to make a name for yourself and that even the world's greatest products need it.

➡ In your marketing, use the universal mechanisms of influence. Do so ethically, not only because this is right, but because it is the most intelligent course of action for the long-term interests of your business.

➡ Also, bear in mind that these mechanisms are useless unless you make an irresistible offer that is of real interest to your prospects.

➡ Be aware of the enormous value you can add by providing quality information and use it to create your own 'tribe' of fans, while your competitors have to make do with customers.

➡ Use SPIN Selling questions to help your customers understand exactly what their needs are and how you can meet them, and make the most of your customer testimonials, especially those recorded on video, which is the most powerful and credible.

➡ Use up-selling, cross-selling, and down-selling techniques to boost your sales with a minimum of input and make an effort to recover abandoned carts.

➡ Ask yourself the question: which non-rival businesses have the same sort of customers as mine? Then seek them out and suggest you form partnership arrangements.

➡ Launch your products online, having first tested your offer in a webinar. This is the most effective way of selling on the web.

To help you put the activities described in this chapter into practice, visit http://en.olivier-roland.com/marketing to receive an email with a series of activities and challenges that will give you the necessary motivation.

CHAPTER 15
DELEGATING TO ACCUMULATE
The Key to Greater Effectiveness and Contentment

Outsourcing is vital for your success, as well as your work-life balance and wellbeing. Take a look around you: each of the objects you see is the result of teamwork. Even 'lone wolves' of genii – Leonardo da Vinci, Thomas Edison, Steve Jobs, et al. – gathered a team to help them with a significant part of their work.

One of the mistakes most commonly made by business owners is to become 'solopreneurs' rather than entrepreneurs. They find it impossible to entrust some of their tasks to others for one or more of the following reasons:

- They think they can do things better.

- They want to have everything under their control.

- They think it will be too expensive.

- They have their noses to the grindstone and don't take time to consider when and how to delegate.

Each of these attitudes is wrong for various reasons. The truth is that delegating is the key to establishing a real business rather than creating a job for yourself, working *on* your business, not *in* your business. Do you understand the difference? Take a few moments to think about it. No, really, I mean it: take time to think about it. If at first, you don't get the point, don't worry. When I first came across this distinction in 2008,[285] it was something I had never even considered, despite my eight years' experience as an entrepreneur.

YOUR BUSINESS AS A SYSTEM THAT WORKS FOR YOU

Working *in* your business means having to solve recurring problems. You are constantly firefighting. You gain some experience, so the same fire breaks out

---

285   In the classic business book *The E-Myth*, by Michael Gerber.

again, you are better placed to put it out. However, you won't have formalized this skill or tried to pass it on to someone else who could cope with the problem if you're not there. Moreover, you won't be spending much time working to prevent fresh emergencies, as your priority will be day-to-day management rather than anticipating future developments.

Working on your business means ensuring that a problem you have dealt with once isn't repeated or, if it happens again, can be dealt with even in your absence. You put out the fire and document how you dealt with it by writing a procedure that can be easily consulted. But, above all:

- You think about the cause of the fire.

- You amend existing procedures to ensure it doesn't happen again.

In short, working in your business means performing necessary technical tasks yourself. Working on your business means putting in place procedures that will enable other people to perform these tasks, i.e., delegating them.

Portrait of a 'one-person-band' solopreneur

Solopreneurs base their businesses on their technical skills, which they have developed in a previous job or separate part-time activity and decide they would prefer to work on their own account. Therein lies the weakness of this approach. I know what I am talking about because this was how I set up and ran my first business for eight years, based on my pre-existing experience in IT.

People who act this way (most would-be businesspeople) don't realize that they are not establishing a business but creating a job for themselves. It's certainly an improvement on being an employee; many self-employed people are happy with their new status for the rest of their careers and wouldn't go back to working for someone else. But having the technical competence to do your particular job doesn't necessarily mean you will have the skills needed to manage a business. For example, a plumber or a computer programmer may be an expert in their field but poor in personnel management, accounting and finance, business strategy, sales, etc.

Moreover, the solopreneur who adopts this 'job-creation' approach will typically be jealously devoted to their occupation and their business and will tend to want to keep full control. Many never take on an employee precisely because they fear losing control and having to deal with areas in which they lack competence – personnel management, payroll, etc. – if they recruited other members of staff.

They are also reluctant to outsource. Most enterprises in the USA,[286] the UK,[287] and Canada have no employees.[288]

Many entrepreneurs who do recruit staff keep a tight grip on tasks that ought to be entrusted to others. In the end, they become micro-managers: they position themselves at the center of the web, so their employees are controlled by them at all times and have to report to them at frequent intervals. When these entrepreneurs go on vacation – if they ever do – they are constantly making and receiving calls. If they switch off their mobile phones, they may receive dozens of voicemail messages every day.

Why? Because their employees can't function without them. They find themselves all at sea, having neither the authority nor the information they need to manage the smallest problem independently.

The fundamental problem, apart from the unwillingness to delegate, is that all the expertise and know-how is locked in the brains of a company's human capital: the brains of the employees, but above all that of the business owner. When they are absent, the expertise is lacking, and the others need to access it. This is why they will be calling them to solve problems and put out fires wherever they arise.

Again, I know what I am talking about. My firm couldn't function without me, and when I went on vacation, which was a rare event, I was always getting voicemail messages about things – both major and minor. I even received calls from customers who were panicking because my employees couldn't handle their problems.

But don't misinterpret what I am saying: some one-person bands are excellent at what they do and achieve great things. But not even the best of them can achieve the same degree of sophistication and harmony as a full-scale orchestra.

Portrait of an 'orchestral conductor' entrepreneur

This is how someone intending to work on their business will set about establishing an enterprise. They view their technical skills as secondary. The main thing, as far as they are concerned, are the skills involved in managing a business and selling their products or services, i.e., the skills required to devise the best possible sales strategy in double-quick time, to recruit competent staff and manage them efficiently.

---

286 US Census Bureau.
287 'Small businesses and the UK economy,' Matthew Ward and Chris Rhodes.
288 'Key Small Business Statistics,' Government of Canada, 2019.

Obviously, technical competence in the field in which the business operates won't come amiss. Most business owners who adopt this approach have at least the minimum of what it takes but, except in certain fields, this isn't the most important thing. They know that the value they bring to their enterprise isn't as a worker or additional specialist, but as someone who will direct the whole thing, more like the conductor of an orchestra. Their aim is to ensure that everyone can play in harmony and to the best of their capacities.

The conductor, therefore, needs to view their enterprise as a set of processes, systems, and gears. By this, I don't mean that they should have a mechanical vision of things and see their employees as robots – far from it. But they will see everything that works and doesn't work in their business as processes that can be improved and, above all, as operations that don't need to be designed specifically for them. It will be possible to delegate and outsource everything that ensures the business can offer products and services, market them, and turn a profit.

Perhaps you are saying: 'That's all very well, but that's the way big companies do things! To set up my small business, I don't need to do all that. After all, lots of self-employed craftspeople adopt the approach I am talking about!'

That's true but, between you and me, most craftspeople are really hard grafters. They don't necessarily fit 100 percent into the one-person-band pattern, as many of them recruit employees and delegate a minimum of their work, but that's not nearly so efficient as adopting a business approach from the word go.

The real key to the orchestral conductor approach, apart from thinking in terms of systems, is setting up procedures that will enable their team to tap into their expertise without having to call on them directly. And, as we shall see, this approach applies perfectly to a VSE (Very Small Enterprise), an SME (Small or Medium-sized Enterprise), or a startup. Does that mean you can simply delegate and automate everything, then relax on the beach sipping a piña colada while the systems you have introduced, and the employees and service providers you have recruited, work on your behalf?

Yes, it's quite possible.

Even if it's not exactly what you wanted: many entrepreneurs are passionate about what they do and have a strong desire to focus on their key skills and passions – the things that create real value for the business and its customers. But how does this attitude of working on your business, rather than working in your business, work practically in the small enterprise environment, and what are the techniques and methods you need to make the business work for you? Let's now explore that in more detail.

The franchising model

We have seen how those who work on a business work on their enterprise's systems. A system is a process that produces a reliable result. It isn't necessarily a machine. A system may be no more than a single individual who knows what they are doing. Where your business is concerned, for example, the accountancy firm to which you delegate your accounting operations may be seen as the 'accounting system': you supply documentation and the answers to a few questions, and in return, the accounting system provides you with:

- Completed administrative forms for your signature

- All the necessary declarations, made in your name, addressed to various government departments, which will then deduct the taxes and other charges you are required to pay

- An annual profit-and-loss account and balance sheet

- If appropriate, pay slips

In short, you supply a modicum of information, then the bulk of a long and difficult (but very necessary) task is performed for you, regularly and reliably. This is the advantage of a system. Your business is a system, in turn, composed of many subsystems, which will typically include:

1. Administration

2. The creation of products and services

3. Marketing and sales

4. Recruitment and personnel management

5. Customer support

Each of these systems needs to function as efficiently as possible: if even one of them is defective, the business will become sick and may even die. It's exactly like the human body: the failure of a single major organ – heart, lungs, kidneys, etc. – can lead to a breakdown of the whole system and eventually death. To work on your business, you need to work to improve its various systems. There are two keys to this:

1. Standardization

2. Delegation or outsourcing

One technique that can facilitate your task and put you in the right frame of mind is franchising. To do this, you need to, daily and for each activity, imagine that your business is the starting point, the prototype for a network of thousands of similar enterprises.

Just think about it: you establish a business, it works well, better than its competitors, so you decide to set up similar businesses in several towns. Obviously, you can't personally manage every business in every town: you will need to entrust the management to people who will look after these enterprises on your behalf. How can you ensure that these managers will follow the good practices that have made for the success of your initial business?

Think about that.

Never mind the fact that you have only recently started your project, are wondering how to attract customers, and have doubts as to whether you can make your business a success. How would you ensure that your manager in a town hundreds of miles away follows the good practices that you have established? This simple question will jolt you from an I-work-in-my-business way of thinking to I-work-to-create-a-system-that-works-for-me mode.

This means you will need to set everything out so that your future franchisees can copy exactly the procedures you have laid down in your initial business. You will therefore need to describe how your different systems operate, in writing, so that anyone with a minimum of competence in their field can move in, study the procedures and immediately know how to go about things.

Do this even if you have absolutely no intention of setting up a thousand similar businesses. This is the ambition you should keep in mind and make your own: 'My present business is the prototype of thousands of future enterprises. For the franchise to work, this prototype must be as efficient as possible. I need to analyze each of its components and improve them one by one until my business is as perfect as possible and can then be duplicated in exactly the same format thousands of times over.'

If you adopt this approach, you will be much more attentive to how all the systems can be improved in your business. And you are much more likely to work *on* your business than *in* your business. It is, therefore, very important that you think in terms of systems.

To help you do this (this change of perspective doesn't come naturally), think of all the systems around you that generally work to perfection. Think of the complexity of the human body. Think of the minimal breakdown rates of automobiles, aircraft, television sets, and computers. Your business systems must be similarly efficient. You need to consider all the tasks you perform as integral parts of a system.

EXERCISE FOR THINKING IN TERMS OF SYSTEMS

Imagine and describe all the stages of one of the following three systems:

- The whole sequence of actions required to drive an automobile from point A to point B.

- The whole sequence of actions required to find a prospective customer, present your product to them, and conclude a sale.

- The whole sequence of actions required to recruit a competent candidate to work in your business.

In performing this exercise, it is very important not to omit any action, even the simplest. For example, if you choose to describe the sequence of actions required to drive an automobile from point A to point B, describe all the tasks you need to perform, including pressing your key to open the central locking system, pulling on the handle to open the door, sitting in the driver's seat, insert the key in the ignition, and so on. You must describe absolutely everything, from A to Z.

Example of a system: Videos

Let's take a look at a system I introduced in my business. In February 2014, when I was preparing to spend two months in the Philippines, I thought it would be nice to set myself a little challenge to show that you can do great things for your business while living in a distant corner of the world. I, therefore, decided to make one video each day during the 60 days of my trip and publish them on my YouTube channel.[289] I so enjoyed this challenge that I not only succeeded in making my 60 videos but ended up making 465 videos in 465 days, without missing a single day.

At first, the process was simple: I shot the videos on my iPhone and posted them directly online on YouTube, without any editing. That was the challenge.

---

289 The French version can be viewed at https://en.olivier-roland.com/youtubefr/ and the English version at https://en.olivier-roland.com/yten/

Then I decided to go for greater quality by adding music, sound effects, text, etc. My videos also included calls to action, offering people a book in return for subscribing to my newsletter (perhaps you remember the section in Chapter 12 on creating a customer magnet?). But I didn't want to go to all the trouble of editing and preparing the YouTube videos myself. So I set up a system that enabled me to devote my efforts to creating the videos and delegate the rest of the work.

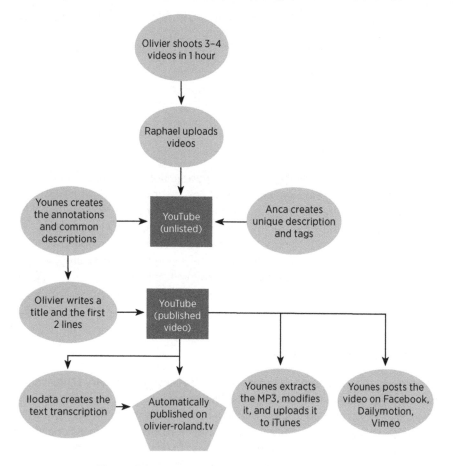

Figure 13: Delegating tasks in a promo video workflow

You will see that the only time I intervened after the shooting sessions was to write the title of the YouTube video and the first two lines of the description. Why did I perform these tasks myself, rather than delegating them? Because:

1. These were activities in which I could really add value.

2. They took no more than two minutes in total.

The title and the first two sentences are, in fact, vitally important, as they determine whether people click to watch the video or not. I was the best copywriter on the team, but everything else was handled by them. This meant that a 10-minute video took me between 15 and 20 minutes to shoot, then I did a further 2 minutes' work on YouTube.

The video was viewed thousands of times on all video platforms, was transformed into a podcast, also listened to thousands of times, and a transcription attracted thousands of readers. In the process, I created content that will work for me for years to come. So I achieved maximum effect for minimum input. And that's what you need to do as much as possible when establishing systems.

DEFINING PROCEDURES

Writing procedures may seem a long and painstaking business, and generally, it is. But it is definitely worthwhile. There is also a simple trick, which I'll share a little later in this chapter, to make it much more enjoyable, and you can always delegate the work involved.

The ideal approach: Documenting everything from the word go

Documenting what you do will provide the basis, the solid foundation, for automating your business. And I must insist that you document all your enterprise's systems. This will ensure that everyone starts from the same baseline and has the same reference points for communication. It must begin with your very first employee or service provider. It means that every customer who calls your business will be treated the same way, whoever answers the telephone. The quality of the welcome you give to customers is especially important and must always be up to standard. It must not be random or dependent on someone having time to pick up the receiver at that particular moment.

How do you document a system? With procedures. There is nothing very exciting about the process, but it really can bring pleasure, prosperity, and peace of mind. It will make all the difference between a business that demands you work 70 hours a week and one that requires only a reasonable number of hours, earns you a fair return on your work, motivation, ambition, and risk-taking. Not to mention allows you to enjoy a peaceful vacation without anyone needing to contact you.

How do you establish procedures? Analyze each system within your business and break it down task by task, as you did in the exercise in the previous chapter. Document each task to establish carefully defined procedures. At the same time, think about each process and how you can improve it. There will be procedures for absolutely everything in your business:

- Taking a phone call from a customer

- Receiving a customer in person

- Preparing a product before shipment

- Performing a service on a customer's premises: working method, tools employed, etc.

Everything, absolutely everything, must be documented. This may seem very boring. And clearly, it isn't the most exciting thing you will be doing in your business. But tell yourself that every hour you spend devising procedures will save you weeks of work later on. And may well spare you serious problems. Maybe at present, you can't see the benefits of it. But it is much easier to work out procedures as you go when you are setting up your business because you will already be putting systems in place and describing them.

The realistic approach: Defining procedures for employees and service providers

You might say, 'These procedures are supposed to describe "good practices," i.e., processes that are already tried and tested. How do you go about it when you start out and have no idea of the best way of doing something? And is it realistic to think that, when setting up an enterprise, you can find time to write up procedures when you have to run the whole business yourself?'

The answer to the second question is clearly no unless you have an iron discipline and devote time at least once a week to thinking about how your business is functioning and how you can improve it. But let's be realistic: most entrepreneurs are too involved in simply keeping the show on the road. So the best thing you can do is to identify the tasks you can delegate and entrust them to external service providers at an early stage. This will motivate you to write up procedures, which has two major advantages:

1. Simply writing down how a task is to be performed will concentrate your mind and enable you to see immediately if there is a better way of dealing with certain aspects of the process.

2. When you ask someone to follow a procedure, something magical happens if they make mistakes:

- Either the person has followed the procedure, in which case all you need do is correct it to ensure the problem never arises again or reduce its impact if it were to recur.

- Or they have not followed the procedure, in which case they are undeniably at fault, and will be much more careful to follow the procedure to the letter next time. If your service provider continues to ignore procedures, you will quickly become aware of it and may well decide you no longer need their services.

Moreover, thanks to the magic of the Internet, finding competent and value-for-money service providers has never been so easy. You can delegate important tasks such as your logo design, presentation brochure, or business card for as little as $5 on some sites, as I will now explain.

Write up procedures yourself or outsource the work?

Perhaps you will say: 'Yes, but there are systems for which I have absolutely no competence. If I were to try and write up a procedure, I would be completely out of my depth!' For example, if you had to write up the way a car works, you wouldn't describe the engine system. Quite right, here you are putting your finger on something very important. In the beginning, you will obviously have only a limited understanding of the various systems and will therefore have to describe them as best you can. Once you have a team or begin to outsource to service providers, there are two very important things you should do:

1. When you are writing up procedures yourself, always submit them to your employees or service providers.

   Ask them to critique the procedures and let you know how they could be improved. It is really important to ask them to tell you when they feel that a procedure is inadequate in some way. If they write the procedures themselves, it will take a load off your back and free you to concentrate on more creative work.

2. Entrust the documentation of a system to the person in your enterprise best qualified to manage it.

   This second point is important: you are not always the best person to write up procedures. If, for example, you run a chauffeur-driven limousines hire business, you may have a mechanic in your business who knows exactly how limousines work, can repair them, and ensure they are in tip-top condition. In this case, he or she is the person who should write up the procedure on 'How to maintain, repair, and keep a limousine in perfect running order.'

Perhaps you think this isn't a very good idea. What if the mechanic leaves the firm or has an accident? Then there will be no one in the company who can implement the procedure. And if you have to take on another mechanic, he or she will know how to look after a limousine anyway! Well, not necessarily. The procedure drawn up by your first mechanic will also be intended for other mechanics, who will have the necessary technical know-how to make good use of it. Your mechanic knows by heart all the breakdowns your limousine is likely to suffer and exactly how to remedy them as efficiently as possible without any messing around. They may have spent hours and hours working out the most appropriate solution for such and such a problem.

There is a world of difference in productivity and efficiency between a mechanic with in-depth knowledge and long experience of your vehicle, and a replacement you have just recruited, straight out of school, who has a good theoretical knowledge of engines and vehicles in general but no familiarity with your particular limousine. If your first mechanic has kept all this expertise locked up in his head and hasn't written it down anywhere, the new person will have to start from square one, and it may be months or years before he has acquired the same level of competence.

On the other hand, if the former mechanic has drawn up a full procedure with precise descriptions of the problems most likely to arise and how to deal with them, the new person will need only to read the manual to acquire, in just a few hours, the fruits of their predecessor's hard work and experience. Do you understand the huge difference in terms of business efficiency?

Something was invented a few thousand years ago that has completely changed the life of the human race: writing. By writing things down, human beings can accumulate and transmit knowledge in a vastly more efficient way. And yet, most enterprises still live in the hunter-gatherer era: i.e., know-how is transmitted orally. So don't remain in the Stone Age! Get the power of the written word behind you.

Once again, your entire business is a system. Its objective is to earn more money than it expends. All its subsystems are interrelated components and should be geared toward this same goal. Procedures, too, are part of the overall money-making system.

They ensure that the knowledge of competent people is available to everyone. When a newcomer arrives to perform a pre-existing function, they shouldn't have to reinvent the wheel. Nor should they need to take up a large part of the time of the person they have come to replace or support. They will spend part of their time reading up the procedures manual. They may possibly need to ask a few additional questions, but not so many that your specialist will be overwhelmed. And if your specialized member of staff is unable to train the newcomer because they are in hospital, have died, or lack the resources to do so, you won't be completely at sea.

You will have the essentials of their know-how, experience, and expertise in written format and so readily available to all.

Now imagine that you are the one going on vacation. Exactly the same applies. If all the advice and instructions you give your employees every day are not set out or summarized in writing somewhere, how can you expect them to get on with their work without you? Sooner or later, they will come up against an obstacle. Usually, you are there; all they need do is ask you a question and get the information they require. Now, they are going to have to call you… Not the best way to have a break from work!

If you have written procedures describing the chief situations they will have to face – methodically explaining all the steps required to deal with such problems and achieve the best possible outcomes – the number of calls you receive will be drastically reduced. At the same time, you will have an automated business that continues to produce good results without needing to be present.

I trust you have now understood the vital importance of having procedures in place. First, analyze your systems and each of their components. Try to improve them. Describe how these components function and summarize it all in a simple procedure intended for your employees.

A few tips on the art of writing procedures. You should follow a four-rule model:

1. Procedures must always add value for your customers, your employees, and your suppliers. They should consist of concrete, directly applicable expertise.

2. Procedures must be comprehensible even for people with only a minimum of competence in the field concerned. In the case of the mechanic, for instance, you will ask them to describe the procedure clearly and simply, so it can be understood and followed by a new mechanic just out of school… but not so your chief accountant can repair the engine!

3. All procedures must be gathered together and centralized in a single Procedures Manual. If someone needs to consult a procedure, they won't have to spend hours hunting for it. You can, of course, do all this digitally by setting up a Wiki, a blog, or a website. I would recommend a Sync file,[290] enabling you to share and synchronize files and folders among an unlimited number of devices. This is the simplest app for a beginner.

4. The aim of every procedure is to produce predictable, standardized customer service.

---

290 https://en.olivier-roland.com/sync/ Sync provides the same service as Dropbox, but with greater security: not even Sync can access your documents, which are encrypted from end to end. This affords you greater protection if the service is hacked.

A simple way to get started

How should you begin the task of analyzing and documenting? Whenever you encounter a problem and work out a solution, I suggest you write down both the problem and the solution you have adopted, step-by-step. That's a procedure.

In the future, when you or one of your employees encounters the same problem again, all you need do is consult the procedure and action it. And if you find a better solution, you or your employee can update the procedure.

This is one of the advantages of written procedures: when it comes to memorizing, they are much more effective than the human brain! Of course, when you find a solution to a problem, you are absolutely sure you will never forget it. Then months or years pass, and the problem arises again. All you can remember is that you had found a solution, but you will have only a vague memory of the solution. The result? An enormous waste of time and productivity. And a great deal of frustration.

When you find a solution to a thorny problem, you'll generally feel pleased with yourself. So use this positive energy to write down a description of it.

Moreover, once a procedure has been recorded in writing, your employees will no longer be able to say: 'Wait a moment, no... The instructions you gave me last week were such and such. I interpreted them as meaning...' Oral instructions are inevitably filtered through memory and interpretation. But when an instruction is written down, misunderstanding is rarer and imperfect memories are not an issue.

Are you beginning to get a better understanding of the distinction between working *in* a business and working *on* a business?

When you work on your business, you see it as a structure, a system consisting of subsystems you can always improve. You are aware of all these subsystems and ensure that they function in the best possible way. When there is a dysfunction, you identify it the moment it arises. You remedy it. You improve.

If you work in your business, you won't have this vision. You resign yourself to living from hand to mouth, firefighting on all fronts, just doing a job.

HOW TO HAVE FUN WITH PROCEDURES

OK, I can't promise you will have the time of your life using these techniques, but there is a far less lengthy and boring way of recording procedures than writing them.

Record your procedures on video

When you need to describe tasks performed on a computer, you can simply record your screen while commenting on what you are doing. Subsequently, your employee or service provider will be able to watch the video and follow step by step the procedure you have recorded. So record it when you are doing a 'live' demonstration for a service provider or employee, which will give you 80 percent of the advantages with 20 percent of the effort.

Think of the huge benefit of making these videos. When you limit yourself to explaining a task verbally:

- An employee can ask you questions then and there, but, subsequently, if there is a stage they don't understand, they will have to keep coming back to you until they have fully mastered the task.

- If an issue arises when you are absent, they will either have to disturb you or wait for you to become available, not being able to get on with the task or not performing it as well.

- If they forget a stage in the process, as often happens, they will have either to ask the same question again, down tools while they wait for instructions, or perform the task less well.

On the other hand, if your employees have access to video recordings, such problems are easily dealt with. Now, in your opinion, how much extra time do you think it takes to make an oral presentation and record your screen as you go instead of just making an oral presentation? Between two and five seconds! Just the time required to activate the recording software. Do you think this extra time will pay for itself? You can be pretty confident the answer is yes.

If the task you describe isn't performed on a computer, you can record it in audio or video format using your smartphone. Simple and effective.

Software applications for recording your screen:

- Camtasia[291] (PC and Mac)

- ScreenFlow[292] (Mac)

---

291 http://en.olivier-roland.com/camtasia/
292 http://en.olivier-roland.com/screenflow/

Nowadays, I rarely record written procedures. My service providers are sufficiently familiar with my working methods and tools for me to send them a short email with a brief description of the request that they can work up into a full procedure. I can also say to them quite simply: 'I'm looking for result X. Can you work out the best way of achieving it, then record a procedure?'

As your service provider or employee will generally be more competent than you in the task you are delegating, this is a better solution than doing your own research into how a task should be performed. You can also pay for them to take an online training course or buy them a book on the subject, then ask them to adopt the techniques being taught, apply them to a particular task and produce a report for you.

HOW TO OUTSOURCE AT A LOW COST THANKS TO THE MAGIC OF THE WEB

Imagine being able to delegate the majority of:

- Repetitive tasks that take a lot of time

- Tasks you are not very good at

- Tasks which don't earn you anything in the short term

- Tasks you really hate

And for as little as $3 an hour? Wouldn't that make your life less fraught and enable you to devote more time and energy to developing your business?

Does that seem too good to be true? But you know me by now, so you must think I have something useful to say on the matter. And you are right. Thanks to the Internet, many jobs no longer need to be done in a particular place but can be performed remotely. This means you can have, literally, a whole army of people working for you, from their own homes or from anywhere on the planet, without having to buy or rent offices and all the related equipment.

So you can offer work to people who live in countries where the cost of living is much lower than in the West... and therefore where wages and the rates payable for services are also much more affordable. Before you accuse me of exploitation, or even of modern-day slavery, if you take an extreme view, let's look at the reasons why outsourcing to such countries is perfectly ethical, and indeed a boon for developing countries and their inhabitants. Then, if I haven't lost you en route (and, if I have, I wish you well; it was good to have you onboard), I will explain how to outsource efficiently to these countries in a way that makes everyone happy: service providers, customers, and you as a business owner.

Why outsourcing to low-cost countries is ethical

1. It creates jobs in countries that need employment opportunities

The first reason is that just by giving work to service providers in these countries, you create employment. You enable people who are less fortunate than you to get decent work and earn a living for themselves and their families. Of course, this may lead to job losses back home – though not necessarily. I'll return to this subject under point 2 – but you can't deny that these countries are more in need of jobs than we are.

Outsourcing to these countries is a much more effective way of helping their people than making donations to NGOs because you are enabling people to become self-reliant and to increase their skills by doing real jobs, rather than maintaining the infernal system of welfare handouts.[293] For them, therefore, it is a solution that furthers sustainable development.

Of course, nothing is entirely black or entirely white. But relocating jobs abroad isn't such a negative phenomenon as the media would like to have us believe. I fully accept that in our own countries, some things are far from perfect. Still, you only have to diverge from the tourist trail in developing countries to realize that, in comparison, our problems are relatively benign.

2. It creates wealth in your own country

Of course, using service providers located in the developing world reduces the number of jobs back home. But just think for a moment: if you can have three people working full time for your enterprise – for the cost of one employee in your own country – won't that generate more value for your customers, for yourself, and for your country's economy? Certainly, it will.

With this additional staffing, your business will grow faster and earn more money, and consequently, you will pay more in tax, thus increasing your country's wealth.

---

293 There are, however, cases in which charitable donations are vitally important, especially in the case of humanitarian disasters. So please do not misrepresent or misinterpret what I am saying!

3. Outsourcing to these countries is the very opposite of exploitation

A criticism that is often made of outsourcing to developing countries is that it amounts to exploitation. But we are not talking about outsourcing to Chinese child laborers who work for 12 hours a day in sweatshop conditions. In our case, we are giving work to people who will be able to do it at their own pace, from home or elsewhere, while earning a higher wage than local standards, enabling them to live comfortably and meet their families' needs. Indeed, this kind of outsourcing enables many people to work in far better conditions than if they were to take on a 'normal' job.

THE EXAMPLE OF YOUNES

My personal assistant Younes performs many one-off and repetitive tasks that would take me ages: moderating comments on my blogs, managing my training course communities, editing most of my videos, managing my blogs' Facebook community, handling and publishing transcripts of my videos, managing after-sales service emails, and so on.

He lives in Agadir, Morocco. Do you know what the legal minimum wage is in Morocco? Go on. Say a figure. Or perhaps think a figure if you would feel strange talking to your book.

At the time of writing, the minimum wage in Morocco is 2,570.86 AED (dirhams) a month, the equivalent of $265. The working week is 44 hours (over six days a week). In other words, an hourly rate of $1.39, with just one day's rest a week.

When Younes began working for me, he was finishing his studies and so worked part-time. I paid him $3 an hour, just over twice the Moroccan minimum wage, not at all bad for a student.

Then, he couldn't find work that matched his qualifications and had to make do with an unskilled job that he hated, 44 hours a week, earning the minimum wage. When he told me this, as I was very satisfied with his services, I looked for other tasks I could put his way and suggested he might work for me half of the time, increasing his wage to $5 an hour. This had a transforming effect: he immediately left his day job and was able to work from home (or anywhere else he pleased), earning more from working half time for me than from working 44 hours a week in a dead-end job.

> I gradually entrusted him with more and more tasks, raising his wages accordingly. He currently earns 10 times the Moroccan hourly minimum wage, so he can live very comfortably, and has taken on three assistants to whom he can delegate certain tasks. His long-term aim is to recruit more staff and develop a company providing services to French-speaking entrepreneurs.

HOW DO YOU OUTSOURCE?

Starting the quick and easy way

The simplest way is to register with Fiverr[294] or its European equivalent People per Hour.[295]

Fiverr started as an Israeli website designed to connect you with thousands of service providers worldwide willing to do a job for $5. Or rather, willing to sell you a basic product or service for $5, and (in many cases) offering you the option of additional services. You will be amazed at the number of things you can buy: a cover for a book or report, a unique article you can publish on your website, an animated video to illustrate a musical composition, a video presenting your company, a 'cartoon' version of your face to use in your communications, the design of a logo, a 3D image of a product for your e-commerce site, a brand name (or your own name) drawn on just about any surface you can imagine, and so on.

Not to mention the improbable but original gifts you can order: a video of a groovy singer giving a rendition of 'Happy Birthday' dedicated to someone you love; the same sung by a Fijian on a tropical beach to the sounds of a ukulele; a clip of a well-known journalist announcing someone's birthday on television...

In short, Fiverr and People per Hour are ideal marketplaces for taking your first small steps in the world of outsourcing. Go and have a look, order something that tickles your fancy, and pay the $5 or €5 it will cost you. That will build up your confidence when it comes to something more substantial. Take it step by step.

---

294 http://en.olivier-roland.com/fiverr/
295 http://en.olivier-roland.com/people-per-hour/

AN EXAMPLE OF HOW YOU MIGHT USE FIVERR

When my YouTube channel was beginning to take off, I ordered an analysis of it by a specialist I found on People per Hour. The report cost me €50 (yes, not everything costs €5!) and I was impressed by its quality.[296] One of the recommendations was that I should have a YouTube banner. So I went onto Fiverr, ordered a banner from four different providers – for $5 each – and chose the one I liked best. Here is the result:

Clearly, you could get something better but remember: it took me just five minutes to order this banner, and it cost me $20. That's real 80/20 stuff.

When I did this, my channel was getting 50,000 views a month. When I reached 200,000 views, I engaged a graphic designer to take care of the design of all my blogs and web platforms. I could have launched a competition on 99designs to get a better banner. But for the time being, this design was quite adequate.

Remember: things don't need to be difficult or complicated. Or expensive. The important thing as you move ahead is to do those things that require minimum effort but get you maximum results.

Taking things further: 'Grown-up' outsourcing sites

You can outsource many services using Fiverr and People per Hour and find providers who do a good job, but if your needs are more advanced, you will have to visit other sites. The one I use and would recommend is Upwork,[297] but there are plenty of others: Freelancer, Guru, The Freelance Nation, among others.

These are platforms that put service providers based all over the world in contact with customers/clients. In other words, you can find service providers for thousands

---

296   This is not always the case on these two sites, far from it.
297   http://en.olivier-roland.com/upwork/ resulting from a merger between Elance and oDesk.

of different tasks, working in almost every country in the world, at prices ranging from a virtual assistant in India charging $2 an hour to an expert in US law working for $500 an hour, and all levels in between.

To date, Upwork has more than 10 million service providers on its books, who are earning more than $1 billion a year through the site. If you know how to search and are persistent, you will find quality providers who can add amazing value to your business while saving you no end of time.

Posting a request is free, though depending on the site you can make a priority request that will allegedly be seen by more people for a fee of between $20 and $30. I have used this function only once and wasn't aware of any significant difference, so I would recommend using the free option, at least initially. When you post a request, it appears in the site's 'catalog,' and service providers will begin making bids. Depending on the nature of the project, your requirements, and the price range you are offering, you may receive dozens of bids or... none at all.[298] You can then select one or more providers, possibly after corresponding with them to clarify certain points, for example, via Skype. You then have two options:

1. You pay a fixed price agreed in advance with the service provider when the project is completed

When you post your request, you indicate a price range, then providers will make bids for the project. When you have agreed on terms with your chosen service provider, the sum is debited from your account and paid into a secure third-party account managed by the site. This is reassuring for the service provider, who knows that they will get paid if they do a good job. And it is also reassuring for you because the funds won't be released until the project has been delivered, and you approved it. If you are not satisfied, you inform the site. One of Upwork's employees will scrutinize your project, all the correspondence between you and your service provider, and the product or service as delivered and will make a decision. This gives everyone peace of mind. In any case, disputes of this kind are extremely rare: since 2009, I have outsourced more than 100 tasks, functions, and projects on Upwork,[299] costing a total of $213,468, and I have never had a problem requiring this kind of adjudication.

You can check on the progress of the work by breaking the project down into stages, for example, when it is 25, 50, and 75 percent completed. At each stage, the provider sends you a report or shows you a prototype or model, and if you are

---

298   The fewest service providers who bid for one of the 100 or so projects I have outsourced over the
        years was two. But it is theoretically possible that you might post a project that attracted zero interest.
299   Initially on Elance and oDesk, two platforms which then merged to form Upwork.

happy that the project is progressing as it should, you can release a proportion of the funding.

In this case, you allocate a maximum number of hours per week and set a maximum duration for the project. The site's software automatically records the number of hours spent on your project: the service provider informs the site when they begin and stop working on your behalf by clicking on a dedicated button. The software takes screenshots at regular intervals and supplies statistics on the use of the mouse and keyboard, with the agreement of the service provider, which enables you to check that the number of hours logged is correct, and generally discourages cheating. This is a practical way of doing things: the software counts the hours, your account is automatically debited every week, and the site issues an invoice. This avoids cheating and time-wasting. As with the pay-per-project function, you can ensure that satisfactory progress is being made by arranging reports at different stages.

Hundreds of graphic artists at your service with 99designs

In early 2000, a few months before I founded my first business, I needed a logo. But how could I go about finding a good graphic designer at a time when the Internet was still in its infancy? There weren't a huge number of options. I could consult the business phone directory or ask one of my acquaintances for a recommendation. I went for the second solution and had meetings with three graphic artists who were required to get back to me, each with several proposals. One came back with two proposals, the other two with five each: 11 possible logos in all. The logos designed by a particular artist were often similar to one another in style. While I was hesitating about which one to choose, an entrepreneur colleague told me that one of the logos I had been offered was a free Clipart motif available in Microsoft Office! The designer in question was asking €1,200 for it. So I ruled him out and chose my logo from among the nine remaining proposals, paying around €1,100.

Fast forward to 2012, when I was selecting the final logo for my blog. I'm happy to tell you that:

- I was able to choose the logo from among 198 proposals.

- I asked my readers and friends to vote on my shortlist of 10 or so logos.

- The total amount paid for the winning logo was $499.

What had changed between 2000 and 2012 that so greatly improved my customer experience? Online platforms had emerged, putting clients in touch with graphic designers, in particular, 99designs.[300] The procedure is quite simple:

- As a potential client/customer, you create an account free of charge.

- You define a project, specifying exactly what you want: logo, visiting card, website, icon, button, smartphone application design, social media banner, brochure, flyer, t-shirt, label, book cover, you name it.

- You then fill in a form describing exactly what you want.

- You decide what price you are prepared to pay.

- You can opt to guarantee that you will pay for the winning design, and I would recommend that you do so. Knowing this, more designers will participate. If you eventually decide not to use any of the designs, the amount you promised will be distributed among the participants.

- Then you wait for the designs to roll in. Mark and make comments on them so that all the participating designers will know what you are looking for.

- After a few days, the time allotted for the competition is up. You can select the logos that appeal to you most and ask your friends and colleagues to vote on them.

- Then you choose the winner and take possession of the files.

Figure 14: Above is the winning logo for my blog Books That Can Change Your Life: silhouettes of birds flying off into the sunrise, representing the books – a design of amazing power and simplicity.

Every entrepreneur should use these types of websites. But a word of caution: I'm not suggesting you should use 99designs or a similar platform when you are getting started. The price of a package comprising a logo, business card, and letterhead is only a few hundred dollars, but it would be a lot cheaper to contact four or five service providers on Fiverr. If you have borrowed several thousand dollars for your

---

300 http://en.olivier-roland.com/99designs/

business, OK, you can spend $500 on a package of this kind. Otherwise, remember your Lean Startup principles: don't invest more than $30 or $40 until you have evidence that your new business is profitable.

The art of successful outsourcing – practical advice

Here are some practical tips, gleaned from my reading on the subject and years of experience:

- Clearly indicate the final result you want to achieve. One of the most common mistakes entrepreneurs make is to not give sufficiently clear instructions concerning the project or task they have decided to outsource.

- Include a simple test in the description. I always ask a simple question unconnected with the project in my descriptions. My favorite is: 'What is the language of Sweden?' This enables me to check that the service provider really reads the instructions and can follow them: this eliminates many cowboys. Moreover, this question is a kind of trap: the official language of Sweden is obviously Swedish, but five minority languages are also recognized: Finnish, Meänkieli, Lappish, Romany, and Yiddish. Most service providers will simply answer Swedish, and I don't blame them. But if one of them also specifies the existence of these minority languages, they win additional points: I know immediately that they will go the extra mile in meeting my requirements.

- Make the service provider think a bit. If yours is a one-off project, rather than a series of recurring tasks, ask these two questions in your description:[301] 'How long do you think it will take you to complete this project?' and 'Break down the project into stages. How long will it take you to complete each stage?' This forces providers to think more carefully about how they will organize themselves. Comparing the different assessments will also be very instructive.

- Ask for a few extra details, for example, why you should select him/her in particular, and the number of hours a week they can devote to the project. I also like to ask the service provider to state their best price. This may well discourage excessive quotations at this stage.

- Don't hesitate to engage several service providers in the early stages. Give them a small task in 'real conditions,' then retain the one who performed best for future assignments.

---

301 These two questions are suggested by Chris Ducker in his book *Virtual Freedom*.

What can you outsource?

At the rates being charged, even individuals can afford to outsource certain tasks, such as market research, travel organization, and even things they do in regular paid employment![302] These are the categories offered by Upwork at present, which may, of course, change over time:

Web, Mobile & Software Dev

All Web, Mobile & Software Dev
Desktop Software Development
Ecommerce Development
Game Development
Mobile Development
Product Management
QA & Testing
Scripts & Utilities
Web Development
Web & Mobile Design
Other - Software Development

IT & Networking

All IT & Networking
Database Administration
ERP / CRM Software
Information Security
Network & System Administration
Other - IT & Networking

Data Science & Analytics

All Data Science & Analytics
A/B Testing
Data Visualization
Data Extraction / ETL
Data Mining & Management
Machine Learning
Quantitative Analysis
Other - Data Science & Analytics

Engineering & Architecture

All Engineering & Architecture
3D Modeling & CAD
Architecture
Chemical Engineering

Design & Creative

All Design & Creative
Animation
Art & Illustration
Audio Production
Brand Identity & Strategy
Graphics & Design
Logo Design & Branding
Motion Graphics
Other - Design & Creative
Photography
Physical Design
Presentations
Video Production
Voice Talent

Writing

All Writing
Academic Writing & Research
Article & Blog Writing
Copywriting
Creative Writing
Editing & Proofreading
Grant Writing
Resumes & Cover Letters
Technical Writing
Web Content
Other - Writing

Translation

All Translation
General Translation
Legal Translation
Medical Translation
Technical Translation

Admin Support

All Admin Support
Data Entry
Personal / Virtual Assistant
Project Management
Transcription
Web Research
Other - Admin Support

Customer Service

All Customer Service
Customer Service
Technical Support
Other - Customer Service

Sales & Marketing

All Sales & Marketing
Display Advertising
Email & Marketing Automation
Lead Generation
Market & Customer Research
Marketing Strategy
Public Relations
SEM - Search Engine Marketing
SEO - Search Engine Optimization
SMM - Social Media Marketing
Telemarketing & Telesales
Other - Sales & Marketing

Accounting & Consulting

All Accounting & Consulting
Accounting
Financial Planning
Human Resources
Management Consulting
Other - Accounting & Consulting

Figure 15: Categories offered by Upwork at the time of writing

Lots of categories there! Where outsourcing is concerned, if something can be done remotely and is legal, you are sure to be able to find someone on one of these platforms that will do it for you. Many jobs can be done remotely nowadays. The practice isn't yet very widespread, mainly because many people in the corporate world haven't cottoned on yet... or they think there are insurmountable obstacles,

---

302 Check with your employer whether you are permitted to do so before delegating tasks you are asked to perform as part of your job!

like not being able to exchange banter while waiting for the coffee machine. But what tasks can the owner of a VSE with few or no employees effectively outsource? Here is a broad range of possibilities:

- Accounting work: This is a boring, complex, and time-consuming activity unrelated to the core work of your business. Delegate it at the earliest opportunity.

- Design work: Get four or five service providers to design a logo for you via Fiverr, select the best candidate, and ask him/her to design your visiting cards, too. Then use an online service to print your cards.

- Miscellaneous tasks, using a generalist virtual assistant, the equivalent of a secretary. Some examples of the tasks you might delegate to him/her:

  - Moderating comments on your websites

  - Managing social media posts

  - Responding to comments on your platforms and on social media

  - Managing and checking safeguards for your websites in particular (e.g., on Dropbox)

  - Collecting testimonials from your customers in a Word file

  - Managing emails: After some training and following a detailed procedure, your assistant will be able to reply to most of your emails, passing on only the ones that need your personal attention. Where he/she cannot handle particular emails, gradually identify standard types, refine the procedure, and give additional training so that he/she can deal with them in the future.

  - Possibly handling phone calls

  - Taking care of invoicing, using online software[303]

  - Arranging refunds (if you are offering customer satisfaction guarantees or selling by mail order)

  - Partial or total management of after-sales service, either by email of using dedicated software[304]

---

303   Such as E-Tag: http://en.olivier-roland.com/e-tag/
304   Such as Zendesk: http://en.olivier-roland.com/zendesk/

- Creating free content using a marketing manager. Do you remember what I told you about information being the under-exploited resource of the web (*see p.323*)? It is quite possible to delegate the creation of content relevant to your audience. Go to https://en.olivier-roland.com/externaliser-contenu/ and tell me the email address to send you a special supplement on this subject).

- SEO, or the art of optimizing your site, so your website gets a top ranking with search engines.

SUMMARY

For the intelligent rebel who has decided to act

➡ Understand the difference between working *in* and working *on* a business. It's the difference between being a one-person band and being the conductor of an orchestra.

➡ See your business as the prototype of a network of franchises, even if you don't intend to multiply your small personal enterprise.

➡ Write procedures. If you find this boring, record your procedures on video by recording your screen or filming yourself with your camera. If you can, delegate the writing of procedures to your employees and service providers.

➡ Outsource on a grand scale.

➡ Begin simply by calling on low-cost service providers in developing countries. By providing people in these countries with decent work they really need, you will be contributing far more to the development of these countries than by making charitable donations. Then outsource more and more, always asking your employees/service providers to record procedures so that the expertise of the business isn't locked away in their heads.

➡ You can even automate your business, completely or to a very large extent, if that is what you really desire.

To help you implement the activities discussed in this chapter, go to http://en.olivier-roland.com/outsourcing to receive an email with a series of activities and challenges that will give you the motivation you need.

CHAPTER 16
BUSINESS SENSE
How to Double Your Results Every Six Months by Running Your Business Scientifically

*'Improve by 1 percent a day, and in just
70 days, you're twice as good.'*

ALAN WEISS

AN EDIFYING EXAMPLE OF THE POWER OF THE SCIENTIFIC BUSINESS

**DAVID OGILVY DISCOVERS THE 'SCIENTIFIC BUSINESS,'
BY CLAUDE HOPKINS**

New York, 1938. A young British salesman has just arrived in the USA, full of ambition, eager to learn all he can about advertising and establish his own agency. He meets Rosser Reeves, a pioneer in the field who went on to become one of its great exponents, inventing the Unique Selling Point (USP) I mentioned in the section on slogans (*see p.235*)[305] and acting for Eisenhower in the 1952 elections. Feeling a fatherly affection for the young man, Reeves lends him an old manuscript he has been keeping in a safe, *Scientific Advertising*, by Claude Hopkins. Reading this text, the young Ogilvy feels like a Judean shepherd discovering the Ark of the Covenant.

In his book, Claude Hopkins, who earned so much for his agency that they paid him an annual salary equivalent to $4 million in today's values, shared his recipe for effective advertising based on tried-and-tested principles. The reason the book, written in 1923, had laid dormant

---

305 He was behind M&M's famous slogan 'Melts in your mouth, not in your hand.'

in a safe for two decades was that the director of Hopkins's agency considered it too valuable to be published![306]

Ogilvy was, therefore, privileged to read the book five years before its eventual publication. He made good use of it, becoming one of the 20th-century's most influential ad men, referred to in *Time* magazine in 1962 as 'the most sought-after wizard in today's advertising industry' and a few years later, as 'the father of advertising.'

So aware was he of the power of scientific advertising that he called it his 'secret weapon.' Like Warren Buffett, who expressed amazement in 1984 that the value investing method that had made him rich was not better known, Ogilvy expressed astonishment in 1986 at the lack of popularity of his method. Addressing a professional audience, he said: 'For forty years I've been a voice crying in the wilderness, trying to persuade my advertising colleagues to take [*this method*] seriously.'

What then is this much-vaunted method? Scientific advertising. And what does it consist of? Accurately measuring the thing which, in an advertisement, really increases sales. At this point in my book, you are familiar with the importance of testing your hypotheses as simply and efficiently as possible. This is precisely the foundation of scientific advertising and scientific business. But how could Claude Hopkins measure the performance of his advertisement in the early 20th century? Simple. He used reply coupons.[307]

Imagine an advertisement for a product in a magazine. Include a reply coupon in the advertisement, to be returned postage-free to your company to receive documentation or, better, a sample of the product.

Put a different reference number on the coupon for each variant of the ad. If advert A, published in 5,000 copies of the magazine, results in 50 returned coupons and advert B, also published in 5,000 copies, harvests 80, you know which of the two is the more effective.[308] And if there is only one difference between the

---

306 Source: *The King of Madison Avenue: David Ogilvy and the Making of Modern Advertising*, by Kenneth Roman, 2010.

307 Another possible method is direct mailing: sending out mailshots through the post.

308 In direct mailing, to take a similar example, you send mailshot A to 5,000 people and variant B to another 5,000, then your measure the returns to see which of the two is more effective.

two advertisements, for instance, the heading, you know that the heading is the differentiating factor. You can then conduct a second test, keeping the heading but changing another element of the advert, e.g., including a photograph or replacing one photograph with another.

Hopkins used this method when launching the Pepsodent brand of toothpaste in 1911 – a brand still going strong today – so successfully that the journalist Charles Duhigg, a Pulitzer Prize winner, credited Hopkins with popularizing the previously neglected practice of toothbrushing in America.[309]

But this was by no means a foregone conclusion: in advertising, it is notoriously difficult to 'educate' people into performing preventive actions. Human nature is such that it is far easier to sell a remedy to an urgent problem than a product that will prevent the problem from arising in the first place. Hopkins tackled the difficulty by publishing multiple variants of his advertisement to test his hypotheses. Despite his 15 years' experience, he made many mistakes. As he says in his autobiography:[310]

> *I spent much time to learn [what worked for Pepsodent]. I wasted some money. But I always knew immediately, by my keyed coupons, the effects of my every appeal. I learned my mistakes in a week. I never spent much money on any wrong theory. I discovered quickly the right and the wrong.*

When Hopkins found that this worked at a local level, he quickly tested it in other towns. Within a year, Pepsodent was being sold all over the USA. Within four years, all over the world. All thanks to what Hopkins called his 'relentless testing.'

I'll let him have the final word:

> *What is the lesson? It is that none of us can afford to rely on judgment or experience. [...] We must test our undertakings in the most exact way possible. Learn our mistakes and correct them.*

This is the basis of scientific advertising and of scientific business: testing hypotheses, measuring, improving. This may seem obvious, yet few entrepreneurs adopt this approach, which is undoubtedly the most important aspect of their work.

---

309 In his book *The Power of Habit: Why We Do What We Do in Life and Business*, Random House, 2012.
310 *My Life in Advertising*, 2012 (1927).

The *Harry Potter* books have been one of the greatest successes of all time, translated into some 75 different languages and selling more than 450 million copies worldwide. A work that has reached almost half-a-billion readers, transcending many different cultures, must surely have been lighted on immediately by publishers with decades of experience behind them, capable of recognizing the universal appeal of its plot? But no. The first Harry Potter volume was rejected by no fewer than 12 publishers before it was taken up by Bloomsbury.

This instance is by no means unusual in the publishing world. You may have heard, for example, of the sad story of *A Confederacy of Dunces*. Its author, John Kennedy Toole, tried for years to get it published, suffering rejection after rejection. Finally, depressed, he committed suicide in 1969 at the age of 31. His mother discovered the manuscript and embarked on a crusade to get it published, finally succeeding in 1980. The book was an instant best-seller, winning its author a posthumous Pulitzer Prize in 1981.

Still not convinced? These two examples could be multiplied many times: of the 195,000 books published every year in the USA, only 5 percent sell more than 5,000 copies.[311] This means that, in 95 percent of cases, decades of experience don't enable the publishers to make the right choices. What lesson can we draw from this? The same as we deduced from the example of Claude Hopkins: experience and intuition is not to be trusted; testing is infinitely better.

By conducting simple, practical experiments, you can beat old-timers who rely on intuition they have never taken the trouble to test, and which very often turn out to be misguided. For this reason, the best thing you can do is to put in place a sales funnel.

THE SALES FUNNEL OF THE SCIENTIFIC BUSINESS

This diagram is referred to as a 'sales funnel.' At every stage, every business has a conversion rate, i.e., the percentage of people it manages to move on to the next stage.

---

311   According to *The 4-Hour Work Week*, by Tim Ferriss.

Figure 16: A basic diagram of how a business operates

Let's imagine a business known to 10,000 people, of whom just 2,000 are prospective customers. It has managed to convert 10 percent of these prospects into customers, 30 percent of its customers into regular customers, and 30 percent of its regular customers into fans. Let's assume that its customers spend an average of $100 on each purchase and that typical customers make just one purchase per year, regular customers make five purchases per year, and fans 20 purchases. This gives the following result:

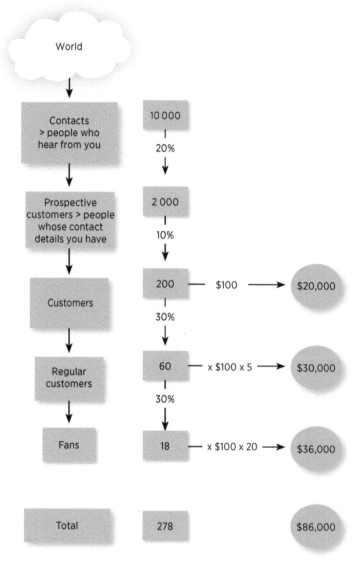

Figure 17: Sales funnel result

The final turnover is, therefore, $86,000.

Let's now assume that, by conducting tests, the business can improve its conversion rate at each stage by 10 percent. Instead of having 2,000 prospects, it, therefore, has 2,200 and succeeds in converting 11 percent of these prospects into customers, 33 percent of its customers into regular customers, and 33 percent of its regular customers into fans. These customers spend an average of $110 on each purchase.

Regular customers make a purchase 1.1 times a year, regular customers five times a year, and fans 20 times.

The turnover then increases from $86,000 to $140,602. This is just by improving performance by 10 percent at each stage, without any increase in the number of people aware of your business (if this figure is also increased by 10 percent, the final turnover amounts to $155,510). Can you now see how important it is to carry out tests at each stage?

To simplify

If you can't be bothered with a sales funnel, at least remember this basic principle, which few entrepreneurs can explain in simple terms: there are only three ways of boosting a business's sales. Just three:

1. Increasing the number of customers

2. Increasing the average value of customers' purchases (the contents of their shopping cart)

3. Increasing the number of times customers come back for more

Let's assume you have 1,000 customers who spend an average of $100 each time they make a purchase and make purchases twice a year. This gives a turnover of:

$$1{,}000 \times 100 \times 2 = \$200{,}000$$

If we increase each of these factors by just 10 percent, we get a turnover of:

$$1{,}100 \times 110 \times 2.2 = \$266{,}200$$

Business turnover has increased by 33.1 percent. And an increase in all these factors of 25 percent will almost double your turnover, lifting it to $390,625. Very simple, but the results can be amazing.

The A/B test as a foundation of the scientific business

In Chapter 12, I shared the principles of A/B testing or split testing, on which a scientific business relies heavily to improve its results. But what should you test? Here is an 80/20 selection:

- Titles of:
  - Emails
  - Blog articles
  - Sales pages
  - Product information pages
- Buttons inviting the customer to take action:
  - Color
  - Wording
  - Size
  - Whether or not to use images
- Reducing the content of a page to give more prominence to the main calls to action

Here are a few examples of interesting split-tests.

'Follow me on Twitter'

Blogger Dustin Curtis tested several versions of a call to action inviting his readers to follow him on Twitter. The winning version 'You should follow me on Twitter here' performed 173 percent better than the control 'I'm on Twitter.'

Reducing options

Tim Ferris carried out a test for the website DailyBurn, called Gyminee at the time. He simply reduced the number of clickable links on the homepage from 25 to five to see if it increased the number of registrations. The result was crystal clear: there was an increase in registrations of 20.5 percent.

Free or not?

On my blog *Books That Can Change Your Life*, I tested the following two calls to action to promote a free book in exchange for registering for my mailing list:

- You can receive a copy of *Zen et Heureux* – Click here
- You can receive a copy of *Zen et Heureux* for free – Click here

The performance of the version that didn't include the word 'free' was 27.7 percent better than that of the version that did. (Subsequently, when the same text was tested with the wording of the link changed from 'Click here' to 'Next step,' the latter version performed 10 percent better.)

In my experience, the word 'free' has a negative effect on performance. Is that always so? Let's see from the following example.

Free or not 2?

The Basecamp company wanted to try out a split-test tool to see if it could increase the conversion rate of the sales page of their Highrise product.[312] They therefore tested several different titles and subtitles on this page.

The text they started with turned out to be the least effective:

Open a Highrise account
Pay as you go. 30-day free trial
on all accounts. No hidden costs.

And the final version was 30 percent more effective than the original:

30-day free trial for all accounts
Registering takes less than 60 seconds.
Choose a plan to get started!

In this case, highlighting the 30-day free trial increased the conversion rate. You might say: 'OK, but maybe it was the subtitle that boosted the number of conversions?'[313] And you would be quite right to ask the question. It isn't a good idea to test several different elements at the same time.[314] But this was the first – admittedly imperfect – test the company had carried out, and in a very short time they were able to increase sales of their product by 30 percent.

Do you think you could do better? What (imperfect) test could you put in place straight away to increase your conversion rate?

---

312 A communication software application for businesses.
313 As it happened, all the variants using this title performed better than the original, whatever the subtitle. So it is highly probably that featuring the 30 free days increases sales.
314 Unless the software is capable of handling a 'multi-variable' test, in which case it will be able to differentiate exactly which elements improve performance. But to begin with I would recommend a simple A/B test, changing only one element (always the same) from one variant to the next.

For a cent more or less

Have you ever wondered why you are always seeing prices stated as 99 cents rather than being rounded up? Well, it's because this method works.

Many studies have shown that it is, in fact, very effective. Gumroad, a marketing platform that enables creatives to sell their films, music, and books,[315] has analyzed the conversion rates of all products sold via their site, and here are the results:

Price ($)	Conversion rate	Price ($)	Conversion rate
1.00	1.88%	0.99	3.06%
2.00	2.39%	1.99	5.2%
3.00	2.11%	2.99	3.44%
4.00	2.39%	3.99	3.21%
5.00	3.84%	4.99	4.67%
6.00	1.42%	5.99	1.56%

Do you see a theme emerging here? 'Psychological' prices beat 'normal' prices hands down. Sometimes as much as doubling sales performance. Just for a measly penny/cent difference. How come? It is mainly lowering the figure on the left, the first we read, that produces this phenomenon. Changing $2 to $1.99 is effective but reducing $1.99 to $1.89 doesn't have the same effect.[316]

But wait a minute. Does this method work in all cases? Not really. The results I have just shared with you certainly show the power of 'psychological' pricing... for small amounts. Other studies show that this method may work for larger amounts... or it may not.

One of the chief aims of this book is to show you which methods work, but you need to adopt the attitude of the healthy skeptic and test them to see if they work for you. What could you test today to see if you can improve your pricing? Go on, do it now.

---

315 'A Penny Saved: Psychological Pricing,' Nichols T., 2013: https://medium.com/@gumroad/a-penny-saved-psychological-pricing-57e6acb3ae14
316 This at least is what the research shows in most cases. See 'Penny Wise and Pound Foolish: The Left-Digit Effect in Price Cognition,' Majoc T. and Morwitz V., *Journal of Consumer Research*, 2008.

In 2009, researchers tested the impact on sales of three different ways of displaying prices on a restaurant menu:

1. 19 $

2. 19 dollars

3. 19

When clients were presented with menus that didn't mention dollars, whether in written form or by a dollar symbol, they spent 8.15 percent more on average.[317] This is very easy to test on the web. But make very sure that people understand that the figure displayed is, in fact, the price.[318]

Effective 80/20 tools for optimizing your business

To decide on a course of action and increase your conversion rate, it is very important to measure each stage accurately. You can do this manually, of course, and I would encourage you to do so if you run an offline business. However, the beauty of an entirely online business is that many of the calculations can be automated.

Let me set out the details of my business model. I am in the information market, along with publishers, newspapers, and magazines. My sales funnel is as follows:

- **Traffic:** I publish free content on my blogs, YouTube channel, and social media. People find me via search engines, other sites which reference me, or social media, and they 'consume' this content: they read, listen to or watch it, depending on the format. These people are my contacts or my audience.

- **Prospects:** For those who want to take things further, I offer additional free content in a more 'packaged' form (often a book) in exchange for them joining one of my email lists and agreeing that I may contact them from time to time about free content and commercial offers. They can, of course, unsubscribe at any time with just one click. The people who register on my lists are my prospects. They have given me permission to contact them, and I have their contact details (their email address at the very least).

---

317 'Menu Price Presentation Influences on Consumer Purchase Behavior in Restaurants,' Yang S.S. et al., *International Journal of Hospitality Management*, 2009.
318 Depending on your national legislation, it may be illegal not to display the currency concerned alongside the price. Seek advice from a lawyer. Similarly, if you are selling in a number of countries using different currencies – which is very likely on the Internet – it is definitely not a good idea.

- **Customers:** For those who want to go further still, I offer paid content in online training or digital books created by one of my partners or me. People who buy these products are obviously customers.

- **Fans:** Finally, for many different reasons, some of my customers become fans – what I am offering meets their special needs, they have taken my advice with life-changing results, etc. These fans buy almost all the products I create, sometimes even when they don't really need them. For them, it is a way of thanking me for the way they have benefited from my input. They, of course, are the people most likely to spread the word about me and often the first to share more widely the free content I publish.[319] They are also the most likely to send me customer testimonials, and in the best possible format: video. As we have seen, video testimonials are one of the best ways of increasing your sales, as they are very persuasive where prospective customers are concerned.

At each of the stages I have just described,[320] there are software applications for measuring results, and I can configure them to monitor my objectives automatically and give me a conversion rate for each. Having to do this manually would take a lot of time and energy, both of which most entrepreneurs would prefer to devote to other tasks. This way, it is easy: it might take me five minutes to create an objective in Google Analytics, then the tool will do all the measuring work, night and day for years. And there are other software tools to help you analyze the performance of your business:

The autoresponder

An autoresponder is undoubtedly the most powerful tool a business can use. It enables you to:

- Collect your prospects' email addresses (and their full details and other information if you so wish) using dedicated forms or entire pages (*see LeadPages, p.229*).

- Send personalized emails (with the name of the prospect, for example) in two different ways:

  - In a predefined sequence after the prospect has joined your list. For instance, you might create a series of 12 messages (or 112!), the first sent

---

319   But there are also 'free fans' who don't buy any of my products for various reasons, but 'consume' all the free content I offer and share it widely.
320   Except for the percentage of customers who become fans.

immediately after registration, and the others at intervals as you decide (e.g., the second after three days, the third after X days, etc.).

– Directly to all or a part of your list. You write an email, send it, and Bob's your uncle! It lands in the inboxes of thousands of prospects.

To date, despite the power of such social media as Facebook, Instagram, YouTube, and Pinterest, the autoresponder is still the best tool for contacting your audience, for three main reasons:

Reason 1: You own it 100 percent

First of all, your list of emails belongs to you and you alone. No one can take it away from you. This isn't the case with a Facebook, Instagram, or YouTube audience, which may change from one day to the next if the company decides you are not respecting its conditions and closes down your account (this happens more often than you might think) or be difficult to reach without having to pay for the privilege (it is now estimated that on average Facebook will show a post to less than 5 percent of followers for free).

Reason 2: It's the best way to get your audience to take action

All the tests that colleagues and I have conducted show that people react more positively to an email than a Facebook post, a tweet, a blog article, or any other online message. When I say 'react,' I mean 'follow your calls to action,' when you invite your audience to perform a specific act: click on a link, reply to an email, share a video, purchase a product, etc.

This doesn't prevent you from sending an email AND publishing an article, a tweet, a video, or other messages. It's just that, except on rare occasions, an email is more effective. There are several reasons for this. First, even if your email is in competition with all the other emails a person receives or consigned to the recipient's spam folder, once they have opened it, it is the only thing on which their attention is focused – unlike a Facebook post or a tweet, which is drowned in the raging sea of the Internet. Second, on the whole, people consult their email inbox more than anything else. According to the McKinsey Global Institute, Americans spend roughly 650 hours per annum on their emails, i.e., slightly more than one hour 45 minutes a day.[321]

---

321 'Re:Re:Fw:Re: Workers Spend 650 Hours a Year on Email,' Weissmann J., *TheAtlantic.com*, 2012.

Reason 3: It's the best way to find out what works with your audience (and make improvements)

Three indicators are clearly displayed by any autoresponder worth its salt:

1.   The opening rate

2.   The click rate

3.   The rate of people who have reported the email as spam

If you have a list of 100,000 people and only 1 percent, i.e., 1,000 people, open your emails, your list will be worth less than a list of 4,000 people with an opening rate of 50 percent. In the first case, you are effectively able to reach 1,000 people; in the second, you can reach 2,000.

But the click rate is the most important measurement, i.e., the percentage of people on your list who effectively click on the links contained in your email. The purpose of an email sent by your business is, in 99 percent of cases, to get your audience to do something, and, in the overwhelming majority of cases, this 'something' has to be done on a webpage. The main exception is when you ask your audience to reply to your email, which I advise you to avoid if your list consists of more than 1,000 contacts; it would be better to use a survey app.

A good autoresponder also enables you to perform split-tests easily, i.e., send two almost identical emails to your audience with one or a limited number of differences. You could, for example, test a different title with the same email to see if it increases the opening rate. Or you could test one image as opposed to another, or to no image at all, to see if this increases the click rate.

I'm talking about Active Campaign because I use it, but any self-respecting autoresponder will offer these functionalities. Mailchimp, too, is well-respected and deserves to be, as it is free for up to 2,000 subscribers, in exchange for displaying an advert at the foot of each email. Clearly, then, when choosing an autoresponder, make sure that it offers these basic functions and carry out some split-tests to find out what enhances the performance of your email marketing.

Creating registration pages and forms: LeadPages

To transform your contacts into prospects, you need to get them to fill in a form with (at least) their email address. You can use the forms of your autoresponder and place them on a blog, on Facebook, or a conventional website, in addition to carrying out split-tests on the forms and measuring their performance.

Active Campaign and most good autoresponders allow you to place forms almost anywhere on a website, and in particular:

- At the end or beginning of each article (with a plugin on a WordPress blog, for example)

- In the sidebar

- In the articles or on the pages

And they provide the form that is by far and away the most effective in terms of conversions: the lightbox. Your form is made to pop up on your website after a period of time you have set, usually a few seconds, and dims out the rest of the webpage, thus presenting your offer without distraction. This method outperforms all others by a factor of two or three.

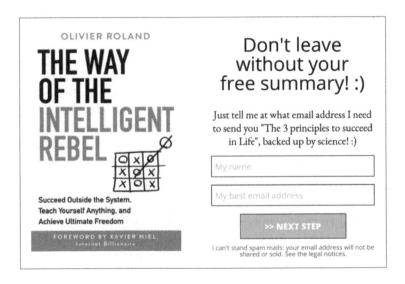

Figure 18: Example of a lightbox that appears after a few
seconds on my website Books That Can Change Your Life.

The lightbox that appears after a few seconds on my Zen Habits website. This type of lightbox may seem invasive, but my tests show that it doesn't affect the time people spend on the site or the number of pages they view, and it considerably increases the number of registrations.

Another possible type of form is the exit pop-up, which appears when a visitor is about to close the page. However, this type of lightbox isn't provided by most autoresponders, so you will have to use third-party tools.

Then, there are pages devoted exclusively to registration on email lists, known as squeeze pages or landing pages. For these, I use a tool called LeadPages, which enables you to create an attractive, well-designed, and, above all, effective squeeze page very simply by choosing from a catalog of motifs and modifying them with just a few clicks.

The great thing about LeadPages is that it measures the performance of all its customers' squeeze pages, and it is possible to sort the models in terms of performance to ensure that the model you choose performs well.

Visual Website Optimizer

There are specialized A/B test applications you can use to improve the performance of all your web pages. The one I use is Visual Website Optimizer.

In the case of a WordPress blog, it can be installed with a few clicks in the form of a plugin and then enables you to test almost everything via an excellent, entirely visual interface. For example, you can test different versions of the title of an article and measure which elicits the most clicks from visitors, from the home page or the side navigation bar. It is also very easy to use on non-WordPress websites and allows you to carry out A/B tests on a marketing funnel, with very precise measurements of the conversion rate at each stage.

Another function it provides is a 'heat map,' which superimposes a 'hotspot map' on your site, showing the points over which visitors' cursors have hovered most. Though not free, this app is an excellent investment for any serious entrepreneur wanting to make their online business truly scientific. There are other apps for performing this task, of which the best known is Optimizely.

SUMMARY

For the intelligent rebel who has decided to act

→ Shrewd entrepreneurs know that a small improvement at each stage of their business sales funnel results in phenomenal growth overall. And that a daily improvement of 1 percent results in a doubling of performance after 70 days.

→ To continually improve your business performance, use the various tools presented in this chapter to carry out A/B tests, and measure the results.

To help you implement the measures advocated in this chapter, go to http://en.olivier-roland.com/deux-fois-plus, and we will email you a series of motivational activities and challenges.

CONCLUSION

Keeping One Step Ahead by Preparing for the Future

'The 21st century will be, in terms of technological advances, the equivalent of three 20th centuries.'

RAY KURZWEIL, AUTHOR, INVENTOR, AND FUTURIST

Ray Kurzweil bases his reasoning on a truth everyone can see: technological progress is accelerating. A few centuries ago, someone could live their whole life without seeing a single technical improvement. Today, this is unimaginable and wonderful for those who have the flexibility and openness of mind to embrace it! We belong to a privileged generation that has seen the Internet emerge from nowhere and revolutionize our daily lives, the economy, and society. Maybe you also experienced the previous revolution, when computer technology burst onto the scene, albeit with few practical applications in the early days.

We shall experience many revolutions of this kind in the 21st century, at closer and closer intervals, sometimes simultaneously, and in many fields: medicine, transport, energy, and so on. In each case, the applications will at first be limited, not particularly interesting, then suddenly they will completely change our lives, so much so that we will wonder how we managed in the past. All of these revolutions will be built on the foundations of earlier ones, reinforcing and extending them.

WHY THIS RAPID ACCELERATION?

Two of the main reasons are:

1. Innovations are based on previous innovations, resulting in more and more effective tools, facilitating the creation of even more sophisticated ones.

2. The human population is increasing. There were one billion of us in 1800, more than seven billion in 2011. We are also increasingly educated, and more and more of us use the scientific method. At the same time, fewer people work in agriculture, which frees them up for more creative tasks. To take the example of the USA, 90 percent of the population was working

in this sector in 1790, as against 50 percent in 1870, and under 2 percent today.[322] Worldwide, the proportion has declined from 44 percent in 1991 to 28 percent in 2018 and continues to fall year on year.[323]

This means more brains are seeking solutions to our problems, with a consequent speeding up of scientific progress. Moreover, it is interesting to note that the population explosion is due to the explosion in innovation we owe to the scientific revolution. Take a look at this mindboggling diagram showing the estimated growth of the world's population over the last 12,000 years.

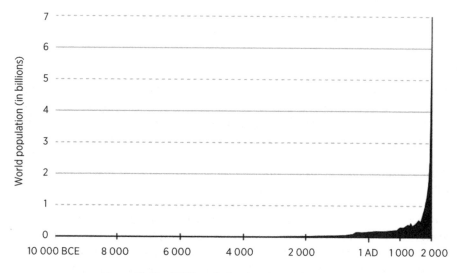

Figure 19: The UN Population Fund (UNFPA) predicts
that there will be nine billion of us by 2043.

EXPONENTIAL VS. LINEAR

Another very important reason for these recent revolutions is the progress made in the field of transistors. These follow a 'law' which has nothing to do with physics but has proved to be remarkably constant over the last five decades, partly because the industry uses it to set its objectives: Moore's law.

This states that the number of transistors placed on a given surface doubles every two years, all other things being equal. This means not only that processors are

322 'Employment by major industry sector,' US Bureau of Labor Statistics
323 'Employment in agriculture,' The World Bank.

increasingly powerful but also that any technology using transistors benefits accordingly. This is why the capacity of hard discs, flash drives, RAMs, etc., regularly increases while their size diminishes, photographs become sharper and sharper, and screens become larger with higher resolution. Because it doubles every year, the development of IT is exponential. To understand the enormous difference between exponential and linear growth, take a look at this diagram.

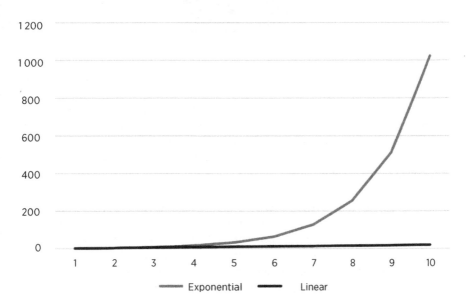

Figure 25: Exponential vs linear growth

By starting with the same figure 2 and doubling it each time (exponential curve), as opposed to adding two each time (linear growth), after 10 iterations, we get a total of 1,024 for an exponential progression, as opposed to 20 for a linear progression! Do you see what an enormous difference this makes? In transistors, growth is exponential, with the result that the timescales of new developments get shorter and shorter.

If you are still to be convinced, compare this:

With this:

The first device is an Osborne 1, the first 'portable' computer,[324] released in 1981. The second is an iPhone 12, first marketed 40 years later. The iPhone 12 was 745 times faster,[325] had 62,500 times more memory and more than 1 million times more storage space, was 100 times lighter and 500 times less bulky, and cost roughly six times less[326] than its ancestor. Not to mention the quality of its screen, wireless connections, and inbuilt camera, and the countless apps available which no one would have dreamed of in 1981.

Can you imagine what your car would be like today if it was 745 times faster and 100 times lighter, had an 62,000 times greater range, and was six times cheaper than the cars produced 40 years ago? This is the power of exponential compared to the linear growth of the kind we see with transistors. Transistors are now found almost everywhere and will become even more omnipresent, leading to exponential growth in many sectors where progress is still linear, such as medicine and energy.

Medicine? Oh, yes. And it's already happening. Let's take a simple example to illustrate my point.

The sequencing of the human genome

The Human Genome Project started in 1990 with the aim of sequencing human DNA in its entirety for the very first time. It was completed in 2003 at the cost of $3 billion.

In parallel, in 1998, a private company, Celera Genomics, undertook the same task. They also finished the sequencing in 2003, for a total cost of $300 million!

---

324 Today we would probably say it was 'transportable.'
325 And is a thousand times more powerful, its processor being much more powerful than that of the Osborne, even at the same frequency.
326 Adjusted for inflation.

In other words, one-tenth of the cost of the public project in a little more than a third of the time.

How did they manage it?

By using a more efficient method, made possible by the exponential development of computing power. In 1998, the computers at Celera's disposal were 32 times more powerful than those used by the public project in 1990, at no additional cost. Since then, the cost of sequencing a complete genome has continued to fall exponentially: from $100 million in 2001 to $10,000 in 2014.[327] In early 2019, the Veritas company was offering full sequencing of the genome of all private clients for $999. Soon it will be within the reach of everyone, and will become routine.

Combined with research revealing the risks associated with different genes and combinations of genes, this will lead to customized medicine for all, rather than today's 'mass' healthcare. You will know what diseases you are susceptible to and against which you should take preventive action if you are hypersensitive to a particular drug or not sensitive enough. At a later stage, there will be drugs tailored to your special needs, taking into account the specifics of your genome.

And this is only the beginning. We shall see other incredible innovations in the years ahead. Let's take a look at one that has the potential to revolutionize the whole medical establishment… and plenty of other fields of activity.

The Watson computer

2011, Los Angeles: We are on the set of a television studio, *Jeopardy!* The rules of the game are simple: a candidate chooses from a selection of categories, the game-show host reads out an answer, and the candidates have to guess the corresponding question. All in all, a normal day for a pretty ordinary show, wouldn't you say?

Not really. On this occasion, February 14, 2011, one of the three candidates was Watson, a supercomputer invented by IBM. After beating Garry Kasparov at chess in 1997 with their Deep Blue computer, IBM was looking for a new challenge.

And *Jeopardy!* was a much more complex challenge than winning at chess: in this case, they had to get a computer to understand spoken language, and quite a complex language at that, formulating questions corresponding to given answers. And Watson wasn't competing with amateurs. Its first opponent was the all-time

---

327   According to the National Human Genome Research Institute.

Jeopardy! champion Brad Rutter, unbeaten during the 19 seasons and tournaments in which he had taken part. Its other opponent, Ken Jennings, was no less redoubtable, having won the game 74 times in a row, second only to Brad Rutter, the man who had won more than anyone else in a televised game (apart from the lottery), more than $4 million.

And yet, despite the difficulty of the task and the extraordinary expertise of the other two candidates, Watson won hands down: in two matches, the computer won $77,147, as against a mere $24,000 for Jennings and $21,600 for Rutter (who thus suffered his first-ever defeat).

Since then, AI has notched up a long series of victories: in 2016, Google's AlphaGo beat the world champion of Go, a far more complex game than chess, by four matches to one. Before 2015, the best AI struggled to reach an amateur level in this game.

In 2019, Google AI repeated its exploit by beating – by nine games to one – two professional players of Starcraft 2, a game with even more combinations than Go, in which the opponent doesn't have a perfect view of the battlefield due to the fog of war.

In 2018, IBM's Debater Project, a follow-up to Watson, engaged in debate with the world debating champion. For the time being, this AI is generally unable to beat a human being in debate, though it sometimes does, and it is amazing to hear it articulate logical speech and answer its opponent's arguments.[328] What point will this technology have reached in 10 years?

IBM has also developed more useful applications for Watson, beginning in the medical field: the first commercial sale of Watson was in 2013, to the Memorial Sloan Kettering cancer research center. This is how Watson works: a doctor or nurse asks the system a question, describing the patient's symptoms and other factors. Watson then searches a medical database, the patient's medical history, and any available genetic and hereditary information before suggesting a list of probable health conditions and the recommended treatments, with a confidence score. IBM says that 90 percent of the nurses who use Watson follow its directives.

This is, of course, a massive issue: in the USA alone, it is estimated that medical errors cause between 44,000 and 98,999 deaths a year, and more than a million injuries and complications.[329] And medicine is only the beginning: IBM is planning

---

328   Search for 'Project Debater' on YouTube to see the latest debates.
329   'To Err Is Human: Building a Safer Health System,' Institute of Medicine Committee on Quality of Health Care in America, National Academies Press, 2000.

to sell its system to clients in many other sectors of the economy: finance, scientific research, legal affairs, etc.

And Watson (in common with its rivals) is already in the cloud. Now, imagine a free or very affordable service you can consult from your smartphone. You describe your symptoms and pass your finger over a sensor that is an integral part of the device. The sensor automatically measures dozens of parameters, such as your blood pressure, heart rate, temperature, blood glucose level, and so on, and informs the diagnostic software. This software cross-references your symptoms with your complete medical history and your DNA, quickly gives a diagnosis, and suggests the most appropriate remedies, making sure they are compatible with your genetic peculiarities and any other medicines you are currently taking.

What will be the role of doctors in a world of this kind? No doubt, it will be very different from the role they currently play. And how many of today's doctors, in your opinion, are aware that their occupation is in danger of being severely shaken up – we say disrupted in startup language – within the next 10 or 20 years?

In 10 years, your smartphone, its sensors, and all other digital computers and peripherals will be 32 times more powerful. And in 20 years, 1,024 times more powerful than today. Very few doctors realize what this exponential technological development may signify. And they will be taken by surprise, like many other people. Because they will not be the only ones. Let's take an example closer to hand to make this point clear.

Of taxis, beavers, and Uber

We have all seen the efforts made by traditional taxi companies to put a spoke in the wheels of Uber, in almost all countries, from the USA to the UK. Despite a few successful court cases here and there, the results are plain for all to see. It was like watching beavers building a dam of twigs in the hope of stopping a tsunami.

Uber is a textbook case of the radical and total disruption digital technology can cause in an industry living in a bygone era and unable to foresee the exponential growth of a new rival. And this total wipe-out has a remarkably simple explanation: customers prefer the service Uber provides because it is better in every way than a traditional taxi service. You can order a car in two clicks; the drivers are friendly; it is usually less expensive, and you don't need to carry cash around: the fare is automatically charged to your card. What more could you want?

Looking further ahead, taxi companies' dam-building appears even more futile. The advent of automated vehicles is just over the horizon. What will taxi companies do in eight, 10, or 12 years, when there are millions of autonomous electric vehicles you can call up from your smartphone?

IN CONCLUSION

Take a few moments to observe or visualize the electronic devices you are currently using: television, computer, smartphone, tablet, maybe a smartwatch, games console, etc. Now close your eyes and recollect the devices you were using 20 years ago (or as far back as you can remember if you are too young to think back so far).

What TV were you watching? What sort of mobile did you have? Did you have just one? And what about computers? Were you using the Internet 20 years ago? If not, how did you manage?

Truth to tell, the devices that were part of our daily lives then are now completely and irremediably obsolete. We thought they were indispensable, but now they make us smile. In any case, you couldn't now make a present of them to anyone without it being taken as an insult or a joke.

You see what I am getting at? In 20 years, with progress accelerating, all the electronic devices you are currently using will seem even more obsolete than those you were using twenty years ago. What's more, services as revolutionary as the Internet was in its time will have made their appearance.

Think of it for a moment. What does this mean for shrewd entrepreneurs and intelligent rebels? That the world is changing ever more quickly. That it is vain to try to resist the march of progress. Shrewd entrepreneurs will, on the contrary, embrace and take advantage of it to add value for themselves and others. And to avoid being in the company of those who didn't see what was coming and take to the streets to defend a world that no longer exists, you need to be constantly renewing your mind. Engaging in lifelong learning, experimenting, and launching new projects. By foreseeing and embracing change. And even instigating it within your own sphere of influence. Because the future belongs to those who stride boldly forward, while others mark time.

I hope this book will have taught you some techniques and motivated you to step forward competently and with confidence.

So act and succeed.

And may you be successful.

TAKE ACTION.
AND SUCCEED.

RESOURCES

In addition to the works quoted and recommended in this book, here is a small selection of books of vital interest for intelligent rebels.

Business

The 4-Hour Work Week, Tim Ferriss
Given the number of times I have quoted from this book, you will undoubtedly expect me to list it here! You may or may not agree with this book, but any active or aspiring entrepreneur should have read it. So there you are.

The E-Myth Revisited, Michael Gerber
This is a classic, perfectly describing the trap into which many entrepreneurs fall, creating a prison for themselves when they were searching for freedom.

Marketing

Getting Everything You Can Out of All You've Got: 21 Ways You Can Out-Think, Out-Perform, and Out-Earn the Competition, Jay Abraham
Behind this long-winded title is concealed one of the greatest books on marketing ever written, a real nugget.

Influence: The Psychology of Persuasion, Robert Cialdini
The classic work on influencing people, a topic covered in detail in Chapter 14.

The Ultimate Sales Machine, Chet Holmes
An excellent and pithy book (I wrote the preface to the French edition). It presents several very effective 80/20 methods for increasing a business's sales. The art of recruiting superstars is one of them.

Made to Stick, Chip and Dan Heath
A handbook on disseminating messages that buzz and attract people's attention.

Simplicity and the art of living

Walden; or, Life in the Woods, Henry David Thoreau
An American philosopher's autobiographical account of two years lived in the wild – an inspiration to strip down your life and find satisfaction in simple pleasures.

Willpower and discipline

The Willpower Instinct, Kelly McGonigal
Willpower: Why Self-Control is the Secret to Success, Roy F. Baumeister
These two books, which I referred to in Chapter 4, are both classics, admirably summarizing 20 years of research on self-control and discipline.

Health

Fantastic Voyage: Live Long Enough to Live Forever, Ray Kurzweil and Terry Grossman
Don't be put off by the clickbait title. This is one of the best books on how to live a long and healthy life and be full of energy, happy and relaxed. As a bonus, it gives an insight into the positive and negative consequences of information breaking into the world of health.

Anticancer, David Servan-Schreiber
An excellent complement to the previous book, explaining how to take responsibility for your health parallel with the conventional health system.

Education for the intelligent rebel

Obviously, the list of 99 books that fit into the 24 categories of the Personal MBA is an invaluable resource. The full list is available at http://en.olivier-roland.com/personal-mba.

You can find summaries of the various books on my blog https://books-that-can-change-your-life.net/.

Other resources

Evernote: An excellent tool for note-taking in all circumstances, automatically saving your jottings in the cloud and synchronizing with all your devices. It can search for material in photographs of text taken with your smartphone (with amazing precision). I use it five or six times a day. You can throw away your conventional notebook! Free for up to 2G: http://en.olivier-roland.com/evernote/.

'Learn How to Learn' course by Barbara Oakley on Coursera. Excellent free online training: http://en.olivier-roland.com/learning-how-to-learn/.

ABOUT THE AUTHOR

Laurent Breillat

Olivier Roland dropped out of school at the age of 19 to create his first business, and he never looked back. He is now a serial entrepreneur, blogger, YouTuber, startup investor, best-selling author, amateur archaeologist, diver, amateur pilot, globetrotter, international speaker, and philanthropist – among his many hats. He has built a global audience of more than 450,000 fans convinced by his method, while traveling the world for six months a year for more than 10 years.

When Olivier was in school he often felt out of place, inadequate, and unmotivated. He thought for a long time that this was a problem and a weakness, until he realized that it could be a strength if he played his cards right, because being a rebel means being free to break from the traditional model and create your own reality.

Olivier is now on a mission to show that you don't need to be brilliant in school to be brilliant in life. In fact, he believes a lot of Intelligent Rebels are embers ready to blossom and make beautiful fires full of heat and light... but they've been watered all their lives.

He wants this book to be the breeze that blows on some of these embers and helps them to ignite.

 Olivier Roland English

 @olivierrolanden

 Olivier Roland English

https://en.olivier-roland.com/

HAY HOUSE

Look within

Join the conversation about latest products,
events, exclusive offers and more.

f   Hay House

🐦   @HayHouseUK

📷   @hayhouseuk

❤   healyourlife.com

We'd love to hear from you!